Get the eBook FREE!

(PDF, ePub, Kindle, and liveBook all included)

We believe that once you buy a book from us, you should be able to read it in any format we have available. To get electronic versions of this book at no additional cost to you, purchase and then register this book at the Manning website.

Go to https://www.manning.com/freebook and follow the instructions to complete your pBook registration.

That's it!
Thanks from Manning!

Practical Recommender Systems

Practical
Recommender
Systems

KIM FALK

MANNING
SHELTER ISLAND

For online information and ordering of this and other Manning books, please visit www.manning.com. The publisher offers discounts on this book when ordered in quantity. For more information, please contact

Special Sales Department
Manning Publications Co.
20 Baldwin Road
PO Box 761
Shelter Island, NY 11964
Email: orders@manning.com

Manning Publications Co.
20 Baldwin Road
PO Box 761
Shelter Island, NY 11964

Development editor:	Helen Stergius
Production editor:	Janet Vail
Copy editors:	Katie Petito and Frances Buran
Proofreader:	Elizabeth Martin
Technical proofreaders:	Valentin Crettaz and Furkan Kamaci
Typesetter:	Dottie Marsico
Cover designer:	Marija Tudor

ISBN 9781617292705
Printed in the United States of America

To the loves of my life:
my wife, Sara, and my son, Peter,
the small Superhero

brief contents

contents

preface

When I finished university in 2003, it was with the threat that no computer scientists would be needed in Europe because everything would be developed in countries where salaries were much lower. That never materialized, thank goodness, for many reasons. I'd venture that one of the larger issues was that companies underestimated the problem of developers not understanding the culture where their software was going to run. Software requests were implemented, but the functionality was different from what customers expected.

Today, there's a similar menace for people interested in machine learning and data science. But now the threat is not low salaries, but software as a service (SaaS), where you upload data and then the system does the work for you.

I'm as concerned as anyone else that machines don't understand domains and people. Machines aren't intelligent enough yet that you can take humans out of the equation. Things are moving quickly, but I venture that anyone who is reading this book will be able to work with recommenders until the end of their career.

Where did I drop into the mix? I was working as a software engineer in Italy and was moving to England and needed a job that required more thought than doing CRUD operations on a database. Luckily, I was contacted by a great recruiter from RedRock Consulting Ltd. They matched me with a recommender system provider, where I worked on the engine. And that was it; I was lost in machine learning ("lost" in the sense of being really interested and engaged). In addition to working on recommender systems, I also started trawling for knowledge on the internet and read myriad books on the subject and related topics.

Today you can't throw a stick without having at least 10 people try to teach you something about machine learning. I find it amusing when I see one-page or one-hour tutorials that claim to teach you all you need to know about machine learning. I can create a similarly effective tutorial on how to be a fighter pilot:

You take off and you fly using the stick. If you need to shoot, you press a button. Then, you land before you run out of gas.

A fighter pilot tutorial like that will probably be great to get you started—it's where I started. But don't fool yourself: understanding machine learning is complex. Add to that the human factor, which always makes things a bit wobblier.

To get back to my story, I worked with recommenders and was happy about it, and then I changed jobs. In my new position, I was supposed to continue working on recommender systems, but that project was delayed. At that point I was nervous I wouldn't be working with recommenders anymore, but that was when Manning offered me the opportunity to write a book about recommender systems. What could I do, other than jump at the task? Immediately after I signed the contract, the recommender project started after all. Writing this book has been a great learning experience, and I hope you'll benefit from and enjoy it.

The goal of the book is to introduce you to recommender systems—not only the algorithms, but also the recommender system ecosystem. The algorithms aren't too complex, but to understand and run them requires understanding the users who are to receive the recommendations. The book's contents have evolved during writing, because I've tried to fit more and more in. I hope reading this book will provide everything you need to know to get started on recommenders and give you a solid foundation to build on as you learn more.

acknowledgments

I want to mention and acknowledge two groups of people here: those who actively worked on the book and those who suffered and supported my constantly distracted presence for the last three years while this book project has been under way.

It might be my name on the cover of *Practical Recommender Systems*, but this book couldn't have come into existence without the great work of the people at Manning. I want especially to thank Helen Stergius for her relentless help and guidance as my development editor. She and all the others have translated my slightly dyslexic writing into something that teaches people to implement recommenders.

I also want to thank Furkan Kamaci and Valentin Crettaz, my technical proofreaders, and all the reviewers who took the time to read the early versions and helped the manuscript become more connected. They include Adhir Ramjiavan, Alexander Myltsev, Alvin Raj, Amit Lamba, Andrew Collier, Fazel Keshtkar, Jared Duncan, Jaromir Nemec, Martin Beer, Mayur Patil, Mike Dalrymple, Noreen Dertinger, Olivier Ducatteeuw, Peter Hampton, Simeon Leyzerzon, Søren Lind Kristiansen, Steven Parr, Tobias Bürger, Tobias Getrost, and Vipul Gupta.

Many libraries, systems, and packages have been used to write this story, and I'm very grateful to the communities that helped me. I'm also thankful for the tools the open source communities have provided so everything didn't need to be implemented from the ground up.

Most important, I want to thank my wife, my son, my mother-in-law, the rest of my family, and my close friends for their support, love, and, most of all, patience. It hasn't been easy for them to have a family member and friend who's always sneaking away to write while moving to a new house and seeing our homes in Italy shaken to pieces by earthquakes. Not to mention that said writer started not one, but two, new jobs in the process. Thank you, and I promise no new projects for at least a couple of years. Love to all of you!

about this book

Are you envious when Amazon recommends its products or when Netflix is spot-on with a recommendation for a user? Then here's your chance to learn how to add these skills to your repertoire. Reading this book will give you an understanding of what recommender systems are and how to apply them in practice. To make a recommender work, many things need to perform in concert. You need to understand how to collect data from your users and how to interpret it, and you need a toolbox of different recommender algorithms so you can choose the best one for your particular scenario. Most importantly, you need to understand how to evaluate whether your recommender system is doing its job well. All this and more is hidden within this book.

Who should read this book

Practical Recommender Systems is primarily intended for developers who are interested in implementing a recommender. The book takes a practical approach and attempts to explain everything in normal, everyday language. There will be math and statistics, but both will be accompanied by figures and code. New data scientists will also benefit from this book as an introduction to recommender algorithms and to the infrastructure needed to get them up and running. Managers will find this book useful to get an overview of what a recommender system is and how it can be used in practice.

To get the full value out of the book, you should be able to read code in a programming language such as Python or Java, you should understand an SQL query, and you should have a basic understanding of higher math and statistics. Figures and code listings that explain concepts can get you only so far.

How this book is organized

The book is divided into two parts, one focusing on the recommender system infrastructure and the other on algorithms.

In part 1, you'll learn how to collect data and how to use it when you add a recommender system to your application:

- Chapter 1 is an overview of recommendations and outlines key elements. It provides a broad understanding of what a recommender system is and how it works.
- Chapter 2 is about how to understand users and their behavior, and covers ways to collect data from users.
- Chapter 3 introduces web analytics and shows how you can implement a dashboard where you can keep track of your recommenders.
- Chapter 4 discusses how behavioral data can be transformed into ratings.
- Chapter 5 looks at non-personalized recommendations.
- Chapter 6 outlines the problem of new users and products and gives simple solutions.

In part 2, we look at the recommender system algorithms and how to use the data a system collects to calculate what things to recommend to a user:

- Chapter 7 discusses formulas for calculating similarity between users or content items such as movies.
- Chapter 8 introduces personalized recommendations using collaborative filtering.
- Chapter 9 presents metrics for offline evaluation recommenders and outlines ways to make recommendations online.
- Chapter 10 introduces content-based filtering, which finds similarities in content using different types of algorithms such as Latent Dirichlet Allocation and TF-IDF.
- Chapter 11 returns to collaborative filtering, which was introduced in chapter 8, but is discussed now using dimensional reduction methods.
- Chapter 12 presents a way to mix types of recommenders.
- Chapter 13 introduces ranking algorithms and methods for learning to rank recommendations.
- Chapter 14 rounds out the book with a look into the future, topics to learn next, books to further your understanding, and thoughts about algorithms and context.

The book is designed to be read from cover to cover, because many things refer to earlier chapters, but it can also be understood by reading only selected chapters.

Downloads

The code required to run the example site called MovieGEEKs can be downloaded from the publisher's website at www.manning.com/books/practical-recommender-systems and can also be found on Github.com at https://github.com/practical-recommender-systems/moviegeek. The website is implemented using the Django platform. We will use two data sets: one is auto-generated, while the other is downloaded from MovieTweetings. All installation instructions can be found on the GitHub site.

Code conventions

This book contains many examples of source code both in numbered listings and inline with normal text. In both cases, source code is formatted in a `fixed-width font` to separate it from ordinary text. Sometimes code is also **in bold** to highlight code that has changed from previous steps in the chapter, such as when a new feature adds to an existing line of code.

In many cases, the original source code has been reformatted; we've added line breaks and reworked indentation to accommodate the available page space in the book. In rare cases, even this wasn't enough, and listings include line-continuation markers (➥). Additionally, comments in the source code have often been removed from the listings when the code is described in the text. Code annotations accompany many of the listings, highlighting important concepts.

Book forum

Purchase of *Practical Recommender Systems* includes free access to a private web forum run by Manning Publications where you can make comments about the book, ask technical questions, and receive help from the author and from other users. To access the forum, go to https://forums.manning.com/forums/practical-recommender-systems. You can also learn more about Manning's forums and the rules of conduct at https://forums.manning.com/forums/about.

Manning's commitment to our readers is to provide a venue where a meaningful dialogue between individual readers and between readers and the author can take place. It is not a commitment to any specific amount of participation on the part of the author, whose contribution to the forum remains voluntary (and unpaid). We suggest you try asking the author some challenging questions lest his interest stray! The forum and the archives of previous discussions will be accessible from the publisher's website as long as the book is in print.

about the author

KIM FALK is a data scientist who is experienced building data-driven applications. He's passionate about recommender systems and machine learning in general. He has trained recommender systems to provide movie choices to end users as well as ads to people, and has even helped attorneys find case law content. He's worked with Big Data solutions and machine learning since 2010. Kim often speaks and writes about recommender systems. You can find him at http://kimfalk.org.

When he isn't teaching machines to stalk people, Kim is a family man, father, and trail runner with his German Pointer.

about the cover illustration

The figure on the cover of *Practical Recommender Systems* is captioned "Amazone d'Afrique," or an Amazon from Africa. The illustration is taken from a collection of dress costumes from various countries by Jacques Grasset de Saint-Sauveur (1757–1810), titled *Costumes de Différents Pays*, published in France in 1797. Each illustration is finely drawn and colored by hand.

The rich variety of Grasset de Saint-Sauveur's collection reminds us vividly of how culturally apart the world's towns and regions were just 200 years ago. Isolated from each other, people spoke different dialects and languages. In the streets or in the countryside, it was easy to identify where they lived and what their trade or station in life was just by their dress. The way we dress has changed since then, and the diversity by region, so rich at the time, has faded away. It is now hard to tell apart the inhabitants of different continents, let alone different towns, regions, or countries. Perhaps we have traded cultural diversity for a more varied personal life—certainly for a more varied and fast-paced technological life.

At a time when it is hard to tell one computer book from another, Manning celebrates the inventiveness and initiative of the computer business with book covers based on the rich diversity of regional life of two centuries ago, brought back to life by Grasset de Saint-Sauveur's pictures.

Part 1

Getting ready for recommender systems

The environment is everything that isn't me.
—Albert Einstein

Using recommender systems and, in fact, most machine learning methods in production isn't only about implementing the best algorithm, it's about understanding your users and the domain.

Chapters 1–6, part 1 of *Practical Recommender Systems*, introduce you to the recommender system ecosystem and infrastructures. You'll learn how to collect data and how to use it when you add a recommender system to your application. You'll learn the difference between a recommendation and an advertisement, and between a personal recommendation and a non-personal one. You'll also learn how to gather data to build your own recommender system.

What is a recommender?

It's a jungle out there as far as understanding what a recommender system is, so we'll start this book looking into what problems it solves and how it's used. Here's what we'll cover:

- Understanding the task a recommender system is trying to emulate
- Developing insight into what are nonpersonalized and personalized recommendations
- Developing a taxonomy of how to describe recommenders
- Introducing the example website MovieGEEKs

Get a cup of coffee and a blanket and make yourself comfortable for this introduction to the world of recommendations. We'll ease into it, first looking at real-world examples before moving into the computational intricacies of a recommender system in the following chapters. You might feel tempted to skip ahead, but don't. You need the basics to understand what the result of your recommender engineering efforts should be.

1.1   Real-life recommendations

I lived for years in Italy, in Rome. Rome is a beautiful place with many food markets—not the central ones found in guidebooks that are full of knock-off Gucci bags (yes, Gucci bags in food markets)—but the ones that are outside the tour bus route, the ones where the locals shop and where farmers sell their products.

Every Saturday we went to see a greengrocer named Marino. We were good customers, real foodies, so he knew that if he recommended good things to us, we'd buy them—even if we had strict plans to buy only what was on our list. The watermelon season was great, the many types of tomatoes offered a fountain of various

3

flavors, and I'll never forget the taste of the fresh mozzarella. Marino, at times, also recommended that we *not* buy something if it was not top quality, and we trusted him to give us good advice. This is an example of *recommendations.* Marino recommended the same things repeatedly, which is okay with food, but that isn't the case for most other types of products, such as books or movies or music.

When I was younger, before Spotify and other streaming services took over the music market, I liked to buy CDs. I went to a music shop that catered mostly to DJs, and I walked around and gathered a stack of CDs, then found a spot at the counter with a pair of headphones and started listening. With the CDs as context, I had long conversations with the man behind the counter. He checked which CDs I liked (and didn't like) and recommended others based on that. I valued the fact that he remembered my preferences well enough between visits and didn't recommend the same titles to me repeatedly. This is also an example of *recommendations.*

Getting home from work (now that I'm older), I always look in our mailbox to see if we've got mail. Usually, the mailbox is full of advertisements from supermarkets, listing things that are on sale. Typically, the ads show pictures of fresh fruit on one page and dishwasher powder on the next—all things that supermarkets like to recommend that you buy because they claim it's a good offer. These aren't recommendations; they're *advertisements.*

Once a week, the local newspaper is among the mail. The newspaper features a top 10 list of the most watched movies at the theater that week. This is a *non-personalized recommendation.* On television, much thought goes into placing commercials with the right television content. These are *targeted commercials* because it's thought a certain type of people are watching.

In February 2015, Copenhagen Airport officials announced the placement of 600 monitors around the airport to show commercials based on the viewer's estimated age and gender, along with information regarding the destinations at the nearby gates. The age and gender were inferred using cameras and an algorithm. The press release about the advertising provided this description: *"A woman traveling to Brussels wants to see nice watches or an ad for a finance magazine, for example. A family going on vacation might be more interested in ads for sunblock or car rentals."*[1] These are *relevant commercials* or *highly targeted commercials.*

People usually perceive commercials on television or at the airport as a nuisance, but if we go online, the limits to what we consider invasive become a bit different. There could be many reasons for this, which is a whole topic in itself.

The internet is still the Wild West, and although I think that the advertising at the Copenhagen Airport is quite invasive, I also find it irritating when I see advertisements on the internet that are directed at a target group that I'm not part of. To target their commercials, websites need to know a bit about who you are.

---

[1] For more information, see http://mng.bz/ka6j.

In this and later chapters, you'll learn about recommendations, how to collect information about the recipients of the recommendations, how to store the data, and how to use it. You can calculate recommendations in various ways, and you'll see the most used techniques.

A recommender system isn't only a fancy algorithm. It's also about understanding the data and your users. Data scientists have a long running discussion on whether it's more important to have a super-good algorithm or to have more data. Both have flip-sides; super algorithms require super hardware and lots of it. More data creates other challenges, like how to access it fast enough. Going through this book you'll learn about the tradeoffs and get tools to make better decisions.

The previous examples are meant to illustrate that commercials and recommendations can look similar to the user. Behind the screen, the intent of the content is different; a *recommendation* is calculated based on what the active user likes, what others have liked in the past, and what's often requested by the receiver. A *commercial* is given for the benefit of the sender and is usually pushed on the receiver. The difference between the two can become blurry. In this book, I'll call everything calculated from data a recommendation.

1.1.1 *Recommender systems are at home on the internet*

Recommenders are most at home on the internet because this is where you can not only address individual users but can also collect behavioral data. Let's look at a few examples.

A website showing top 10 lists of the most sold bread-making machines provides *non-personalized* recommendations. If a website for home sales or concert tickets shows you recommendations based on your demographics or your current location, the recommendations are *semi-personalized*. Personalized recommendations can be found on Amazon, where identified customers see "Recommendations for you." The idea of the personalized recommendation also arises from the idea that people aren't only interested in the popular items, but also in items that aren't sold the most or items that are in the long tail.

1.1.2 *The long tail*

The long tail was coined by Chris Anderson in an article in *Wired* magazine in 2004, which was expanded into a book published in 2006 (Hyperion).[2] In the article, Anderson identified a new business model that's frequently seen on the internet.

Anderson's insight was that if you've a brick-and-mortar shop, you've a limited amount of storage and, more importantly, a finite space to show products to your customers. You also have a limited customer base because people have to come to your shop. Without these limitations, you don't have to sell only popular products as with the

---

[2] For more information on the magazine article, see https://www.wired.com/2004/10/tail/. For information on the book, see https://en.wikipedia.org/wiki/The_Long_Tail_(book).

usual commerce business model. In brick-and-mortar shops, it's considered a losing strategy to stock non-popular products because you need to store many items that might never sell. But if you've a web store, you can store an infinite number of products because rental space is cheap or, if you sell digital content, it doesn't take up any space at all, costing little or nothing. The idea behind the long-tail economy is that you can profit by selling many products, but only a few of each, to many different people.

I'm all for diversity, so I think it's great to have a huge catalog of products, but the question that's difficult to answer is how do users find what they want? This is where recommender systems make their entrance. Because these systems help people find those diverse things that they wouldn't otherwise know existed.

On the web, because Amazon and Netflix are considered the giants both in content and in recommendations, these companies are used in numerous examples throughout this book. In the following section, you'll take a closer look at Netflix as an example of a recommender system.

1.1.3   *The Netflix recommender system*

As you likely know, Netflix is a streaming site. Its domain is that of films and TV series, and it has a continuous flow of available content. The purpose of Netflix's recommendations is to keep you interested in its content for as long as possible and to keep you paying the subscription fee month after month.

The service runs on many platforms, so the context of its recommendations can differ. Figure 1.1 is a screenshot of Netflix from my laptop. I can also access Netflix from my TV, my tablet, and even my phone. What I want to watch on each platform varies—I never watch an epic fantasy film on my phone, but I love them on TV.

Let's begin this walk-through by looking at that startup page. The front page is constructed as a panel containing rows with subjects such as Top Picks, Drama, and Popular on Netflix. The top row is dedicated to what's on my list. Netflix loves this list because it indicates not only what I've watched and what I'm watching now, but also what I (at least at one point) have shown an interest in watching.

Netflix wants you to notice the following row because it contains the *Netflix Originals*—the series that are produced by Netflix. These are important to Netflix for two reasons, both financial:

- Netflix has spent big money to produce original content and the programs are, in most cases, found only on Netflix.
- Netflix must pay content owners when users watch their content. If that owner is Netflix, not only does it save them money, it puts money in their pocket.

The last point also illustrates something to consider: even if everything is personalized on the page, the fact that the Netflix Originals are on the second row probably isn't a result of me watching them, but rather a pursuit of an internal business goal.

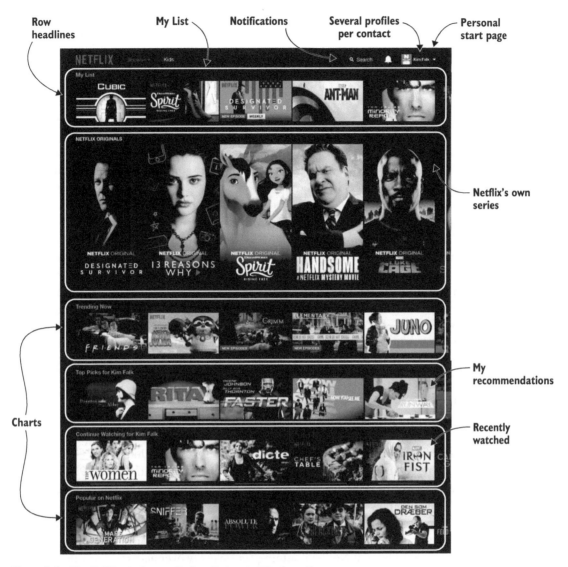

Figure 1.1 The Netflix start page (before it changed the layout)

CHARTS AND TRENDS

Next is the Trending Now list. Trending is a loose term that can mean many things, but here it includes content that's popular within a short period. The bottom row, Popular on Netflix, also has to do with popularity but over a longer period, maybe a week. Trends and charts will be discussed in detail in chapter 5.

RECOMMENDATIONS

The fourth row is the list of Top Picks for me, which match my profile. This list contains what most people would call recommendations. It shows what the Netflix recommender system predicts what I'd like to watch next. It looks almost right. I'm not into bloody, gory movies, and I'd rather not see any dissections of bodies at all. Not all the suggestions are to my liking, but I assume that it's not only my taste that Netflix uses to build this list. The rest of my household also watches content using my profile at times. *Profiles* are Netflix's way of letting the current user indicate who's watching.

Before introducing profiles, Netflix aimed its recommendations at a household rather than one person.[3] It tried to always show something for mom, dad, and children. But Netflix has since dropped that, so now my list doesn't include any children's shows. But even if Netflix is using personal profiles, I think it imperative to consider who's watching—not only the person with the profile, but also anyone else. I've heard rumors that other companies are working on solutions enabling you to tell the system that other people are watching too. This is to allow the service to deliver recommendations fitting all members of the audience. To date, I haven't seen any in play.

Microsoft Kinect could recognize people in front of the TV by using face/body recognition. Microsoft took it a step further by identifying not only household members, but also other people from its full catalog of users, allowing Kinect to recognize users when they're visiting other homes. Although a sign of audience recognition, Kinect for Xbox One was discontinued in October 2017, representing the end of the Kinect product line.

ROWS AND SECTIONS

Back to the Top Picks of Netflix. You can find more details on the content by hovering your mouse over one of the suggestions. A tooltip appears with a description (see figure 1.2) and a predicted rating, which is what the recommender system estimates I'd rate this content. You might expect that the recommendations in the Top Picks all have a high rating, like the one in figure 1.1, but looking through the recommendations, you can find examples of items with a low predicted rating, as shown in figure 1.3.

The ways of the Netflix recommender are many, so there are numerous possible explanations as to why Netflix recommends an item that it predicts I won't rate highly. One reason could be that Netflix is aiming for diversity over accuracy. Another reason could be that even if I won't rate a movie maximum stars, it might still be something that I'm in the mood to watch. This is also the first hint that Netflix doesn't put much value on ratings.

The titles of each row are different; some are of the type Because You Watched Suits. These lines recommend things that are similar to *Suits*. Other rows are genres such as *Comedies*, which, curiously enough, contains comedies. You could say that the row titles are also a list of recommendations; you could call these *category recommendations*.

---

[3] "Netflix Recommendations: Beyond the 5 stars (Part 1)," http://mng.bz/bG2x.

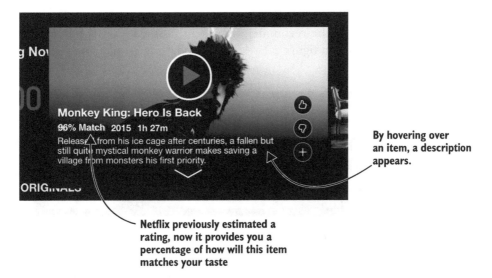

By hovering over
an item, a description
appears.

Netflix previously estimated a
rating, now it provides you a
percentage of how will this item
matches your taste

Figure 1.2 A Netflix Top Pick with a predicted match

Low-predicted match
between the Top Picks

Figure 1.3 A Netflix Top Pick with a low predicted rating

This could be the end of the story, but then you'd miss the most important part of the Netflix personalization.

RANKING

Each of the row headlines describes a set of content. This content is then ordered according to a recommendation system and presented in order of relevancy or *rank*, starting from the left as illustrated in figure 1.4.

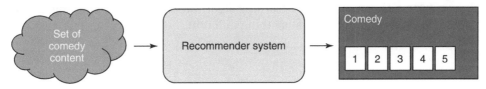

Figure 1.4 Each Netflix row is ordered by relevance.

Even in My List, which contains the content I've selected myself, the content is ordered according to the recommender system's estimate of its relevance for me. I added the screenshot in figure 1.1 yesterday. Today my list has a new order, as shown in figure 1.5.

Figure 1.5   Netflix orders my list by relevancy.

The Netflix recommender system also tries to recommend content that's relevant at a specific time or in a particular context. For example, Sunday mornings might be more for cartoons and comedies, whereas evenings might be more for "serious" watching of a TV series such as *Suits*.

Another row that might be surprising is Popular on Netflix, which shows content that's popular right now. But Netflix doesn't say that the most popular item is the one all the way to the left. Netflix finds the set of most popular items and then orders them according to what you consider most relevant now.

BOOSTING

A point to ponder is why Netflix has ranked the show *Designated Survivor* high in My List, considering that I'm already watching it. But Netflix had a notification indicating that a new season of *Designated Survivor* is out. This could explain why this show appears.

Boosting is a way for companies to put a finger on the scale when suggestions are calculated, and Netflix wants me to notice *Suits* because it's new content, meaning it has a freshness value. Netflix boosts content based on freshness; *freshness* can mean that it's new or it's been mentioned in the news. Boosting is covered in more detail in chapter 6 because it's something that many site holders request as soon as the system is up and running.

> **NOTE**   There's a machine-learning algorithm family called boosting, but what I'm referring to here is something different.[4]

---

[4] For more information, see https://en.wikipedia.org/wiki/Boosting_%28machine_learning%29.

SOCIAL MEDIA CONNECTION

For a short period of time, Netflix also tried to use social media data.[5] Back then, you'd find something like what's shown in figure 1.6 on your Netflix page.

Figure 1.6   **Netflix wants to know what my friends are watching.**

Netflix encouraged you to enable Facebook Connect, thereby allowing Netflix access to your list of friends as well as other information. One of the advantages for Netflix was that it was able to find your friends and make social recommendations based on what they liked. Connecting with Facebook could also make watching films a much more social experience, which is something that many media companies are exploring.

In this day and age, people don't sit down to watch films passively. They multitask, watching a movie while sitting with a second device (such as a tablet or a smartphone). What you're doing on the second device can have a large influence on what you watch next. Imagine that after you watch something on Netflix, a notification pops up on your phone that one of your friends liked a film, and presto, Netflix recommends that as the next thing to watch.

This social feature was, however, removed in the 2015-2016 timeframe, with the argument that people weren't happy with sharing their films with Facebook's network. In the words of Neil Hunt, the Chief Product Officer at Netflix, "It's unfortunate because I think there's a lot of value in supplementing the algorithmic suggestions with personal suggestions."[6]

TASTE PROFILE

With a page that's built almost entirely based on suggestions, it's a good idea to provide as much input as possible on your tastes. If Netflix doesn't have a clear sense of your taste, it can be hard for you to find what you want to watch.

In 2016 Netflix had options that helped users build their profiles. The Taste Profile menu, shown in figure 1.7, enabled you to rate shows and movies, to select genres by saying how often you felt like watching, for example, *Adrenaline Rush* content as illustrated in figure 1.8, or to check whether your ratings matched your current opinions.

---

[5] "Get to know Netflix and its New Facebook Integration," http://mng.bz/6yHM.
[6] "It's your fault Netflix doesn't have good social features," http://mng.bz/jc7M.

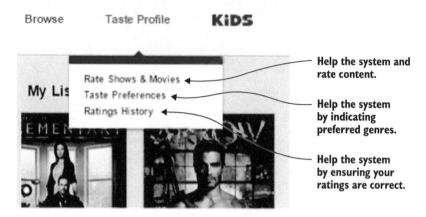

Figure 1.7   Example of how the Netflix taste profile looked in 2015

Figure 1.8   The Netflix Taste Preferences menu

The manually inputted Taste Preferences enable Netflix to provide better suggestions. Asking the user for help with the taste profile is a method often used to allow the system to give suggestions to new users. But, as with so many things, there's often a difference between what users say they like and what they indeed like.

Seeing taste preferences is usually the first step in getting to know a user. And as the user uses the system more, Netflix was able to collect usage data, which is often more trustworthy. Netflix has now removed this feature.

1.1.4   *Recommender system definition*

To be sure we're all on the same page, table 1.1 provides several definitions.

Table 1.1 Recommender system definitions

Term	Netflix example	Definition
Prediction	Netflix guesses what you'll rate an item.	A prediction is an estimate of how much the user would rate/like an item.
Relevancy	Orders all rows on the page (for example, Top Picks and Popular on Facebook) according to applicability.	An ordering of items according to what's most relevant to the user right now. Relevance is a function of context, demographics, and (predicted) ratings.
Recommendation	Top Picks for me.	The top N most relevant items.
Personalization	The row headlines in Netflix are an example of personalization.	Integrates relevancy into the presentation.
Taste profile	See figure 1.8.	A list of characterizing terms coupled with values.

With these definitions in place, we can finally define a *recommender system*.

> **Definition: recommender system**
>
> A *recommender system* calculates and provides relevant content to the user based on knowledge of the user, content, and interactions between the user and the item.

With this definition in place, you might think that you've figured it all out. But let's go through an example of how a recommendation could be calculated and how it would work. Figure 1.9 shows how Netflix might produce my Top Picks row. Here are the steps of how Netflix might calculate my Top Picks:

1. A request for the Top Picks list is received.
2. The server calls the recommendation system, which consists of a pipeline of methods. This step is called *retrieve candidate items*. It retrieves the items from the catalog database that are most similar to the current user's taste.
3. The top five items (normally it could be 100 items or more) are piped into the next pipeline step, which is to calculate prediction.
4. Prediction is calculated using the user preferences retrieved from the user database. It's likely that the calculation will remove one or more items from the list due to a small predicted rating. In figure 1.9, items C and E are removed.
5. The significant items are output from the calculated prediction, now with a predicted rating added to them. The result is piped into an order-by-relevance process.

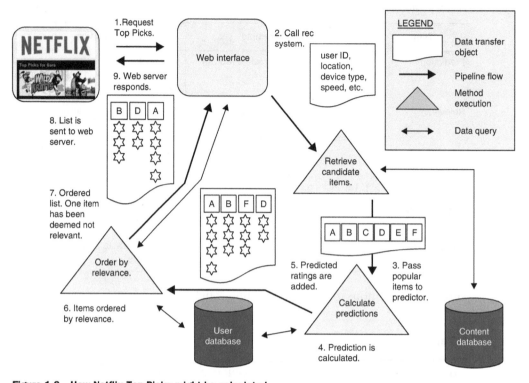

Figure 1.9   How Netflix Top Picks might be calculated

6 The revelant items are ordered according to the user's taste, context, and demographics. The process might even try to add as much diversity to the result as possible.

7 The items are now ordered by relevance. Item *F* was removed because the relevance calculations showed that it wouldn't be relevant for the end user.

8 The pipeline returns the list.

9 The server returns the result.

Looking at figure 1.9, it's evident that there are many aspects to consider when working with recommender systems. The preceding pipeline is also missing the parts of collecting the data and building the models. Most recommender systems try to use the data shown in figure 1.10 in one way or another.

Figure 1.9 also illustrates another fact to take into consideration: the rating prediction is only a part of a recommendation system. Other things can also play an important role in what your system should display to the user. A big part of this book is about predicting ratings, and that's important, even if I made it sound like something negible here.

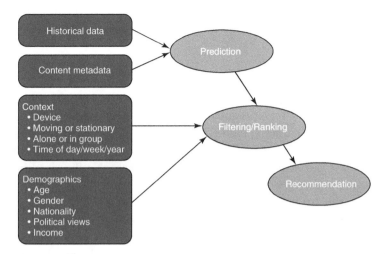

Figure 1.10   Data can potentially be used as input data for a recommender system.

1.2   Taxonomy of recommender systems

Before starting to implement a recommendation system, it's a good idea to dwell a bit on what kind of recommender system you want to roll out of the garage. A good way to start is by looking at similar systems for inspiration. In this section, you'll learn a framework for studying and defining a recommender system.

In the previous sections, the Tour d'Netflix provided an overview of what a recommender system can do. This section explains a taxonomy to use to analyze recommenders. I first learned about it in Professor Joseph A. Konstan and Michael D. Ekstrand's Coursera course "Introduction to Recommender Systems,"[7] and have found good use for it ever since. *Taxonomy* uses the following dimensions to describe a system: domain, purpose, context, personalization level, whose opinions, privacy and trustworthiness, interfaces, and algorithms.[8] Let's look at each of those dimensions.

1.2.1   Domain

The *domain* is the type of content recommended. In the Netflix example, the domain is movies and TV series, but it can be anything: sequences of content such as playlists, best ways to take e-learning courses to achieve a goal, jobs, books, cars, groceries, holidays, destinations, or even people to date.

The domain is significant because it provides hints on what you'd do with the recommendations. The domain is also important because it indicates how bad it is to be wrong. If you're doing a music recommender then it isn't that bad if you recommend

---

[7] For more information, see www.coursera.org/learn/recommender-systems-introduction/.

[8] The taxonomy concept first appeared in *Word of Mouse: The Marketing Power of Collaborative Filtering* by John Riel and Joseph A. Konstan (Business Plus, 2002).

music that isn't spot on. If you're recommending foster parents to children in need, then the cost of failure is quite high. The domain also dictates if you can recommend the same thing more than once.

1.2.2   Purpose

What is the purpose of the Netflix site, both for the end user and for the provider? For end users, the use of Netflix recommendations is to find relevant content that they want to watch at that specific time. Imagine that you didn't have any ordering or filtering. How would you ever find anything in the Netflix catalog when it has more than 10,000 items? And the purpose for the provider (in this case, Netflix) is ultimately to make customers pay for the subscription month after month by providing content they want to watch, right at their fingertips.

Netflix considers the amount of content viewed as a deciding factor in how they're doing. Measuring something else instead of your direct goal is called using a *proxy goal*. Using a proxy goal is something you should be careful about because it can inadvertently end up measuring other effects than what you wanted—more time spent on the Netflix platform could mean frustrated customers who search and search without finding what they're looking for, or they may have found it, but the site keeps stalling.[9]

Behind the scenes, there might also be considerations to balance things in such a way that Netflix pays the least money possible for what you're watching. Netflix probably pays less to offer 10-year-old episodes of *Friends* than a newer series or, even better, a Netflix original series where they don't have to pay a license fee to anybody.

A purpose could also be to give information or to help or educate the user. In most cases, however, the purpose is probably to sell more.

What type of customers would you rather serve: consumers who arrive once and expect good recommendations or loyal visitors who create profiles and return on a regular basis? Will the site be based on automatic consumption (for example, the Spotify radio station, which keeps playing music based on a song or a single artist)?

1.2.3   Context

The *context* is the environment in which the consumer receives a recommendation. In our example, it can be the device the customer uses to view Netflix or the current location of the receiver, the time of day (or night), and what the consumer is doing. Does the user have time to study the suggestions or is a quick decision needed? The context can also include the weather or even the user's mood!

Consider a search for a cafe on Google Maps. Is the user sitting at an office computer and looking for a good coffee bar, or is the user standing on the street as it starts to rain? In the first scenario, the best response would identify good quality cafes in a wider radius; in the second scenario, recommendations would ideally contain only the

---

[9] I recommend *Weapons of Math Destruction* by Cathy O'Neil (Broadway Books, 2016) if you want to know more about how wrong things can go when you use proxy goals.

nearest place to drink coffee while the rain passes. Foursquare is an example of an app where you can find cafes. We'll look at Foursquare in chapter 12.

1.2.4 *Personalization level*

Recommendations can come at many personalization levels, from using basic statistics to looking at individual user data. Figure 1.11 illustrates these levels.

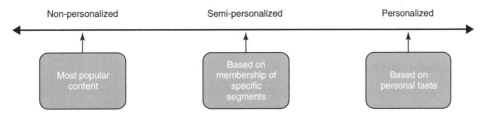

Figure 1.11 Personalization levels

NON-PERSONALIZED

A list of the most popular items is considered a *non-personalized recommendation*: the chances are that the current user might like the same items as most others do. Non-personalized recommendations also include showing things ordered by date, such as showing the newest items first. Everyone who interacts with the recommender system receives the same list of recommendations. And they can also include when a cafe suggests drinks Friday afternoon, cappuccinos in the morning, but brunch on weekend mornings.

SEMI/SEGMENT-PERSONALIZED

The next level of recommendations divides users into groups—the *semi/segment personalized recommendations*. You can segment groups of users in many ways: by age, by nationality, or by distinct patterns such as business people or students, car drivers or bicycle riders.

A system selling concert tickets, for example, recommends shows based on the user's country or city. Here's another case: if a user is listening to music on a smartphone, the system might try to deduce whether the device is moving or not. If it is moving, the person might be exercising or they might be driving or cycling. If the device is stationary, the consumer may be sitting on a sofa at home and the appropriate music might be different.

This recommender system doesn't know anything personal about you, only you as a member of a group or segment. Other people who fit into the same group will get the same recommendations.

PERSONALIZED

A *personalized recommendation* is based on data about the current user that indicates how the user has interacted with the system previously. This generates recommendations specifically for this user.

Most recommender systems also use segments and popularity when creating personalized recommendations. An example of a personalized recommendation is Amazon's Recommended for You. The Netflix starting page is an extreme example of personalized recommendations.

Usually, a site applies various types of recommendations. Only a few sites, such as Netflix, offer everything personalized. On Amazon, you'll also find Most Sold Items, which is nonpersonalized, as well as the Customers Who Bought This Also Bought This list, which provides *seeded recommendations*. These are recommendations based on a seed, which could be the current item that a user is viewing.

1.2.5   *Whose opinions*

Expert recommenders are manual systems whose experts recommend good wines, books, or similar. These systems are used in areas where it's generally accepted that you need to be an expert to understand what's good.

The days of expert websites are mostly over, however, so the *whose opinions* parameter isn't used much nowadays. Almost all sites use the opinions of the masses. They say that there's no rule without an exception; a few expert sites still remain. An example is the sommelier's recommendation on the wine site called www.vivino.com, shown in figure 1.12. Vivino is turning to recommender systems to recommend wines as well. Vivino added the recommender system to their app in 2017 to help users find new wines to taste based on their rating history.[10]

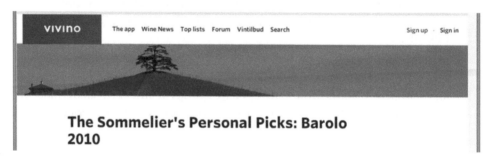

Figure 1.12   Vivino.com provides expert wine recommendations (the recommendations are omitted to save space).

1.2.6   *Privacy and trustworthiness*

How well does the system protect users' privacy? How is the collected information used? For example, in Europe, it's common to pay money into a pension, which is handled by a bank. Often these banks offer different kinds of retirement savings plans. A system that recommends these should have strict rules for privacy. Imagine

---

[10] For more information, see http://mng.bz/1jFR.

filling in an application for a retirement savings plan and describing that you've back problems, and a minute later receiving a phone call from a chiropractor with great offers to handle your exact problem. Or even worse, you buy a special bed for people with back problems, and an hour later you receive an email that your health insurance premium has gone up.

Many people consider recommendations as a form of manipulation because they present choices that customers are more likely to pick than if they were offered a random selection. And most shops are trying to sell more, so the fact that stores that use recommendations to sell more makes people think they're being manipulated. But if that means watching a film that would entertain rather than bore, then I say it's okay. Manipulation is more about the *motive* for showing a particular item rather than the *act* of showing it. If you've recommended inappropriate and non-optimal medicine because the vendor buys the website owner better dinners, then that's manipulation, which should be frowned upon.

When the recommendation system starts performing and an increase in business is measured, many might find it tempting to inject vendor preferences, overstocked items, or maybe preferences for which brand of pills customers buy. Beware: if customers start feeling manipulated, they'll stop trusting your recommendations and eventually find what they need somewhere else.

> *The moment that recommendations have the power to influence decisions, they become a target for spammers, scammers, and other people with less-than-noble motives for influencing our decisions.*
> —Daniel Tunkelang[11]

Trustworthiness indicates how much the consumer trusts recommendations instead of considering them as commercials or attempts at manipulation. In the Netflix example, I talked about how predictions can be discouraging for users if the estimated prediction is far off the user's actual rating. This is about trustworthiness. If the user takes the suggestions seriously, the system is trustworthy.

1.2.7   Interface

The *interface* of a recommender system depicts the kind of input and output it produces. Let's look at each.

INPUT

Netflix once enabled users to enter likes and dislikes by rating content and adding preferences on genres and topics. This data can be used as input to a recommender system.

The Netflix example uses *explicit input*, where you, the consumer, manually add information about what you like. Another form of input is *implicit*, where the system

---

[11] For more on the role taste and trust play in recommendations, see www.linkedin.com/pulse/taste-trust-daniel-tunkelang.

tries to deduce taste by looking at how you interact with the system. Chapter 4 handles feedback in more detail.

OUTPUT

Types of *output* can be predictions, recommendations, or filtering. For example, Netflix outputs recommendations in many ways. It estimates predictions, provides personalized suggestions, and shows popular items, which normally is in the form of a top 10 list (but Netflix even personalizes that).

If the recommendations are a natural part of the page, it's called an *organic presentation*. The rows shown on Netflix are an example of organic recommendations: Netflix doesn't indicate that these are recommendations; they're an integral part of the site.

The examples illustrated in figure 1.13 are nonorganic. Hot Network Questions uses a form of non-personalized recommendations by not explicitly stating that what's shown. Amazon displays nonorganic personalized recommendations in its Recommended for You list, and the *New York Times* employs nonorganic recommendations showing the most emailed articles.

Figure 1.13   Examples of nonorganic, non-personalized recommendations: Hot Network Questions from Cross Validated, Most Emailed from the *New York Times*, and a personalized Recommended for You list from Amazon

Certain systems explain the recommendations. Recommenders with that ability are called *white-box recommenders*; those that don't are called *black-box recommenders*. Figure 1.14 shows examples of each. The distinction is important to consider when choosing an algorithm because not all provide a clear path back to the reasons for a prediction.

Deciding whether you want to produce a white-box or black-box recommender can put constraints on which algorithms you use. The more your system needs to explain, the simpler the algorithm. Often you can consider the decision as shown in figure 1.15. The better the quality of the recommendation, the more complex and the harder to show explanations. This problem is known as *model accuracy-model interpretation trade-off*.

I once worked on a project where extreme emphasis was placed on explainability and quality. To solve this, we had to build another algorithm on top of our recommender system to allow for good quality recommendations while also having a system that connected the evidence with the result.

Figure 1.14 Black-box (from Netflix) and white-box (from Amazon) recommendations

Figure 1.15 Explainability vs. quality of recommendations

Recommender systems have become extremely common in recent years, so there are many examples to look at. Often the recommender systems are implemented for movies, music, books, news, research articles, and most products in general. But recommender systems also have a place in many other areas, such as financial services, life insurance, online data, job searches, and in fact, everywhere there are choices to be made. This book primarily uses websites as examples, but there's no reason not to work in other platforms.

1.2.8 Algorithms

A number of algorithms are presented in this book. The algorithms fall into two groups, and they depend on the type of data you use to make your recommendations. Algorithms that employ usage data are called *collaborative filtering*. Algorithms that use content metadata and user profiles to calculate recommendations are called *content-based filtering*. A mix of the two types is called *hybrid recommenders*.

COLLABORATIVE FILTERING

Figure 1.16 illustrates one way of doing collaborative filtering. The outer set is the full catalog. The middle set is a group of users who have consumed similar items. A recommender system recommends items from the smaller, front-most set, assuming that if users liked the same things as the current user, then the current user will also like other items this group has consumed. The group is identified by the overlap between what the individual users have liked and what the current user liked. Then the gap of content, which the current user is missing, will be recommended (the part of the middle circle that isn't covered by the circle representing the current user's likes).

Many ways exist to calculate collaborative filtering recommendations. You'll see a simple version in chapter 8 and a not-so-simple one in chapter 11, where we talk about matrix factorization algorithms.

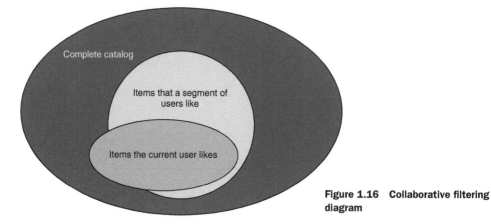

Figure 1.16   Collaborative filtering diagram

CONTENT-BASED FILTERING

Content-based filtering uses the metadata you have on the items in your catalog. Netflix uses descriptions of its movies, for example.

Depending on the specific algorithm, the system can calculate recommendations either by taking the items the user has liked and finding similar content, by comparing the items and user profiles, or, if there's no user involved, by finding similar content between items. When there's a user profile, the system calculates a profile for each user that contains categories of the content. If Netflix used content-based filtering, it could create a user profile of genres like thrillers, comedies, drama, and new films, and give values to them all. Then a film gets recommended if it has similar values as the user.

Here's an example. User Thomas likes *Guardians of the Galaxy*, *Interstellar*, and the TV series *Game of Thrones*. Each is rated according to a five-point system. Table 1.2 shows one way of looking at the three selections.

Table 1.2 Rating system for two films and a TV series

Movies and TV	Sci-Fi genre	Adventure genre
Interstellar	3	3
Game of Thrones	1	5
Guardians of the Galaxy	5	4

Based on this information, you build a profile of Thomas indicating Sci-Fi: 3, Adventure: 4. To find other films to recommend, you look through the catalog to find films similar to Thomas' profile.

HYBRID RECOMMENDER

Both collaborative filtering and content-based filtering have strengths and weaknesses. Collaborative filtering needs much feedback from the users to work properly, while content-based filtering needs good descriptions of the items. Often recommendations are produced as a mix of the output from the two types of algorithms we talked about previously, plus other types of input, which could be the distance from a place or the time of day.

1.3 *Machine learning and the Netflix Prize*

A recommender system is about predicting what content a user needs right now. You can predict this in many ways. Building recommender systems has become a multidisciplinary sport that takes advantage of computer science fields such as machine learning, data mining, information retrieval, and even human-computer interaction. Machine learning and data-mining methods enable the computer to make predictions by studying examples of what it should predict; consequently, recommendations can be constructed by using these prediction functions.

Many recommender systems are centered around machine-learning algorithms to predict user ratings of items or to learn how to correctly rank items for a user. One reason that the field of machine learning is growing is that people want to solve the recommender system problem. The aim is to implement algorithms that enable computers to suggest our secret desires, even before we know them ourselves.

Many claim that the catalyst for this interest in applying machine learning to recommender systems was the famous Netflix Prize. The *Netflix Prize* was a competition hosted by Netflix that offered $1,000,000 to anyone who could come up with an algorithm that improved their recommendations by 10%. The competition began in 2006, and it took almost three years for somebody to win it. In the end, it was a hybrid algorithm that won. You'll recall that a hybrid algorithm runs several algorithms and then returns a combined result from all of them. You'll learn about hybrids in chapter 11.

Netflix never used the winning algorithm, probably because it was so complicated that the performance hit on the system couldn't justify the improvements. Sadly, we don't have Netflix to play with while learning about recommender systems. Instead, I've implemented a small demo site called MovieGEEKs to show off the things described in this book. The site requires much tweaking before it can be production-ready. Understanding recommender systems is its key purpose.

1.4 The MovieGEEKs website

This book is about how to implement recommender systems. It will provide you with the tools to do that, no matter which platform you want to use for your recommendation system. But to do anything interesting with a recommender system, you need data and to get a feel for how it's working it's not enough to look at numbers.

This book focuses on websites, but that doesn't mean that everything written here doesn't apply to any other type of system. This is a short introduction to the framework in which we'll do our dance.

The MovieGEEKs website (http://mng.bz/04k5) is built using a Django website. I encourage you to download MovieGEEKs and use it as you read through the book because it will help you understand what's going on. The fact that it's a Django site or something else isn't so important; I'll point you to where to look as we work through the examples.

> **Django website and framework**
>
> If the words *Django web framework* sound strange to you, take a look at the Django documentation at www.djangoproject.com/start/overview/.

You'll download the website once. It contains all the functionality described in this book. Here's the fictional scenario that we'll be following.

Imagine that you have a customer who wants to take his DVD selling online. I imagine an old DVD rental shop that was in Bath, in the United Kingdom, with an owner who wants to try movie selling on the internet. The store sadly no longer exists (see figure 1.17).

The shop was anything but electronic; it was managed with small paper cards and, although you might think that sounds impossible, it all seemed to work! In real life, I don't think the owner would ever have taken his business online, but one of the unique things about this place was that you'd always get superb recommendations. The owner would do a monthly review—expert opinion recommendations—and the people who worked there always knew everything there was to know about films.

I like to think of recommender systems as an attempt to give personal service to people on the Net. The following is a brief description of what the fictive owner wants.

Figure 1.17   The facade of On the Video Front, our fictional business

1.4.1   *Design and specification*

To get started, you'll need to put down several overall points for the design. The main page of the site should show visitors the following:

- A tiled area of movies
- An overview of each film, without leaving the page
- Recommendations as personal as possible
- A menu containing a list of genres

Each movie should have its own page with details as follows:

- Movie poster
- Description
- Rating

Each category should have a page containing the following:

- Same structure as the homepage
- Recommendations specific to the category

1.4.2   *Architecture*

You'll use Python and the Django web framework to implement this site. Django lets you split a project into different applications. Figure 1.18 shows a high-level architecture and provides an illustration of which applications will build the site.

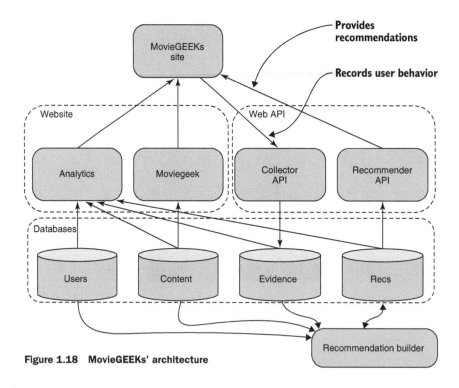

Figure 1.18   MovieGEEKs' architecture

Let's do a quick walk-through:

- *MovieGEEKs*—This is the main part of the site. Here the client logic (HTML, CSS, JavaScript) is placed along with the Python code responsible for retrieving the movie data.
- *Analytics*—The ship's bridge, where everything can be monitored. This part will use data from all the databases. The analytics part is described in chapter 4.
- *Collector*—This handles the tracking of the user behavior and stores it in the evidence database. The evidence logger is described in chapter 2.
- *Recs*—This is the heart of this story and is what will add the edge to this site. It'll deliver the recommendations to the MovieGEEKs site. The recommendations part is described in chapter 5 and the rest of the book.
- *Recommendation builder*—This pre-calculates recommendations, which will provide elaborate recommendations to the user. You'll meet the recommendation builder for the first time in chapter 7.

Each of these components or applications contain exciting data models and features. This will thoroughly entice future visitors.

MovieGEEKs is a movie site mainly because a data set is available that contains a long list of content—movies, users, and ratings. Even more important, the content includes URLs that translate into movie posters, which makes working with it much more fun.

Figure 1.19 shows the MovieGEEKs homepage, or landing page. When the user clicks a movie, a pop-up appears that gives more information and a link to even more details.

Figure 1.19   The landing page of the MovieGEEKs site

That's it! Simple, but it'll do the trick. Go ahead and download it now. For installation instructions, refer to the readme on GitHub at http://mng.bz/04k5. The Movie-GEEKs site uses a data set called MovieTweetings. This data set consists of ratings on movies that were contained in well-structured tweets on Twitter.[12]

1.5   *Building a recommender system*

Before moving on, let's look at how you'd build a recommender system. Assuming you already have a platform in the shape of a website or an app where you want to add a recommender system, it'd go something like the cycle shown in figure 1.20.

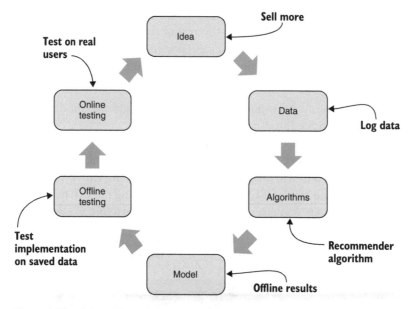

Figure 1.20   A data-driven approach to building a recommender system

Start with an idea that you want to sell more by adding recommenders. You'll collect behavioral data and use that data to build an algorithm, which creates a model when it runs. The model can also be considered as a *function*, which will, given a user ID, calculate recommendations.

   You'll try out this model on historical data to see if you can use it to predict a user's behavior. For example, if you have data showing what users bought last month, then you can create the model using the three first weeks of data to see how well the model recommends things that the users bought in the last week of your month of data. It might be better at predicting what the user has bought compared to a baseline recommender system, which can be as simple as a method that returns the most popular items. If it's doing well, you can expose it to part of your users and see if you can track

---

[12] For more information, see https://github.com/sidooms/MovieTweetings.

improvement. If you see improvement, then it can go into production; otherwise, it's back to the drawing board.

You should now have an idea of what a recommender system is, an understanding of what's needed as input, and what it can produce. Knowing the basis of a recommender system gives you the foundation for chapter 2, which shows how to collect data from users.

Summary

- Netflix uses recommendations to personalize its site and to help users select things they like.
- A recommender system is a common term for many different components and methods.
- A prediction is different than a recommendation. A prediction is about projecting what rating a user would give content, while a recommendation is a list of items that's relevant to the user.
- A recommendation context is what happens around the user (the user's environment) when a recommendation arrives. Items that might not be predicted to have the highest ratings can be recommended if they suit the context.
- The taxonomy described in this chapter is handy when you're looking at other recommender systems or trying to design your own. It's good to go through this taxonomy before starting to implement your own recommender system.

User behavior
and how to collect it

This chapter invites you to delve into the interesting subject of data collection:

- You'll start by returning to the Netflix site to identify events, which can provide evidence to build a case for what a user likes.
- You'll learn how to build a collector to gather these events.
- You'll learn how a collector can be integrated into a site such as MovieGEEKs to fetch events similar to the ones identified on the Netflix site.
- With a general overview in place and an implementation, you'll step back and analyze general consumer behavior.

Evidence is the data that reveals a user's tastes. When we talk about collecting evidence, we're collecting events and behavior that provide an indication of the user's tastes.

Most books on recommender systems describe algorithms and ways of optimizing them. They start at a point where you already have a large data set to feed your algorithms. You'll use one such data set in the MovieGEEKs site. This data set contains a catalog of movies and ratings from real users. A data set doesn't magically appear. Gathering the right evidence takes work and consideration. It'll also make or break your system. "Garbage in, garbage out," that famous programming saying is also true for recommenders.

Sadly, data that's good for one system might be unsuitable for another. For this reason, we'll have a serious discussion about data that *could* be usable, but I cannot guarantee that everything described will work in exactly the same way in your environment. In this chapter and throughout the book, we'll look at many examples of how to approach data collection for your own site.

Generally, two types of feedback are produced by users of a system: *explicit* (ratings or likes) and *implicit* (activity recorded by monitoring the user). A user can provide explicit feedback in the form of a certain number of stars, hats, smileys, or any other icon illustrating how much the user likes a product. Usually the scale is between one and five (or one and ten). User ratings are often the first thing people think about when talking about evidence. Later in this chapter, you'll look at ratings, but they're not the only thing that indicates what a user likes.

Ron Zacharski's *A Programmers Guide to Data Mining* presents a great example that illustrates the difference between implicit and explicit evidence.[1] He shows the explicit evidence of a guy named Jim. Jim states he's a vegan and enjoys French films, but in Jim's pocket is a rental receipt for Marvel's *The Avengers* and one for a 12-pack of Pabst Blue Ribbon beer. Which should you use to recommend things? I think it's an easy choice. What do you think Jim wants recommended when he opens the online ordering site for his local takeout place: vegan food or fast food? By collecting user behavior data, you can understand what users like Jim want.

You'll find there's no substitute for good evidence. Let's look at what Netflix could record, and how they could interpret it.

2.1 How (I think) Netflix gathers evidence while you browse

Let's return to Netflix for an example of evidence. Everything on the Netflix landing page is personalized (the row headlines as well as their content), with the exception of the top row, which is an advertisement that everybody probably sees or perhaps only users similar to me. Figure 2.1 shows my personalized Netflix page.

The rows are different for each user; the headlines range from familiar categories such as Comedies and Dramas to highly tailored slices such as Imaginative Time Travel Movies from the 1980s.[2] On my page, the first couple of rows contain recently added content, suggestions, and popular content. On that day, the first personalized row title is Dramas, which indicates that between the genres (or row headlines), Netflix predicts that drama best matches my interests. The Dramas row contains a list of content that Netflix considers interesting to me within that category. Figure 2.2 illustrates the Netflix content shown in my Drama list.

Hovering the mouse over the row, I can make it scroll sideways, showing other content in the Dramas genre. When I scroll over the content of the Dramas row, what

---

[1] A free download of this book is available at http://guidetodatamining.com/.

[2] This example comes from Netflix. I'd love to know what's inside that category because I'm sure I'd want to watch all the films, but besides the *Back to the Future* films, what could possibly be in there? Look at this article for more details on Netflix's colorful categories at http://mng.bz/xCvj.

The first
personalized
row

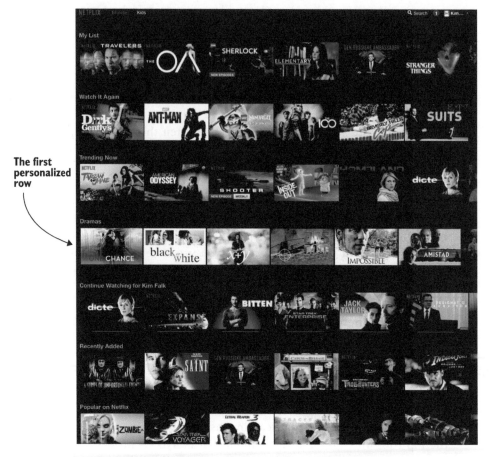

Figure 2.1   **My personalized landing page on Netflix. On this day, Drama occupies the top spot.**

does this say about me? It could mean that I'm writing a book and trying to make screenshots, but most likely it suggests that I enjoy dramas and want to investigate this list further.

If I see a movie that looks interesting, I can place my mouse over it to view details. Moreover, if those details are intriguing, I can click to go to the films's page. If it still sounds good, I'll either add it to My List or start watching it.

You could say that for any e-commerce site, looking at details means that I'm interested; only the act of watching (and finishing) a film is equivalent to buying. But for a streaming site, this isn't where it ends. If a visitor starts watching a film, it's a positive event, but if they stop after three minutes and never restart the film, then it shows that the visitor didn't like what they saw. If they restart the movie later or within a certain timeframe, it might mean that they liked it even more than when they'd watched it the first time.

Figure 2.2　Netflix Drama row, where you can either scroll the dramas using the arrow or click the row title and get a complete listing.

OFTEN THE PURPOSE ISN'T WHAT IT SEEMS

Often the purpose of e-commerce sites is to make people buy products, even if the product the customer is buying might not be exactly what they want. That depends on the site's affiliation to the product. If Amazon sells you a poor quality T-shirt, for example, you'd say that the brand of the T-shirt is bad, but you might go back to Amazon and buy another T-shirt. If you buy a T-shirt from, say, a Gap website, and you didn't like the quality, then you'll probably go to another site.

Subscription-based sites are a bit different. Mofibo (https://mofibo.com/), an e-book streaming service available in Danish, Swedish, and Dutch markets, provides recommendations as inspiration and discovery, but with a catch—it's important to Mofibo that the reader knows what kind of book it is before starting to read it. Because Mofibo pays a fee every time a reader opens a new book (not per page, but per book) and, although Mofibo wants you to read as much as possible, it also wants to minimize the number of books it must pay for.

2.1.1　The evidence Netflix collects

Let's try to imagine what goes on behind the curtains at Netflix and what data they collect. Say it's Saturday night at Jimmie's place. Jimmie has Netflix user ID 1234, and after finishing nuking the popcorn in the microwave, he opens Netflix and does the following:

- Scrolls the Drama (ID 2) row
- Hovers the mouse over a movie (ID 41335) to get details
- Clicks to get more details about the movie (ID 41335)
- Starts watching the movie (ID 41335)

While he watches the movie, imagine what happened on the Netflix server. Table 2.1 shows several of the events that could be collected from this user, along with interpretations of what they could mean. Moreover, I've added a column containing an event name to connect table 2.1 to the log described later.

Table 2.1   **Examples of evidence from Netflix**

Event	Meaning	Event name
Scrolling a themed row	User is interested in the theme, here Dramas.	`genreView`
Placing the mouse over a film to request an overview of content	User is interested in the movie (a drama), thereby showing interest in this category.	`details`
Clicking the film to request the details of content	User is more interested in the movie.	`moreDetails`
Adding the film to My List	User intends to watch the movie later.	`addToList`
Starting to watch the film	User "purchases" the movie.	`playStart`

As table 2.1 illustrates, all these events are evidence to the system because they uncover interests of the user. Table 2.2 shows how the evidence might be recorded by Netflix.

Table 2.2   **How Netflix probably logs evidence**

userId	contentId	Event	Date
1234	2	`genreView`	2017-06-07 20:01:00
1234	41335	`details`	2017-06-07 20:02:21
1234	41335	`moreDetails`	2017-06-07 20:02:30
1234	41335	`addToList`	2017-06-07 20:02:55
1234	41335	`playStart`	2017-06-07 20:03:01

There'll probably be a long list of other columns such as device type, location, speed, and weather, that can all be used to better understand the user's context. I'd also venture that the number of log events for this scenario would be many more, but let's keep the example simple. The list of events types is probably much longer as well.

Now that you have a general idea what evidence is, you can start looking into the implementation of an evidence collector. An *evidence collector* is used to collect data like that found in table 2.2. To ensure that you're not thinking that this can work only with media streaming sites, let's look at another scenario.

GARDEN TOOLS SITE EXAMPLE

I once had a colleague who spent all his breaks surfing the internet for garden tractors or for anything that ran on gasoline that he could use in a garden. Let's imagine this former colleague had a short break and opened his favorite (imaginary) site called Super Power Garden Tools. He did the following:

- Selected the Garden Tractor category
- Clicked a green monster that can pull up trees

- Clicked Specifications to see the size of the trees it can pull up
- Bought the green monster

These events were the same as picking a movie; the importance of buying an expensive product might be more significant than watching a movie, but I hope you get the picture.

2.2 *Finding useful user behavior*

Sites with high user involvement enable the site owner to collect large amounts of relevant data, whereas sites with mostly one-time visitors need to focus on relationships among the content instead. Don't despair if you don't have a streaming service with lots of user interaction to collect data from; chances are that there's still plenty to collect.

Ideally, a recommender system collects all data about a user when they interact with the content—down to measuring brain activity, adrenalin released in the blood when exposed to an item, or how sweaty the user's hands get. The more we live our lives connected, the more realistic this scenario might sound.

In the movie *WALL-E*, humans have devolved into shapeless things who live all their lives in a chair in front of a screen, where everything about them is fed into a computer. (Come to think of it, I spend most of my days sitting in front of a screen. But at least I move between screens.) Because most people have other things to do besides being hooked up to a recommender system, we need to lower expectations a bit. But with the web, we've become closer to users than any physical store ever could, so it's possible to learn many things.

CONTENT AFFILIATION TO PROVIDER

In chapter 1, one of the dimensions in the taxonomy was purpose. Purpose is important because it might result in particular strategies for calculating suggestions, as well as what you want to suggest.

Take, for example, a film: if you watch a bad film on Netflix, it tells you something about the quality of the content on Netflix and, therefore, says something bad about Netflix. If Amazon sells a Blu-ray disc of a bad film, you probably wouldn't think any less of Amazon, but if you were looking for the film and couldn't find it, that would make you think less of Amazon. I mentioned this in section 2.1 with the T-shirt analogy, but a good point is worth making twice.

The purpose of Netflix is to show good films that you like. Amazon shows you things to buy; whether you like them isn't so important. Amazon spends many resources on asking customers to write reviews and rate content, so it might not be completely fair to say it doesn't care, but for the sake of example, it will do.

2.2.1 *Capturing visitor impressions*

To better illustrate the events that occur in the lifetime of a consumer/product relationship, I've divided it into the following steps, illustrated in figure 2.3:

1 Consumer browses. As in a physical shop, the consumer looks around to see what's there, with no specific goal. What's noteworthy is where the consumer pauses and shows interest.

2 Consumer becomes interested in one or more products. It might be that the consumer knew from the start that they were looking for something specific or it might be by chance.

3 Consumer adds product to basket or a list with the intent to buy.

4 Consumer buys products.

5 Consumer consumes product. For example, the consumer watches the film or the consumer reads the book. If it's a trip, the consumer goes on the trip.

6 Consumer rates the product. Sometimes consumers return to the shop/site to rate the product.

7 Consumer resells product or otherwise disposes of it. The consumer lifetime of the product is finished; it's disposed of, deleted, or resold; in which case, the product probably goes through the same cycle again.

We'll look at what can be collected at each of these steps a bit later. But note that explicit feedback in the shape of a rating is done in step 6 or later. That's late in the process. Therefore, even if ratings are always the first thing people talk about, you should record data prior to that.

2.2.2 *What you can learn from a shop browser*

Now to go into detail about what's happening in steps 1–3 in figure 2.3. A *browser* is a customer who looks through content. They might randomly go through many different things but often pause at content that seems relevant or interesting. In a physical shop, a browser strolls through the store, not showing any direction or purpose. In a sense, the customer is gathering intelligence for later buys.

> **A browser**
>
> A *browser* is a customer looking through content. A browser as I said earlier, should be exposed to as many different things as possible, and suggestions should reflect that. If you could classify that a visitor is a browser, you could use that information to produce suggestions that fit that mood.

What you need to collect here is where the browser stops and investigates. It's also worth keeping track of what the browser sees without showing any interest. But can you be sure that a page view (product view) is always good?

PAGE VIEW

A *page view* in an e-commerce site can mean many things. It can be an indication that the visitor (or browser) is interested, but it could also identify someone who's lost or clicking randomly. In the latter instance, more clicks aren't positive. A lost user shows up as a visit with many clicks but no conversions.

Figure 2.3   Consumer/product relationship lifecycle

On the other hand, a great recommender results in fewer page views. That's because people will find everything they're looking for from the recommended links and products without needing to browse around first.

PAGE DURATION

To determine what a visitor browsing your site is interested in, you can measure the customer's duration on a content page. But is that straightforward? It is if you assume that the customer isn't doing anything else and that the next thing the customer does is to go to a new page by following a link on the current page. Table 2.3 shows one way to interpret the possible meaning of how much time a browser spends on a page.

Table 2.3   Page durations and a possible interpretation

Duration on page	What it means
Less than 5 secs	No interest
More than 5 secs	Interested
More than 1 min	Very interested
More than 5 mins	Probably went to get coffee
More than 10 mins	Interrupted or went away from the page without following a link

Adjust the duration times to fit your domain, but I think most would agree that these interpretations could be true. Which of these is worth saving? Well, all of them. Less than 5 secs is a dislike, 5 secs to 1 min could mean "interested," 1–5 mins could mean the user thinks "this is great," and 5 mins and more is hard to say. All of these depend on the content of the page. It's not an exact science.

EXPANSION CLICKS

Besides page duration, there are other ways to record user interest in the content. Add small control interactions that help you determine what the user is doing. For example, websites often use links to more information, as shown in figure 2.4. This is convenient for the customer, who can get a quick overview or expand the link if

Figure 2.4   When an expansion link is clicked, it's an indication of the visitor's interest. This is an example from Amazon.co.uk.

they're interested. Similarly, a user might scroll down to see reviews or technical details. If a user does one of these things, consider it a sign of interest.

SOCIAL MEDIA LINKS

You can also add social media buttons (figure 2.5) for people who like something so much they want to share it with others. You can't control what happens on Facebook or Twitter, or one of the other social media sites, but you can collect the event of a consumer sharing something.

Figure 2.5 The usual gang of social media links

SAVE FOR LATER

A Save for Later feature that lets users add things to lists is powerful. If a customer finds something of interest, it's a good idea to provide the user the capability to save it for later (if they don't buy it immediately). This can be as simple as having a link for bookmarking the page. Even better, have a wish list, favorites list, or watch list, depending on the type of content. Other signs of interest could be downloading a brochure, watching a video about particular content, or signing up for a newsletter on a specific topic.

SEARCH TERMS

Visiting a website can mean that people are either browsing or that they're looking for something in particular. If the page is laid out well, most customers find what they want quickly. Netflix says that every time someone starts searching, it's seen as a failure of the recommender system because it means people didn't find anything they wanted to watch among the recommendations. I'm not sure I would agree with that because often I use the search function because someone has recommended something that might be outside of what I usually watch. In any case, a search term is one of the best ways of understanding what a customer is looking for.

Figure 2.6 shows a Netflix search window. The site has more movies than are available to watch, so if you search for wonder woman, it shows you similar titles, even though *Wonder Woman* isn't part of the catalog.

Even if the system can't provide the content searched for, registering the event is worthwhile. If a user looks for a film, you know they're interested in something about that content. With this knowledge, your recommender can suggest something similar.

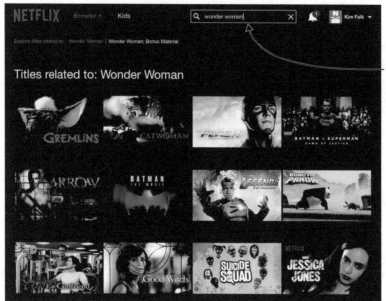

Searching for wonder woman shows that Netflix knows *Wonder Woman*, even if it isn't in the catalog.

Figure 2.6   Netflix search result window, searching on wonder woman

Linking searched items with the resulting consumption

Another thing to consider about *search terms* (what a customer types in the search field) is that it's a good idea to connect what's searched for with what's consumed. Say a user searches for *Star Wars* and looks at *Harlock: Space Pirate*, which has a reference to *Babylon A.D.*, and the user ends up watching that. Maybe it's worth putting *Babylon A.D.* in the search result for *Star Wars*.

2.2.3   Act of buying

Buying something means that the consumer considers the item useful or likeable—or maybe it's a gift. It's not easy to determine whether a purchase is for the buyer and thereby another piece of evidence that can be used to understand the user's taste, or if it's a present and something that should be disregarded.

Figuring out which purchases are presents and which aren't is an interesting problem. An item that's different in taste from the items consumed by the user so far could either be an indication of a new dimension in the user's taste or a present. Either way, it's seen as an *outlier* in the data.

Graphically, an outlier shows up as a point far away from the main body of points, as shown in figure 2.7. Because you can't be sure about what they indicate (present or

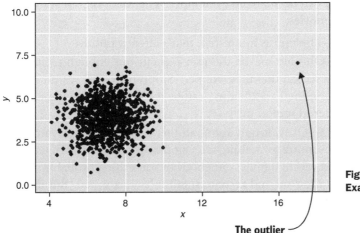

Figure 2.7
Example of an outlier

The outlier

a new interest), it's often better to disregard outliers. Conversely, it could also be a first indicator of a new trend, which is an opportunity that could be explored.

The act of buying something means that the product was presented in a good way, although it doesn't say anything about whether the consumer likes the product. At least, this is true if it's the first time the consumer buys the product. People might argue that every time a consumer buys a banana, that indicates more stars on the rating for bananas. A first buy might not be much of an indication of approval, but a second buy is. Either way, a buy can be regarded as something positive.

2.2.4 *Consuming products*

When something is bought, the shop loses contact with the product and the ability to track how it's used—if it's not a streamed product or service provided from the website.

ENDOMONDO
Movies and music aren't the only content that's consumed online. Endomondo (www.endomondo.com) is another example of a site providing online services. The social fitness sports network allows users to collect statistics about their activity using a sports tracker.

Endomondo keeps track of how much you use its features, a basis for the company to recommend similar services or to understand where they should develop new ones. Telephone companies also measure how consumers use their phones; they can track us in scary ways. The following section discusses what you can learn from streamed products.

STREAMED PRODUCTS
In the case of streaming services, music, film, or even books, all user interactions can be considered an implicit rating. Listening to a song is an indication that the user

likes it. But this data can be analyzed even more. The following list shows user interactions with music or movies:

1   *Start playing*—The user is interested; that's already positive.

2   *Stop playing*—Oh wait, maybe the user was curious enough to start playing but thought it was so bad that they stopped. Stopping a song within the first 20 secs (or a film within the first 20 mins) can be a bad sign. Stopping close to the end can be considered something else.

3   *Resume playing*—Okay, forget about all the negative implicit ratings the system registered. Resuming something after stopping can mean various things. If playing is resumed within 5 mins, somebody or something probably interrupted the consumer, so the stop and resume shouldn't be counted. But if the consumer stops and then resumes 24 hrs later, the consumer probably likes the content.

4   *Speeding*—If the user skips something in the middle, it's probably not a good sign—but only if it's the first consumption. If it's the tenth time a film has been watched, for example, skipping a boring scene probably doesn't make the overall perception of the film worse. The technical proofreader of this book noted that with music, he often skips through songs to understand a song, or whether it's worth listening to. Songs have less context, so with skipping, you can get a sense of whether you'll like the content or not. This wouldn't work with movies.

5   *Playing it to the end*—We have a winner! This is a good sign—it might not be something that the user would rate high, but if they sat through the whole thing, it probably means that they'd watch similar films. (Played to the end means played until the film ends and the credits start rolling.)

6   *Replaying*—Replaying content might mean something good for film and music, but for a site offering educational videos, it can also mean that the topic was too difficult.

These steps work on most streaming products. How to collect evidence from streamed products depends on the type of player that's used.

In the case of Endomondo, which is also a kind of streaming service, these steps and explanations don't really hold. In this sense, if you start Endomondo and indicate that you started running (by pressing the Play button), it probably doesn't have anything to do with how much you like the app if you pause it after 10 k; that may mean that you should get in better shape.

2.2.5   Visitor ratings

Finally, you've arrived at what everybody talks about—the ratings. Netflix has a motto:

> *The more you rate, the better your suggestions.*

That might be a truth requiring modifications, as you'll see later. Most recommender systems use ratings, but those user ratings are usually weighted against user behavior. These systems use ratings only as a starting point. What you want is to capture the behavior of users.

Many sites enable users to review content that they've viewed, bought, or used. This enables the system to gain a better understanding of what users like and thereby what to suggest in the future. Adding a certain number of stars (or hats, smileys, or something else) determines a rating, but behind the scenes that's only a number on a scale. Amazon, as with most places, tries to help you with what each number of stars means by providing tooltips. Figure 2.8 shows an example of a book review on Amazon.

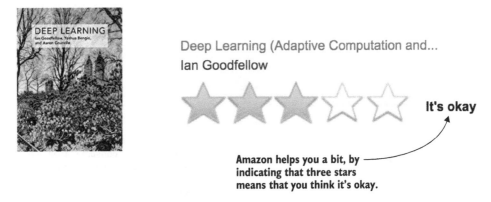

Figure 2.8 **When rating something on Amazon, it provides hints as to what the number of stars means.**

On Amazon, as the user passes the mouse over the stars, a description is shown. In this case, four stars means in effect, "I like it." In addition to ratings, certain sites, such as TripAdvisor, encourage users to write a review.

You could say that a five-star rating plus a written review counts as more than a five-star rating alone, because the person who writes the review puts more thought into it. The same is true for one-star ratings. But if a person accompanies all ratings with a written review, then it doesn't mean more. Could buying something and not rating it indicate something about your preference?

A SENSE OF CONTROL

When just-add-water cake mixes (figure 2.9) first arrived in stores, they were a huge failure. The product seemed perfect for busy consumers: the only thing they had to do was to add water. Through consumer studies, it was discovered that the problem wasn't that the process was easy, but that it was *too* easy. Baking a cake is about creating, but pre-preparing everything made the process too easy; it took away the consumer's sense of control. The manufacturers said, "All right, we'll let them add eggs also." It was less expensive to produce and the consumer felt empowered. When the cake mixes were introduced again, with instructions to add water and eggs, they were a huge success.

Many sites let users add their preferences for the very same reasons: to give the consumer a sense of control over what the system believes is that consumer's taste. Netflix states that many people indicate that they like documentaries and foreign

Figure 2.9 Chocolate cake mix. When introduced, the consumer needed to add only water. But it wasn't a success until consumers were instructed to add water and eggs.

movies but watch American sitcoms. Then what should Netflix suggest: things that make you feel bad about your choice of entertainment or things that you want to watch?

This is one of the reasons it's hard to use data sets with ratings to test whether a recommender system is good. Data sets can test whether your prediction calculations work, but not whether the system will attract more users.

SAVING A RATING

When a user adds a rating, it's an event, and that event should still be saved among the evidence as any other event. It might also be worth saving directly in your content database, so you can show average ratings when you present the content to the user.

NEGATIVE USER RATINGS

Things get a bit tricky if you as a consumer want to indicate that you dislike certain content because to review something you have to give it at least one star. Zero stars means no rating at all. If you hate something, you don't want to give it any stars, not even one. In a sense, not rating it is better than "I hate it," which you can indicate on Amazon with one star as shown in figure 2.10.

Not liking something can mean not bothering to rate it. But if something really irritates you, you might want to release your frustration somewhere, and that's often in the form of a negative review.

The rating in figure 2.10 is not mine. I definitely recommend *Deep Learning* (The MIT Press, 2016) if you have a background in machine learning. Otherwise, you might be better off starting with *Grokking Deep Learning* by Andrew Trask, (Manning, 2016).

Deep Learning (Adaptive Computation and...
Ian Goodfellow

⭐☆☆☆☆ I hate it

Figure 2.10 At Amazon you show you hate something with one star. Not that I dislike this one. If you want to get into *Deep Learning*, then this is the book to read.

VOTING

Many sites have had success creating a community around users voting whether something is good or not. For example, TripAdvisor's only service is the rating of hotels and restaurants. Another such example is Hacker News (https://news.ycombinator.com/), where the users are responsible for adding content, which can be links to articles and blog posts about "anything that good hackers would find interesting." When something is added, you can *up-vote* it. The more up-votes it gets, the higher it stands on the page (it's almost as simple as that; you'll take a better look at the algorithm later). Sites that use voting are called *reputation systems*.

2.2.6 *Getting to know your customers the (old) Netflix way*

With a page that's almost completely built based on suggestions, it's important to gather as much input as possible about a consumer's tastes. If Netflix thinks that your tastes are different, finding what you want to watch can be difficult. This is another point for people who claim that recommender systems are manipulative. Because the system doesn't provide equal opportunity for all content, it therefore manipulates you. I understand the argument, but I disagree.

Netflix once offered the user the capability to assist in creating a taste profile.[3] This feature is no longer available, but when it was, you could find it in the Taste Profile menu shown in figure 2.11. It let the user rate shows and movies and select genres by indicating how often the user felt like watching, for example, *Adrenaline Rush*. Netflix could then check whether the user's ratings matched their current opinions.

Netflix used this manual input of a taste detail to offer better suggestions. Asking the user for help with the taste profile is a method often used to enable the system to give suggestions for new users.

---

[3] For more information, see https://help.netflix.com/en/node/10421.

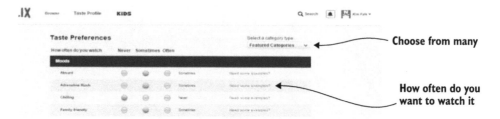

Figure 2.11   Netflix Taste Preferences, 2015. The feature is no longer available.

2.3 *Identifying users*

Collecting data on users works only if you have a way of uniquely identifying customers. The best way to do that is to make the customer log in on your page so you've positive identification. Another alternative is to use cookies.

Usually sites start out by setting a cookie and connecting all information to that cookie. If the user then provides identification by logging in or by creating a profile, all information from the cookie is transferred to that account. Be careful with cookies because the computer could be a public or a family computer used by several people. Saving data to the cookie ID over several sessions can be misleading.

If you don't have logged-in users, there's also a cross-device problem, which means that even if you recognize a user on one device, your system can't recognize the same user across different devices. Certain services can help you with this but always with uncertainty. Try to make users register and log in when possible. It goes without saying that personalized recommendations can only work if you recognize the user.

2.4 *Getting visitor data from other sources*

Your site is unique, and the data that can be collected on your site is the data that's best suited to reveal the behavior of your customers. But what if you could cheat a bit and get data from somewhere else?

Social media is a good place to start, and, if you're lucky, a visitor on your site has liked something that matches the content in your catalog. Depending on your content, the social media site could be Facebook, LinkedIn, or similar sites. Many will think that, yes, connecting to Facebook is good, but if you aren't dealing with films or books, what's the purpose of adding data from Facebook? Most sites, however, will benefit from getting something as simple as the age of a visitor or where they live.

There might be other ways to gain knowledge too. A recommender of pension plans could benefit from knowing whether a customer reads finance books, for example. That would be an indication that the customer is interested in the stock market and will probably be more interested in pension plans enabling the customer to have more control over a portfolio.

Another thing to consider is that many algorithms calculate recommendations based on similar users. If the system has the same data about many users, even if that data might not be relevant for the content of your site, it still enables the system to find similar users that can then be used to create recommendations. I'm sure a car dealership site can find that there's a special kind of film that most SUV owners like, or that a makeup site can recommend something based on age and gender. People who work in IT probably like gadgets instead of phones, and train drivers might like sunglasses.

2.5   *The collector*

We're now going to look at an evidence collector implemented for the MovieGEEKs website. We'll look at the essential parts and then leave it to the interested reader to explore the details within the code.

Because of performance and reliability of your website, it's better not to add evidence collection to your current (web) application. Instead, add it to a parallel structure that supports what you want to achieve. This lets you move the evidence collector to another server if the users go wild after adding your recommender system or the load on your site gets close to its limit—for scalability.

This evidence collector has two logical parts:

- *The server side*—In our example, the server side is built using a Django web API that works as an endpoint and can be used by anything that a user is in contact with. Mostly this means a web page, but it could also be an app on a phone or any kind of device connected to the internet—anything that collects relevant events. When the server receives a notification that an event has occurred, its only job is to save it. A web API is an HTTP address configured to receive this kind of message and can be implemented essentially by any type of framework.
- *The client side*—There won't be a client part in the traditional sense because there're no web pages that can be requested. The client side consists of a simple JavaScript function that posts evidence to the evidence collector on the server.

With a collector in place, you'll be prepared to start collecting data either on Movie-GEEKs site or on your own. To relate the evidence collector to the rest of MovieGEEKs architecture, figure 2.12 highlights elements of the evidence collector in the architectural diagram from chapter 1.

You might be thinking, why not use Django logging to save all the hassle of adding another app? But consider this:

- Django logging works on server-side code execution, so you have no way of saving user behavior (except by putting it in a kind of session state and saving it in the next request). All the events such as hover and scroll would be lost.
- The collector lets you receive evidence from everywhere, not just a website. The future is around the corner, where evidence is something that you record from phone apps or other strange gadgets that are coming out, as well as from physical shops.

Because the data collected is simple, it's often best to save it in a comma-separated (CSV) file. In this way, it's easier to move it around if the system that uses it is somewhere

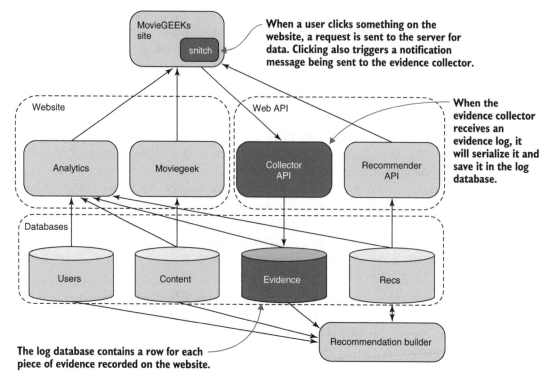

Figure 2.12   MovieGEEKs' evidence collector and logger architecture

else. The CSV file can then be fed to a service that ingests the data at a speed the system CSV can handle. That way, you always have a buffer to ensure that you aren't overloading your system. Because a CSV file isn't easy to query, and while learning about recommender systems, it's important to query the data. Instead, you'll use a database.

2.5.1   Building the project files

Getting the site up and running is fairly easy. You need to download or clone the GitHub repository at http://mng.bz/AU9X. After the download completes, follow the instructions in the readme.md file.

2.5.2   The data model

It's important to collect most kinds of interactions. The previous section indicated that all you need are three things: user ID, content ID, and event type. You really need a few more things to make it work, as listed in the data model shown in figure 2.13.

    The session_id uniquely identifies each session. Later, you can add more to this model such as device type or context. But for now, you can start with this.

Logger	
date:	datetime
user_id:	varchar(64)
content_id:	varchar(16)
event:	varchar(200)
session_id:	integer

Figure 2.13   Data model of an evidence logger

You'll find plumbing around the logger, which you're welcome to look into, but it's a web API that's open for one type of request containing the data as shown in figure 2.13. You'll virtually tag along on a request a bit later on, when we talk about how it's hacked into the MovieGEEKs website. But first, let's look at what you should do on the client side.

> **A note on time**
>
> Recording time is always a bit tricky because you must take into account different time zones. Using all local time zones means that you can have problems with the order of events, because events happening at the same time in different time zones will be farther apart. But recording local times means that you can work with phrases such as "in the afternoon" on a global basis, rather than having to look at different time intervals for each time zone.

2.5.3 The snitch: Client-side evidence collector

Evidence can be collected as events from anything that interacts with the user, from a phone app to a device you put in your shoe when jogging.

The event logger is a simple JavaScript function that calls the event collector. It doesn't do anything if there's an error, because this isn't something end users can do anything about. In a production environment, it's worth keeping track of whether evidence is being recorded, but this probably isn't the right place to do it.

The snitch should be in the project where you want to collect data. You'll find a file called collector.js in the /moviegeek/static/js folder containing the function shown in listing 2.1, which creates an AJAX call to the collector.

Listing 2.1 Creating an AJAX call to the collector: /moviegeek/static/js/collector.js

```
function add_impression(user_id, event_type, content_id,
                        session_id, csrf_token)
    {
        $.ajax(
            type: 'POST',
            url: '/collect/log/',
            data: {
                "csrfmiddlewaretoken": csrf_token,
                "event_type": event_type,
                "user_id": user_id,
                "content_id": content_id,
                "session_id": session_id
            },
        fail: function(){
                console.log('log failed(' + event_type + ')')
            }
        })
    };
```

Makes an AJAX call

A CSRF middleware token that allows your site to call a site from a different domain.

To be RESTful, the message sent is a POST because you're adding something to the db.

Shows the three important data elements

Shows a unique session ID

If it fails, then write something out to the browsers debug console. Don't show the user anything.

The calls from the function in listing 2.1 will eventually be received by the log method in /moviegeek/collector/view.py shown in the next listing.

> **Listing 2.2   Receiving calls from listing 2.1: /moviegeek/collector/view.py**

```
@ensure_csrf_cookie
def log(request):

    if request.method == 'POST':
        date = request.GET.get('date', datetime.datetime.now())

        user_id = request.POST['user_id']
        content_id = request.POST['content_id']
        event = request.POST['event_type']
        session_id = request.POST['session_id']

        l = Log(
            created=date,
            user_id=user_id,
            content_id=str(content_id),
            event=event,
            session_id=str(session_id))
        l.save()
    else:
        HttpResponse('log only works with POST')

    return HttpResponse('ok')
```

This method is only interested in POST type messages.

Creates a timestamp to add to the created field

Saves a log entry in the database

Responds nicely even if it isn't a POST message

2.5.4   Integrating the collector into MovieGEEKs

The MovieGEEKs app covers the examples shown in table 2.4. The examples are similar to the ones listed in table 2.1, which depict a use case on the Netflix site. I've added the table again here with a new column showing the event data that will be collected.

Table 2.4   MovieGEEKs evidence points

Event	Meaning	Evidence
Clicking a genre such as Drama	User is interested in the theme (here, Dramas).	(Kimfalk, drama, genreView)
Placing the mouse over a film such as Toy Story (requests an overview of the content)	User is interested in the movie.	(Kimfalk, ToyStory, details)
Clicking the film (requests details of the film's content)	User is further interested in the movie.	(Kimfalk, ToyStory, moreDetails)
Clicking Save for Later	User intends to watch the movie.	(Kimfalk, ToyStory, addToList)
Clicking the Buy link	User watches the movie.	(Kimfalk, ToyStory, playStart)

LOGGING GENRE EVENTS

The following events have been implemented in the templates/moviegeek/base.html file. The first event to log is the user clicking a genre. The genres are listed on the left side of the screen as shown in figure 2.14.

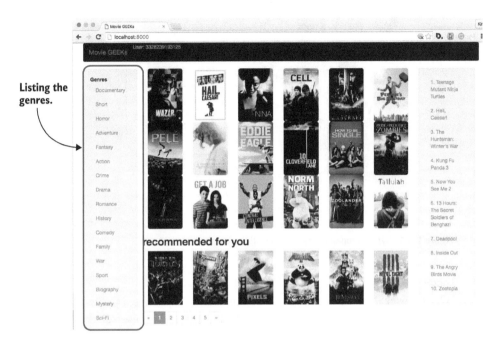

Figure 2.14 MovieGEEKs homepage

To register clicks on a genre, an `onclick` attribute is added to each link. When the active user clicks a genre, it fires an HTTP POST request to the collector. We won't go too much into the code because it's quite repetitive, but look at figure 2.15 to understand what happens when a user clicks a genre.

1 User clicks a genre.
2 The `onclick` event executes, which calls the JavaScript function in listing 2.1.
3 The `add_impression` function executes.
4 The HTTP request is received by the web server, which delegates it to the MovieGEEKs site.
5 The MovieGEEKs site does a lookup in the URL list and delegates everything that has the URL /collector/ to the collector app.
6 The collector app matches the log/ to a view method.
7 The view method creates a log object.
8 Using the Django ORM system, writes the log object to the database.[4]

---

[4] For more information, see https://docs.djangoproject.com/en/1.9/topics/db/.

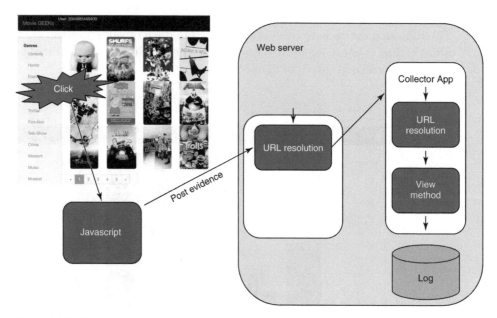

Figure 2.15   What happens when a user clicks a genre

LOGGING POPOVER EVENTS

When a user clicks a film, a popover appears. A *popover* is a fancy name for a big tool-tip. Figure 2.16 shows what one looks like. Because the user clicks, this indicates that the user might be interested in the film and is, therefore, something you should log. This is done by adding an event handler that calls the collector every time a popover is shown.

LOGGING MORE DETAILS EVENTS

A user who finds the information in the popover box interesting can click the More Details link. This is also something to note because it shows further interest in the movie.

LOGGING SAVE FOR LATER

Instead of clicking More Details, the customer can add an item to a list. That's an important event because it indicates that the user is planning to buy or consume it later. This functionality is good to have. It's a link on the details view, which records an event that you'll call `saveforlater`. You can also record other events, but these suffice for the purpose of this example.

2.6   *What users in the system are and how to model them*

Before moving on, you also need to think a bit about users. We've talked about the behavior of users, but what other things might be useful to consider when representing what users know and care about. As mentioned earlier, when it comes to knowing

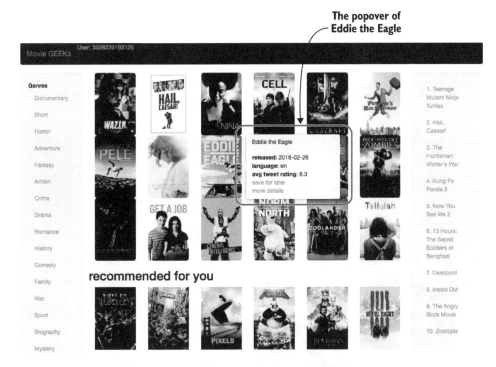

Figure 2.16 MovieGEEKs front page with popover

consumers, many other things can be relevant. You need a user model that you can translate to a database table and use in addition to the evidence.

What could be relevant to know about a user? Again, the answer is, as always, *it depends*. I hate that answer because it's one of the most useless replies, up there with "yes, but no" and "it was once true, but not now." Assuming you're of the same conviction, let's pretend that answer doesn't exist and look at different scenarios where you can say something about what would be relevant. Another answer could be "everything"; in theory, everything could be pertinent to recommending products.

If you're implementing a recommender system on a website such as JobSite (www.jobsite.co.uk), then it's relevant to gather information such as current position, education, years of experience, and so on. If you're looking at a pension site, you probably need the same things as JobSite, but also health data (such as how often you've been to the hospital and what medicine you're taking) will also be of interest. Book sites could also use all the things mentioned previously, because these are all things that say something about books you might be interested in reading. But most book sites probably will use things such as taste and buying habits.

If you shouldn't say "it depends," then let's say "everything" and take it from there. Let's say that Pietro is created in your system (see figure 2.17). What information would be good to store on Pietro? If you had the possibility to retrieve the information in figure 2.17, what should you save in your database? In this day and age where storage is so economical, why not save all of it. You'll see what you can do with it in future chapters.

Figure 2.17   A new user called Pietro

Ideally, you want to keep a list of key-value pairs next to the user identifiers such as user ID, email address, and possibly other additional information. Again, remember you're doing a recommender system, so typically you'd also save a shipping address, and things like that. But for the purpose of the MovieGEEKs site, that isn't so important. This information gives you a data model like the one shown in figure 2.18.

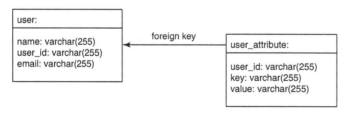

Figure 2.18   Generic data model

There are a couple of things to aim for. You want

- Flexibility to save everything
- Simplicity to make code readable

But these are pointing in opposite directions. You should, therefore, do a less flexible, but easier-to-use implementation (somewhere in the middle ground of what we discussed earlier). You can create a table containing most of the previous attributes, plus one that contains any extras you might need later. Your data model for a user might look like one shown in figure 2.19.

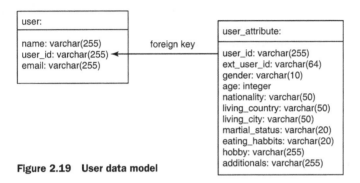

Figure 2.19   User data model

Continuing with our user Pietro, you'll save the data shown in figure 2.20. This data model isn't too flexible, but until you need a flexible data model, it's better to keep the level of complexity as low as possible.

If you have regular visitors, your log might already have something to show you about your visitors, and that's great. Nevertheless, it's always good to have user information to check how your algorithms work. Chapter 3 introduces personas and shows how to autogenerate evidence for them.

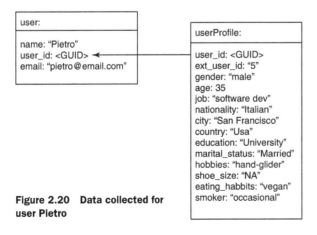

Figure 2.20   Data collected for user Pietro

Summary

- Log user behavior using a web API. This would possibly run in a different web application than that of the site to ensure that it won't cause the site to suffer in performance if the user triggers many events.
- Connect a snitch to a website by attaching a call to all events happing on a site.
- Good evidence provides information to the system about a user's taste. It's good to record all events because they might turn out to be useful later.
- Implicit ratings are deduced from the events triggered by the user, while explicit ratings are the actual ratings a user inserts.
- Implicit ratings are usually more reliable but only if you understand what each event means.
- Explicit ratings aren't always reliable because they can be biased due to social influences.

Monitoring the system

3

This is one of the shorter chapters but still contains considerable information:

- We'll begin with what all data-driven applications should start with—analytics.
- I'll attempt to convince you of the great value of analytics, and we'll look at how to implement an analytics dashboard.
- I'll introduce personas and why they're useful.
- Using these personas, you'll learn different ways to represent user taste.

In the previous chapters, you learned what a recommender system produces and what you can learn from users visiting a site. At this point, you should understand what you want to achieve and what evidence you'll need to do that. Now you're missing only the two parts in the middle as shown in figure 3.1.

To understand the two middle steps, you need to find a way to understand what your users are up to. Taking the log data that the collector described in the previous chapter, you now need to find a way to reduce the data for each user to a

Figure 3.1 Data flow from evidence to recommendations. You start with your evidence, which you can aggregate into website usage. With that, you can start to understand the user's tastes, which can work as input to the recommender system to produce recommendations.

preference. To do this, there are scripts that auto-generate interactions, which will provide the data that I've based the discussion on. Then you're going to learn about simple analytics, something that you can set up and continuously view.

I've always thought of analytics as a continuous, poor-man's data analysis; it gives you information about your data, but it only scratches the surface of what's happening. Nevertheless, in your case that might be enough, as you'll see in this chapter. The reason for resorting to analytics in a book on recommender systems is that you need a way to understand what's happening and to measure whether all your efforts will have any impact. Making recommender systems is such fun that you might not care, but the people who're paying you will want to know if the recommender has any effect.

You'll begin your journey into analytics by learning the theory behind what you want to show. Then, when you've seen the light, you'll look at it in the context of the MovieGEEKs site.

3.1 Why adding a dashboard is a good idea

As I was earning my degree as a computer scientist, we used to make fun of the students working with visualizations, calling them "circus computer scientists."[1] After university, I was never a big fan of anything containing colorful graphical interfaces. I preferred the undisturbed "beauty" of data in a table.

As I got into bigger data sets and data analytics, I saw the errors of my ways and understood the importance of data visualization. After working with large data sets for many years, I've become a firm believer that running a data application without any visual representation is like driving with your eyes closed: you feel great, but you'll realize that something is wrong only after it's already too late.

3.1.1 Answering "How are we doing?"

Let's start out with a question, "How's your website doing?" How would you answer? Where's your focus? Is it money? Number of visitors? Average response time? Or something different altogether?

By adding recommender systems, what do you expect to improve? The first result will be that your colleagues will be much happier, because working with recommender systems is the best thing since the invention of web shops. But what will it change? That's the question of this chapter. Having a data dashboard is paramount in understanding how your website is doing, how you can use the data you're collecting, and if the site is improving.

You want to start with a benchmark showing the current performance. This is so important that I think you can't implement a recommender system without having an analytics dashboard to keep an eye on things. I definitely recommend that you build the analytics part of your site before adding a recommender system.

---

[1] In Danish, it's *cirkus datalog*, which sounds a bit better than circus computer scientist.

In the following segments, we'll look at a dashboard implemented with Movie-GEEKs, so you can see an example of how to track the stream of events and customer behavior. First, let's talk more about what you want to achieve.

DASHBOARDS

Most companies aren't too keen about telling the world how they track behavior or monitor performance, mainly because it can be a business disadvantage and it can give hackers hints as to what weaknesses the company could have. In addition, if your users know too many intimate details of your recommender system algorithm, the user's behavior could become less spontaneous. This could induce biases in the results or even make users do things to push certain recommendations in a specific direction.

In this time, when everything should always be more personalized, site owners need to know their users and what they're doing on the site to enable data-driven decisions and to react quickly to changes. Visualizations help you gain a better understanding of the data. Mind you, what you'll do in this chapter is only the beginning and should be extended when you get a better understanding of the system!

THE MOVIEGEEKS DASHBOARD

The MovieGEEKs analytics dashboard looks like the one in figure 3.2. It's a good idea to know these types of things before you start implementing your recommender system.

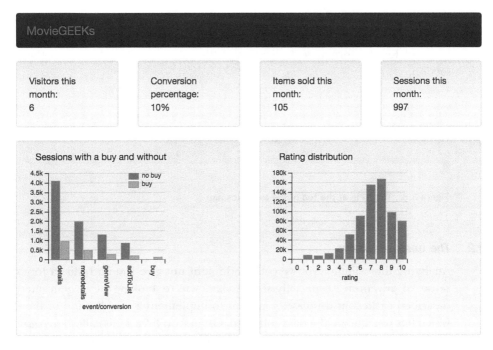

Figure 3.2   The MovieGEEKs analytics dashboard

3.2   *Doing the analytics*

Whether a website is performing in measures of response time (or responsiveness) is a significant factor in the success of the site. But that's the topic of so many books. Here, you're concerned with the business part of a website because that tells you whether you're showing good recommendations.

> **Disclaimer**
>
> No matter how good the recommender is, it's only as good as the content. With good content, it'll never be able to recommend anything to a vegetarian at a butcher shop.

3.2.1   *Web analytics*

What you're going to do is often called *web analytics*. Web analytics is split into two categories: off-site and on-site. *Off-site analytics*, which is about the potential of the website, focuses on opportunity, visibility, and voice.

- *Opportunity*—Indicates how big the potential of the site is in terms of the number of visitors the sector has in total.
- *Visibility*—Indicates how easy it is to find the site.
- *Voice*—Indicates how much people are talking about the site.

This chapter concentrates on *on-site analytics*, which is concerned with how visitors behave on your site (see figure 3.3). In this category, the focus is on conversions, drivers, and Key Performance Indicators (KPIs), which are explained in the following section.

| Visitors this month: 10 | Conversion percentage: 52% | Items sold this month: 1019 | Sessions this month: 1007 |

Figure 3.3   The KPIs at the top of the analytics app

3.2.2   *The basic statistics*

Analyzing the evidence you've collected might not give you an Indiana Jones magical sense of adventure, especially if the data you're looking at is generated data as described earlier. In this case, you want to implement a visualization of the evidence, which lets you analyze the data collected. Often, you'll find this called *summary statistics*.

The top row of the dashboard shows important numbers about the current state of your site—the KPIs. KPIs can be anything that evaluate the success of your website. What might those be?

First, it's important that people visit your site (because on the internet, it's not "Build it and they will come"), so the initial KPI is the number of visitors. Next is the conversion rate, described in more detail later in this section. Then the number of items or content sold this month. Numbers regarding money, such as total revenue, can also be important, but not for this scenario. It's definitely worth noting though that the profit on different items is different, so success criteria can also be that you sell more of the profitable items.

The numbers in the dashboard are configured to provide statistics for the previous month, but they also could be daily or weekly, or even hourly if you have enough traffic and time to sit and watch. You can also use a sliding window that displays statistics from (now – 1 month) until (now). Alternatively, you can say this month, this week, and so forth. It's not terribly important what you do, as long as it's consistent.

Another thing to consider when creating your dashboard is that if you want to keep an eye on how it develops, it can be a good idea to display a chart that shows the values of KPIs over a historical period, such as the last six months, rather than one value.

3.2.3 Conversions

Imagine that you have a website for a new religion, and visitors can subscribe to the religion by paying a monthly fee. When a person signs up, that's a conversion in a sense, but the type of conversion that you're interested in most is a paying customer. In electronic commerce, *conversion marketing* is the act of changing site visitors into paying customers.

I know you're all here with pure intentions and ambitions to create the best customer experiences you could ever dream possible, and the mere mention of KPIs and business conversions are words of disgrace that make you want to slam this book shut—but wait a minute! You're back at the *purpose* again, which is what marketers try to measure with conversions and KPIs.

Conversion rate is an often-used KPI that's defined as follows:

$$Conversion\ rate = \frac{Number\ of\ goal\ achievements}{Number\ of\ visits}$$

The conversion rate is a dear child and has many names. You'll find it called the *goal conversion rate*, when we talk about goal completions, or *commerce conversion rate*, when a goal is a transaction in which something is bought.

Want to make your colleague the marketer happy like Stef in figure 3.4.? Say that you can calculate the website's conversion rate.

Online marketing is all about conversions. When a user does what you want, you say that the visitor converted or that you had a website conversion. Conversions are defined differently by individual marketers and con-

Figure 3.4 Stef the Marketer

tent creators and can be many things, usually related to selling something. For content creators, a conversion can also be about indicators that their content has been read, such as users signing up for a subscription, downloading a newsletter or software, or filling out a lead/contact form. But be careful about sounding too confident because next your colleague will start talking about ROI (return on investment), and that isn't covered here.

To make things even trickier, the word *conversion* comes from the idea of a conversion funnel. A *conversion funnel* shows the path users take before they convert. Let's imagine how a funnel, illustrated in figure 3.5, might look for a company such as Amazon.

Many people open Amazon's homepage, look, and maybe click around a bit. They may move on to look in one of the departments, such as clothing, and might search for shirts and go through the results before finally selecting a funky Hawaiian shirt to purchase. Each event that pushes the user a step down the funnel is called a *value event*. At Netflix, a value event can be that a user watched a film. On Match.com, a wink is a value event on your journey to eternal love or paying your next monthly subscription.

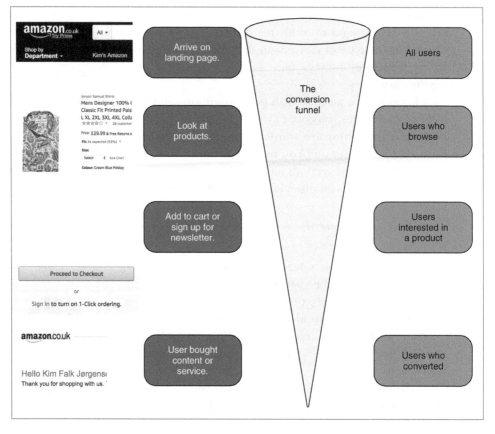

Figure 3.5   A conversion funnel based on logging in at Amazon.

It's called a *funnel* because it starts out wide, then narrows. The same occurs with site visitors: a (hopefully) large number of visitors come to your site (the wide part of the funnel), some will add something to a wish list or will share a product, and part of those will buy something (the narrow part of the funnel).

Converting is marketer lingo, but what if you look at it from a user's point of view? A conversion is what the user wants. For example, a user who comes to Amazon is there to find something to buy or wants to sign up for an interesting newsletter. You're free to claim what you want, even though you may be manipulated or pushed.

Amazon is a place for buying content, so if you go there, it's mostly for buying, and as such, you expect to be helped to get to the best possible things to buy. Later you'll look into topics that don't align with the goals of these two groups, but for now let's stay in the world where everything comes together, and people are holding hands.

In the MovieGEEKs site, the evidence collector is capable of registering conversion events. What about your site? Spend two minutes considering

- What is a conversion on your site?
- What is the conversion rate in your system?

Goals can change. On a car dealership site, you wouldn't expect a customer to convert on every visit, but on Amazon you'd want most visits to end in a conversion (and it does for me, at least). Think about which image in figure 3.6 depicts a match to your site.

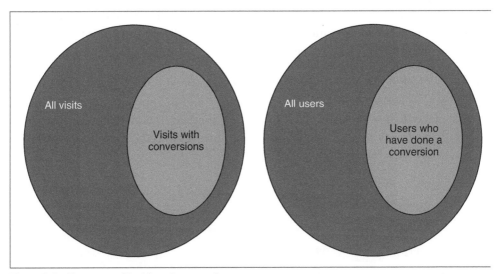

Figure 3.6 Two ways of looking at conversion

If you chose the image on the left, it means that you've an Amazon type of website. Your hope is that a customer makes a conversion per visit—or at least somewhere close. If you chose the one on the right, you're more like the car dealership site. You want to have a visitor converting in the lifetime of their contact with the site. For the car dealership site, it's not important whether a customer visits the site hundreds of times, only that they buy a car in the end. In this second case, the conversion rate is calculated using this formula:

$$Conversion\ rate = \frac{Number\ of\ goal\ achievements}{Users}$$

MovieGEEKs is a site of the first type. Looking at the set of visits, the conversion rate will be the number of sessions in which a buy event occurs divided by the total number of session IDs. This translates to the following SQL code.

Listing 3.1   SQL script to calculate conversion rate

```
select count(distinct(session_id)) as visits,
       count(case when conversion > 0
                 then 1 end) as conversions     ◁          Counts the cases where a
from                                                       session contains one or
( select session_id,                            ◁          more conversions
         sum(case when event = 'buy'
                 then 1                          An inner query calculates for
                 else 0 end) as conversion       each session whether a
  from collector_log                             conversion happened
  group by session_id
) c
```

Using the latest generated data, this returns `"999;97"`, which means that the conversion rate is around 10% (more exactly, 0.097). As mentioned earlier, it might be difficult to relate to this number, but keep it in mind, because this is the rate that you want to improve with your recommendations.

3.2.4   *Analyzing the path up to conversion*

You're happy when a conversion happens, and the purpose of the recommender is to make the user convert. Now if you do a query to find all the event types stored in the database, along with a count of the number of times those events occurred, the results could look like the following:

genreView	1527
details	4953
moredetails	2034
addToList	976
buy	510

This listing shows the query.

Listing 3.2   SQL calculating the distribution of events

```
select event, count(1)
from collector_log
group by event
```

This query gives you a hint as to how often each type of event occurs. What you need to look at again is how often these events happen in buy sessions and in non-buy sessions. This can be checked using listing 3.3, which groups the sessions so that for each session a row indicates the number of buy, details, and moredetails events that happened for the session.

Listing 3.3 SQL script calculates how many times each event happens in each session

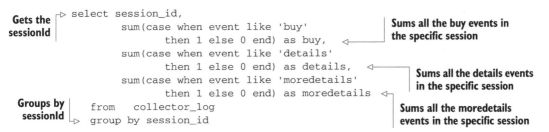

Now that you've broken the sessions into events, you can take the next step and see what happens in sessions where things are bought. One way to accomplish this is to reuse the preceding query and add a filter to show only the sessions in which something was bought. Figure 3.7 shows the result.

But that doesn't get you to what you want, because you want to know what interactions were on each. You want to see what interactions were done before buying something.

session_id	buy	details	moredetails
441115	0	3	5
794948	0	3	1
403960	0	2	1
42483	1	3	6
794776	1	2	1
794784	0	0	0
885466	0	9	2
933590	0	12	8
794855	0	1	0
404058	0	7	2
885591	1	15	3

Figure 3.7 Sessions where a buy event occurs

3.2.5   *Conversion path*

A *conversion path* is the path a user and specific content take together on their way to a buy conversion (and to live happily ever after). More precisely, a conversion path is the sequence of pages and actions a user takes from the time of arrival at the landing page (the first page that's seen) until the conversion.

This is different from a conversion funnel. A conversion funnel is made of predefined goals that have to happen for the user to convert. A conversion path isn't only a linked list of events but also includes a linked list of pages. MovieGEEKs isn't the best website to describe this because it provides only a limited set of events. Often a website will have a much longer list of events including the following:

- View content
- View details
- Look inside
- Like content
- Share content
- Sign up for newsletter
- Search result click
- Campaign link
- Add to cart
- Add to favorites list (this will be added in the following chapter)
- Rate
- Write review
- Buy

A conversion path could be much more interesting than what MovieGEEKs provides because there you have only five events. You're interested in the conversion path because events are often key indicators of where the relationship between the user and content is going (ironically, this analogy works great for dating sites). A key indicator could be that most users who use Search to find a movie end up buying it. You could interpret that event as something that pushes the implicit rating up an extra notch. How can you calculate these paths?

For each user, you want all the sessions in which a buy has happened; and for each buy, you want a count of the events that occurred on the item that was bought. Trying to come up with this information in my head makes me dizzy, but let's move slowly and see if we can do it.

First, you find all the buy events for each user, session, and content as shown in the next listing. Let's assume that everything that's done with a specific item is done before it's bought. This might be cheating, but it saves building complex calculations.

Listing 3.4 SQL script finding pairs of users and content

```
select session_id, user_id, content_id
from collector_log
where event = 'buy'
```

This query gives you a list that you can then use to join with the original table, so that you get only the events that happened in a session where that user did something with content that ended up as a purchase. This brings you to the next query as shown in listing 3.5.

Listing 3.5 SQL script finding events leading up to a buy

```
select log.*
from (
    select session_id, content_id
    from collector_log
    where event = 'buy') conversions
JOIN collector_log log
ON conversions.session_id = log.session_id
and conversions.content_id = log.content_id
```

This results in the output shown in figure 3.8.

id	created	user_id	content_id	event	session_id
40094	2017-07-03 17:10:45+02	3	2096673	buy	794776
40372	2017-07-03 17:10:45+02	1	1489889	addToList	885444
40367	2017-07-03 17:10:45+02	1	1489889	genreView	885444
40360	2017-07-03 17:10:45+02	1	1489889	buy	885444
40376	2017-07-03 17:10:45+02	6	1489889	buy	42456
40323	2017-07-03 17:10:45+02	6	1489889	moredetails	42456
40615	2017-07-03 17:10:46+02	1	1291150	buy	885445
40543	2017-07-03 17:10:46+02	1	1291150	moredetails	885445
40710	2017-07-03 17:10:46+02	6	1985949	buy	42462
40806	2017-07-03 17:10:46+02	6	1489889	buy	42463
40751	2017-07-03 17:10:46+02	6	1489889	details	42463
40724	2017-07-03 17:10:46+02	6	1489889	details	42463
40715	2017-07-03 17:10:46+02	6	1489889	details	42463
41613	2017-07-03 17:10:49+02	2	2120120	genreView	403980
41234	2017-07-03 17:10:48+02	2	2120120	genreView	403980
41228	2017-07-03 17:10:48+02	2	2120120	buy	403980
41276	2017-07-03 17:10:48+02	1	3110958	buy	885463
41386	2017-07-03 17:10:48+02	1	1083452	buy	885466

Figure 3.8 Snippet of the result of running the script shown in listing 3.5, listing all events that happened in a session where there was a buy

But you don't need the buy events because you know they're there. The final query looks like this.

```
select log.session_id, log.user_id, log.content_id
from (
    select session_id, content_id
    from collector_log
    where event = 'buy') conversions
JOIN collector_log log
ON conversions.session_id = log.session_id
and conversions.content_id = log.content_id       ┐  You should disregard
where log.event not like 'buy'              ◄──────┘  buy events.
order by user_id, content_id, event
```

You're not interested in chronological order right now, so this query provides the needed details.

3.3   *Personas*

Personas—the cornerstone of user-centered design and marketing—are fictive people created to represent different stereotypes that correspond to groups or segments in your user community. This section presents several personas; these are not a product of web analysis but were created to span an area of the content in the MovieGEEKs data. (The people pictured in this section and used throughout the book volunteered to be featured. Normally, as I said, personas are fictive people.)

The personas are used throughout the book exactly as marketers would use them. Later, you can look at the results of your algorithms and verify that the results correspond to their type. Without further ado, meet your new best friends.

Sara Comedy, action, drama 	Jesper Comedy, drama, action 
There's always room for another romantic comedy, except when I want to see a CSI-style series.	I'm up for laughs and will choose a comedy most days but will watch drama and rarely an action movie.
User ID: 400001	User ID: 400002

Therese Comedy		Helle Action	
Anything that makes me laugh is a hit. User ID: 400003		Anything with superheroes and anything that blows up User ID: 400004	
Pietro Drama		Ekaterina Drama, action, comedy	
The more complicated the drama, the better it is. User ID: 400005		Nothing beats drama, but I sometimes watch action, and rarely a comedy. User ID: 400006	

Each of these personas has unique tastes. A way to quantify these preferences is to indicate the number of hours, out of 100, each will spend on each genre. Using this, you can describe each user as a tuple containing a number for each genre. For example, you can represent Sara's tastes as 60 hrs of comedy, 20 hrs of action, and 20 hrs of drama, or taste = (60, 20, 20). Now doing this for each user, you get the numbers shown in table 3.1.

Table 3.1 Persona preferences

	Action	Drama	Comedy
Sara	20	20	60
Jesper	20	30	50
Therese	10	0	90
Helle	90	0	10
Pietro	10	50	40
Ekaterina	30	60	10

Another way of illustrating tastes is to plot them in a diagram as shown in figure 3.9. An advantage of plotting tastes in this fashion is that it makes it easy to find similar tastes (or to see that you created two users with the same tastes, as was the case when I first made the graph).

Certain companies go so far as to make posters describing the personas and require all the features to be described based on one of these personas. This creates many odd scenarios because you end up discussing what one persona would do in a specific scenario, as if everybody were best friends with the personas. (And worse, at seasonal parties, I've even heard people discussing who had an affair with whom.)

Armed with these personas and their tastes, you'll move on to auto-generate evidence data that can be used. Generating data seems like cheating a bit, but in this case, it's a good way to start out with a data application, because you know what data you're working with. But remember, you should never expect things to be exactly the same in the real world.

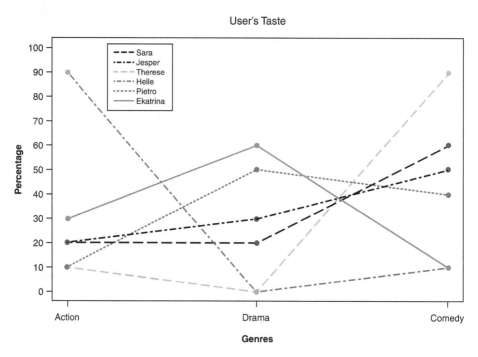

Figure 3.9   Chart of users' tastes

The analytics part of the MovieGEEKs site also has a page for each user (figure 3.10). Figure 3.10 shows what the system knows about Helle. To the left is a list of the highest-rated movies. The chart shows a normalized view of how many movies Helle has rated, and the difference between the average rating of the genre and Helle's average ratings across all genres.

Looking at figure 3.10, you can see that Helle has rated several movies in the action genre but the average of those are the same as the overall average (no bar at "Action"). It also seems that she's positive about Sci-Fi films even if she didn't rate that many.

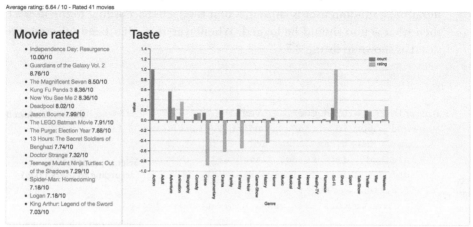

Figure 3.10 This is the profile of Helle. She's into action movies. Here it seems she's also into adventure, but that's because many of the action films she likes are categorized both as action and adventure.

The chart in figure 3.10 shows two types of data. The blue (darker) bars shows how many movies of each genre Helle has rated, while the orange (lighter) bars show the difference from the average rating. This data won't show up before you have read chapter 4 and run the scripts mentioned there. To see figure 3.10 in color, please refer to the electronic versions of this book.

3.4   *MovieGEEKs dashboard*

As a reminder, you can get the code of the MovieGEEKs site from GitHub at http://mng.bz/04k5 either by cloning or downloading it. Follow the readme.md for setup instructions. The database has no data, so you should also run the popu-late_logs.py, to which I give a short introduction here.

3.4.1   *Auto-generating data to your log*

In this and the next couple of chapters, you'll learn about implicit feedback. Usually that isn't something you can download from the internet, but something you'd collect on your site. Since the MovieGEEKs site doesn't have many users, I've created a script that fills in part of the data and saves it into the Log database, so that it looks as if it were collected by the collector. To run it, execute the following at the command prompt:

```
>Python3 populate_logs.py
```

The script auto-generates logs for the six persona users. The core of the script is a `for` loop that iterates over the range from zero to the number of events wanted. At each iteration, a random user is chosen, a film is selected according to the user's taste, and then what action should be logged. When everything has been selected, the event is saved as shown in listing 3.7.

Listing 3.7   Selecting a random user and film: populate_logs.py

```
for x in range(0, number_of_events):                        ⎤ Selects random user
    randomuser_id = random.randint(0, len(users) - 1)       ⎦
    user = users[randomuser_id]
    selected_film = select_film(user)      ◁──── Selects random film
    action = select_action(user)                 (according to users taste)
    if action == 'buy':            ◁────
        user.events[user.sessionId].append(selected_film)

                                          A movie can only be bought once in
                                          this data, so if it's a buy action, you
    l = Log(user_id=str(user.userId),     add the movie ID to a list for the user.
            content_id=selected_film,
            event=action,
            session_id=str(user.get_session_id()),
            created=datetime.datetime.now().strftime("%Y-%m-%d %H:%M:%S"),
            visit_count=0)              ◁────
    l.save()                                Creates a Log object,
                                            and initializes it with
                                            the data received
```

Selects action → (points to `action = select_action(user)`)

Saves the Log object → (points to `l.save()`)

3.4.2   Specification and design of the analytics dashboard

The analytics dashboard is something that most site owners dream about, and you should try to make several of those dreams come true. Your site should contain a dashboard that shows

- Number of visitors and what actions they take
- Number of visits resulting in buys (the conversion rate)
- The most sold products

3.4.3   Analytics dashboard wireframe

The dashboard looks like figure 3.11. At the top of the dashboard are the KPIs. They tell you the number of visitors who have dropped by within a period, currently last month. (Because the log population script works with only six users, it will show six visitors until new users are created by playing with the site. Figure 3.11 shows seven users; the site created one new user for me when I browsed it.) The second component shows the conversion rate, which is calculated from how many sessions ended in a buy, then the number of items sold this month, and then the total number of sessions this month.

The bar chart on the left in the figure shows the number of times the different events occurred. The buy events are calculated as events on content that have been bought in the same session. The chart on the right displays the distribution of ratings,

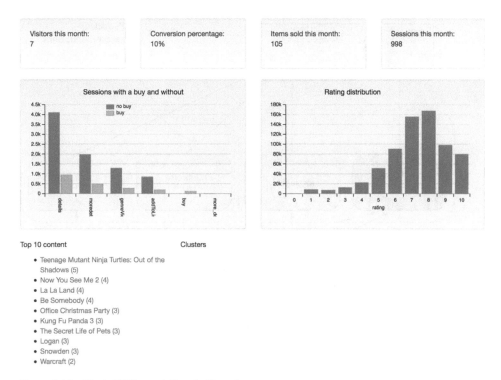

Figure 3.11   MovieGEEKs analytics dashboard

meaning each bar shows how many movies would have that specific rating (this won't appear before you run the populate_ratings.py script). At the bottom is a list of the top 10 most bought movies.

3.4.4   Architecture

The analytics app, illustrated in figure 3.12, is another app in your Django project. Like all websites, it consists of two parts: frontend and backend. Both parts have work to do: the backend queries the database, and the frontend visualizes the results of these queries. The analytics app isn't something that should be accessible to the end user, but the security around that isn't something that we worry about in this book.

As you can see, everything is kept separate from the MovieGEEKs site, which makes it easy to use the same architecture with any kind of site.[2] This is considered best practice and lets you use this app for sites not implemented in Django.

The analytics app contains several views, but only a few views in a traditional sense because they return a web page. The rest are used as a web API to retrieve data. The first traditional view, called an index, returns an HTML page like the one shown in

---

[2]   The analytics dashboard is drawn inside the MovieGEEKs site, but it is doesn't actually share any parts and could easily be running somewhere else.

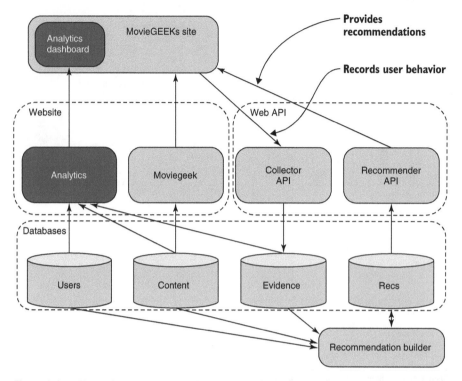

Figure 3.12   The architecture of MovieGEEKs with the analytics parts of the system highlighted

figure 3.13. The *json* views return data and thereby feed the website with the data for each of its components.

The top row, shown in figure 3.13, has four KPIs, which describe numbers that you might want to keep an eye on as mentioned earlier. The first one is the number of users who visited your site. The next is the famous conversion rate. Then you have the number of products sold and finally the number of unique visits (a *unique visit* means how many sessions, so the same user can have many visits).

A NOTE ON MONTHLY VIEWS

The KPIs are calculated for the last month, but could be daily or weekly, or even hourly, if you have that much traffic. You can also use a sliding window (figure 3.14) to always calculate for the last month, or you can say this month, this week, and so forth. What you do isn't terribly important, as long as it's consistent, so you can see if you're improving over time.

In this chapter, you looked at analytics and how to implement a dashboard that shows simple information about how a website is performing. Having a dashboard that shows you how your site is doing will be a great help when doing recommender systems. You're now finally ready to start looking at how to calculate ratings. Following that, you'll start creating non-personalized recommendations.

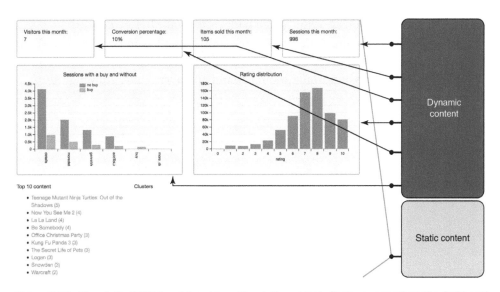

Figure 3.13 The static HTML is retrieved from the static content. Each component on the dashboard retrieves data from a different endpoint.

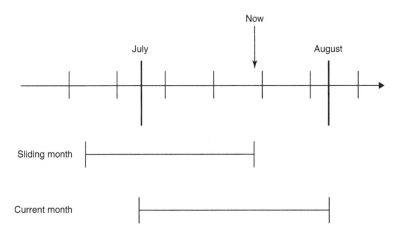

Figure 3.14 Different periods of time

Summary

- Key performance indicators are good because they can be benchmarked and easily used to see whether your site is improving.
- A visitor is converted when they perform a goal or do something that you're hoping for.

- The conversion funnel shows a series of steps you want the user to take. The conversion path is the actual path visitors take before converting.
- Understanding your site's conversion funnel is important so you can understand how close users are to converting.
- Analytics is important to understand and always have running.

Ratings and how to calculate them

Hello, this is your persona speaking, proceed to learn the following:

- Creating user-item matrices.
- Revisiting explicit ratings to discover why they aren't always good.
- Diving into the mystery of implicit ratings and its creation.
- Learning about an implicit ratings function that translates evidence into ratings.

In this chapter, you'll transform your users' behavior to a format that you can use as input for the recommender algorithms. You'll start by looking at the user-item matrix, which is where most recommender algorithms start. Then you'll take another look at explicit ratings, the ratings that users add themselves. Implicit ratings are the core of your system, and you'll look at those next: first, you'll review what they are and then you'll learn how to calculate them from your evidence.

Figure 4.1 shows the flow of data we've talked about so far. Data collection happens when visitors interact with the site. Preprocessing is what you're going to do in this chapter. Model building and recommendation construction are handled in later chapters.

In this chapter, you'll convert web behavior to content ratings, which you'll use for the recommenders in later chapters. This type of rating is called *implicit* because they're deduced.

Figure 4.1   Data processing model for recommender systems

Implicit ratings are used more and more because people seem to be unsure about what they like, and they tend to do (or watch) things that they'd otherwise tell their friends (or websites) that they don't like. I've watched films on Netflix that I then tell everybody who asks that I hate, but I still watched them. Another good reason for using implicit ratings is that the information is much easier to collect than explicit ratings. That's why I'm a great fan of implicit ratings, which you've probably guessed.

Having read the previous chapters, you should have considered the following:

- What's the purpose of your site (the goals that you want users to achieve)?
- What events lead up to these goals?
- How many times has each of these events happened?

Keep those things in mind as you continue through this chapter. You're going to start by looking at what most recommender algorithms expect as input—the user-item matrix. The idea of this chapter is to take the behavioral data and turn it into exactly such a matrix.

4.1   User-item preferences

A user-item matrix can be thought of as a table that has a row for each user and a column for each item (or the other way around). In literature, this is called a *matrix*, and we'll stick with that. In the junction between a user and a content item, a number indicates the user's sentiment toward the content item.

4.1.1   Definition of ratings

A *rating* is, for example, the number of stars on Amazon.com or Glassdoor (www .glassdoor.com/index.htm, a site where people can rate their workplaces), or a list of hearts in my local newspaper's movie reviews. Behind the scenes, a rating is a number on a scale—say, between 0 and 5—that can be translated into a graphical representation when shown to the end user.

More formally, a rating is something that glues together three things: user, content, and the user's sentiment toward the content item as shown in figure 4.2. This figure shows what's saved after Jimmie had watched, liked, and rated season 1 of *Game of Thrones* with four stars. In a database, ratings are implemented as a junction table, which connects a user to a content item.

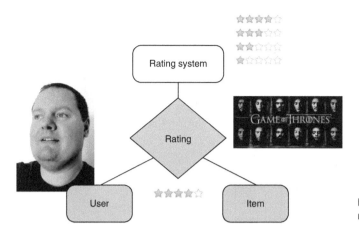

Figure 4.2   User content relationship

4.1.2   User-item matrix

An example of a user-item matrix is shown in table 4.1.

Table 4.1   A simple example of how a user-item matrix could look if there were only 6 users and 4 movies in your system

	Indiana Jones	Microcosmos	Avengers	Pete's Dragon
Sara	4	5		
Jesper	4		5	
Therese	5			3
Helle	4			5
Pietro		3	4	3
Ekaterina	3		3	3

An empty cell indicates that there's no recorded interaction between the user and the item. Remember that there's a difference between an empty cell and a cell containing a zero. The latter represents the user giving a rating of zero to an item; the empty cell means that there has been no rating for the item.

Those empty cells might not look like much, but they're the core of most traditional recommender systems. Most recommender systems attempt to predict what the user would put in those if they rated the corresponding items. Too few empty cells and the user has exhausted all content; too many and the recommender won't have enough data to understand what the user likes.

If you find yourself in conversation with people about the user-item matrix (which is something that occurs all the time, right?), then a good topic to bring up is the sparsity problem. It's a bit like bringing up baby-feeding habits when talking to new parents;

they'll light up and talk for hours. (New parents also speak of a sparsity problem, but it's probably a different one than the following.)

SPARSITY PROBLEM

A user-item matrix isn't always as populated as the one shown in table 4.1. In fact, usually nonempty cells are rare because many internet shops have numerous users and plentiful items. But most users only buy one or a few items, so you're much more likely to see a user-item matrix like the one in figure 4.3.

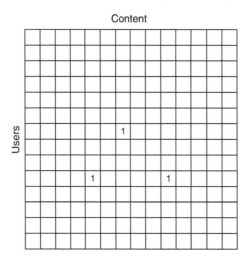

Figure 4.3   Sparsity table, a user-item matrix

The user-item matrix is input to the recommender algorithms that you'll see later. It's definitely not a good thing to have a matrix that looks like a Danish beach in wintertime. I can attest to the fact that it's a lonely place to be (see figure 4.4).

In chapter 8, we'll talk about a family of recommender algorithms called *collaborative filtering*. This family of algorithms uses the user-item matrix to find similar users. If the matrix is sparse (or empty), it provides little information, and it's difficult to calculate recommendations. In chapter 5, you'll look at how to provide recommendations even if you have a sparse matrix. For now, let's focus on how to populate this matrix either from *explicit ratings* (added manually by users) or *implicit ratings* (calculated from the evidence you collect).

Figure 4.4   Danish beach on a cold winter day

4.2 Explicit or implicit ratings

For the ratings matrix shown so far in this chapter, the data inside supports the examples in this chapter. The example app gets ratings from two sources; the most important one being the MovieTweetings data set.[1] The other part is calculated from the user's behavior persisted in the database, which is auto-generated in this case as described in chapter 3.

In a real app, the data could come from either ratings added by users explicitly if a ratings system were implemented, data collected based on the user's behavior, or data from a mix of the two. Figure 4.5 shows examples of the difference between explicit and implicit ratings.

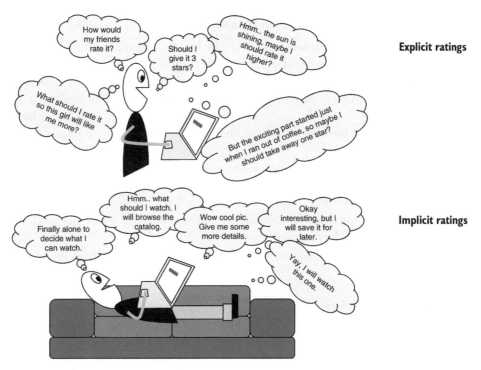

Figure 4.5   The difference between explicit and implicit ratings. Many things can influence what you rate and what you eventually watch.

On a movie site such as MovieGEEKs, if a user bought something and then rated it, the rating is probably trustworthy. Or is it? I've enjoyed films that I rated low, so what if the user buys two similar films and rates both low? How much would you then trust the ratings?

These are domain-specific questions, so it isn't easy to give general answers. But since the user keeps buying films that he rates low, then you should probably show

---

[1]   For more information, see https://github.com/sidooms/MovieTweetings.

more films that he would rate low also. But an HBO user (another subscriber-only online streaming service) rates something that's only available on HBO, so without seeing it, do we trust it? Always have a critical eye on what data is showing you.

> **The truth about users' tastes**
>
> It's important to remember that the log data you collect is evidence, and you need to foster an objective view of what users do on the site. Translating it into ratings and opinions is a subjective process, which is something that has to be tweaked not only for each domain but also for each recommender algorithm.

4.2.1 *How we use trusted sources for recommendations*

Are your fellow users trustworthy sources for recommendations? Certain sites also have users selling things, which means that people have an incentive to make themselves look better and make the competition look worse. For example, somebody got a crazy idea and wrote a book on recommender systems. And he was the boss of a big company (not all of this is true), and then he said all his 2,181 employees had to give a positive review of his book or they'd be fired. Then the Amazon page could look like the one in figure 4.6.

That's probably an extreme example, but I have seen a situation where a c-level person wrote a book and then gave it as a present to all his employees afterward. Or people saying something is bad because the package was broken when it arrived in the mail. I'm not saying that you shouldn't trust the reviews on a site, but think about what incentive the users have to give good ratings or bad ratings. No matter whether it's explicit or implicit ratings, they can be faked, so remember that.

Figure 4.6 The fake Amazon page of this book. I leave it as an exercise for the reader to figure out which book pages I cut-and-pasted together.

4.3   *Revisiting explicit ratings*

When a user manually gives a content item a rating, it's called an *explicit rating*. The easiest way for a system to populate the user-item matrix, in theory at least, is to ask users to do it themselves. Only they don't, even if you give them the opportunity.

How many people review the books they buy or the movies they watch on Netflix? And even when they do, you can't always be sure that their ratings reveal their true opinions. People are influenced by what their circle of friends say and do. What's being rated when a user rates? The next time you rate something, think about it: are you rating the complete package or was it a detail that you didn't like that made you give it a low rating? Maybe you loved the film, but the DVD's cover was ugly, so you rated it low. Do you rate a good lawnmower low because of the way a screw is attached?

When you finish this book, I hope it inspires you to not only write recommender systems but also to spread the word that this is an excellent book. If so, then a way to do that is by giving it a high number of stars, for example, on Amazon (not trying to mentally imprint anything here—blink, blink). That's an explicit rating. An explicit rating can be plotted directly on the matrix.[2] If you have opinionated users, working with their explicit ratings is worthwhile.

Websites like TripAdvisor, Glassdoor, and others have based their sole existence on users' ratings. I mention this to remind you that even if implicit ratings generally show more accurate opinions, explicit ratings still have their place in the world of ratings. We'll get back to explicit ratings later. In the next section, you'll concentrate on the implicit ones.

4.4   *What are implicit ratings?*

Implicit ratings are deduced from monitoring people's behavior. Sounds kind of scary when it's written like that, doesn't it? But remember, you're trying to ease information overload and help users, not stalk and manipulate them into buying more.

Most would agree that when a user buys a product, it indicates that the user has a positive opinion of the item. You can, therefore, deduce a positive rating between the user and that particular item. This is an implicit rating. The same is true when a user streams content or requests more information about a product. These are positive examples of user-content relationships. But a user returning an object is an example of an event that induces a *negative* implicit rating.

To calculate implicit ratings, you take all the events recorded between each user and each item and determine a number indicating how happy the user is with specific content. Another way of thinking about it is that you're trying to deduce the number of stars users would give content they've interacted with (viewed, streamed, bought, and so forth). You can define what each event means, but often the actions of users can be interpreted in several ways, so it's advisable that you create a system that lets you easily tweak the rating calculations.

---

[2] Well, that's not completely true; often you normalize the ratings.

When the data is collected, there are then many ways to use it. Amazon's famous *item-to-item recommendation algorithm* uses only what users buy to create recommendations, but few sites can claim to have more than 200 million active users as Amazon does.[3] Others use the browsing history of all users to recommend similar pages. Which approach better fits your site depends on what you're selling and what customers you have. After reading this chapter, you should have a better idea of which road to follow.

Some sites don't have the concept of "bought" at all. *The New York Times* website, for example, uses your browsing history to recommend new material to you. Figure 4.7 shows the recs from the front page of the site (www.nytimes.com).

Figure 4.7   Recommended for you from *The New York Times*

The New York Times must use implicit ratings because the site doesn't allow users to rate what they like. Moreover, even if it did let users rate articles, what would it mean if users rated an article low? Would it mean that they didn't like the topic, the way it was written, or the specific story?

It's important to mention that even if a rating is high, that highly rated item might not be the best thing to recommend right now. A good example is that I love the mojitos made at a certain cafe I frequent when I'm in Italy. That doesn't mean that I want one for breakfast, even if I've rated the mojitos from the previous evening high several

---

[3] Amazon definitely uses much more than the "buy" events, but the particular algorithm described in Greg Linden, et. al's article, "Amazon.com Recommendations: Item-to-Item Collaborative Filtering" (IEEE Internet Computing, v.7 n.1, p. 76-80, January 2003), they only use the "buy" events. The year 2003, however, was a long time ago. You can view the article at www.cs.umd.edu/~samir/498/Amazon-Recommendations.pdf.

times in a row. Sometimes it's worth dividing the evidence into timeslots and doing different recommenders for each slot. But it's a trade-off between more accurate recommendations and data sparsity.

Always remember *relevance*. Not all applications have a rating system, and it doesn't always make sense to add one. Another good example (in addition to *The New York Times*) is eBay. What information would eBay gain from your rating a rare 1984 Wonder Woman lunchbox that you bought? eBay probably had only one to sell, but it's interested in knowing that you frequently browse comic collectibles and lunchboxes.

Many other sites have content that probably wouldn't benefit from ratings either, but they can still provide recommendations. These could be public sites with informational documents or real estate sites, for example. User ratings also are hard to come by on educational sites, which are another area where more energy is spent on implicit ratings.

4.4.1 People suggestions

Much CPU power is spent calculating how to suggest people to other people. One of the more famous places that does this is good old LinkedIn, which also claims to be the first site to have achieved that (outside of dating sites, I venture).

LinkedIn suggests "People You May Know" that you can add to your network. This is an example of a site where it'd be out of place for people to rate other people. But for sites such as LinkedIn (or Facebook), a calculation must be done to figure out what friends it suggests to you.

We're walking on the edge here. Most people might say that we're leaving the realm of recommender systems and entering the realm of data mining.

4.4.2 Considerations of calculating ratings

In this section, you'll go through a few considerations before calculating ratings. Which approach to use depends on what kind of data is registered and what type of site displays the recommendations.

In chapter 2, you saw that a buy event is something that comes before the user rating. The evil truth is that you don't know anything about this event, and that's the hardest problem to solve. But to make this work, you need to assume that a user buys an item because it looks good. The item might turn out to be garbage, but generally people buy things because they want them. The item might be a present for the user's mother-in-law, but the user bought something once, so why not recommend something else for the next present? Let's go with that and look at the buy events in your evidence.

BINARY USER-ITEM MATRIX

Using buy events, you can make a simple user-item matrix by using this formula:

$$r_{ij} = \begin{cases} 1, & \textit{when a user i bought item j} \\ 0, & \textit{else} \end{cases}$$

Each cell in the user-item matrix contains a 1 if the user (i) bought the item (j) and 0 otherwise. A snippet of such a user-item matrix can be seen in table 4.2. (A similar matrix could be generated by likes: 1 if the user liked the movie, 0 otherwise.)

Table 4.2 **Binary user-item matrix**

Users	Movies			
	Indiana Jones	*Micro cosmos*	*Avengers*	*Pete's Dragon*
Sara	1	1	0	0
Jesper	1	0	1	0
Therese	1	1	0	1
Helle	1	0	0	1
Pietro	0	1	1	1
Ekaterina	1	0	1	1

The web shop that is said to use "bought or not" the most is Amazon. I regularly go to Amazon to look for books on Python or data analysis, but I often end up at the Manning or O'Reilly sites because I find that they provide free access to more books and because they're often half price. I've bought several books from Amazon that I can't read on my PC, only on tablets, and that drives me crazy.

Because I've browsed often on Amazon, Amazon can see in my browsing history that I'm interested in Python and data analysis, but it recommends only the books I've bought as shown in figure 4.8. Recently, I chose a number of books on Microsoft Azure because, to a large extent, they were free.

I bought my first book on Amazon around the year 2000 and have bought many since. But do they all represent my taste? Previously, I was a Java developer, but now I'm over that phase. I'm no longer interested in Java books, so I hope that the items I bought recently are more important than the things I bought 15 years ago. In the next section, we'll look into that.

TIME-BASED APPROACH

Using a binary matrix makes all things black-or-white. But most websites want nuances to enable the recommender system to get a better picture of what the users like.

There's a saying: "Nothing beats your first love." But this isn't true in recommender systems. Here the most recent is given the most importance. Therefore, a way to make the matrix more nuanced is to use a function based on the purchase date. You could go as far as to add the production time of the item also. For example, a purchase completed five minutes ago of an item that was produced (or added to the catalog) five minutes ago will have a higher rating than a buy five minutes ago of an old product. It would also have a higher rating than a buy last year of a product that was new at that time.

Figure 4.8   Amazon shows recommendations based only on what you buy.

Using this approach favors new items. Even if a user buys many old romantic comedy movies and only one new action movie, the action genre will win because old products get punished for being old.

HACKER NEWS'S ALGORITHM

Hacker News (https://news.ycombinator.com) uses a somewhat similar algorithm, which puts importance into recent events and not so much on older ones. These types of algorithms are called *time-decay algorithms*.

Last time Hacker News published any details on how it works, it used the following equation to calculate a news item's ranking. The formula takes the score (how many people upvoted this story minus how many who downvoted it) and divides that with a time decay element, using a term they call *gravity*, which indicates how fast an item's ranking decays:

$$\frac{score - 1}{(Item\ age\ in\ hours + 2)^{Gravity}}$$

There was a time when Hacker News defined gravity as 1.8, but the company tweaks this algorithm all the time. People's tastes change, so what was once the best thing for a user might not be the favorite now. This indicates it's a good idea to let old events count less than new ones.

BEHAVIOR-BASED APPROACH

Big companies like Amazon would probably drown in data if they used more actions than a buy. But for most sites, the binary table shown previously would be quite empty or at least full of zeros. That's why it might be a good idea to broaden the horizon a bit and add other events than buy events.

Using several kinds of events requires a bit more thought because you need to quantify how much a user shows liking through the different events. After the value of each event has been defined, each entry in the user item matrix can be calculated based on all the events that have occurred between the user and the item. This approach is what you'll work on, spicing it up with a bit of a time-based approach.

4.5   *Calculating implicit ratings*

Given the knowledge that you gained from working with the evidence in earlier chapters, what can you say about events? Can you say that actions that led up to a buy mean that a customer was closer to buying? It's hard to tell whether that's always the case, but in most instances it's probably true. Therefore, you'll work through the events that are collected on the MovieGEEKs site, starting with the buy event.

The example site is simple with only Details and More Details events to calculate the implicit ratings. Its "lucky" that there isn't much complexity here. Most sites have many more event types. Now might be a good time to stop and think about what you're calculating because, in a sense, the word *rating* isn't what you're trying to estimate, not even if you call it an implicit rating. Let's look at an example.

My original objective for learning Italian was to read books by Umberto Eco (figure 4.9) in his original language. It was a silly project because I never bothered to read any of his books, even the ones that were translated, before setting out to evening classes in Italian. But it seemed like a good idea at the time. Ten years later, I'm now married to an Italian and speak Italian fairly well, although not well enough to make it enjoyable to read

Figure 4.9   A book by Umberto Eco, an Italian author and literary critic who died in 2016

Eco's books. But that doesn't stop me from hurrying out to buy his books when a new one comes out and try it—at least I did until he passed away—even if I'm not even sure whether I like his books in the end. Yet there are other writers that I do like and recommend to others.

If you were implementing a book site, you'd want to know about all the books that I'd potentially buy, regardless of how I'd rate them. What you're calculating here is a number that indicates how likely your user is to buy, not how high the user will rate the content. Beside insights into my obsession with Eco books, this example should also provide an idea of what you want to find.

4.5.1 *Looking at the behavioral data*

Let's take an example from the MovieGEEKs site. Jesper (user 400002) has a weak spot for Jim Carrey (figure 4.10). He's considering buying *Ace Ventura*. He looks at it once and thinks, "Ahh, maybe it's too expensive." Later he looks again, and then again. Finally, he decides to check out more details, which provide him with the final reason (excuse) to buy it, so he does. The list of events looks like the rows in table 4.3.

Table 4.3 Constructed evidence for Jesper

User ID	Content item	Event
2	*Ace Ventura: When Nature Calls*	Clicks Details
2	*Ace Ventura: When Nature Calls*	Clicks Details
2	*Ace Ventura: When Nature Calls*	Clicks Details
2	*Ace Ventura: When Nature Calls*	Clicks MoreDetails
2	*Ace Ventura: When Nature Calls*	Clicks Buy

Figure 4.10 Jesper loves *Ace Ventura*.

You know that he bought the movie. But if I stopped the story before he made the transaction, you'd still agree that if a user looks at an item three times and clicks More Details once, then it's a positive thing. If Pietro clicks *Ace Ventura* by mistake and never comes back to the page, then that action shouldn't mean too much. But if he did come back, it would be more positive.

A thing that I left out of this example is the timestamp of the events. If clicks are done within a short period of time, they might not mean as much as if the clicks were registered over several days. You could work through many such stories, but the core of the matter is that you can start adding rules that your implicit recommendations should obey, for example:

- Buy => Top rating
- One or more Details view + More Details => Very positive
- Several Details views => Positive
- One Details view => Not sure

In the MovieGEEKs dashboard, there's a chart that shows which actions most often lead to a buy event. If you return to that, you also get a similar picture of how to calculate implicit ratings. Figure 4.11 is a repeat of a portion of figure 3.2. In our case, we're cheating a bit because the chart shows auto-generated data, so the events distribute like this by design. But in a real system, that chart would be a good place to look at what value to attribute to each event.

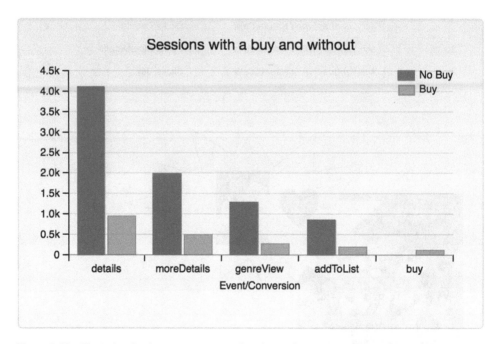

Figure 4.11 Chart showing how many events of each type have occurred in sessions with and without a buy.

To sum up this investigation, and with Jesper in mind, you can define an implicit rating function that outputs a number that shows how much user u will be interested in buying item i. To be more precise, you're interested in knowing how close user u is to buying item i, so that you can use this knowledge to find similar things that the user might buy instead or buy also with item i. With this in mind, consider the following implicit rating of item i for user u:

$$IR_{i,u} = (w_1 \times \#event_1) + (w_2 \times \#event_2) + ... + (w_n \times \#event_n)$$

Where

- $IR_{i,u}$ is the implicit rating.
- $\#event$ is the number of times that a specific event type has occurred.
- $w_1 ... w_n$ are weights that you set based on the previous analysis (and probably tweak again when you start creating recommendations).

SHOULD ALL EVENTS HAVE A POSITIVE WEIGHT?

If actions occur in more sessions that include a conversion event than in sessions that don't, you can give those events a positive score or weight. All interactions between user and content on your site, and in general, give a positive indication of the user being interested in the content and should be treated as such.

You can find exceptions, such as a Dislike button (you haven't added that to the site) as Netflix did, moving away from the star ratings to use a thumb's up or down.[4] The thumbs down can be used to indicate that the user doesn't want to see similar content, which can only be interpreted as adding a negative score or weight to the content.

CALCULATING WEIGHTS

Let's create a function by adding the weights according to what you learned in the example with Jesper and *Ace Ventura*. As I've iterated several times before, it's important not to think that you can start out doing this once and it'll always work.

> **NOTE** It's a good idea to work with the weights and the function when you have a full recommender up and running and then see how the result looks.

First define the following:

- $Event_1$ = buy
- $Event_2$ = moreDetails
- $Event_3$ = details

Now let's try to deduce the weights for this function so that a buy has the maximum rating. Let's say the top rating is 100 (you can normalize it afterward). Table 4.4 shows your assumptions that can be translated into weights.

---

[4] Tom Vanderbilt, "Now Netflix is all Thumbs," http://mng.bz/2GV8.

Table 4.4 Weights on events[a]

Events	Interpretation	Example of value
Clicks Buy	Top rating	$100 = (w_1 \times 1)$
Clicks one or more Details views + More Details	Very positive	$80 < (w_2 \times 1) + (w_3 \times 3)$
Clicks several Details views	Positive	$50 < (w_3 \times 3)$
Clicks one Details view	Not sure	$(w_3 \times 1) < 50$

a. w_1 is the weight for a Buy; w_2 is for More Details, and w_3 is the weight of the Details event.

Having a list of equations looks like an optimization problem, which can be solved mathematically, but the equations have come from assumptions, so you can't trust them as gospel. A way to solve the equations is to come up with weighted values (w_x) that obey the preceding rules:

- $w_1 = 100$
- $w_2 = 50$
- $w_3 = 15$

If you insert these weights into the preceding formula, it looks like the following:

$$IR_{i,u} = (100 \times \#event_1) + (50 \times \#event_2) + (15 \times \#event_n)$$

As a small test, let's try to calculate Jesper's implicit rating of *Ace Ventura:*

$$IR_{i,u} = (100 \times 1) + (50 \times 1) + (15 \times 3)$$
$$IR_{i,u} = 195$$

If you calculate an implicit rating for a film Jesper found slightly interesting, and yet clicked Details, then the equation would be:

$$IR_{i,u} = (100 \times 0) + (50 \times 1) + (15 \times 1) = 65$$

You'll normalize these ratings, which means that you'll adjust them so that later they're between 1 and 10. Something to consider is whether there's a *cut-off*, where the number of times someone triggers an event doesn't add more information—for example, if somebody looks at content details more than a certain number of times. Think about it: if a user clicks Details three times for the same item, does it mean that they're more interested in it than if they'd clicked 10 times?

It could be worthwhile to replace `#eventn` with `min(#eventn, relevant_maxn)` to implement a cut-off. The `relevant_maxn` would be different for each event type. What it says is that the formula returns the number of times an event occurs unless its value is higher than `relevant_max`n.

USING MORE AND MORE RELEVANT DATA

The first time a user returns to your site, your ratings will be based mostly on previous browsing data and not on buy data, so the recs will be based on a fewer number of things. As the user interacts with the site and starts buying, the content with which the user has interacted will narrow down to the user's specific tastes.

4.5.2 *This could be considered a machine learning problem*

Today many companies spend a lot of energy trying to predict which users are ready to buy and when. You have a similar problem: you need to predict how likely a customer is to buy a specific product that the prospective buyer has viewed.

It can't be said for certain that a relationship exists between a user's interactions with the site and what the user will buy, but it seems plausible. If so, certain numbers or a vector could be multiplied with the data collected to produce a *probability*, which indicates how close a customer is to buying something. This is a fair approximation of what you're trying to calculate. If you defined that in machine learning lingo, you'd say that there exists a function like the following:

$$Y = f(X) + \varepsilon$$

Where Y represents the true prediction of a user's closeness to buying a specific item. In theory, this can be calculated by inserting the data that you've recorded with the evidence logger—your features. To save face, you include ε, a parameter called *noise*. ε is an indication that you can't calculate the complete truth from the features, so there'll also be a sense of uncertainty, no matter how close your function f comes to calculating the real rating. The purpose of many machine learning algorithms is to use data to approximate the function f, and I encourage you to try it with your data.

What kind of machine learning could you apply to this problem? You'll want to predict an implicit rating based on various events. To do that, you can only try to predict whether a series of events is leading to a buy or not. To do that, you'll look at classifiers.

A good classifier to begin with is the naive Bayes classifier. This not only provides a classification, but also a probability of how certain it is about the classification. In this case, you can use the probability that the classification is a buy as an implicit rating. For more details about how to use a naive Bayes classifier, see chapter 5 of *Machine Learning Systems* by Jeff Smith (Manning, 2017, https://livebook.manning.com/book/machine-learning-systems/chapter-5).

If you're only here to do machine learning, then read on. Several of the algorithms used to calculate recommendations are machine learning. Those will be handled in detail in this book. Next, let's see how you can implement implicit rating calculations.

4.6 *How to implement implicit ratings*

Enough beating around the bush—let's get code on the table! Let's start with an overview of where you'd want to implement this functionality in the MovieGEEKs site, and then move on to explaining how you go about it. More precisely we'll look at:

- Retrieving data
- Calculating ratings
- Viewing and understanding

To understand the following discussion, it'll be better if you have the MovieGEEKs site running on your machine. You can download it from GitHub at http://mng.bz/04k5. See the instructions on the site for how to install it.

RETRIEVING DATA

To calculate implicit ratings for a specific user, you need to retrieve the log data from the user. What you want is the data to tell you, for each item, how many times the user has interacted with the content. For the example shown with Jesper, you want a row like table 4.5.

Table 4.5 Aggregated view of the sessions leading up to Jesper buying *Ace Ventura*

User ID	Content ID	Details	moreDetails	Buy
400002	Ace Ventura	3	1	1

Having this data and many rows like this lets you calculate the implicit rating. Getting data like this can be done either by retrieving all data from the log containing the specific user ID and content ID, or you can make the database work a bit more and return data in the format shown in table 4.5, which is what's done with an SQL query in the following listing.

Listing 4.1 SQL script to retrieve ratings for a user

Counts how many copies a specific user bought of a specific item

Counts how many times a specific user viewed details of a specific item

Counts how many times a specific user viewed more details of a specific item

```
SELECT
    user_id,
    content_id,
    mov.title,
    count(case when event = 'buy' then 1 end) as buys,
    count(case when event = 'details' then 1 end) as details,
    count(case when event = 'moredetails' then 1 end) as moredetails
FROM    evidenceCollector_log log
JOIN    movies mov
ON      log.content_id = mov.id
WHERE   user_id = '4005'
group by user_id, content_id, mov.title
order by buys desc, details desc, moredetails desc
```

Joins with the movie table to get the title

Uses group by to enable the counts

Filters the user ID to get the data of only one user; here it's user 4005.

Orders things by buys, then details, and finally moredetails

Compares the movie ID with the content ID of the evidence

Having this data in hand (well... in system memory), you can now start calculating the implicit ratings, which should then be saved in the ratings database. The function implemented is as previously shown and can be found in the code in listing 4.2. You can also look in the file moviegeek/ Builder/ImplicitRatingsCalculator.py to find the method `query_aggregated_log_data_for_user` to see the actual code that retrieves the data.

CALCULATING IMPLICIT RATINGS

The calculations are quite simple and don't require much explanation. You load the data from the database and calculate the rating. The rating is calculated using the weights that you deduced earlier as shown in the following listing.

Listing 4.2   Calculating implicit ratings based on the users' events

```
def calculate_implicit_ratings_for_user(userid):         Calls method that
  data = query_aggregated_log_data_for_user(userid)      queries the database
  agg_data = dict()
  maxrating = 0              Creates a dictionary to
                            contain the ratings
  for row in data:                      Iterates through each
    content_id = str(row['content_id'])  content item
    if content_id not in agg_data .keys():
      agg_data[content_id] = defaultdict(int)
    agg_data[content_id][row['event']] = row['count']

  ratings = dict()                        Calculates the implicit
  for k, v in agg_data .items():          rating for the content item

    rating = w1 * v['buy'] + w2 * v['details'] + w3 * v['moredetails']
    maxrating = max(maxrating, rating)      Keeps track of what is
    ratings[k] = rating                     the highest rating so far
  for content_id in ratings.keys():
    ratings[content_id] = 10 * ratings[content_id] / maxrating
  return ratings         Returns ratings
```

Goes through all ratings, divides with maxrating to normalize, then multiplies by 10 to put it on a 0-10 scale

---

The method `query_aggregated_log_data_for_user` is called for each user. The data set MovieTweetings, which you'll use later in this book, has ratings on a scale from 1 to 10, so you'll normalize these ratings to the same scale. Having the implicit ratings on this scale also means that you can use them in place of explicit ratings.

VIEWING THE RESULT

If you fire up the MovieGEEKs app, you can now run:

- `python populate_logs.py`—Adds auto-generated logs into the database. Flip back to chapter 3 for more information on this script. The database now contains data shown in figure 4.12.
- `python -m builder.implicit_ratings_calculator`—Calculates the implicit ratings.
- `python manager.py runserver 8001`—Starts the MovieGEEKs site running on port 8001.

id	created	user_id	content_id	event	session_id
100296	2017-08-14 22:04:06+02	400005	1355644	addToList	441008
100344	2017-08-14 22:04:06+02	400005	1355644	details	441008
100363	2017-08-14 22:04:06+02	400005	1355644	details	441008
100440	2017-08-14 22:04:06+02	400005	1355644	details	441009
100767	2017-08-14 22:04:06+02	400005	1355644	genreView	441014
100831	2017-08-14 22:04:06+02	400005	1355644	details	441014
100992	2017-08-14 22:04:06+02	400005	1355644	details	441019

Figure 4.12   A snippet of the auto-generated data. This is the data related to user 400005 (Pietro) and item 1355644.

In the screenshot in figure 4.13, you'll see that two movies received top ratings of 10/10. If you look at the database (figure 4.12), you'll see that there's no buy event, but the item still got a top rating. That's due to the many interactions that occurred between the user and the content.

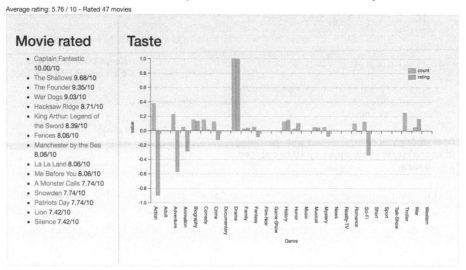

Figure 4.13   Screenshot of the user profile for user ID 400005 (Pietro). "Not in Cluster" means that the user isn't part of any cluster. You'll build clusters in chapter 7.

If you use implicit ratings like the ones described here, you need to take into account that the user hasn't consumed many of the items that you've ratings for. As a result, the items not bought could be included in recommendations. But because a user who has looked at an item as much as in this example, and still not bought it, you probably won't include it in the recommendations.

4.6.1   *Adding the time aspect*

The preceding implementation doesn't include any aspects of time decay. If old behavior is less important than recent activity, it's worth adding that to the mix. It's a bit more effort to include the time aspect, however, because you need to look at each evidence point and add a multiplier that becomes smaller over time.

Adding a time decay can be done with SQL in the database or in code. Certain companies swear by doing everything in SQL because they believe that's the best environment; others say that SQL becomes unreadable with more than 10 lines, so rather than using the database, they move to code. The time decay function you're going to implement uses the following formula.

$$score = \frac{1}{age\ of\ event\ in\ days}$$

In a database, SQL has no elegant way to do this, so you'll do the time decay in code. This also gives you the opportunity to see how you can do everything in code, as opposed to listing 4.1, where you aggregated the data first. Here you'll get all log data from the user using the query in the following listing.[5]

Listing 4.3   SQL to return a specific user's log data

```
SELECT *
FROM collector_log log
WHERE user_id = {}
```

The reason for using days instead of seconds is twofold. First, you want all the events that happened in one day to count the same because movies aren't something you buy several times a day. Second, you want the ratings to decay slowly. By using days, the weight of the events that happened a week before will decay only by one seventh. A music-streaming site like Spotify might want to give more importance to the last hour, or even the last 10 minutes. Figure 4.14 shows the decay algorithm, where you can see a plot of the time decay.

To make sure you understand what's happening, let's consider an example. If Jimmie buys *Game of Thrones* today, the event will have a score of 1; if the purchase was yesterday, the score is 1/2; a week ago is 1/7; a year ago is 1/365. The decay function is shown in the following listing.

Listing 4.4   Calculating implicit ratings using users' events and time decay

```
def calculate_implicit_ratings_w_timedecay(userid, conn):

    data = query_log_data_for_user(userid, conn)          ← Retrieves the data

    weights = {{'buy': w1}, {'moredetails': w2}, {'details': w3} }   ←
                                                          Dictionary of weights
                                                          for each event type
```

---

[5]   If you have a large log, it might be a good idea to put a time constraint on it, such as created > 1 month ago, and define an index on the column's `user_id`.

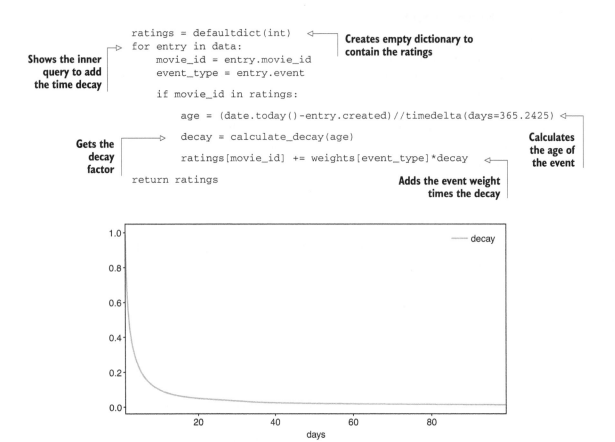

Shows the inner query to add the time decay

Creates empty dictionary to contain the ratings

Gets the decay factor

Calculates the age of the event

Adds the event weight times the decay

```
ratings = defaultdict(int)
for entry in data:
    movie_id = entry.movie_id
    event_type = entry.event

    if movie_id in ratings:

        age = (date.today()-entry.created)//timedelta(days=365.2425)

        decay = calculate_decay(age)

        ratings[movie_id] += weights[event_type]*decay
return ratings
```

Figure 4.14 The function of the decay algorithm

The decay function is shown in the following listing.

Listing 4.5 The decay function

```
def calculate_decay(age_in_days):
    return 1/age_in_days
```

You can try out more complicated time decay algorithms on your own time to see if they improve anything. At this point in the book, it's probably hard to understand what effect changing the decay function has. But the concept is to add an indication of how relevant old things are to users in your recommender system.

If you've a horse you're probably not going to change preferences in horse equipment very often, but if you're looking at a news site, it's likely that old stories won't interest you as much. For movies, one day is a short period, and one month or year may be more likely. For testing your system, however, it makes more sense to use one day.

4.7   *Less frequent items provide more value*

Popular items are often highlighted (understandably) as good items to suggest to people. But if you want to understand which things are important for people, you need to look to the items that few users buy. Consider these examples:

- I buy the movie *Lord of the Rings*, which is number one on the charts (back then), and which every man and his dog have already bought.
- I buy a special collector's extended version of *Lord of the Rings*, which includes a signed poster by the leading stars and of which only 100 copies were produced.

Which event tells you more about my tastes? The first example puts me in a group with half the globe, because most people in the first example don't make me unique compared to others. The second example puts me in an exclusive club with a maximum of 100 members. And those 100 have a specific taste that's likely to be shared.

A different example often used to describe this problem is bananas. Everybody buys bananas, so knowing that the user buys bananas doesn't have much value, as compared to the imported sardines in chili oil, which is a unique product that says something about the buyer. Why am I mentioning this? Well, you could put a filter on the ratings you're calculating and boost the items that are special while the normal ones wouldn't rate so highly. Implementing this can also be a bit tricky, so let's take a quick stab at it.

First, let's define a function that makes sense. This problem is closely related to the well-known *term frequency–inverse document frequency* problem (TF-IDF among friends). It's often used by search engines as a tool to rank a document's value given a user's inquiry. You can consider this a queryless search, where you want to attribute more value to the special items. To understand what content items you'll consider special, you'll look for the IDF instead. The thinking is that if a user buys an item that's popular, it doesn't provide much information about the user's taste. If the same user likes something only few people like, then it could be a better indication of the personal taste of the consumer.

The function can be calculated in several ways. But the following shows one I find more valuable.[6] To find the special items, you can calculate the inverse user frequency (IUF) like this:

$$iuf_{i,u} = \log\left(\frac{N}{1 + n}\right)$$

Where

- n is the number of times item i has been bought by user u.
- N is the number of users in the catalog.

---

[6]   It's mentioned in regard to collaborative filtering in an article by J.S Breese, et al., "Empirical Analysis of Predictive Algorithms for Collaborative Filtering," which I recommend you read. See http://mng.bz/tQhY.

Normalizing in this context means that you put the result on a logarithm scale. Taking the logarithmic of something is done to ensure that there's a big difference among small numbers, while the more numbers grow, the less importance it has, whether it's 1,000 or 2. You can see this in figure 4.15.

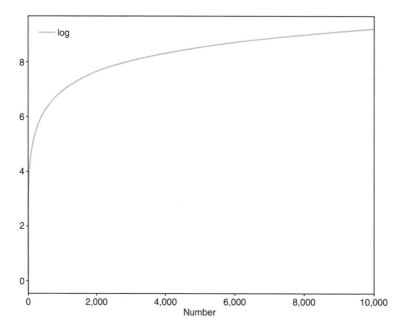

Figure 4.15   The `log` function on numbers from 1 to 10,000. Numbers that go through the `log` function change more when they're small, while the change is smaller when they become larger.

Because the number of users N is constant while calculating the IUF, it's graph would look like the one shown in figure 4.16. The weighted rating calculated by multiplying the two is as follows:

$$wR_{ui} = R_{ui} * iuf_{i,u} = R_{ui} * \log\left(\frac{N}{1+n}\right)$$

If you want to keep these ratings between 1–10, you need to normalize again, the way you did in listing 4.2. It makes it easier to look at these ratings and compare them with the explicit ones. If you think that your site might increase conversions by adding this, this can be implemented both in SQL and on the server.

If you say that you're teaching machines how to predict ratings, then even if there's only one truth, the role of a recommender system engineer or a data scientist is your guide. Remember that if the recommendations that come out in the end seem to fit with the data but not with the users, then one of the knobs to turn is here, where you build the implicit ratings. The implicit ratings that you calculate are the

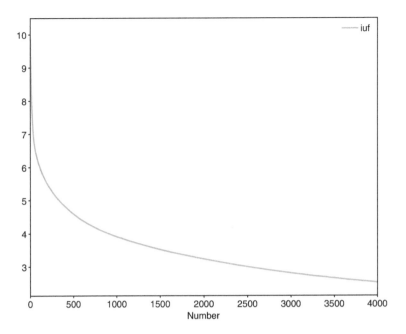

Figure 4.16 The IUF looks like this. If only a few people bought the product, then it would be boosted more, while if many users bought the item, it would be boosted very little.

foundation on which you create the recommenders. Doing it well gives the recommender system the best conditions for predictions, but doing it badly means the recommender system will fail.

Now that you have the dashboard and implicit ratings, you're well on your way to making your recommender system. The next step is to look at how to best save the trinity of user, content, and rating data. This is part of the next chapter, where you'll also see several recommendations. Go look!

Summary

- A user-item matrix is the data format for recommender algorithms. You can populate them by using explicit as well as implicit ratings or by indicating which items were consumed by the user in a binary matrix.
- A rating is the glue that connects a user to an item. It can either be manually entered by the user or calculated based on the behavior of the user.
- The time decay algorithm takes into account that not all information is equally important: old evidence is less important because people tend to change their tastes.
- Inverse frequency factors into the equation because interactions with less popular items provide more information about the user than interactions with popular items.

Non-personalized recommendations

You'll find recommendations in this chapter, but they're not personalized. That doesn't mean that this chapter will be less important.

- You'll learn that using non-personalized recommendations can also show interesting content.

- You'll see examples that show why your site should order content, and you'll learn how to build charts to show users what's popular and that highlight items of interest to other users.

- You'll learn how to calculate association rules by creating itemsets based on the shopping basket and then use those rules to create seeded recommendations.

- You'll see how the recommender component is implemented, which is the core component in the MovieGEEKs example site and the one that provides the recommendations.

Non-personalized recommendations are usually where most sites start because it's easy and doesn't require that you know anything specific about the users. Non-personalized recommendations are good because you can always show those, despite how little you know about the users. People might say that non-personalized recs should only be shown until the system knows enough about the user to show more personalized recs, but always remember that humans are flock animals by nature, so most will be suckers for knowing what content items are the most popular—if for no other reason than to ensure what not to like.

We're handling charts and ordering and association rules in this chapter. We'll start the party by looking at the good old charts, which everybody hates in these context-based days. Charts are simple recommendations based on statistics such as which content sold more. Charts are about ordering your data, and it's natural to continue with a talk about ordering your presentation of the data. We'll look at the implementation of charts and discuss reordering the movies in the MovieGEEKs site. In the second part of the chapter, we'll look at what people put in the shopping basket and use that to create recommendations such as "people who bought X also bought Y," using something called *itemsets* or *frequency sets*. The recommendations we'll look at will be the same for all users interacting with the recommender system; that's why they're called non-personalized recommendations.

After four chapters that are mostly about how to collect data about the users, you might think that it's a bit unfair to put the individual aside and look at the data as a whole. But remember, most sites have many non-identified visitors to whom you want to cater because they're the future customers of your site. And even when you do know the identity of your visitor, it's highly likely that you don't have enough data to calculate personalized recs, and then it's good to fill out the blanks with non-personalized ones.

5.1 What's a non-personalized recommendation?

In chapter 1, we discussed the difference between a commercial and a recommendation. Let's briefly talk about that again.

5.1.1 What's a commercial?

The *deal of the day* from Manning, shown in figure 5.1, is a commercial. It doesn't make it evil because it's a commercial. A *commercial* is something that a vendor publishes because they want content to be exposed to the users, and often people are interested

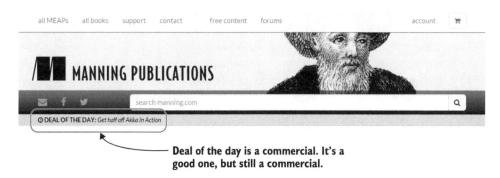

Deal of the day is a commercial. It's a good one, but still a commercial.

Figure 5.1   Manning Publications' (manning.com) Deal of the Day ad

in offers. But, it's something you, as a site owner, should do with caution because bad commercials will drive visitors away. (I have an idea that the internet is full of such commercials, but after spending 30 minutes searching for one, I gave up. I did find a complaint from a guy who felt he got spammed after signing up on a paranormal dating site—it surprised him because he thought it was a serious site). I define a bad commercial as something that's blocking the user from getting on with business, like a popup that can't be closed before a film has been played or redirecting the user to unintended pages.

Often *commercials* are about things that the seller is trying to convince the user is a good offer or cheap (even if it isn't), while a *recommendation* is about finding the user what they want. You could say that finding something cheap is exactly what the user wants. In fact, many sites have made a business out of recommending offers of cheap things. Personally, I go searching for something after I discover I need it, while a coupon site, like cupon.com (figure 5.2), is a bit more like people searching for something they need but don't know it.

Cupon.com uses non-personalized recommendations to recommend more offers. In the top, it lists the popular categories and brands. While the central part of the screen contains lists of vouchers to save money on, it's hard to say how that's calculated. Cupon.com is one of many choices, and I think it's a great way for sellers to get

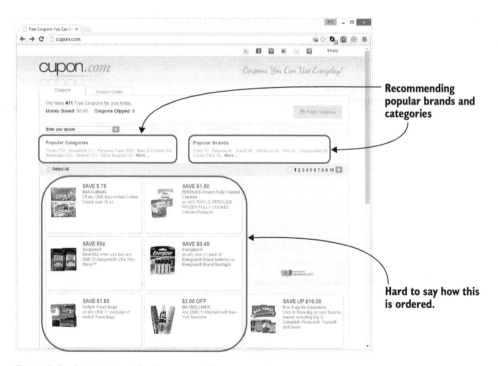

Figure 5.2 Cupon.com collects coupons from everywhere.

in contact with people who are happy to get things cheaper—in quantity, thus spending more money.

5.1.2   What does a recommendation do?

A recommendation, personalized or not, is based on data and calculated from data. To keep the definition from being too murky, we'll restrict it to be computer-calculated based on usage data. That means popular categories at cupon.com are recommendations (by calculating which category is viewed more). Before you start calculating, let's look at examples of what a site can do if it doesn't have any data at all.

5.2   How to make recommendations when you have no data

We talked about it before—no data at all means no recommendations. A recommendation comes from what people like. Again, no data means no recommendations. What can you do then? You can fake it by hand-coding the recs to begin with (this is a purer objective than what we've defined as commercials). You can call it a spotlight, for example, the way they do on DZone.com as shown in figure 5.3. If you don't want (or have the resources) to have somebody set up a spotlight page, you can do a smaller version.

Editors are selecting content that they consider recommendable to the readers.

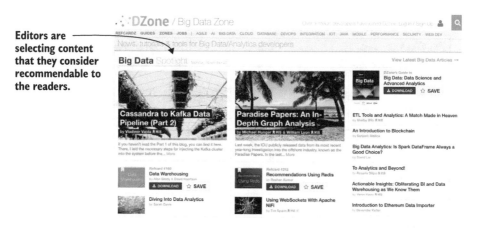

Figure 5.3   DZone has editorial spotlights.

First, what does it mean to present unordered data? An example of that is the Movie-GEEKs page, where the films shown on the first page are the first items that came out of the database. But presenting data like that leaves much to coincidence. Data could be inserted into the database alphabetically or, if you always add data to the end, then the oldest will always be shown first.

> **TIP**   Never use the order set up in the database. Always consider having a default ordering of the content presented.

ORDERING BY PRICE IS USUALLY A BAD IDEA

Before ordering data by price, consider what that means. For cupon.com, that could mean the items with the smallest savings would always be on top, or vice versa. The next option could be to order by the percentage of the savings. For example, if you save $1 on something that costs $10, the item would be shown before something that you save $2 on but costs $100. That's because one discount is 10% while the other is 2%.

USING RECENCY KEEPS THE WEBSITE DYNAMIC

Considering the film website, you don't have any prices so what could you do there? To begin, one of the easiest ways to recommend your items is to order it according to what most people are *most likely* to favor (assuming you know that). You can order movies to show the movies most recently produced or the content most recently updated, for example. In the case of the films, it's probably better to go with the newest ones first. You'll make the site come alive and be more dynamic, as long as the content is alive and dynamic.

Remember that most recent things aren't always the most desirable. If you're selling antiques, you can probably work with ordering the oldest first, such as the PreWarCar.com site (www.prewarcar.com) shown in figure 5.4.

As another example, if your item is a garden tool, then people won't care much about recency ordering, except if you're talking about Weber grills with someone

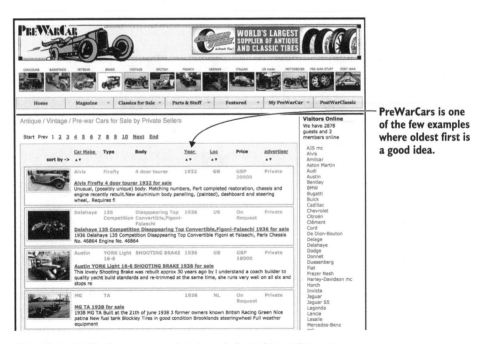

PreWarCars is one of the few examples where oldest first is a good idea.

Figure 5.4 PreWarCar.com, a marketplace dedicated to antique cars

from Denmark. If you're a male Dane, it seems you have to exchange your Weber grill at least once a year, and it can only be bigger. That's due to genius marketing.

5.2.1 Top 10: A chart of items

Back before the internet (yeah, I'm dating myself), we had Top 10s everywhere. We had the Top 10 music chart on the radio every weekend, which we religiously recorded and listened to it on repeat all week. (*Repeat* meaning that you listened to it to the end and then rewound it. Usually the popular songs filled a whole cassette.) The Top 10s were basically the only way to receive recommendations, besides what we heard from friends. When MTV came to Denmark, it was insane... .

Anyway, Top 10 charts, like the ones shown in figure 5.5, have gotten a bad reputation since then, and that's a shame because they do show people what's popular. No matter your personal taste, or how much of an individual you say you are, chances are that you like something on the Top 10.

Top 10 most-emailed articles from the *New York Times* from the Food section. It's is also possible to see the most-viewed articles. Which provides a better signal is hard to say.

Movies with the biggest box office take during a weekend in 2017 in the US. Don't know why earnings is a good measure of quality, but it often used.

Figure 5.5 Top 10 highest earning movies in the US during one weekend in 2017 according to IMDb (imdb.com), and the most-emailed Food section articles at the The New York Times (nytimes.com).

The Top 10 list is all you need, right? Not entirely. A Top 10 chart will satisfy a large group (the majority even), but users aren't alike, making the topic of recommender systems much more fun when tastes are different. It's worth pondering what the Top 10 tells you. If you've a number of users, say 11, and you've 10 films, then the most popular film might be liked by only two people, leaving nine others liking something else more. Always spend time looking at the data.

Let's look at what an implementation of a chart might look like. The chart shows what content items were bought most often, such as the one in figure 5.6. We could also have made a chart on which items are viewed more often or, to use a Facebook term, *liked* more.

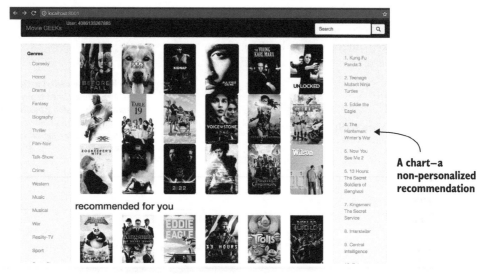

Figure 5.6   MovieGEEKS displays a chart showing what was bought most often.

5.3   Implementing the chart and the groundwork for the recommender system component

You could add the chart quickly, as described in chapter 4. To do things properly and add the functionality in the right place, you'll start by creating the recommender system component, which is where you'll do most of the work in the rest of the chapter.

5.3.1   The recommender system component

A recommender system can be built in many ways, depending on how many recommendations you need to serve, the size of content catalog, and the number of visitors. One thing for certain is that you want it to be a structure that's independent from your website, because you can quickly drown performance.

The solution for the MovieGEEKs site is composed of two components (and a database). The first component, called a *builder*, makes all the precalculations (training) needed to serve the recommendations, while the second component focuses on serving the recommendations. The reason for the builder component is that most recommendations require a great deal of calculations, which requires time, something you don't have when the user's waiting for the page. It's the goal of most recommender algorithms to precalculate as much as possible to make the real-time performance as fast as possible.

Normally you split recommender algorithms into memory-based and model-based recommender algorithms. *Memory-based* means that the recommender accesses the log data in real time, while *model-based* signifies that the algorithm aggregates the data beforehand to make it more responsive. Experience shows that memory-based algorithms only work up a certain point because they don't require many views per minute before it becomes difficult for the servers to keep up.

Looking at figure 5.7, would you do something different, and why? The light boxes contain the components we've already discussed. The dark boxes are the topics of this section. The Recommender API handles requests from the website; the Recs database contains calculated recommendations. The recommendation builder is the component that creates the models and, in some of the algorithms, precalculates the recommendations and saves them in the Recs database.

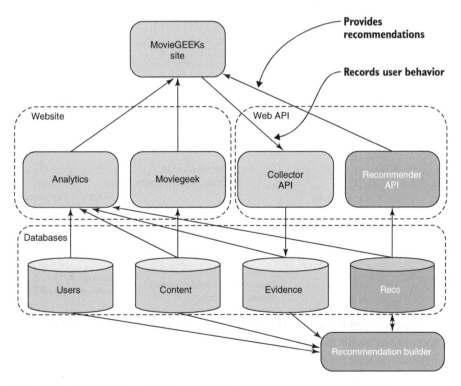

Figure 5.7   MovieGEEKs architecture with the recommender system highlighted

5.3.2   *MovieGEEKs code from GitHub*

Once again, you should consider downloading the MovieGEEKs code from GitHub at http://mng.bz/04k5. Install it following the instructions in the readme file found in the root, so you can try out the things.

5.3.3   *A recommender system*

A *recommender system* is an application that needs access to all your data, depending on what type of recommendations it should produce. Often sites will build an architecture that has a recommender system in a separate instance, and as a safety mechanism has a simple (even hard-coded) fallback recommender, which will keep providing data if the recommender system runs into problems.

> **NOTE**   Always keep the recommender system separate from other parts of your website because it can be quite demanding performance-wise.

In the MovieGEEK site, the recommender system is implemented as a separate Django application. This allows it to run independently on a separate machine when the site goes into production.

5.3.4   *Adding a chart to MovieGEEKs*

A chart is a rather simple thing; you need to count how many of each item has been bought and plot that information. With SQL, it's a matter of grouping by content and counting the buy events in the log. The SQL query in listing 5.1 does one more thing: it adds the title of the movie to the chart. In a live system, it might be worth precalculating the chart once a day because tables can be big and expensive to query every time a chart should be shown.

Listing 5.1   SQL query to get the most sold products

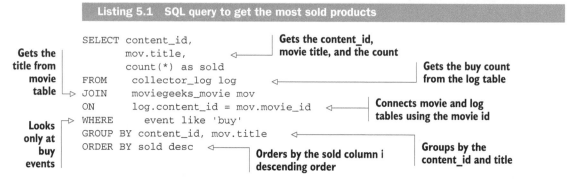

You're querying the log file, which is empty if you recently downloaded the code. But if you run the script moviegeek/populate_logs.py found in the root directory, it auto-generates log data for you. This script is described in more detail in chapter 4.

Being in the spirit of recommenders, let's say this is a recommendation and should therefore be something that should come out of the recommender app. The chart method in recommender/views.py is as shown in listing 5.2. It isn't nice code, but it works.

Listing 5.2   The chart method in recommender/views.py

Calls the popularity recommender method to
retrieve the most bought items

Extracts the
movie_ids to a list

```
def chart(request, take=10):
    sorted_items = PopularityBasedRecs().recommend_items_from_log(take)
    ids = [i['content_id'] for i in sorted_items]      ←

    ms = {m['movie_id']: m['title'] for m in
        Movie.objects.filter(movie_id__in=ids).values('title',
                                        'movie_id')}   ←

    sorted_items = [{'movie_id': i['content_id'],
                    'title': ms[i['content_id']]} \
                    for i in sorted_items]
        data = { 'data': sorted_items }

        return JsonResponse(data, safe=False)      ←      Returns as json
```

Uses the extracted
movie_ids to get
the movie titles

Creates a new sorted items list
that also contains the movie title

The method used in the previous listing calls the following method to extract the data from the log.

Listing 5.3   The `recommend_items_from_log` method in recs/popularity_
recommender.py

```
recs/popularity_recommender.py
def recommend_items_from_log(self, num=6):
    items =
        Log.objects.values('content_id')
    items = items.filter(event='buy').annotate(Count('user_id'))

    sorted_items = sorted(items, key=lambda item: -float(item['user_id__count']))

    return sorted_items[:num]
```

Retrieves the items and counts
how often they were bought

Sorts by
number of
users who
bought

To see the output from the method, type `localhost:8000/rec/chart` as the URL in your browser. I get a chart of the 10 most sold items for MovieGEEKs as shown previously in figure 5.6.

5.3.5   *Making the content look more attractive*

Let's look at MovieGEEKs content (the movies in the database). Earlier we said that you can't allow the database to dictate the order of how you present your content. If MovieGEEKs site displays the movies as they are in the database, it shows you really old films (figure 5.8).

Figure 5.8 Movies as they're ordered in the database

You can play around with the ordering of your database by changing this line in the view file from the following listing:

Listing 5.4 Getting the oldest movies first

```
movies = selected.movies.order_by('year')
```

This line orders movies by year, starting with the oldest first. If you've a thing for black-and-white films, this is great, but I think most people nowadays want to watch more recent ones in color. To display the most recent films in a Django query, add a minus sign in front of the column name as shown in this listing.

Listing 5.5 Getting the newest movies first

```
movies = selected.movies.order_by('-year')
```

This change makes the front page of MovieGEEKs a bit more interesting, as you can see in figure 5.9.

Figure 5.9 Ordering films by most recent

You can also order the movies according to release date, but that doesn't work for other things because customers aren't always looking for the latest one. For example, Netflix often adds new content to its catalog, but it's not always the latest films, so your sort should be based on something else.

If you turn again to gardening tools, you might not get much out of ordering them by production date, but maybe your database will contain data about when gardening tools are typically used. You can use machines to prepare the ground in early fall, later you need tools to put down seeds, even later a gadget to keep weeds away, and so on. Gardening equipment could be ordered by seasonal use, with the current season topmost. With ordering in place, and several non-personalized recommendations made (figure 5.6), it's now time to look at several more concrete recommendations.

5.4   *Seeded recommendations*

Charts are good but generic. One thing that many sites take advantage of is you looking at a specific item, which can be used to create recommenders for associated items. These items could be said to be *seeds.*

Seeded recommendations; isn't that a search? It is, but the idea is that seeded recommendations can be either an item, a product, or an article that you then use as input to find other relevant content. You use items bought together to figure out how to make suggestions. To understand how people buy together, you look in your evidence.

One of the most famous seeded recommendations is the Frequently Bought Together (FBT) category (figure 5.10) when you look at an item at Amazon or almost every other web shop. A way to create these associations between items is called an *affinity analysis* or, in more familiar terms, *shopping basket analysis.* Let's look at how you go about doing that.

Frequently Bought Together

Total price £43.49

Add all three to Basket

☑ **This item:** Frostfire Large 2 Person Instant Popup Tent £24.99

☑ New Set of 2 x 180cm Camping Yoga Roll Eva Foil Foam backed Sleeping Mat Mattress Tent Festival ... £8.69

☑ Yellowstone Essential Mummy Sleeping Bag £9.81

Figure 5.10   An example of Amazon's Frequently Bought Together sales pitch

5.4.1   *Frequently bought items similar to the one you're viewing*

Can you create an FBT recommender by finding all the products that are bought together with the current product and then take the top *X* of that? You could, but as you'll see later, it doesn't work well.

One of the challenges of showing an FBT recommendation is that most products are bought together with other popular items. A classic example is that most people leaving a supermarket in Denmark will have a liter of milk in the bag, so almost no matter what else is in the basket, you could say that those items were frequently bought together with a liter of milk.

As I was writing this, my wife came home from the supermarket with not only one, but two liters of milk (figure 5.11 shows the shopping receipt). Most products in a supermarket that are bought often will also be purchased with milk. This yields

Figure 5.11   What my wife bought (the list contains plastic bag, yogurt, milk, and olives).

frequency sets containing milk and most other products. When two or more items are often seen together it's called a *frequency set.*

You're probably thinking, "Yeah, that's great, but this is only interesting for supermarket owners." Nevertheless, this can be applicable to many different areas.

In the following sections, we'll look at how to calculate FBT products in a simple supermarket example and then move on to implement this in the movie site. Beyond that, you can move to larger items, such as furniture or estate sales, or boat-selling websites—markets that usually sell one item at the time that can have FBT products. For these markets, it's worth thinking about recommending smaller things. I've never bought a boat, but I'd venture that no matter what size the boat, I'll need a life vest. And depending on whether it's a sail boat or a speedboat, I might need special equipment. Even when you're selling large and expensive things, it's worth adding FBT recommendations, or would you call it *frequently needed equipment?*

5.4.2 Association rules

Instead of looking at most popular objects, there's the idea of association rules, something a bit closer to kindness than marketing talk. *Association rules* in the commerce scenario can be thought of as well-meaning advice. Most people hate to come home with a new hard disk only to realize that they don't have any cable to connect it. If you buy things on Amazon, then you're in luck because they remind you that most people buy a cable with the hard drive, as you can see in figure 5.12.

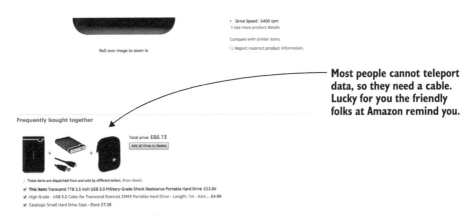

Figure 5.12 On Amazon, external hard disks are frequently bought together with a cable.

Now let's think a bit about how to get these association rules. The short list that follows details supermarket checkouts. (I tried to add an example about Star Wars here, but I don't remember them ever shopping for groceries, so we'll stick to supermarkets.) Let's imagine that you have a supermarket that has only five products: milk, dates, yogurt, carrots, and bread. These are usually called *items* when talking about association rules.

1 { bread, yogurt }
2 { milk, bread, carrots, }
3 { bread, carrots }
4 { bread, milk }
5 { milk, dates, carrots }
6 { milk, dates, yogurt, bread }

Each line is a transaction that contains a number of items. To make an association rule, look at items that are bought together. If you pick milk in this example, then all other products are bought together with milk. Does that offer you much value? No matter what product you have, you can say that other people bought milk together with the current product, so, no, that isn't of much value. Then what?

You'll need to find the products that are always bought together, but not bought with everything else. Any subset of the list of items is called an *itemset*. Bread and milk are an itemset {Bread, milk}, and they can be found in three out of six transactions. Does that make you confident that it's a good idea to recommend milk whenever there's bread in the basket? It should.

Let's define some numbers that can make it easier to decide if a rule is valid or merely a coincidence. The problem about the three-out-of-six itemset from the example is that bread is present in five out of six transactions, so it would be hard *not* to find transactions containing bread. To take that into account, you'll define *confidence* as the number of transactions in which the itemset is divided by the total number of times the first item is present.

Definition: *Confidence*

$$c(X \rightarrow Y) = \frac{|T(X \text{ AND } Y)|}{T(X)}$$

where T(X) is the set of transactions that contain X.

Let's calculate what the confidence rating is that milk will be in the basket when bread is also bought. This can be written like this:

$$c(bread \rightarrow milk) = \frac{|T(bread \text{ AND } milk)|}{|T(bread)|}$$

Next you need to find all the transactions containing first both bread and milk and then only bread.

$$T(bread \text{ AND } milk) = \{milk, bread, carrots\}, \{bread, milk\}, \{milk, dates, yogurt, bread\}$$

$$T(bread) = \{milk, bread, carrots\}, \{bread, carrots\}, \{bread, milk\}, \{milk, dates, yogurt, bread\}$$

Inserting that into the equation, you get

$$c(bread \rightarrow milk) = \frac{|T(bread\ AND\ milk)|}{|T(bread)|}$$

$$= \frac{3}{5}$$

$$= 0.6$$

According to this calculation, you'd be 60% confident that you'll find milk when you see bread in the basket. That seems okay, right? But wait a minute. If you do the same with dates and carrots, the same calculation would give you

$$c(dates \rightarrow carrots) = 0.5$$

While I get that bread and milk often go together, I'm not as confident that people who eat dates also buy carrots half the time they buy dates. There simply aren't enough cases of transactions with dates to support the claim. This leads to a second definition you can use to understand whether there exists an association rule between two items.

> ## Definition: *Support*
>
> $$S(X \rightarrow Y) = \frac{|T(X\ AND\ Y)|}{T()}$$
>
> *where T(X) is the set of transactions that contain X, and T() means all transactions.*

Looking at the two examples gives us the following support:

$$S(bread \rightarrow milk) = \frac{3}{6}$$

$$S(dates \rightarrow carrots) = \frac{1}{6}$$

In other words, evidence that supports the association rule *bread* → *milk* is much greater than for the association rule *dates* → *carrots*, which was also the previous conclusion. This is a nice little example. But if we zoom back to real life, then most shops (at least the ones that survive) have more than six products. And the transactions might well be much larger.

When I began writing this chapter, I asked my friends on Facebook what they bought last time they went to the supermarket, hoping to get some good example data. But the feedback was far too messy to work with. Figure 5.13 also illustrates that association rules can quickly become much more complicated to calculate.

To find association rules you first need to find frequency sets. Figure 5.14 shows the possible frequency sets that could result if you've a set of items containing four

Figure 5.13   Helpful friends on Facebook were quick to respond to my call for shopping data.

elements {milk, butter, dates, bread}. Once again, this is a simple example, but to explain how the implementation is done, we need a diagram (figure 5.14).

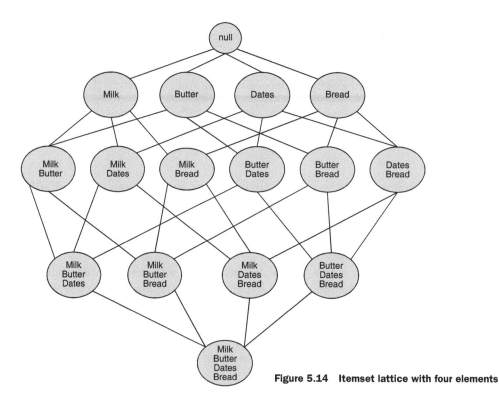

Figure 5.14   Itemset lattice with four elements

Figure 5.14 shows all the possible combinations of the four elements of the itemsets. If you start from the bottom, where you'll find all elements in one itemset, you can ask what needs to be fulfilled for that frequency set to exist? All elements need to occur often together in a transaction, but if all of them need to be present, then each item of the itemset should also be there frequently.

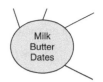

Figure 5.15 Itemset lattice with a low presence of butter

If you go one step up and pick the node (the circle) all the way to the left in the lattice, you find an itemset {milk, butter, dates} as shown in figure 5.15. For this to become a frequency set, milk, butter, and dates need to occur often and together. But the fact that all the items have to occur often means you can take advantage of that to make a fast implementation.

Start by looking at itemsets with only one element to see how frequently they appear. If you find that butter is almost never present, then you know there are no frequency sets with butter. That means that you can cross off all rules that contain butter. The black nodes in figure 5.16 show which elements you can remove from the list by finding butter infrequently. With that in mind, you'll see how you might implement this in the following section.

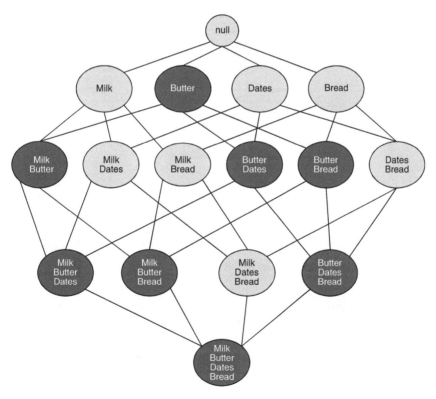

Figure 5.16   The black nodes in the diagram show which frequency sets will never produce any association rules. Because butter is infrequent, none of the nodes containing butter can be frequent.

5.4.3 *Implementing association rules*

The procedure described in the previous section goes something like the following:

1   Settle on a minimum support and minimum confidence level.
2   Get all transactions.
3   Create a list of itemsets, one for each element, and calculate their *support* (number of times it's present divided by the number of transactions) and set *confidence* to one.
4   Build a list of itemsets containing more than one item and calculate support and confidence by inferring that each transaction finds all combinations of items and adds one to the itemset's support.
5   Iterate through the itemsets and remove the ones that don't fulfill the confidence requirement.

Let's translate this into Python code, but we'll wait a bit before setting the minimum support and confidence level, calculating everything to start with.

GET ALL TRANSACTIONS

On the MovieGEEKs site, there's no concept of a basket, so instead we'll say that buys happening in the same session are transactions. You'll get your transactions from the log, which means that you first need to retrieve buy events from the database and then build the transactions based on the session ID as shown in figure 5.17.

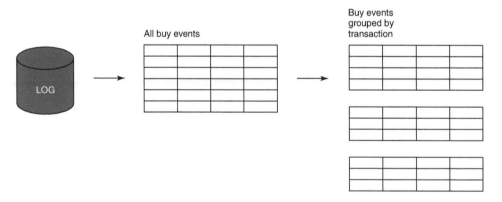

Figure 5.17   Creating transactions from the log data

To get all transactions from your log, select all log entries that contain a buy event as shown in listing 5.6. This is what the `retrieve_buy_events` method does.

Listing 5.6   Retrieving buy events from your log

```
def retrieve_buy_events():

sql = """
SELECT *
```

```
FROM  Collector_log
WHERE event = 'buy'
ORDER BY session_id, content_id
"""
```
Uses an SQL query to get all buy events

```
    cursor = data_helper.get_query_cursor(sql)
    data = data_helper.dictfetchall(cursor)

    return data
```

Now you need to group each of the buy events into a transaction. To do that, you'll feed the data into the `generate_transactions` method as shown in listing 5.7. This method runs through the data and collects each transaction in a dictionary that contains the transaction ID as a key and a couple of session IDs for the transaction.

Listing 5.7 Creating a list and adding it to a dictionary

```
def generate_transactions(data):
    transactions = dict()

    for trans_item in data:
        id = trans_item["session_id"]
        if id not in transactions:
            transactions[id] = []
        transactions[id].append(trans_item["content_id"])

    return transactions
```
Iterates through all rows in the data

Retrieves the transaction_ids (session_id in your case)

If not seen before, creates a list and adds it to the dictionary

Appends the content to the transaction

GET ALL ITEMSETS, SIZE ONE, AND CALCULATE THEIR SUPPORT

You can now calculate the frequency sets. The method shown in listing 5.8 makes it easy to abstract what's going on.

Listing 5.8 Calculating support and confidence for the frequency sets

```
def calculate_support_confidence(transactions, min_sup=0.01):

    N = len(transactions)

    one_itemsets = calculate_itemsets_one(transactions, min_sup)
    two_itemsets =
      calculate_itemsets_two(transactions,
                             one_itemsets, min_sup)
    rules = calculate_association_rules(one_itemsets,
                                        two_itemsets, N)
    return sorted(rules)
```
N is the number of transactions.

Calculates all itemsets of size one

Calculates all itemsets of size two

Calculates association rules

Sorts rules and returns

The method creates two dictionaries: one for the frequency sets with only one element and one for the frequency sets with two elements. The declarations are followed by two calls to methods that populate the dictionaries. Let's look at `calculate_itemsets_one` first.

Listing 5.9   Creating a list of itemsets with only one element

N is the number of all transactions.

```
def calculate_itemsets_one(transactions, min_sup=0.01):

    N = len(transactions)

    temp = defaultdict(int)
    one_itemsets = dict()

    for key, items in transactions.items():
        for item in items:
            inx = frozenset({item})
            temp[inx] += 1

    # remove all items that is not supported.
    for key, itemset in temp.items():
        if itemset > min_sup * N:
            one_itemsets[key] = itemset

    return one_itemsets
```

defaultdict initializes new elements with default values of the type you use as input.

Goes through each transaction

Looks at each item

Goes through all elements

Picks the elements that have support larger than the required support

Because you use the defaultdict, you don't have to worry about initialization.

FrozenSets are a special type of sets. FrozenSets are immutable and can therefore be used as dictionary keys.[1]

---

defaultdict

In the previous listing, there's an import of a defaultdict. This is a dictionary where every new element is initialized to the default value of its declared type. This makes the code a bit more readable. The method runs through all the transactions and, for each transaction it increments, increases the count for each element found in the transactions.

When this is done, the itemsets with one element (found in listing 5.9), are fed into this method, which calculates itemsets with confidence and with support greater than some minimum value. Listing 5.10 shows the calculation for itemsets with two elements.

Listing 5.10   Creating a list of itemsets with two elements

```
def calculate_itemsets_two(transactions, one_itemsets, min_sup=0.01):
    two_itemsets = defaultdict(int)

    for key, items in transactions.items():
        items = list(set(items))

        if (len(items) > 2):
            for perm in combinations(items, 2):
                if has_support(perm, one_itemsets):
                    two_itemsets[frozenset(perm)] += 1
```

Checks if the itemset has support

Iterates through all transactions

Removes duplications

Looks only at the transactions that contain more than two items

Adds the itemset to the list of itemsets

Looks at all the permutations of two items one can build from the list of items

---

[1] For more information, see http://mng.bz/o2h5.

```
                     elif len(items) == 2:
                         if has_support(items, one_itemsets):
                             two_itemsets[frozenset(items)] += 1
             return two_itemsets
```

The transaction only contains two items

Adds the itemset to the list of itemsets

Checks if the itemset has support

The resulting dictionary is iterated once more, and the items that are above the minimal support are added to the output dictionary that's eventually returned. Now you're ready to calculate the association rules (listing 5.11).

Listing 5.11 Calculating association rules

Iterates through all the itemsets of size one

For each itemset of size one, iterates through all the itemsets of size two

Checks if the itemsets of size one are a subset of the itemset of size two

```
def calculate_association_rules(one_itemsets, two_itemsets, N):
    timestamp = datetime.now()

    rules = []
    for source, source_freq in one_itemsets.items():
        for key, group_freq in two_itemsets.items():
            if source.issubset(key):
                target = key.difference(source)
                support = group_freq / N
                confidence = group_freq / source_freq
    rules.append((timestamp, next(iter(source)), next(iter(target)), confidence,
        support))
            return rules
```

If so, sets target to the element(s) that aren't the source

Appends rule

Support is the number of times the itemset has occurred divided by the total number of transactions.

Confidence is the number of times the group occurs compared to how often the source occurs by itself.

It's worth noting that there could be value in also looking at association rules for sets with more than one element on the left of the rule if you want to use it to recommend things when looking at the shopping basket. But calculating it with only one source element makes sense in this case, because you'll use it to show recommendations in reference to one item.

5.4.4   *Saving the association rules in the database*

Now that you can calculate the association rules, it might be worth considering if computing this every time a customer looks at a product is a good idea. What you can do is to calculate the rules offline and then have a place to save them, where you can retrieve those quickly. But the association rules should also be updated, and while the update is going on, this shouldn't disrupt the service.

Can you save the association rules to one table? Well, this could cause problems. Let's take a step back so everyone is following. You have users clicking Details of movies, which query a rules table. This also happens while the system is adding new rules. To avoid having problems while saving new rules, you need a marker that shows which rules are the current ones to retrieve.

A way to get around this is to introduce a version table as shown in figure 5.18. The version table ensures that the system will not mix up different runs of rules. The version table contains a row for each full version of the rules. It means that you can't query the association rules directly, but you'd have to join it with the version table as shown in listing 5.12.

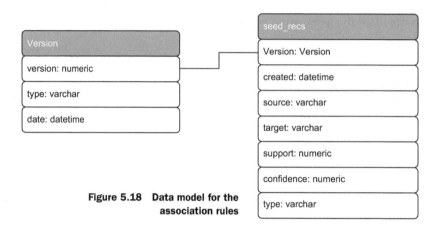

Figure 5.18   Data model for the association rules

Listing 5.12   SQL to retrieve association rules from a specific source's latest version

```
WITH currentversion as
  (SELECT version
     FROM version
     WHERE type = 'association_rules'
     ORDER BY version desc
   LIMIT 1)
SELECT *
FROM seeded_recs recs
WHERE source = '<the source id>'
AND recs.version = currentversion
```

Before you get too excited about the version table, I'd better tell you that it isn't implemented in the MovieGEEKs website.

5.4.5   *Running the association rules calculator*

To run the association rule calculator, you should first generate the log entries that were mentioned in chapter 4 (by running python populate_logs.py). Then you can run the code as shown in the following listing.

Listing 5.13   Calculating the association rules

```
python -m builder.association_rules_calculator
```

This generates the association rules and saves them in the database. And with this, you should understand how association rules work and are implemented.

Let's have a quick look at the MovieGEEKs site to see the rules in action. To retrieve recommendations using association rules, you call the method in listing 5.14; it's Django-specific (and maybe not too interesting to look at if you aren't into Django). But you should still be able to see what's happening.

> ### Listing 5.14 Seeded recommendation rules using association rules

```
def get_association_rules_for(request, content_id, take=6):
    data = SeededRecs.objects.filter(source=content_id) \
               .order_by('-confidence') \
               .values('target', 'confidence', 'support')[:take]

    return JsonResponse(dict(data=list(data)), safe=False)
```

Retrieves objects from the SeededRecs table, where source equals content_id, and orders them by confidence

Wraps in json and returns

The landing page, shown in figure 5.19, now contains the Top 10 chart on the right. (The recommendations on the landing page are also from the association rules, but more on that in chapter 6.) If you click an entry in the chart (in theory, you can click any movie but we build them using a small dataset, so they will only appear in few places), you will see the association rules in action on the Details page.

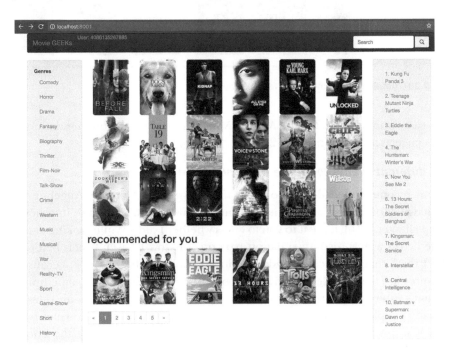

Figure 5.19 Landing page with Top 10 content on the right

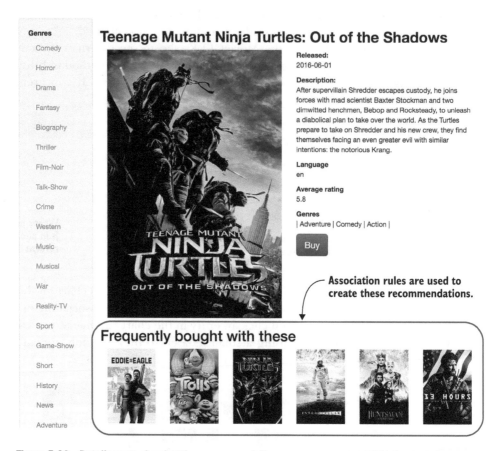

Figure 5.20   Details page showing the recommendations

In my case, when I click *Teenage Mutant Ninja Turtles*, I get recommendations on the Details page as shown in figure 5.20.

5.4.6   *Using different events to create the association rules*

A friend recommended that I look at *Online Consumer Behavior* by Angeline G. Close (Routledge, 2012) to gain more insight into how users behave on the internet so as to beef up chapter 3. (I'll leave it to you to guess whether I did.) While looking at the book, I came across a new recommendation type on Amazon I haven't seen before (figure 5.21). I think that this recommendation does a disservice to the book, because it gives the impression that people looked at the book but eventually bought something else.

What's interesting is that it shows a way to beef up your association rules. Even if not many people bought this book, you could still create association rules by finding all the sessions where a customer viewed a book (for example, like the book *Online Consumer Behavior*) and then look at what was eventually bought. Instead of starting out with frequency sets only containing things bought, you'll have all the sessions with

What other items do customers buy after viewing this item?

Positioning: The Battle for Your Mind Kindle Edition
› Al Ries
⭐⭐⭐⭐✩ 287
$8.99

Qualitative Consumer and Marketing Research Kindle Edition
› Russell W. Belk
⭐⭐⭐⭐✩ 2
$36.00

Figure 5.21   Amazon's recommender: Customers who viewed this went on to buy.

the buy events plus the viewed book. Then when you've found all the supported frequency sets, you can calculate rules that start with the book and use those as recommendations.

This is so exciting that we don't even need to summarize the chapter, and probably you'll want to jump to the next chapter to get started on more ways of constructing recommendations. But summaries are a good way to refresh what you've read.

Summary

- Charts are great and easy to add. You can chart data in many ways, not only by counting which items have been bought most often.
- Its best not to present unordered content. Content should be ordered according to what you think most users are interested in. For movies and books that can mean ordering by the release date, or for coupons, it can be money saved.
- Association rules are based on what is bought together and used to show Frequently Bought Together (FBT) recommendations. The usefulness of the rules is calculated by looking at the indicators support and confidence.
- It's good to save recommendations in the database; that will make the recommender system respond faster. On the other hand, it takes time to calculate them, and they take up space.
- Adding a version number to the recommendations in your database lets you have several versions in the database at one time, which means that you can have one that's used in production and then switch to a new one when your ready to go live. But more importantly, if something happens with the recommendations that you're currently using, you can revert to an older version.

The user (and content) who came in from the cold

Open your arms and put on a big smile; it's time to learn how to greet new customers. In this chapter

- You'll examine the cold-start problem that's related to new customers.
- You'll learn how to segment users, so you can look at semi-personalization.
- You'll look at Redbubble.com as a case for cold-start problems with your newly acquired knowledge.
- You'll look at an implementation of a simple personalize recommender using association rules.

We're off to a cold start in this chapter, so put on your hat and gloves and let's get started. In the previous chapter, we talked about how to get data, and luckily, most websites have data before they start adventures into recommender systems. But even having a lot of data won't solve the problem of how to introduce new things, be that products or users.

6.1 What's a cold start?

Not so surprisingly, if you don't have knowledge of your users, you can't personalize them. And having no personalization is a huge issue because you want to make new visitors feel welcome so they'll become loyal returning customers. Repeat customers are ideal and you'll want to keep them happy, but there's nothing like adding a new one to the list.

This problem is so big that it has a name—it's called *cold start*. It's a term used not only for serving recommendations to new users, but also for introducing new items into your catalog. New items won't show up in any of the non-personalized recommendations because they don't have the numbers to enter into sales statistics, and they won't appear in personalized recommendations because the system doesn't know how to relate those to other items.

Under the umbrella of cold-start problems are also *gray sheep*. These are users who have such individual tastes that even if there's data, there are no other users who've bought any of the products they have.

Personalized recommendations are based on information that binds content with users. Figure 6.1 illustrates the most common connections used when you calculate recommendations. In the following chapters, we'll go more into these connections; here I only want to say that the cold-start problem is about figuring out what to do when you have none or a small number of these types of connections.

The figure indicates that if a user has rated film #1 high, then if one of these connections is present, you can recommend film #2. If there are no connections outgoing from the items the current user has rated high, then you'll have a hard time recommending something to the user.

Luckily, this occurs only when you've new users who haven't yet related to any items (related meaning viewed, bought, and rated). And, as you'll see, customers with unique tastes also cause similar problems. But I'm getting ahead of myself. Let's take it

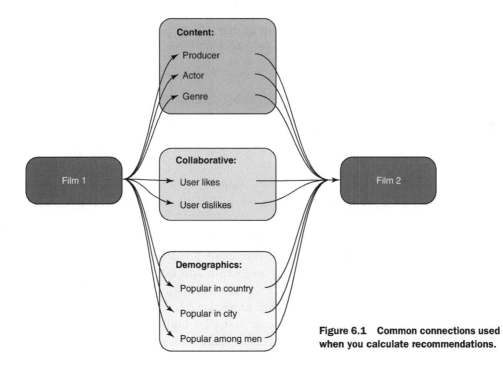

Figure 6.1 Common connections used when you calculate recommendations.

from the top in more detail. We'll start with the easiest one—cold products—and move on from there.

6.1.1   Cold products

A catalog of items doesn't need to be big before new content will disappear into obscurity, like a needle in a haystack. It's therefore crucial that you make extra effort to introduce something new. In most cases, adding new content should be accompanied by a manual process where the site promotes the item, such as sending emails to users with similar interests.

An easy way to make visitors notice new content is by adding a place on your page that shows it. Most people love to check out new stuff. Netflix has its own area for showcasing new arrivals as shown in figure 6.2.

Click to find browse the new arrivals.

Figure 6.2   Netflix shows new arrivals.

Another way is to boost new content so that it looks popular and shows up in your recommendations. Then if it doesn't get consumed, you can slowly let it decay.

6.1.2   A cold visitor

A new visitor that you don't know anything about is also a cold start. When should you start giving a user personalized recommendations? Many scientific papers say that recommendations can't be calculated before a user has rated at least 20 to 50 items. Normally, the customer expects sites to start delivering recommendations long before that.

Some movie sites ask you to rate five items to get started; that isn't an option with most sites. But if a user searches for something, that's a great way to understand what a person wants, then you're completely sure the item is something the user is interested in.

Figure 6.3 shows a search I did on LinkedIn. And right there in the upper corner, where you're most likely to see it, is the Create Job Alert button. Such items could provide good evidence as to what the user wants, and might be enough to classify one or two groups of your content that could be relevant for the user.

When you have enough information to display a recommendation is a tradeoff. It's a matter of deciding whether you want to display high-quality recommendations when you've more data or lower-quality recommendations with less data. Think about it this

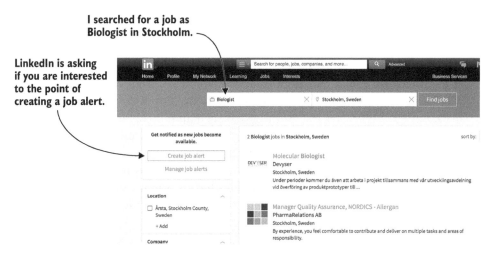

I searched for a job as Biologist in Stockholm.

LinkedIn is asking if you are interested to the point of creating a job alert.

Figure 6.3 LinkedIn sets up a job alert using your search terms, which shows that your search terms were effective in helping find what you were searching for.

way: what's the least amount of data that will suffice for determining someone's preferences? In certain cases, this could be five ratings, like on a movie site, but in other places, it could be different.

When a new user arrives, you know nothing.[1] No data means no personalization. That's easy, but instead of throwing in the towel and leaving to drink some herbal tea, let's see how much you need to know before you can do something.

One thing to keep in mind is that when you have little data on a user, you might not have a correct picture of the user's preferences. For example, imagine that Sara arrives at MovieGEEKs, and she likes to divide her movie watching into something like this: Action, 20%; Drama, 20%; and Comedy, 60% but hasn't rated any movies yet. Today, she knows what she's looking for and goes straight to the Drama category and buys one. The system knows that Sara likes drama, but not how much or whether she only likes drama. If the recommender assumes that it's only drama from here forward, that's only a small part of what Sara likes. But, as mentioned earlier, it's often better to recommend something that's a little off instead of providing no recommendation at all.

In chapter 12, you'll learn about hybrid recommenders, particularly a certain type called *mixed hybrids*. When such a recommender is used, it falls back to the most popular recommendations if personalized recommendations aren't available.

For example, Amazon will, among other things, show you what people are looking at right now. Finding out what people are currently looking at can be done quickly. Look in your log and find the content that's been viewed within the last minute, hour, or day. But there are also other things you can do. Even when you do know something

---

[1] That's a truth with modifications: because you know their IP addresses and, therefore, probably also where they come from. More on that in section 6.3.

about your customers, you can still have a cold-start problem. We call this a gray sheep.

6.1.3   *Gray sheep*

A gray sheep isn't what you think (well, I've no idea of what you think, but at least not what many would think). It also has nothing to do with the sweet, wool-producing animals. Rather, a *gray sheep* is a user who has such an individual taste that even if there's data, there are likely no other consumers—or very, very few people—who've bought any of the products the gray sheep has.

The reason it's here among the cold-start problem is that gray sheep create the same issue of calculating recommendations for users that you don't have any data on. And certain solutions overlap between cold visitors and gray sheep, so it's worth mentioning here as well.

6.1.4   *Let's look at real-life examples*

Take a film, let's call it *X*; no one ever bothered to look at it. And here comes Susan, who may have met somebody who was a statist for 2 min in *X*, which is the only 2 min she ever wants to watch. She has chatted with that person online, she intends to get the film, and so she arrives at the movie site. In this case, Susan probably wouldn't want any films like this again, so recommending similar films would be a mistake—but you don't know that.

Generally, people tend to buy something because they like it. In fact, Susan creates more problems than not for two reasons: the system will spend energy looking for similarities but won't find any and, if Susan does buy something more popular, you suddenly have a link between a popular film and something that was only ever viewed or purchased by one user.

This might end up making your recommender start recommending the film *X* to people who like the more popular film. Only after the user has generated more data will you realize that film *X* is an outlier and disregard it because film *X* has little support. This isn't a problem when we talk about association rules, but when we talk about collaborative filtering, it can be a problem.

AN EXAMPLE OF GRAY SHEEP AND COLD PRODUCTS

Gray sheep sound like odd users that you probably can't recommend anything to, but consider a site such as Redbubble (www .redbubble.com) (figure 6.4). Redbubble is a place where artists can showcase and sell art in many forms, from wall art to T-shirts and hoodies. With a content catalog containing millions of art pieces and a customer base from all over the world, Redbubble has many customers who've bought something that nobody else, or darn few, have bought.

Art is difficult to categorize, so it's hard to say that because somebody likes one piece of art, they'll also like another. If you combine that with the fact that most items are sold only a few times, the result is that it's hard to recommend things even to old customers.

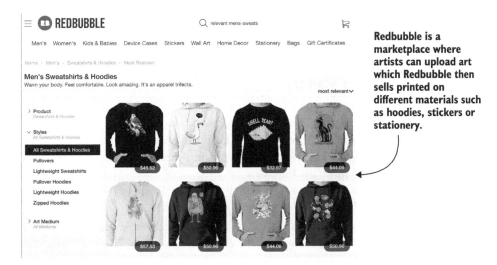

Figure 6.4 Landing page of Redbubble

Most of Redbubble's products stay cold products because few buy each product. You, therefore, can't relate those items to other products. Customers who buy from Redbubble can easily be gray sheep, meaning that they've bought things that haven't been purchased by other people.

Redbubble, in many ways, has the same type of problem as news sites such as Google News, video sites such as YouTube, or magazine sites, such as Issuu (the YouTube for magazines). Artists, moviemakers, or magazine publishers add content without descriptions (such as genre, tags, and so on). When they do add information in the form of tags, people have different opinions about what a tag means. But Redbubble is especially interesting because, while you can read the uploaded content and try to tag it, it's hard to tag art. Look around the Redbubble site and see if you can come up with ways to automatically add tags.

6.1.5 What can you do about cold starts?

In the following sections, you'll look at different ways to make cold starts less problematic.[2] Many of the solutions for cold-start problems (users, products, and gray sheep) relate to one of the algorithms you'll study in the following chapters, so those solutions will be handled then. For example, a cold item is best handled using content-based filtering, which we'll look at in chapter 10. I'll postpone any real attempt to solve this issue until then.

While not solving the cold-start problem, a solution that often comes up is offering to connect with people using social media accounts like Facebook Connect and then

---

[2] I originally wrote "get around," referring to cold starts, but as a reviewer rightfully said, it isn't getting around a cold start—it's about making it less problematic.

extracting data from the user's profile, thereby circumventing the cold-start issue. These profiles won't automatically provide you with data that suits your domain, but it can be a start.

6.2   Keeping track of visitors

Sadly, most users are elusive. They tend to access websites without signing in or logging on from different devices and locations, so it can be a feat to recognize returning customers. This is sad because to understand users you need to know if they're a new user and, more importantly, when they're coming back. You need to track users, new and old, to understand their behavior.

6.2.1   Persisting anonymous users

As soon as a new user arrives at your site, it's a good idea to explain the benefits of registering, either through Facebook or through a registration page or form. While you'll prefer users to register, you'll still want to save an ID for the anonymous sessions, so that you can recognize them if they do return. *Recognizing users* means that you can accumulate information about the person, which will make the system calculate recommendations even before you know who they are.

In the old days when people had one stationary computer and no other devices, it was enough to set a cookie in the user's browser. It's still worth doing but remember, as soon as the user changes browsers or devices, you're lost. This problem is so significant that companies advertise it when they've found a solution to it.[3]

Django enables *anonymous sessions*: sessions where you can place a cookie even if the user hasn't added any information to the system. The session framework lets you store and retrieve arbitrary data on a per site visitor basis. It stores data on the server side and abstracts the sending and receiving of cookies.

Cookies contain a session ID that can be looked up in the database where you store your data. Do set a user ID and save it. That's because as long as the cookie is received, and assuming that there's just one person using the device, your system can identify the user, even if it's only on one device. Storing sessions on the server is something to be careful about, however, because if you have 40 million users, the storage and retrieval of user data becomes a problem. Tracking users is hard, even the returning ones, but assuming you have that problem solved, there are other ways to get around cold starts.

6.3   Addressing cold-start problems with algorithms

Cold starts are still considered a problem because nobody has come up with a great solution and, unlike what certain magazines want you to believe, machine learning doesn't do magic: it infers things from data. If there's no data with a signal, there's no reasonable response. The solution is about finding information in even a sparse data

---

[3]   To see an Adform example, look at blog.adform.com/products/cross-device-audience-management.

set. You want to use the information you already have in the data and relate that to a new user, or rather, the other way around.

In the following sections, you'll use the association rules from the previous chapter, as well as look at creating segments for existing users, and then consider how fast you can make your users fit into a segment. Finally, we'll have a little chat about how you can ask the user what they like.

6.3.1 *Using association rules to create recs for cold users*

Association rules are created by looking at shopping transactions and producing rules that tell the recommender that if a person has put bread in their basket, then butter might be a good thing to recommend. In the previous chapter, these rules were used to make recommendations on items. But what if you stepped back and used these rules in cooperation with what you know about a new user (which isn't much); namely, the list of items browsed. Then you use those as seeds to find relevant rules and, from those rules, you can make recommendations. Figure 6.5 illustrates how this could be implemented.

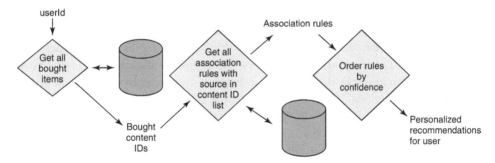

Figure 6.5 Making personalized recommendations with association rules

The system can start when the user views the first item, which could happen in the first session. Then as the number of visits increases, the data could be more and more restricted as shown in table 6.1.

Table 6.1 What events to use

Number of visits	Events to use
0-2	Item views
2-4	More Details buys
4+	Buys

Or you could define it otherwise, starting out by retrieving only association rules based on more valuable information. Something like

- Get all association rules based on user's bought items.
- Get all association rules based on user's bought items plus More Details views.
- Get all association rules based on all user's data.

THE WEIGHTED AVERAGE OF PURCHASED ITEMS

When a user buys their first item, you can use the association rules to provide recommendations based on that item. And, as more items are purchased, you can take weighted averages of the association rules. Let's say a user bought bread and butter, and the system already has the following rules saved:

```
bread => marmalade⁴
bread => butter
bread => gorgonzola cheese
butter => marmalade
butter => flour
eggs => bacon
```

Then, because bread and butter were bought, you'd have a choice among

```
bread => marmalade (and butter => marmalade)
bread => gorgonzola cheese
butter => flour
```

Butter was also bought, so you should have added a `bread => butter` rule also, but since butter was already bought, it wouldn't add any value. If two rules point to the same target, you could calculate a new confidence rating using a weighted average. Or order them and take the best ones, removing duplicates from the list before returning recommendations. If the user is a returning customer, but still so new that you have little data, you could also add weights to each of the rules based on how recently the user bought the item. That way more recent purchases are weighted higher.

A way to make the recommendations look better in the movie scenario would be to add business rules. This means incorporating domain knowledge into the system, which we'll look at next.

6.3.2   *Using domain knowledge and business rules*

Sometimes the recommender can't do everything for you. It can't figure out what to show when people buying cartoons also buy horror movies, for example. Eventually, this ends up as an association rule. Those who bought *Bambi* and *The Texas Chainsaw Massacre* cause the system to offer a chainsaw massacre movie to young people who bought their first Disney show!

One way to avoid this is to filter the content to restrict the recommendations to certain types of content that are considered appropriate to recommend, based on the type of content the user is currently viewing. Data scientists will tell you that it

---

⁴ The rule `bread => marmalade` means that there's a pattern in the data indicating that when you find bread in the basket, you often find marmalade as well.

spoils the algorithm to add such constraints to the output, but I've found that it's often necessary.

Business rules can be defined positively or negatively. You can say, "While viewing the cartoons genre, the system can only recommend cartoons and family films." Alternatively, you can list all the things that shouldn't appear, such as "Never recommend a horror movie based upon someone watching a cartoon."

You have several ways to implement this. Usually it's done by calculating a list of 100 recommendations (if you need 10), then filtering and taking the top 10 of the remaining as shown in figure 6.6.

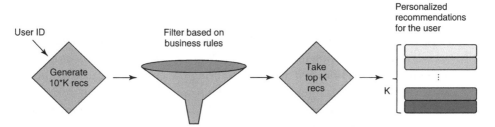

Figure 6.6   Using business rules to provide sensible recommendations

6.3.3   *Using segments*

Cold start is an irritating problem, but little can be done about it. Then again, if you know something about your users, might it be useful for something?

In Denmark, there's a saying, "Similar children play best." I'm not sure I've ever understood the expression because I found that opposites also play well together. But one thing is certain: children with similar tastes best watch TV together. Transforming the old proverb would probably make the people who came up with the original one roll over in their graves, but the transformed proverb is what we're going to use here.

You want to group people with similar tastes, so you can figure out what kind of people like what kind of content. When new visitors arrive, and they're of a certain type, you can recommend content popular with that segment. This is known as *demographic recommendations.* Many people say that doesn't work because people are too different within their demographic groups. But it can get you closer to semi-personalization. Demographics are often not available without the user logging in first, but if they do, you'll have that information and will be a step ahead.

THE OBVIOUS SEGMENTS

Before you bring out the big cannons and start doing *clustering,* which is unsupervised machine learning, let's think about what segments naturally fall out. If you've a visitor, you can often get an IP address, and with an IP address you can often pinpoint where the person is located.

If the person is from Copenhagen and your shop has things that aren't sold in Denmark, then you're better off filtering those items and only showing things that are sold in Copenhagen (which is the capital of Denmark). If you sell clothing, then there'll usually be at least two groups you want to create—male and female. Beyond that, you can also divide users into age groups.

Let's work through an example of how you could take advantage of something like gender. If you have a user database that includes a person's gender, you can filter your request when retrieving buy events from users who are, say, female and create the chart based on those users instead of the whole data set. The same is valid for males. I should note that there's probably a large percentage of males who are classified as women after buying a dress as a gift (I'm one of them) and the other way around.

In your clothes shop imagine that you've an image containing dresses and men's suits. You could make the men visiting your site feel more at ease by filtering out the dresses and only showing men's clothing. Now, this is a bit silly with clothing. Knowing the gender of the visitor is a matter of filtering the content because clothing items are usually tagged with a target gender. But let's move up a level and talk about content, which isn't predefined gender-specific, and you might start seeing the point of this.

For different age groups, for example, look at the *Star Wars* films, which are generally considered boring for people of the generation who were too young to have watched them when they came out and too old to think the next ones were cool. Kids and the generations who watched them in the cinema adore these films. If you knew that people coming into your site were younger than 15 or in the 40-50 range, then you could recommend *Star Wars*, while the group in between may go for Marvel superheroes movies instead.

THE NOT-SO-OBVIOUS SEGMENTS

Let's expand a bit on the obvious segments from the previous section and consider the following: what if there were groups such as "German women who browse in the evening during the weekend and like action" or "American male teenagers who buy horror films during school time." Segments like these aren't so obvious and might be hard to spot even in the data, but it's valuable information for personalizing the site for your users. Segmentation doesn't have to include demographics; it can be based on any kind of data you have on your users.

Usually segments are created by market researchers based on industry practice and wisdom, which in many cases translates to guesswork. Guessing is good, but not always practical. So instead of doing segments by hand, more and more researchers use cluster analysis to find these not-so-obvious segments.

Cluster analysis is a less subjective way of finding the segments and can be done using unsupervised machine learning. A *cluster* is a fancy word for a group with similar traits, so we'll try to find particular types of users who consume specific content.

6.3.4 *Using categories to get around the gray sheep problem and how to introduce cold product*

"Sometimes you need to take a step back to get ahead." This proverb is always irritating when it's thrown at you, but sometimes it's necessary. This is the idea behind the next method of getting around gray sheep and some cold products.

If you've a series of products that only a few people have bought and rated, it's hard to infer recommendations. But if you take a step back and use the metadata of a product, you might be able to find similar products. It sounds confusing, so here's an example.

Turning back to Redbubble, it has one thing going for it: artists tend to create art that falls within the taste of a particular group of users (at least, that's what I assume). A way to get less sparse data is to look at artists instead of art content. To do this, you'd need to group all artwork by artist as if it's one item.

Salvador Dali did many art pieces, two of which are shown in figure 6.7. And if you can imagine that he isn't world-famous and that thousands would buy his paintings, you could look at users who bought the painting to the left as people who also bought *X*, which uses the functionality implemented in the previous chapter. Or you could look at users who bought art by Salvador Dali and who also bought art from artist *X*. And if the buying decision is only based on art works, then recommend the most popular of artist *X*'s art.

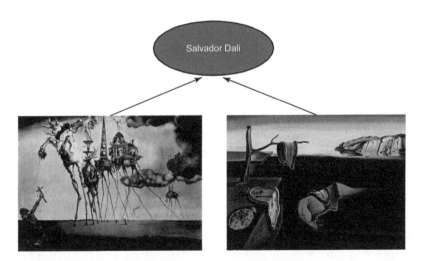

Figure 6.7 Grouping art rather than artists.

In general, this can be abstracted into the method shown in figure 6.8. You can use this logic for sites such as Redbubble, but also many other sites. With music, you can abstract songs to the artist; with news, you can either abstract it to the topic using tags or to the articles by author.

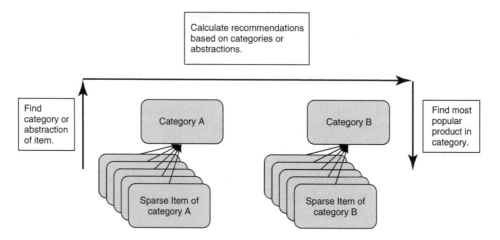

Figure 6.8   Using metadata to get around data sparcity

Remember that the abstraction or classification can't be too general because the association between the categories loses its value. An example of such an association is
action => comedy. You could find plenty of associations in the data but will find little
value in calculating quality recommendations.

A not-so-obvious example would be this: I like the films of J.J. Abrams, so I'd probably watch any movie he made (especially after *The Force Awakens*). People who like him
may also like Richard Marquand, who directed *Return of the Jedi*.[5] If you implement this
(and we're not going to here), you could create association rules based on the abstraction, and then every time you ask for a recommendation, you could use the current
item that the user is viewing. It depends on the data set you're holding if this will work.

A classification could also be the works of Tolkien or cars that run more than 40 km
per liter of gasoline. To implement this, you can alter the association rules described in
chapter 5, and instead of saving the item ID, you can save the author and manufacturer
of each category and then create a special lookup that looks for rules based on the
metadata.

6.4   *Those who doesn't ask, won't know*

One solution to get started is to ask the user what they think about a selected list of
items to get them started immediately. But for most e-commerce sites, it isn't a good
idea to restrict access until a visitor answers several questions, so it might not be worth
doing. You could make it optional, however.

Amazon offers you the possibility to improve your recommendations. This is done
by logging into Amazon and clicking Improve Your Recommendations as shown in
figure 6.9. The way Amazon does this doesn't help us much in this case because you're

---

[5] Okay, in all honesty the films that Richard Marquand did beyond *Star Wars* don't seem to be something I'd
like, but let's continue for the sake of the example.

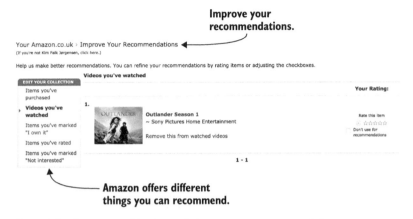

Figure 6.9 Amazon provides a way to improve your recommendations.

trying to collect data about new users, not existing ones (even if you can never get too much data.)

How do you create a page where a user can teach you about their preferences? It isn't as simple as it sounds, because what content should you show—the most popular (the ones that everybody likes) or the least popular (the ones that few people like)? If you choose the latter, most likely you'll spot the gray sheep and not be any closer to understanding the user. The chances are that you're better off guessing the recommendations. Another thing to consider is that if you do pick a popular item, you'll gain the advantage of comparing this user to many others.

To solve this problem, you have to turn to something called *active learning*, and it's cool. But sadly, it's beyond the scope of this book. A good place to go to learn more is in the publicly available article "Active Learning" by Ruben, et al.[6] Active learning for recommender systems is about creating an algorithm that comes up with good examples for the user to rate, which then provides the recommender with valuable information about the person's preferences.

6.4.1 *When the visitor is no longer new*

It's worth putting checks in place if the user is no longer new, something you can do over time. Say that you'll only use the evidence for the last week or the most recent 20 evidence items for this kind of recommendation. Or you might add weights, so that new items have a higher weight. You might also say that when the user has bought five items, you'll only use the buy events as seeds.

Association rules seem to make the most sense when you look at the raw evidence and not the implicit ratings. You could, however, start by using the implicit ratings as seeds and then weight them based on the ratings.

---

[6] Rubens N., M Elahi, M. Sugiyama, D. Kaplan "Active Learning in Recommender Systems." Ricci F., L. Rokach, B. Shapira (eds) *Recommender Systems Handbook* (Springer, 2015).

6.5   Using association rules to start recommending things fast

How would you go about adding association rules to the MovieGEEKs site? You already have a framework in place for the association rules, so you need to take what a user has shown an interest in and then find association rules for each of those items. You can then return the recommenations that you think are a best fit. Not much magic there, but let's see if it does the trick.

Association rules are one way this can be implemented, but any kind of similarity method can be used. For example, you could use content-based recommendations instead, but you don't know about those yet (content-based filtering is discussed in chapter 10), so let's look at association rules first. In terms of the MovieGEEKs site, you'll use the space beneath the other elements on the front page as shown in figure 6.10.

Here's a checklist for adding personalized recommendations:

- Find a good spot on the page.
- Collect and use the list of items the user has interacted with.
- Find the association rules.
- Order by confidence and show the recommended items.

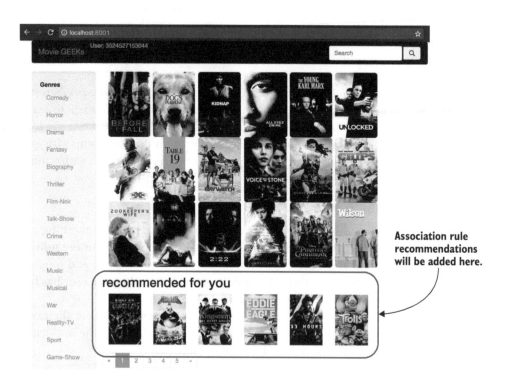

Figure 6.10   Added space for personalized recommendations in MovieGEEKs site

6.5.1 Find the collected items

You'll want these recommendations to start working as soon as the user looks at something, so you'll get data from the evidence log. Implicit ratings can give a better view of a user's preferences, but because you want to service new users, you can't be sure that the system has calculated the implicit ratings yet.

The problem you're trying to solve here is to create recommendations for users you don't know much about, so you'll use all items the user has interacted with, not only the purchased ones. The data is scarce and, in most cases, the user won't have bought anything up to this point.

6.5.2 Retrieve association rules and order them according to confidence

You can use the method you already implemented to get association rules, but that would mean that you'd query the database repeatedly for each item. Instead, you'll create a new method as shown in listing 6.1 that queries the database by itself.

Listing 6.1 Calculating recommendations using association rules

Queries the database for events that are related to the user_id, orders those by created, and returns a unique list of items

```
def recs_using_association_rules(request, user_id, take=6):
    events = Log.objects.filter(user_id=user_id)\
                        .order_by('created')\
                        .values_list('content_id', flat=True)\
                        .distinct()

    seeds = set(events[:20])        ◄——— Takes the newest 20 events

    rules = SeededRecs.objects.filter(source__in=seeds) \
                        .exclude(target__in=seeds) \
                        .values('target') \
                        .annotate(confidence=Avg('confidence')) \
                        .order_by('-confidence')

    recs = [{'id': '{0:07d}'.format(int(rule['target'])),
            'confidence': rule['confidence']} for rule in rules]
    return JsonResponse(dict(data=list(recs[:take])))
```

Gets only the target row

JSONify and return

Creates a dictionary of the result

Shows where the targets are not in the user's event log

Orders by average confidence

Queries the association rules and finds all rules where the source is among the content found in the active user's event log

If duplicate targets found in the result, takes the average confidence

Calling the method in listing 6.2 produces JSON output. To test it, try requesting http://moviegeek.com:8000/rec/ar/5/. It produces JSON that looks like the following listing.

Listing 6.2   Output of http://moviegeek.com:8000/rec/ar/5/

```
{
data:
[
{confidence: 0.006463878326996198,
id: "1291150"},
{confidence: 0.004617055947854427,
id: "1985949"},
{confidence: 0.004562737642585552,
id: "2267968"},
{confidence: 0.004562737642585552,
id: "0475290"},
…
}
```

The values might be different because they're based on a data set that changes.

The response contains more items.

6.5.3   *Displaying the recs*

If you create a new private browser tab (on a PC using Chrome, it's done by typing Ctrl-Shift-n), you'll create a new session (figure 6.11.) so as to mimic the new user. A *private browser tab* means that you hide all your current cookies (and delete new ones when you leave the private tab). It's useful in these cases to see how a site looks when you arrive as a new user. Or when you want to order plane tickets without the air lines

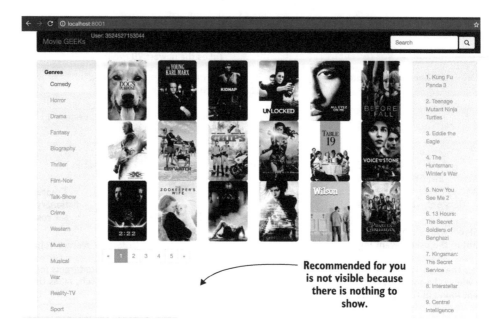

Recommended for you is not visible because there is nothing to show.

Figure 6.11   New private session to illustrate what new visitors see at MovieGEEKs site.

making calculations on which plane you need, which makes it more expensive. … Getting off trail here. … The private browser tab lets you see the MovieGEEKs site as if you were visiting it for the first time.

Looking at the terminal window where you're running the Django app (figure 6.12), it's clear why there are no recommendations. Because it's a new private session, it's considered a new user and the site doesn't recognize the user. Looking further down in figure 6.12, it also indicates that it finds no seeds, meaning no evidence is yet captured.

New id created

```
[06/Sep/2017 21:24:29] "GET /rec/cb/item/3110958/ HTTP/1.1" 200 36
ensured id:  3524527153044 ◁
[06/Sep/2017 21:25:07] "GET / HTTP/1.1" 200 26333
[06/Sep/2017 21:25:07] "GET /static/js/collector.js HTTP/1.1" 200 618
[06/Sep/2017 21:25:08] "GET /rec/chart HTTP/1.1" 301 0
recs from association rules:
[] ◁
[06/Sep/2017 21:25:08] "GET /rec/ar/3524527153044/ HTTP/1.1" 200 12
<QuerySet []>
Collaborative filtering recommendations for user 3524527153044
 []
[06/Sep/2017 21:25:08] "GET /rec/cf/user/3524527153044/ HTTP/1.1" 200 40
[06/Sep/2017 21:25:08] "GET /rec/chart/ HTTP/1.1" 200 765
```

No seeds found

Figure 6.12   Command prompt shows the new user ID being generated.

Let's buy an item (go to http://localhost:8000/movies/movie/3110958/). Click Buy and check that your Django app log output shows a registered evidence item. This takes you to the page shown in figure 6.13.

Returning to the main page, you should see the same recommendations as shown in the frequently bought section in figure 6.13, which is what figure 6.14 shows, although the order of films differs. (It's worth noting that the recommendations have these content IDs: 10, 18, 45, and 9.)

Now to make things more interesting, let's buy another item on the list of association rules so that the recommendations are updated. A bit of a trick exists here. If you bought the most popular item, the confidence of the association rules already used will be much greater than the others, so before you start throwing something out the window if it doesn't change anything, look at the confidence indicator first.

If you look at the previous association rules you can see that if you choose *Y*, then at least one element should change. Go to http://moviegeeks:8000/movies/Y and click Buy. Then go back to the main window and press Refresh (F5 on most machines and browsers). The recs should now be updated.

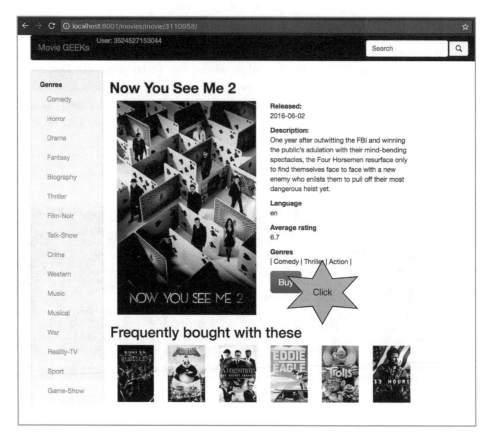

Figure 6.13   Buying *Now You See Me 2*

Recommendations appear after just interacting with one item.

Figure 6.14   Recommendations after interacting with one item.

6.5.4 *Implementation evaluation*

The recommendations implemented here are simple, but the advantage is that you start getting those immediately, which is what you set out to do. And as you get more data you have better ways to extract user preferences, which you'll look at in the following chapters.

Another thing to remember here is that the data on which you're basing recommendations is auto-generated for MovieGEEKs. The generation only looks at genres, so an association such as *Ninja Assassin* and *The Time-Traveler's Wife* seems a bit farfetched given that one is an action film and the other one is a drama.

We've covered many topics in this chapter. Recommender systems encompass many problems, which can be attacked in many ways. Different studies show one is better than the other, but only for specific data sets. It's important to know your options and then see what works best for your site. With this, we end part one of this book. We've looked at all the basics of recommender systems and talked about users and how to understand them. Now it is time to look into the algorithms and understand how the recommenders perform their "magic." As you'll see, there's actually no magic about it, but that doesn't make it less cool.

Summary

- Cold-start problems mean you have to decide what to recommend to new visitors on your site. Introducing new products is also a cold-start problem, which we'll look at in more detail in later chapters.
- Adding a conscious ordering to the data that's presented is a great start and will make many sites look more dynamic.
- Gray sheep are users who don't have individual tastes resembling other users who've bought any of the products they have. Sometimes gray sheep can be helped by abstracting the content into genres.
- Creating recommendations for new users using association rules provides an easy and quick way to add personalization that will start working quickly.
- Segments can be built or generated to make semi-personalized recommendations. Alternatively, demographics can be used to create demographic recommendations.

Part 2

Recommender algorithms

An algorithm must be seen to be believed.
—Donald Knuth

In the first six chapters, you learned about the ecosystem and infrastructure around recommender systems. Now, in part 2, we'll look at the recommender system algorithms. We'll look at how to use the data that a system can collect to calculate what things it can recommend to a user. We'll also discuss how you can evaluate a recommender system and look at the strengths and weaknesses of each algorithm.

Finding similarities among
users and among content

Similarity can be calculated in many ways, and we'll look at most of those. In this chapter

- You'll gain an understanding of what similarity and its cousin, distance, are.
- You'll look at how to calculate similarity between sets of items.
- With similarity functions, you'll measure how alike two users are, using the ratings they've given to content.
- It sometimes helps to group users, so you'll do that using the *k*-means clustering algorithm.

Chapter 6 described non-personalized recommendations and the association rules. Association rules are a way to connect content without looking at the item or the users who consumed them. Personalized recommendations, however, almost always contain calculations of similarity. An example of such recommendations could be Netflix's More Like This recommendation shown in figure 7.1, where it uses an algorithm to find similar content.

In later sections, you'll learn ways of measuring whether two items or two users are similar. You'll first look at how to calculate similarity on binary data (bought versus not bought) and then move on to measure the similarity between users based on their ratings (and items based on how the same users rate them). You can use the tools that measure similarity as an instrument to understand the similarities among your catalog's content. In chapter 8, you'll put that to good use when implementing collaborative filtering algorithms.

In this chapter, you'll also learn how to cluster users into segments of similar taste. You'll use this to provide a way for the users to browse. And in chapter 8, you'll see examples where clustering can optimize collaborative filtering algorithms. This is a bit of a tooling chapter, but it's an essential one, both for recommender systems and for many machine-learning algorithms. Before we jump in, let's consider the recommendations in figure 7.1.

In Netflix you can get *More Like This* recommendations, which is probably found by calculating similarity.

Figure 7.1 More Like This personalized recommendations on Netflix based on the TV series *The Flash*

In the figure, it's clear that it isn't only about showing things that are similar to the first recommendation, *Doctor Strange*. If we want to attribute a label to *Doctor Strange*, I'd say the first thing that comes to mind is Superhero, which relates to *Captain America: Civil War* and *Wonder Woman*. But what about the two other movies? Are they similar in other ways?

In this chapter, we'll look at calculating the similarities among content and among users using different metrics. We'll start with the intuitive explanation of what similarity is and then move on to ways of calculating it.

7.1 Why similarity?

We must talk about similarity because you want to find items like the ones you like, or you want to find users who like what you like. How do you define *similarity*? For example, how do you answer the following: on a scale of -1 to 1, how similar are two people?

Your first response is probably to ask, "In what sense similar?" Let's narrow the scope and base the similarity on their tastes. The answer could be many things. One could say that two people have similar tastes because they both like films with Tom Hanks, science fiction films, or simply all-evening movies.[1] But then, even people who like sci-fi have different tastes. Maybe one person likes *Star Trek* and another *Star Wars*. Are they similar?

Looking at the data you have on hand narrows the possibilities of using the ratings to understand a user's taste. But similarities can also be found using additional information such as metadata about the content or the demographics of the user. This chapter looks at how to answer how similar things are. In the scientific literature, few similarity functions are said to give good results, so we'll go through each in the following sections. You'll also look at optimizing the number of similarity calculations between users by finding segments of similar users.

7.1.1   What's a similarity function?

You can calculate similarity in many ways, but the overall problem can be defined as follows: Given two items, i_1 and i_2, the similarity between them is given by the function $\text{sim}(i_1, i_2)$.

This function's return values will increase the more similar the items are. We can say that the similarity between the same item is $\text{Sim}(i_1, i_1) = 1$, and two items that have nothing in common will be $\text{Sim}(i_1, \text{nothing in common with } i_1) = 0$. Figure 7.2 illustrates two examples of similarity functions. It's worth thinking about which you should choose. Which is better depends on your domain and data.

Similarity measurement is closely related to the calculation of the distance between items. Generally you can say that the relationship between similarity and distance is the following:

- When distance gets larger, the similarity goes toward zero.
- When distance goes toward zero, the similarity goes toward one.

7.2   *Essential similarity functions*

As mentioned earlier, there's no right or wrong similarity method. Different methods work better on different data sets, but there are several guiding points, which are discussed in this section.

We'll start by looking at the *Jaccard similarity*, which is used to compare sets. In your case, a set can be the set of movies a user has bought. We'll then look at similarities between ratings; the first is one dimension in the form of the similarity between two users' ratings of one film. This can be generalized to measure how similar users are when they rated many films. To do this we'll use Pearson and Cosine similarity functions. Each similarity method needs a specific kind of data, as shown in table 7.1.

---

[1]   In Denmark, we have a term called *helaftensfilm*, which means an all-evening movie, and something that you pay extra to go to see, compared to normal-length films. A *helaftensfilm* is a film that is longer than two hours and 45 minutes.

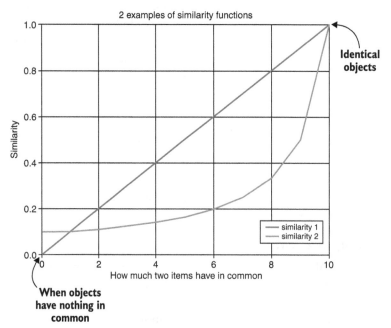

Figure 7.2   Two different similarity functions. A straight line indicates a similarity of 0.5 if it has half the features in common. The curved line returns a similarity of approximately 0.20.

Table 7.1   Different data types

Data type	Data example	Similarity
Unary data: This can be data containing only likes or only transactions of items bought.	User 1 likes movie 2 User 2 likes movie 2 User 3 likes movie 1	Jaccard similarity
Binary data: Data where there are two possible values. Like/dislike for example.	User 1 dislikes movie 1 User 1 likes movie 2 User 2 likes movie 2 User 3 likes movie 1	Jaccard similarity
Quantitative Data	User 1 gave 4/10 stars to movie 2 User 2 gave 10/10 stars to movie 2 User 3 gave 1/10 stars to movie 1	Pearson or cosine similarity

Before getting started, we'll name a few things in table 7.2 that will make it easy to describe the similarity functions.

Table 7.2 Elements of a similarity function

Name	Definition	Example
r_{ui}	Rating of user u for *item*	$r_{sara,star\ trek} = 4,5$ indicates that Sara rated *Star Trek* 4,5
r_u	Average rating of the user u.	The mean of all the ratings given by user u. If Peter rated *Star Trek* 4, *Star Wars* 3, then $r_{Peter} = 3,5$
$P_{a,b}$	Set of items rated by both a and b	The set of items, if you have Sara and Peter from the previous examples. $P_{sara,Peter} = \{Star\ Trek\}$ since they both rated that movie.

7.2.1 Jaccard distance

This was originally coined *coefficient de communaté* by Paul Jaccard, who came up with this distance measure to indicate how close two sets are to each other. You'll also find it under the names *Jaccard index* or *Jaccard similarity coefficient*.

Two sets? What does that have to do with users and content? Well, if you say that each movie is a bag containing all the users who bought the movie, then you have sets of users—one for each movie. Then you can compare two movies by looking at the two sets of users.

Data sets such as the one described previously can be produced from the user transactions, which can be turned into a list where each row indicates whether or not a user bought a product (1 = bought, 0 = not bought). Or if the user likes the content item, you have a unary data set, which can be illustrated in a table such as table 7.3. It's a unary data set because a 1 is information and 0 is no information.

Table 7.3 Unary user-item matrix (1 = bought, 0 = not bought)

	Comedy	Action	Comedy	Action	Drama	Drama
Sara	1	1	0	0	0	0
Jesper	1	1	1	0	0	0
Therese	1	0	0	0	0	0
Helle	0	1	0	1	0	0
Pietro	0	0	0	0	1	1
Ekaterina	0	0	0	0	1	1

To find the similarity between two items, calculate how many users bought both items, then divide by how many users bought either one (or both). Written more formally, it's

$$similarity_{Jaccard}(i,j) \;=\; \frac{\#users\ that\ bought\ both\ items}{\#users\ who\ bought\ either\ i\ or\ j}$$

where i represents item 1 and j represents item 2.

To calculate the similarity between two movies, you count the number of equal bits (number of times where the user has repeated a similar event with each movie) as shown in table 7.4. The table shows four rows out of six where users did the same thing, which means the Jaccard similarity between the two is 4 / 6. If you look at the movies in table 7.4 where no users reacted, the Jaccard similarity is 2 / 4 = 0.5, meaning that they're only a little bit similar.

Table 7.4 Similarity Between *Men in Black* and *Star Trek*

	Men in Black	*Star Trek*	1 if similar 0 if not
Sara	1	1	1
Jesper	1	1	1
Therese	1	0	0
Helle	0	1	0
Pietro	0	0	1
Ekaterina	0	0	1
			Sum = 4

The Jaccard similarity is plotted in the previous figure as similarity 1 (see figure 7.2). Whether 0.5 is a high similarity is domain-specific, so you should play around with the similarity function and see what fits your domain. Later, we'll look at how users are similar in the MovieGEEKs site using Jaccard's similarity algorithm. For now, if you've more details in your data set, you can do additional similarity calculations. Let's look at a few of those.

7.2.2 *Measuring distance with L_p-norms*

A general way of measuring distances is with L_p-norms, so in this section, we'll look at two different measures—the L_1- and the L_2-norms. If your data set is a bit more detailed than the one used in the MovieGEEKs example, with ratings indicating how much people like the content viewed, you could use a long series of other functions to calculate distances and similarities, rather than just the Jaccard measure.

L₁-NORM

What is similarity? I ask again (and, hopefully, answer this time). If you want to find if Pietro and Sara have similar opinions about a film like *The Secret Life of Pets*, you could ask them how they'd rate it on a scale of 1-10. Pietro thought it was an okay film, so he gave it a 6, while Sara, a lover of dogs and cartoons, rated it as 9 because it was a nearly perfect film for her. Figure 7.3 illustrates the ratings for both Pietro and Sara.

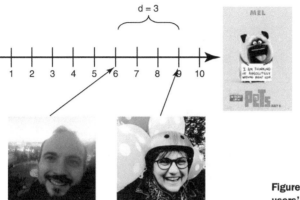

Figure 7.3 Similarity of two users' ratings on one film

Based on only one film, it's easy to measure how similar two users are, even if it doesn't give any real indication of their actual tastes or preferences. You can calculate the difference between the two like this:

$$distance(Sara, Pietro) = \left| r_{sara} - r_{pietro} \right|$$

where

- r_{sara} is Sara's rating.
- r_{pietro} is Pietro's rating.

With this formula, the distance is 9 - 6 = 3. Because the maximal distance between the two ratings is 9, you can make it a similarity (1 when the distance is minimum and close to 0 when the distance is maximum) with this calculation:

$$similarity(Sara, Pietro) = \frac{1}{\left| r_{sara} - r_{pietro} \right| + 1}$$

Here, I've added 1 to the denominator to avoid the division-by-zero exception if two ratings are the same. Returning to the distance method again, for two movies, as shown in figure 7.4, you can calculate the difference between each rating and sum them to end up with the following formula:

$$Sum\ of\ Absolute\ Difference(SAD) = \sum_{i=1}^{n} \left| r_{sara,i} - r_{pietro,i} \right|$$

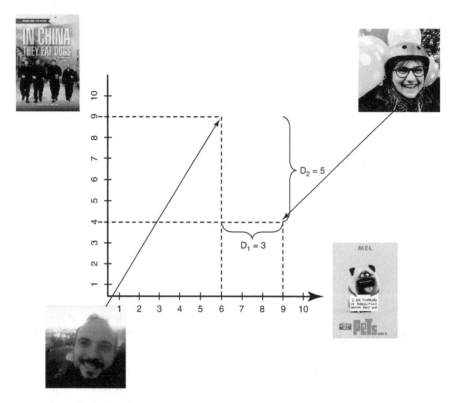

Figure 7.4   Similarity of two users based on ratings of two films. Pietro rated *In China They Eat Dogs* a 9, while Sara rated it a 4, so the difference $D_2 = 5$, while $D_1 = 3$ comes from the difference in their ratings for *The Secret Life of Pets*.

This way of measuring distance or similarity goes by the sexy name of *Manhattan distance*. It's part of what's called *taxicab geometry.*[2] In more established circles, however, it goes by the name of *L_1-norm.* The idea is that if you want to measure the distance between two street corners in Manhattan, you drive a grid, rather than measure as the crow flies.

According to the L_1-norm, you'd calculate a similarity measure of $3 + 5 = 8$. Often, you'll run into the *mean absolute error* (MAE), which is calculated using the average of the L_1 norm. As shown in the following formula, the only thing new here is that you divide the sum by the number of items to get the average distance between ratings:

$$Mean\ absolute\ error\ (MAE) = \frac{1}{n} \sum_{i=1}^{n} \left| r_{sara,i} - r_{pietro,i} \right|$$

We'll return to MAE in chapter 9, where you'll evaluate recommender systems. For the sake of similarity, let's move on to the next norm.

---

[2]   For more information, see https://en.wikipedia.org/wiki/Taxicab_geometry.

L₂-NORM

The big brother of L_1-norm is the L_2-norm, which geometrically can be considered the distance between two points not travelled by a taxi in Manhattan but by the crow, going directly from one point to the next. Basically, it stems from the famous Pythagorean theorem, $a^2 + b^2 = c^2$, which says that the square of the hypotenuse (the side opposite a right angle in a triangle) is equal to the sum of the squares of the other two sides. If you don't know much about Pythagoras or this theorem, it's no problem because we're immediately moving on.

The L_2-norm is known as the *Euclidian norm*. It's defined as follows:

$$distance\,(Sara,Pietro) \;=\; \|r_{sara} - r_{pietro}\|_2 \;=\; \sqrt{\sum_{i=1}^{n} |r_{sara,i} - r_{pietro,i}|^2}$$

When you use machine learning, and you'll want to, you'll come across the Euclidian norm. It's often used as a measure of how well your algorithm is performing. It takes the average of the norm, called the *root mean square error* (RMSE), which is also a known fellow:

$$Root\ Mean\ Squared\ Error\ (RMSE) \;=\; \sqrt{\frac{\sum_{i=1}^{n} |r_{sara,i} - r_{pietro,i}|^2}{n}}$$

Again, you can create the similarity by inserting 1 over the sum of squared differences. While you can use these formulas, it isn't something that's regarded as a good solution in recommender systems. They're here because you'll use them when you evaluate the algorithms. The following section explains a good way to measure similarity instead.

7.2.3 *Cosine similarity*

Another way of looking at content is to see the rows of the rating matrix as vectors in space, and then look at the angle between them. I know that sounds a bit "spacey," but it'll make perfect sense once you look at the following example, where we slim down your data to what's shown in table 7.5.

Table 7.5 A slimmed-down rating matrix

	Comedy	Action
Sara	3	5
Therese	4	1
Helle	2	5

You'll then plot the data into the coordinate system shown in figure 7.5. This works for more than two items as well, but because each item will be another dimension and there are no decent ways of illustrating higher dimensions, we'll stick with two and hope you believe me when I say it can be expanded quickly to more items.

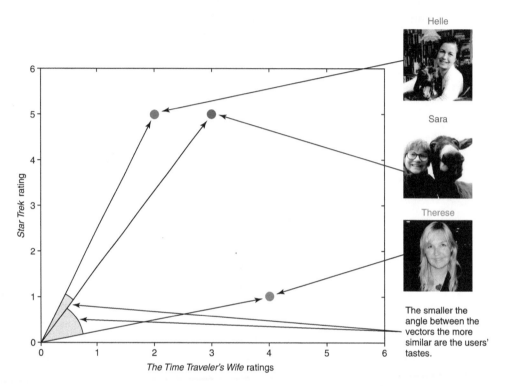

Figure 7.5   You can measure similarity by looking at the angles between the rating vectors.

From the angles between the vectors, it's easy to see that Sara and Helle are much closer than Therese and Sara when it comes to ratings. Because of that, you can assume that the tastes of Helle and Sara are more similar.

A small issue exists here that always makes you stare at vectors for a long time. If you look at figure 7.5 and imagine that there's a user who rated both films a 6 and another one who rated both a 1, their vectors would point in the same direction. They'd therefore have a similarity of 1. This can be a problem when calculating similarity using the angles between vectors; but in practice, it's not a problem I've seen.

Let's go for a test run by computing several similarities. But instead of users, we'll look at item similarity. Amazon has shown us that item-item collaborative filtering is much more efficient for the simple reason that they've more customers than items. By calculating item similarity, however, there are fewer things to calculate.

COMPUTING ITEM SIMILARITY

Looking at item similarity means that you look for similarity between the columns (see table 7.6) instead of rows as in the previous section.

Table 7.6   Looking for item similarity

	Comedy	Action	Comedy	Action	Drama	Drama
Sara	5	5		2	2	2
Jesper	4	5	4		3	3
Therese	5	3	5	2	1	1
Helle	3		3	5	1	1
Pietro	3	3	3	2	4	5
Ekaterina	2	3	2	3	5	5

The function to calculate the angle among column ratings is done using the cosine formula that most kids learn in school and then forget it when they leave. In case you forgot what you learned in school, here's the formula again:

$$sim(i,j) = \frac{r_i \cdot r_j}{\|r_1\|_2 \|r_j\|_2} = \frac{\sum_u r_{i,u} r_{j,u}}{\sqrt{\sum_u r_{i,u}^2} \sqrt{\sum_u r_{j,u}^2}}$$

It's beautiful, isn't it? Sadly, we have to change the function a bit because we're talking about comparing different users' ratings, and people use different rating scales when they're rating (a happy rater gives higher marks than a sad one). You need to take that into account. Badrul Sarwar and friends came up with an adjusted cosine similarity to offset this drawback by subtracting the user's average rating.[3] Luckily, that doesn't make the formula any less beautiful:

$$sim(i,j) = \frac{\sum_u (r_{i,u} - r_u)(r_{j,u} - r_u)}{\sqrt{\sum_u (r_{i,u} - r_u)^2} \sqrt{\sum_u (r_{j,u} - r_u)^2}}$$

---

[3] Badrul Sarwar, et al., "Item-based Collaborative Filtering Recommendation Algorithms," (http://files.grouplens .org/papers/www10_sarwar.pdf).

7.2.4   *Finding similarity with Pearson's correlation coefficient*

If you take the ratings you looked at in the last few sections, you've an idea of whose are similar. But if you plot them in a diagram with the items along the *x*-axis and the ratings along the *y*-axis and then draw a line from point to point, it's even more visible; you can clearly see which ratings are similar and which aren't (figure 7.6).

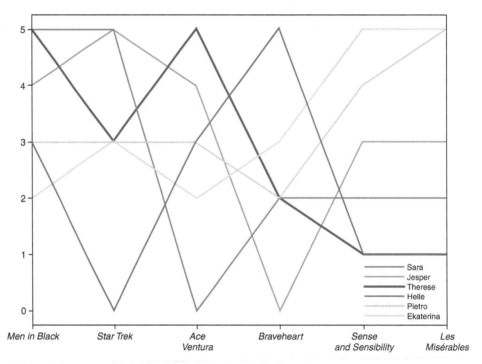

Figure 7.6   Charting the ratings of MovieGEEKs users. The vertical axis shows ratings and the horizontal axis is a list of films. The films are those rated in table 7.6: *Men in Black, Star Trek, Ace Ventura, Braveheart, Sense and Sensibility*, and *Les Misérables*.

Pearson's correlation coefficient looks at these points and measures how different each point is on the average: *very different* means that it returns something close to -1, while *very similar* means something closer to 1. Note that these findings range from -1 to 1, not 0 to 1 as you saw earlier in table 7.4.

The algorithm calculates how much the two lines correlate between two users. If their trends are identical (they go up and down together), it'll be 1 or close to that. Here, getting a 0 means that there's no connection at all, while -1 means that what one user likes, the other dislikes.

With Pearson's correlation coefficient, the ratings are normalized by subtracting the item's average rating from each rating as shown in the following equation:

$$sim(i,j) = \frac{\sum_{e \in U}(r_{i,u} - \overline{r}_i)(r_{j,u} - \overline{r}_j)}{\sqrt{\sum_{e \in U}(r_{i,u} - \overline{r}_i)^2}\sqrt{\sum_{e \in U}(r_{j,u} - \overline{r}_j)^2}}$$

where is the set of users which have rated both *i* and *j*.

Don't worry if it looks a bit scary; it isn't. It's addition and multiplication, as you'll see when we implement it later in the chapter. Let's take this for a test run and see how similar Jesper and Pietro are in taste.

7.2.5 *Test running a Pearson similarity*

Table 7.7 shows how Jesper and Pietro rated the six films.

Table 7.7 Ratings of Jesper and Pietro

	Comedy	Action	Comedy	Action	Drama	Drama
Jesper	4	5	4		3	3
Pietro	3	3	3	2	4	5

To calculate the Pearson similarity, you need to

1. Calculate the average ratings
2. Normalize the ratings
3. Put the results into the formula

CALCULATING THE AVERAGE RATING

First, for each user, you need to calculate the average rating by adding all ratings and dividing by the number of ratings:

- Jesper: *(4 + 5 + 4 + 3+ 3) / 5* = 3.8
- Pietro: *(3 + 3 + 3 + 2 + 4 + 5) / 6* = 3.33

Notice that Jesper has rated five films, while Pietro has rated all six. You still use the number of ratings for each user to calculate the average. You're deducting the average to make the ratings comparable.

Because Jesper only gave ratings between 3 and 5, then you can deduce that when he rated something a 3, he probably didn't like it much. When he used the rating 5, it was for something he liked a lot. But if he gave ten other movies a rating of 1, his average would be much lower, which would push the value of a rating of 3 to be much more positive. It could also indicate that Jesper only sees films he's somewhat indifferent to, but for the similarity calculations to work, assume that he's used only ratings 3 and 4 to describe his taste.

> ### Note on implementation
> Remember when you have an array of ratings similar to Jesper's, you need to calculate the mean of the items that were rated. If you look at Jesper's ratings, you'd have the following array [4, 3, 0, 4, 4]. If you use a normal mean operation on that, you'll get 15 / 5. Although the zero doesn't affect the sum (15), it still counts in the total number of ratings (5).

NORMALIZING THE RATINGS

As mentioned previously, a certain user's rating should always be viewed in relationship to that user's other ratings. To compare the ratings of two users, you need to normalize their ratings. *Normalize* means a broad range of things, but in its simplest form, it means that you adjust the scale of certain values to be comparable or on the same level.

To normalize ratings, you subtract the rating average of each user from their ratings. For example, to subtract the average from the ratings of Jesper and Pietro, you'd calculate $((r_{Jesper,i} - r_{Jesper})$ and $(r_{Pietro,i} - r_{Pietro})$ as shown in table 7.8. By doing that, you'll have the essential building blocks for calculating the similarity according to Pearson.

Table 7.8   Pietro's and Jesper's normalized ratings

Jesper	0.20	1.2	0.2		-0.8	-0.8
Pietro	-0.33	-0.33	-0.33	-1.33	0.67	1.67

Normalizing the ratings around 0 means that the ratings get a positive or negative feel to them. For example, a rating of -0.75 sounds negative compared to a rating of 3. It probably should be viewed as negative as such, but for an optimistic guy, the scale goes from likes a little to likes a lot, while for another, it could go from absolutely hate to like a little.

PUT THE RESULTS INTO THE FORMULA

Let's set $nr_{a,i} = r_{a,i} - r_a$, transforming the Pearson correlation into the following, which is the same but uses the normalized ratings instead:

$$sim(a,b) = \frac{\sum_{i \in P}(nr_{a,i})(nr_{b,i})}{\sqrt{\sum_{i \in P}(nr_{a,i})^2}\sqrt{\sum_{i \in P}(nr_{b,i})^2}}$$

Inserting the normalized ratings, you get the following:

$$= \frac{(0.2)(-0.33) + (1.2)(-0.33) + (0.2)(-0.33) + (-0.8)(0.67) + (-0.8)(1.67)}{\sqrt{(0.2)^2 + (1.2)^2 + (0.2)^2 + (-0.8)^2 + (-0.8)^2}\sqrt{(-0.33)^2 + (-0.33)^2 + (-0.33)^2 + (0.67)^2 + (1.67)^2}}$$

Now it's a matter of calculating (or rather copying and pasting into your web browser to do the calculation for you):

$$sim(jesper,pietro) = \frac{-2.4}{\sqrt{2.8} \times \sqrt{3.56}} = -0.76$$

This result shows what you saw from the beginning: that Jesper's and Pietro's tastes aren't at all similar. You could say they're close to opposites.

7.2.6 *Pearson correlation is similar to cosine*

Pearson's correlation coefficient and cosine similarity look alike and, in fact, in later chapters you'll see that the cosine similarity function will be extended into the adjusted cosine similarity function. *Adjusted* means that you add the normalization of ratings, which makes it the same function as Pearson's. The only difference between the adjusted cosine and Pearson's correlation is that the Pearson function uses items that two users have rated, while the cosine similarity function uses all rated items by either or both, setting the ratings to zero when one of the users doesn't rated an item.

In the previous example with Jesper and Pietro, the two similarity functions produce the following result:

$$sim_{\text{Normalized Cosine}}(\text{Jesper,Pietro}) = -0.62$$
$$sim_{\text{Pearson}}(\text{Jesper,Pietro}) = -0.75$$

One thing to notice is that if you calculate similarity between a user with few ratings and one with many, then the cosine would push the similarity toward zero. Why? If there are many items that don't overlapping, it doesn't affect the numerator because if an item isn't rated by one of the users, then the product will be zero, not adding any value, while in the denominator for each rating is squared.

7.3 *k-means clustering*

As you'll see in the next chapter, calculating the similarity between users or items is the Achilles heel of the neighborhood collaborative filtering algorithms. That's because it requires that the algorithm have an opinion about how similar the currently active users are to all other users or how similar items are to all other items in the system. Because of this, it's a good idea to divide the data set into smaller groups, so you only need to calculate similarity in groups with fewer users.

Figure 7.7 shows the data divided into four clusters. Consider that every time a person comes to your site, you potentially need to compare all the users in your system with the active user. If you have clusters, you can look up which group the user resides in, and presto!— you've cut away three-fourths of the users.

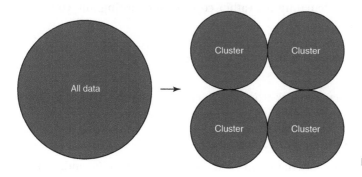

Figure 7.7   Clustering data

7.3.1   *The k-means clustering algorithm*

Clustering is also called *segmentation*. We talked about it in an earlier chapter when we discussed non-personalized recommendations. At that time, we talked about using segmentation to find groups of users that are similar to a new visitor based on demographic data. The purpose here is more of an optimization because you want to find clusters of users to narrow down how many times you calculate user-user similarity.

If user *X* comes to your site, you'd potentially have to iterate through all the users in the database, but if you can divide the users into clusters, you can look up which cluster the user is part of and calculate similarities between those users as part of a smaller group. Although this is the general idea, there's a risk that your cluster doesn't contain the most similar users. Even so, let's try clustering. You'll use k-means clustering, which is one of the popular algorithms for segmentation.

HOW DOES THE K-MEANS CLUSTERING ALGORITHM WORK?

K-means clustering is what's called an *unsupervised machine learning algorithm*. It's unsupervised because you don't give it any examples of what the correct input-output pairs would look like. It's also a *parametric algorithm* because you need to give it a parameter, *k*, for it to run. Adding one parameter sounds simple, but it's hard to get the right one and, sadly, the difference can be that you don't get nice groups of users.

The parameter *k* is used to tell the algorithm how many clusters it should find. In the following section, you'll learn how k-means clustering works using a simple Python implementation to solve the following problem: Divide users Sara, Dea, Peter, Mela, Kim, Helle, Egle, Vlad, and Jimmie into two groups based on how much they liked two films. The data is as follows:

- Sara = [7,1]
- Dea = [10,0]
- Peter = [0, 6]
- Mela = [1, 4]
- Kim = [5,3]
- Helle = [9,9]
- Egle = [2,1]

- Vlad = [4,4]
- Jimmie = [6,8]

It should be clear how to group the first two because they like one film and not the other, while the rest can be a bit difficult to place. Figure 7.8 shows how they look in a plot.

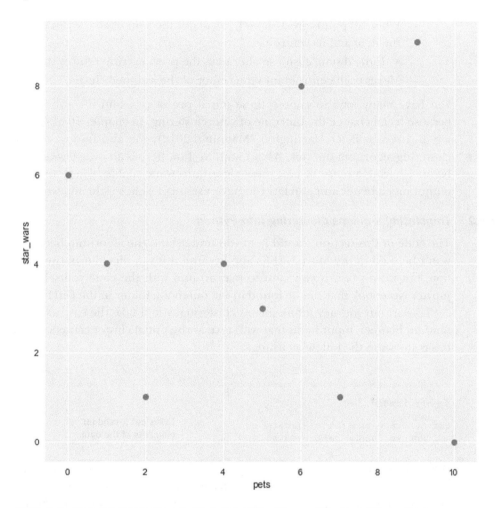

Figure 7.8 Each dot represents a user's rating of *Star Wars* and *The Secret Lives of Pets*.

The k-means clustering algorithm works by finding *k* points, called *centroids*, which satisfy the theorem that the sum of the distances between all items and their assigned centroids are as small as possible. As I write this I'm watching a sprinkler watering the flowers. Why? It takes much consideration about where to place the sprinkler because water in Denmark is precious, so I need to find *k* spots where it'll water everything but use as little water as possible. The k-means clustering can be used for that too because it produces centroids that would show the best place to put the sprinkler.

The algorithm goes through the following steps:

- Selects *k* places as the centers of the clusters.
- Loops over the following:
  - For each data point in the set, finds the centroid with the shortest distance.
  - When all points are assigned, calculates the sum of all the distances between the item and its centroid.
    - If the distance isn't smaller than the previous run, returns the clusters.
  - Moves each centroid into the center of the assigned cluster.

You have many ways to choose these initial prototypes, and it's an important step because it can change the outcome of your clustering. In chapter 10 of *Machine Learning in Action* by Peter Harrington (Manning, 2012), you also find ways to make the clustering algorithm smarter. What I want to show here is an overview of how it works because having a sense of how these algorithms work enables you to understand the output much better and also lets you have a sense of what's right and wrong.

7.3.2   *Translating k-means clustering into Python*

The code in this section should help you understand the algorithm better. The code won't be used in the MovieGEEKs app because this is a nice illustrative implementation, but it isn't fast. If you want to play around with the code yourself, look at the Jupyter Notebook that can be found in the notebook folder in the GitHub project.[4]

To start our journey into k-means clustering, you'll take the easy way, selecting at random between input items that will serve as the initial cluster centers. The code for this is shown in the following listing.

Listing 7.1   Generating centroids

```
import random

def generate_centroids(k, data):
    return random.sample(data, k)
```
Takes out k-random elements of the data

FOR EACH DATA POINT IN THE DATA SET, FIND THE CENTROID WITH THE SHORTEST DISTANCE

The next thing to do is to calculate the distance between the items in the data and the centroids and find which is closer. The distance algorithm you'll use here is a well-known fellow: the Euclidian norm as described earlier. The formula is the following:

$$\left\| r_{sara} - r_{pietro} \right\|_2 = \sqrt[2]{\sum_{i=1}^{n} \left| r_{sara,i} - r_{pietro,i} \right|^2}$$

---

[4] For more information on the Jupyter Notebook, see http://mng.bz/KMfU.

This formula can be implemented as shown in the next listing.

Listing 7.2 Calculating the distance between two vectors

```
import math

def distance(x,y):
    dist = 0
    for i in range(len(x)):
        dist += math.pow((x[i] - y[i]), 2)
    return math.sqrt(dist)
```

Iterates through each dimension

Adds the squared difference between the vectors in that particular dimension

Returns the square root of the sum

You can use the `distance` method to decide which cluster each element should be a part of as shown next (listing 7.3). The method returns the centroid with the smallest distance to the item (the most similar one).

Listing 7.3 Assigning a data item to a cluster

Runs through each cluster center and returns the one that's closer to the item

```
def add_to_cluster(item, centroids):
    return item, min(range(len(centroids)),
                key= lambda i: distance(item, centroids[i]))
```

When all points are assigned, the `distance` method calculates the sum of all the distances between the item and its centroid. The sum is used to compare the iterations of the algorithm. The second iteration compares the sum of the distances in the second setting with the previous one. If the earlier one is better, then the algorithm stops; otherwise, it does another iteration.

For each iteration, the centroids are moved. This can be done in many ways, but in this listing the centroids are moved to the center of all the points in its cluster.

Listing 7.4 Moving centroids to the center of the cluster

```
from functools import reduce

def move_centroids(k, kim):
    centroids = []
    for cen in range(k):
        members = [i[0] for i in kim if i[1] == cen]
        if members:
            centroid = [i/len(members) for i in reduce(add_vector, members)]
            centroids.append(centroid)

    return centroids
```

Loops through k clusters to create new centroids

Finds all members of this cluster. (Remember each item was a tuple of two elements—the actual vector and the cluster assignment.)

... adds all vectors and divides it by the number of vectors. You'll get a point which is in the center of the cluster.

If the cluster isn't empty...

The add_vector method in listing 7.5 is simple. It iterates through the vectors and adds each element as shown in this listing.

Listing 7.5   Utility method

```
def add_vector(i, j):
    return [i[k] + j[k] for k in range(len(j))]
```

Now let's look at the whole k-means algorithm.

Listing 7.6   The k-means clustering algorithm

```
def k_means(k, data):
    best_weight = math.inf    ◄———— Shows the best weight so far is infinity

    centroids = generate_centroids(k, data)   ◄———— Generates the centroids

    while True:
        iteration = list([add_to_cluster(item, centroids) for item in data])

        new_weight = 0

        for i in iteration:                      ◄——————  Calculates the distance
            new_weight += distance(i[0], centroids[i[1]])   between each item and
                                                            its centroid

        if new_weight < best_weight:    ◄—
            best_weight = new_weight
            new_weight = 0                        If the new weight is better than
        else:                                     the best weight, it continues;
            return iteratiasd+on                  otherwise, it returns.

        centroids = move_centroids(k, iteration)   ◄———— Recalculates centroids

k_means(k, data)   ◄———— Runs the clustering
```

Appoints each point to a cluster (annotation pointing to the `iteration = list(...)` line)

Having the clusters in place means that you can reduce the number of users you need to compare when calculating similarity to the other members of the clusters. Figure 7.9 shows an execution of the algorithm that ran for four iterations.

The result of the run was the three clusters shown in table 7.7. It seems okay, for a small toy example.

Table 7.9   Examples of clusters

Cluster	Members
0	Peter = [0, 6] Mela = [1, 4] Vlad = [4,4] Kim = [5,3] Egle = [2,1]
1	Helle = [9,9] Jimmie = [6,8]
2	Sara = [7,1] Dea = [10,0]

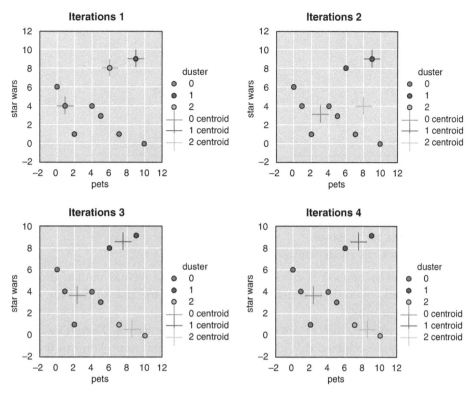

Figure 7.9 The four iterations the k-means clustering went through before it settled.

Pick random values and see if you can convince yourself that this would work. For example, which cluster would a new user who loves *The Secret Lives of Pets* but is so-so on *Star Wars* ([10, 4]) belong to?

NOTE OF WARNING

Before moving on, I think it's only fair to tell you that when you see an example like that in table 7.7 (Pietro's and Jesper's normalized ratings), it's easy to believe that k-means clustering is a magical beast that responds to your every bidding. That isn't so. K-means clustering, as with most other machine-learning algorithms, is difficult to make work correctly. It often responds with results that aren't understandable or usable.

Examples in books are simple and constructed to teach how it works, but sadly how it doesn't work is much harder to describe and is often left to the reader to discover. Figure 7.10 shows other results I got when I began with different starting points.

I'm afraid I'm not going to offer much more assistance. In the next section, you'll see how k-means are implemented in the MovieGEEKs site to get quick lists of similar users. At least that will show you a more realistic example of how to implement it.

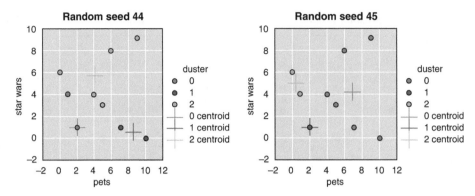

Figure 7.10   Results of k-means clustering that don't look good

HOW TO USE THE CLUSTERS

You can use the clusters in two ways:

1   *Looking up users in existing groups.* If you need to find similar users to say, Kim, then you look up which cluster he's in and use that to find the other users in the group.

2   *Placing new users in groups.* What if a new user arrives? Then it's a matter of finding the centroid that's closest to the new data point. You can then use that to find which cluster to add the new user to.

It's tempting to implement clusters now that it's fresh on your mind, but let's follow the flow of the chapter and go back to the start and add similarities to the Movie-GEEKs site and then clusters.

7.4   *Implementing similarities*

It only makes sense to look at users who've rated many of the same items as the current user. To be even pickier, you need users who not only rated many of the same items but also rated them the same as the active user. Those are the ones you'll use to recommend.

If you look at the sets, it looks like what's drawn in figure 7.11, showing which itemsets are important for user-collaborative filtering.

In short, you want to find users who have much—but not everything—in common with the active user. How can you do that? If you were using SQL, you'd start by doing something like that shown in listing 7.7 when looking for users similar to a user with id = 4.

Listing 7.7   Getting candidate users using SQL

```
WITH au_items AS (
SELECT
   distinct(movieid), rating
FROM
```

Gets all the items that the current active user has rated

```
   public.ratings
WHERE
   userid = '4')

SELECT userid, count(movieid) overlapping
FROM public.ratings
WHERE movieid IN (SELECT movieid from au_items) and
userid <> '4'
AND  overlapping > min
group by userid
order by overlapping desc;
```

Finds all users who've rated one or more of the same items the active user has rated

Only finds ratings on movies that the active user has rated

Groups by ID

Requires the overlap to be more than min number of items.

Orders by overlapping item

Users that aren't the active user

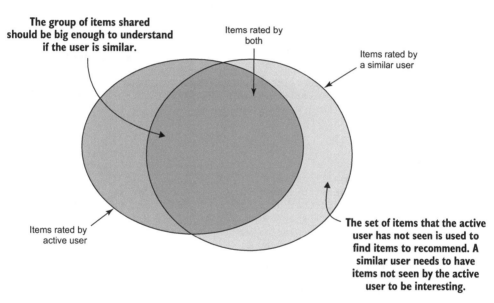

The group of items shared should be big enough to understand if the user is similar.

Items rated by both

Items rated by a similar user

Items rated by active user

The set of items that the active user has not seen is used to find items to recommend. A similar user needs to have items not seen by the active user to be interesting.

Figure 7.11   Showing which itemsets are important for user-collaborative filtering

To make this query in Django, you can use the QuerySet and your procedure will look like the following listing. You'll find this query in the /recommender/views/py file on GitHub.

Listing 7.8   Getting candidate users using Django ORM

```
ratings = Rating.objects.filter(user_id=user_id)
sim_users = Rating.objects.filter(movie_id__in=ratings.values('movie_id')) \
        .values('user_id') \
        .annotate(intersect=Count('user_id')).filter(intersect__gt=min)
```

This is a slow query but considering that you cut away a big chunk of users that wouldn't have been similar to the current user, maybe it's worth the wait. And with this list, you can now say that you only want to look at the 100 most similar users or the users who have at least a certain number of similar items.

Looking around for advice on where to cut the list, I found that Michael D. Ekstrand and others at GroupLens suggest using somewhere between 20-50 users.[5] My feeling is that's a high number for most data sets, but on the sample data set, it might be a good number. I challenge you to test it.

Next, we'll look at how to implement the Pearson similarity that you learned about earlier. The method in Listing 7.9 compares two users and calculates their similarity. Again, you'll find this code in the /recommender/views/py file on GitHub.

Listing 7.9 Implementing Pearson's similarity method

```
def pearson(users, this_usr, that_usr):
  if this_usr in users and that_usr in users:
    this_sum = sum(users[this_usr].values())
    this_len = len(users[this_usr].values())        Finds the users'
    this_usr_avg=this_sum/this_len                  average rating

    this_keys = set(users[this_user].keys())
    that_keys = set(users[that_user].keys())        Merges the two
    all_movies = (this_keys & that_keys)            movie sets into one

    dividend = 0
    divisor_a = 0
    divisor_b = 0

    for movie in all_movies:
        nr_a = users[this_user][movie] - this_user_avg    Normalizes user ratings
        nr_b = users[that_user][movie] - that_user_avg    by subtracting the mean
        dividend += (nr_a) * (nr_b)
        divisor_a += pow(nr_a, 2)
        divisor_b += pow(nr_b, 2)

    divisor = Decimal(sqrt(divisor_a) * sqrt(divisor_b))
    if divisor != 0:
      return dividend/divisor                   Puts everything together and
                                                calculates Pearson coefficient
    return 0        Returns zero if the divisor
                    is always zero
```

7.4.1 Implementing the similarity in the MovieGEEKs site

To make it easier to play with the similarities, you'll look at how it's implemented in the MovieGEEKs site admin part. Did you look at the MovieGEEKs site (http://mng.bz/04K5)? It has an analytics part that, in turn, contains a page for each user_id. You can find it at http://localhost:8000/analytics/user/100s.

---

[5] GroupLens (https://grouplens.org), a research group at the University of Minnesota, has produced a lot of good research on recommender systems.

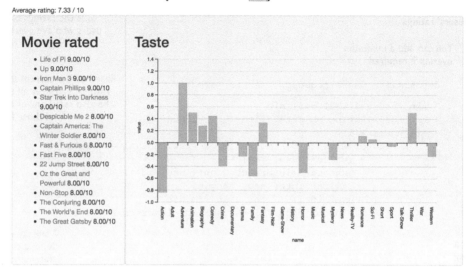

User Profile id: 100 (in cluster: 14)

Average rating: 7.33 / 10

Movie rated

- Life of Pi 9.00/10
- Up 9.00/10
- Iron Man 3 9.00/10
- Captain Phillips 9.00/10
- Star Trek Into Darkness 9.00/10
- Despicable Me 2 8.00/10
- Captain America: The Winter Soldier 8.00/10
- Fast & Furious 6 8.00/10
- Fast Five 8.00/10
- 22 Jump Street 8.00/10
- Oz the Great and Powerful 8.00/10
- Non-Stop 8.00/10
- The Conjuring 8.00/10
- The World's End 8.00/10
- The Great Gatsby 8.00/10

Taste

Figure 7.12 The top of the user profile page of user 100

Look for the user with ID 100. User 100 likes many different genres; for example, adventure, animation, and thrillers as the chart shows in figure 7.12 or on the site.

Your task here is to implement the next section on the page, the one that shows similar users. You can see it in figure 7.13.

Users similar to user 100

Jaccard sim
- 100:1
- 26790:0.27
- 51171:0.26
- 49813:0.26
- 32605:0.25
- 21906:0.24
- 25492:0.24
- 24091:0.24
- 49621:0.24
- 43781:0.23

Pearson sim
- 41244:1
- 100:1
- 32303:0.99
- 31805:0.99
- 18449:0.98
- 40537:0.97
- 7291:0.97
- 40636:0.96
- 15738:0.96
- 34127:0.95

Figure 7.13 Similar users to user 100, calculated by Jaccard's simularity on the left and Pearson's correlation on the right

In the MovieGEEKs site, the similarity is considered part of the recommender system, so I added a `similar_users` method to the recommender API as shown in listing 7.10. The `similar_users` method requires a `user_id` and a type. The type enables you to extend it easily with other types of similarity calculations. I'll leave it up to the interested reader to see the configuration around it, so I'll skip directly to the Python code of the method.

Listing 7.10 `similar_users: /recommender/views.py`

Gets all the current users' ratings

You can add a minimum overlap if required.

Gets the ratings of all the users who'ave overlapping ratings with the user

Based on the current users' ratings, retrieves all users who also rated one or more of those films.

Extracts all the user_ids

Builds a user-rating matrix

A sneaky way of doing a case statement in Python. If you want to add another similarity method, you add the name and the name of the method.

Iterates through all the users

Adds a user to the list of similar users

Gets a reference to the func described in the input, and executes it

Checks whether the similarity is more than 0.2. Changes to this require more or less similarity.

Returns as JSON

```python
def similar_users(request, user_id, type):
    min = request.GET.get('min', 1)
    ratings = Rating.objects.filter(user_id=user_id)
    sim_users = \
        Rating.objects.filter(movie_id__in=ratings.values('movie_id'))\
            .values('user_id') \
            .annotate(intersect=Count('user_id')) \
            .filter(intersect__gt=min)
    users = {u['user_id']: {} for u in sim_users}
    dataset = Rating.objects.filter(user_id__in=users.keys())

    for row in dataset:
        if row.user_id in users.keys():
            users[row.user_id][row.movie_id] = row.rating
    similarity = dict()
    switcher = {
        'jaccard': jaccard,
        'pearson': pearson,
    }
    for user in sim_users:
        func = switcher.get(type, lambda: "nothing")
        s = func(users, int(user_id), int(user['user_id']))
        if s > 0.2:
            similarity[user['user_id']] = s

    data = {
        'user_id': user_id,
        'num_movies_rated': len(ratings),
        'type': type,
        'similarity': similarity,
    }
    return JsonResponse(data, safe=False)
```

The Pearson method is described in detail in listing 7.9. Here, the `jaccard` method is used. For a detailed description, see section 7.2 earlier in the chapter. You'll find this code segment in the file /recommender/views.py.

Listing 7.11 The jaccard method

```python
def jaccard(users, this_user, that_user):
    if this_user in users and that_user in users:
        intersect = set(users[this_user].keys()) \
& set(users[that_user].keys())
union = set(users[this_user].keys()) |\
  set(users[that_user].keys())
```

Calculates the intersection between the two users

Calculates the union between the two users

```
return len(intersect)/Decimal(len(union))        ◁──┐  Returns the
    else:                                             │  Jaccard correlation
return 0
```

I did a small test to see if the Pearson similarity and k-means clustering worked the same way. I sampled a few of the users that I found in the list of similar users to user 2, with 0.87 and 0.85 similarity, respectively, and they were all in cluster seven. You can't prove that it works in all cases. however, by looking at only one example, but it gives you a good indication that the implementation is consistently either wrong or right.

The user similarities that we looked at here don't require any special training. In chapter 8, you'll look at item similarity and calculate all the similarities beforehand.

7.4.2 Implementing the clustering in the MovieGEEKs site

Using a clustering algorithm in your site will be a bit of a leap of faith for now, but don't worry about that. Here, you'll implement the solution using the clustering algorithm that's part of the Scikit-learn library.[6] It's also a k-means algorithm, but supposedly it's faster and better tested than our little example, so we'll go with that. You'll add the clusters to your analytics part of the MovieGEEKs site (figure 7.14) in two places, first on the main page at http://localhost: 8000/analytics/. No clusters will be shown before you've calculated them, however.

The script implemented for the MovieGEEKs site does the same as the script you saw in listing 7.6, only now it loads data from the database, calculates the k-means, and then saves a row in the Cluster table for each user_id, with its corresponding cluster_id, as shown in listing 7.12. You'll find the script in /builder/user_cluster_calculator.py.

Listing 7.12 UserClusterCalculator script

```
class UserClusterCalculator(object):

def load_data(self):                            Gets all the user_ids
    print('loading data')                       from the ratings table
    user_ids = list(                                              Gets all the
        Rating.objects.values('user_id')                          content_ids
            .annotate(movie_count=Count('movie_id'))              from the
            .order_by('-movie_count'))          ◁──               ratings table
    content_ids = list(Rating.objects.values('movie_id').distinct()) ◁──
    content_map = {content_ids[i]['movie_id']: i
                   for i in range(len(content_ids))} ◁──
    num_users = len(user_ids)                             Creates a mapping
    user_ratings = dok_matrix((num_users,                 between the
 len(content_ids)),                                       content_ids and a list of
dtype=np.float32)    ◁──                                  integers to make it
                         Creates an instance of dok_matrix work with the sparse
                         (dictionary of keys matrix)[7] with the matrix implementation
                         dimensions according to number of
                         users and content
```

---

[6] Scikit-learn is a free software machine learning library for Python. For more information see http://scikit-learn.org/stable/index.html.

[7] For more information on the dictionary of keys matrix, see http://mng.bz/5bK4.

```
for i in range(num_users):                    ◄─────────────┐
    # each user corresponds to a row, in the order of all_user_names
    ratings = Rating.objects.filter(user_id=user_ids[i]['user_id'])
    for user_rating in ratings:
        id = user_rating,movie_id
        user_ratings[i, content_map[id]] = user_rating.rating
    print('data loaded')
                                              Iterates through all the
                                              users and adds data to
    return user_ids, user_ratings                     the matrix

def calculate(self, k = 23):
    print("training k-means clustering")

    user_ids, user_ratings = self.load_data()
                                              Creates an instance
                                              of the k-means
    kmeans = KMeans(n_clusters=k)        ◄───┤ clustering algorithm
    clusters = kmeans.fit(user_ratings
                                         ◄───  Does the magic
.tocsr())                                      (clustering)

    plot(user_ratings.todense(), kmeans, k)

    self.save_clusters(clusters, user_ids)

    return clusters                           Deletes all clusters
                                              already saved in the
def save_clusters(self, clusters, user_ids):  database to make
    print("saving clusters")                  room for new ones
    Cluster.objects.all().delete()       ◄─────────
    for i, cluster_label in enumerate(clusters.labels_):
        Cluster(
            cluster_id=cluster_label,          Saves the
            user_id=user_ids[i]['user_id']).save()  ◄──── clusters

if __name__ == '__main__':
    print("Calculating user clusters...")

    cluster = UserClusterCalculator()
    cluster.calculate(23)
```

This script can be run from the command line (or directly from PyCharm, which I'm using). From the command line simply write the code as shown in the listing below.

Listing 7.13   Running the clustering

```
python -m builder.user_cluster_calculator
```

On a MacBook from 2014, it takes a couple of hours, so go and get a little exercise and a snack before moving on.

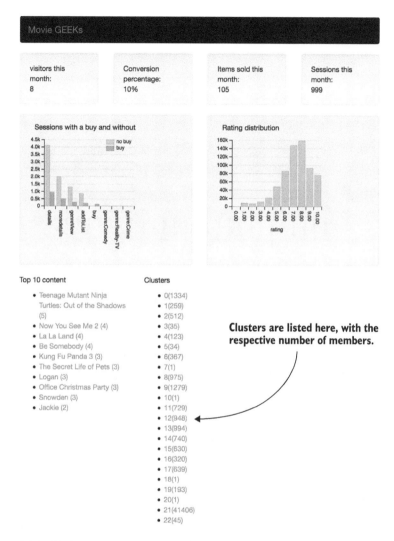

Figure 7.14 The loading page for MovieGEEKs site with the analytics dashboard and the list of clusters

In addition to the view on the loading page of the analytics for MovieGEEKs site, you can click one of the clusters (for example, the first one), and you'll get the view shown in figure 7.15. It shows a chart of the normalized distribution of ratings for all the cluster members, plus a list of all its members.

It's a chapter in itself to describe and discuss how you understand and verify whether your clustering algorithm works to your advantage. But using clusters can be a way to optimize the algorithms described in the following chapter, and you can use clustering algorithms to narrow down the search for similar users so you can calculate recommendations faster.

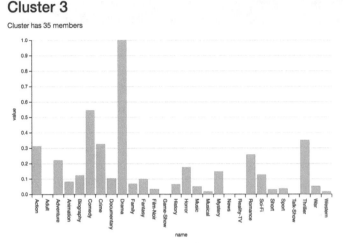

Cluster 3

Cluster has 35 members

2365 6087 7527 10041 10049 10311 13950 14587 15291 16321 17773 20732 21104 21520 22445 25239 26526 30882
31000 32491 32541 32922 33736 35319 36466 40187 40864 40992 41561 41629 43510 44751 47288 50612 51564

Figure 7.15 Screenshot from MovieGEEKs analytics that shows a cluster

Similarity and distance are everything in recommender systems and in many machine-learning algorithms. Data scientists often spend much time transforming data from categories or text into a format that can be used to calculate similarities, so it's important to have a good mental picture of similarity functions.

In this chapter, we talked about data that can be visualized, such as two-dimensional quantitative data. It's great for showing examples, but rarely what you see in real life. My advice is to get well-acquainted with the two-dimensional data similarity examples you looked at here because they'll help you better understand more complex situations.

Summary

- Measuring similarities between sets can be used to calculate similarity between users where the data is transactional, such as a buy or a like data rating.
- Quantitative data is interesting when it comes to users who provide ratings, either implicitly or explicitly.
- L_p-norms can be used on quantitative data and are also the starting point for talking about other types of correlation methods, such as the Pearson correlation and cosine similarity, which look similar but have different interpretations.
- K-means clusters are great in toy examples, but always be careful about checking the results. As you saw, they can easily end in a suboptimal state, which would create strange recommendations to users. (The example you looked at came with a warning reminding you that examples are constructed to explain the algorithm, but it hides the fact that many algorithms are difficult to make work according to the executor's needs. Consider yourself warned.)

Collaborative filtering in the neighborhood

Collaborating makes things easier, so let's collaborate our way through this chapter.

- You'll start by revisiting the rating matrix.
- You'll look at the theory behind collaborative filtering.
- Collaborative filtering is done in several steps, and you'll look at each and learn about the choices that need to be addressed.
- You'll learn how collaborative filtering is implemented in MovieGEEKs.

This chapter introduces collaborative filtering and goes into detail about the branch of it called *neighborhood-based filtering*. Collaborative filtering is an umbrella of methods. What unites those is the selection of data. These filtering methods only use ratings (implicit or explicit) as the source for creating recommendations.

I dedicate two chapters, this one and chapter 10, for collaborative filtering. Chapter 10 covers learned models using matrix factorization to find hidden features, also known as *latent features*. Chapter 9 covers content-based filtering.[1]

In this chapter, you'll learn about the history of recommenders and see different ways collaborative filtering has been used. The core of collaborative filtering we'll look at in this chapter, neighborhood-based filtering, is based on the similarities between users and items, calculated with functions like the ones covered in chapter 7.

---

[1] I also use collaborative filtering in chapter 12, which covers hybrid recommenders as one of the feature recommenders, and again in chapter 13, which covers ranking algorithms. But that isn't the focus of those chapters.

Up to now, you've only created simple, non-personalized recommenders. It's time to get up close and personal with personalized recommendations. The recommendations created so far were based on auto-generated collected behavior but, from now on, you'll use a real rating data set called MovieTweetings and build recommendations based on it.[2] I recommend checking out the data set at GitHub to familiarize yourself with it.

The collaborative filtering algorithm is simple; there are only a few things that need to be in the pipeline to produce recommendations. In each of the pipeline steps, you've a list of choices that affect the outcome. We'll look at each step in detail to make sense of it all.

When you're finished with this chapter, you'll know how to implement the item-item collaborative filtering algorithm used by Amazon—at least the one published in 2003.[3] I'm surprised that Amazon hasn't come up with something different by now. The algorithm is used to produce Amazon's Recommended for You page. Mine is shown in figure 8.1. As you can see, I've bought books on statistics and Django. The overall idea is to find items that are rated similarly to the items already rated or bought.

Neighborhood collaborative filter-based algorithms were the first algorithms to be categorized as a recommender systems algorithm. Let's start with a bit of history.

Figure 8.1   My Recommended for You page at Amazon.com

[2] For more information about the MovieTweetings data set, see https://github.com/sidooms/MovieTweetings.

[3] G. Linden et al., *Amazon.com Recommendations: Item-to-Item Collaborative Filtering*. Available online at http://ieeexplore.ieee.org/abstract/document/1167344/.

8.1 Collaborative filtering: A history lesson

Most people consider themselves unique and don't like to be segmented into a particular type. But that's exactly what using collaborative filtering to calculate recommendations is all about. In all its simplicity, collaborative filtering recommends a list of items for you. The list is created based on people who like the same things as you, but who also like something that you haven't yet consumed.

8.1.1 When information became collaboratively filtered

Our story starts around 1992 at the Xerox PARC (Palo Alto Research Center), when they realized that the number of emails sent had exploded, "...resulting in users being inundated by huge streams of incoming documents."[4] I can't help thinking that in 1992 they truly had seen nothing yet, but as in so many other cases, Xerox PARC was ahead of its time—maybe also in information overload.

The mail system they built was based on the assumption that you always have a few users who'd read everything immediately and then endorse those items of interest, while most users would read only what looked intriguing. The mail system was called Tapestry, a name you'll often read in recommender system literature.

Two years later, the GroupLens project, a collaborative effort between MIT and the University of Minnesota, created "an open architecture for collaborative filtering of Netnews."[5] GroupLens (https://grouplens.org) wanted to solve the same problem of information overload and wanted to enable people to rate newsgroup messages. This time, the system was built on the assumption that people who previously agreed with the ratings were likely to agree with them again.

Xerox and the GroupLens group laid the foundation for most of what we now know as recommenders. The following section largely describes what GroupLens did originally, along with the improvements that have been suggested since then.

8.1.2 Helping each other

The assumption on which collaborative filtering is based is that together we can be better, and together we'll better understand each other. Sounds beautiful and a bit cheesy, like the ending of an epic Hollywood film, but this is the idea behind collaborative filtering. Also, you need to assume that people principally keep their tastes over time and that if you agreed with somebody in the past, you'll likely agree with them in the future. Let's try to be more concrete before we dig into the theory of collaborative filtering and how to calculate it.

In chapter 6, you looked at recommendations that were based on what people had bought in the past by looking at their shopping baskets; now you'll concentrate on the user. You could say that we're asking the question, "If the user was a shopping cart what would be in it?"

---

[4] D. Goldberg et al., *Using Collaborative Filtering to Weave an Information Tapestry* (1992). Available online at http://citeseer.ist.psu.edu/viewdoc/summary?doi=10.1.1.104.3739.

[5] For more information, see http://ccs.mit.edu/papers/CCSWP165.html.

Bookshops and libraries often have posters saying, "If you liked this popular book *X*, then you should also try this (maybe not so popular) book *Y*." These posters are directed toward a large group of people and often work well; they're similar to a filtered chart. Instead, what you want to do is to create individualized content lists or at least lists for small groups of like-minded users. You don't want to print them out and hang them on your walls, but rather create and present them instantly when a user arrives at your website.

Neighborhood-based filtering can be handled in two ways. You could find users with similar film tastes as yours and then recommend films they've liked but that you haven't seen; this is *user-based filtering* (in figure 8.2, start in the upper-left corner then go right and down). Alternatively, you can find items similar to items that you already like (start in the upper-left corner, then go down and to the right in figure 8.2); this is *item-based filtering*. Both similarities between users and items are calculated based on the ratings.

The user-based path means looking at similar users. My good friend Thomas and I have known each other for many years, and I'm fairly sure he likes movies similar to the ones I like. If I want to go to the cinema, I can text him for advice. If I've a group of friends with similar tastes to mine, I could ask all of them and then use all of their responses. The group would collaboratively filter the current selection of movies for me and tell me which to recommend.

For example, say you watched the new *Star Trek* movie, and you want to watch something similar. You ask all your friends what they thought about *Star Trek* and whether they can give you names of other films they liked as much. I would ask Helle, who I know likes science fiction, and she'll tell me that she also liked *Rogue One: A Star Wars Story*, while Pietro has no love for science fiction, so he naturally hates it and

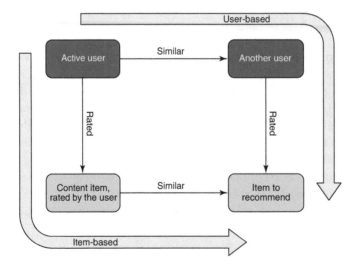

Figure 8.2   The two ways of performing neighborhood-based filtering. One method uses similar users, while the other uses items similar to items the active user liked.

promises me that he'll never waste any more time on another film like *Rogue One*. Having these two testimonies means that I can deduce that the two films are similar (one person likes both of them and one doesn't like either). Because I liked *Star Trek*, I'll probably also like *Rogue One*. In this way, my friends have collaboratively helped me find the next film I should go see in the cinema (if I weren't spending all my evenings writing this book).

In short, either you find similar users to the active user and then recommend the films they liked that the active user hasn't watched, or you find the liked items of the active user and come up with similar items to recommend. To make all this work, you're back at the rating matrix to describe users' preferences.

8.1.3 The rating matrix

A way to represent users' tastes is to list all the content they've expressed an opinion about. Usually, this data is kept in a user-item matrix, which you learned about in chapter 7, and which we'll revisit here.

Matrix is a fancy word for a table with numbers, like the one shown in table 8.1. Each cell indicates a user's sentiment toward an item. Usually, a rating such as 5 or 10 is a good rating (depending on what rating scale you're using), and a rating close to zero is a bad rating or a dislike.

What you want to calculate are predictions for each of the empty cells in this matrix—numbers that correspond to a particular user's predicted future sentiment toward specific content—using the data already present in the matrix. Does that mean that you want all the data to be present? Not really, because that indicates that the user has rated or consumed all the content you can offer already, which is good in one way, but then they have to go somewhere else to get more. If the matrix is too empty, then you have the cold-start problems I talked about at length in chapter 6.

Table 8.1 Example of a rating matrix. Notice that Sara hasn't rated *Ace Ventura*, and Jesper and Helle haven't rated *Braveheart*.

	Comedy	Action	Comedy	Action	Drama	Drama
Sara	5	3		2	2	2
Jesper	4	3	4		3	3
Therese	5	2	5	2	1	1
Helle	3	5	3		1	1
Pietro	3	3	3	2	4	5
Ekaterina	2	3	2	3	5	5

How does this fit into what I said about finding similar users and items? If you look at the table, you can see Sara and Therese have similar tastes, so to find a good movie to recommend to Sara, you could choose a movie Therese likes and Sara hasn't seen. Or you could say Sara liked *Men in Black* and find which films have been rated similarly. If you look at *Ace Ventura*, the same people liked it (Jesper and Therese) and the same people (Helle, Pietro, and Ekaterina) didn't, so those ratings can be considered similar. This is simplified, and you should remember that normally there are more empty cells than filled ones, so collaborative filtering requires a bit more to do it. What does it take to make a program do this for you?

8.1.4   *The collaborative filtering pipeline*

When talking about machine learning and predictive applications, you typically talk about a *pipeline*, which is a serialized pipe of (possibly parallelizable) things that need to be calculated in a certain order before predictions can be made. The pipeline in figure 8.3 gives an overview of the steps to take.

You learned in chapter 7 that there are several ways to calculate similarity. Step 1 in figure 8.3 shows one way. Later, you'll learn about which function should be used. Using one of the ways to calculate similarity described in chapter 7 allows you to create a list of the active user's similarities with all the other users. Step 2 orders the other users. In step 3, you select a neighborhood to use to calculate the predictions. Again, there are different ways you can decide which is the neighborhood, but for now think of it as a close group of users who are similar to the active user. Later in this section, we'll look at the ways this can be done.

In Step 4, you use similarities for the users in the neighborhood along with these users' ratings of the item to predict. Here the predicted rating is 3.48. Predicted ratings can either be used as is or you can calculate many ratings, then order these and return the top-*N* predicted ratings to get the top-*N* recommendation.

The goal of most systems is to do as much as possible before the user visits, expecting recommendations. Let's look at what you can do.

8.1.5   *Should you use user-user or item-item collaborative filtering?*

Which collaborative filtering should you use? Start by looking at the first collaborative filtering algorithm, which finds similar users and uses that to calculate recommendations. An average user doesn't have many item ratings, which means that adding a new rating can change the system's calculation of the user's taste.

It's considered unwise to do a pre-computation of which users are similar. Items are considered more stable in the sense that the same types of people like the same types of items, and studies have shown that you can pre-calculate similarities for items. That's important when you're talking about a catalog the size of Amazon (you can think about both the size of the Amazon River or Amazon the internet store!).

Look at figure 8.2 again. Consider that you want to calculate as few similarities as possible. If you've many more users than items, then you should go for item-based filtering; otherwise, user-based filtering is more economical.

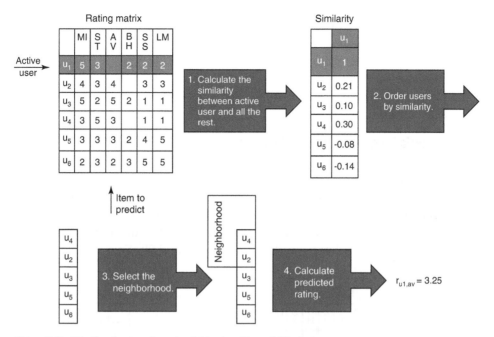

Figure 8.3 Pipeline for user-based neighborhood-based filtering

You may come across the term *user-user-based filtering* in your quest for knowledge. The reason why people are still talking about user-user-based filtering is that it's a better way to give recommendations. If you do item-to-item filtering, you'll find items similar to what user A, for example, has already rated, but similar items won't provide the serendipity that similar ratings can provide.

With user similarity, the hope is that your data will connect a user with other users with different peculiarities in their tastes and provide surprising, but good recommendations. If you want to explain why you gave those recommendations, then item-based filtering makes this task easy. That's because the system can say you get a recommendation for movie *Y* because you liked movie *X*, which is similar to movie *Y*. Whereas user-based filtering requires a bit more ingenuity to explain why the recommendations are shown while keeping the privacy of the other users.

8.1.6 Data requirements

Does the data match the needs of collaborative filtering? I've noted numerous times when there are no clear rules on which recommender algorithm you should use. While that's still true, I've advice before you venture into the exciting world of collaborative filtering. To calculate recommendations, the data needs to be well connected:

- If no users have rated content, then no recommendations will be made.
- Users who don't have overlapping tastes with other users won't receive good recommendations.

A way to implement collaborative filtering is by first finding all the items that are rated by several users (more than two users at least). Then calculate the number of users who are connected to one or more of those items. These are the users who'll receive recommendations; the rest won't.

The good thing about collaborative filtering is that your system doesn't need any domain knowledge. But remember that you do need domain knowledge to create a good recommender system.

8.2   Calculating recommendations

We've looked at both user- and item-based filtering. I'll continue talking about user-based filtering, but more than likely, the implementation that you'll end up with will use item similarity, especially if the data set you have has approximately 45,000 users and only 25,000 items. The item similarity pipeline is a tiny bit different; you still take the same steps as you saw in figure 8.3, but you're looking at items rather than users. Figure 8.4 shows the steps you'll take for item-based filtering.

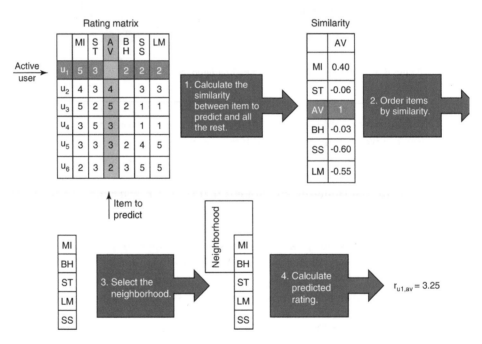

Figure 8.4   The item-based filtering pipeline

8.3   Calculating similarities

The first thing you need to do is settle on a similarity function, which you learned about in chapter 7. There are different schools of thought about which similarity function to use. The one we'll look at uses the cosine similarity from chapter 7. It provides a matrix of similarities that, for each item, provides a list of similar items.

8.4 Amazon's algorithm to precalculate item similarity

It's assumed that item similarity is stable, so item similarities can be calculated before-hand or offline. Amazon was one of the first, and probably biggest, user of this algorithm, and they published a paper describing their method.[6] Greg Lindens, the builder of much of Amazon.com's early recommendation system, describes a pseudo-algorithm for how to do item-item collaborative filtering:

```
For each item in product catalog, I₁
    For each customer C who purchased I₁
        For each item I₂ purchased by customer C
            Record that a customer purchased I₁ and I₂
    For each item I₂
        Compute the similarity between I₁ and I₂
```

Using this algorithm, you'll end up with a data set where you can look up similar items for the current item, making it faster to calculate the predictions. The Amazon article refers to an article by B. M. Sarwar et al.,[7] which is also a great source for learning about item-item collaborative filtering.

Now for our example. Table 8.2 is the same as table 8.1 and is reprinted here for your convenience.

Table 8.2 (A repeat of table 8.1) Example of a rating matrix. Notice that Sara has not rated *Ace Ventura*, and Jesper and Helle have not rated *Braveheart*.

	Comedy	Action	Comedy	Action	Drama	Drama
Sara	5	3		2	2	2
Jesper	4	3	4		3	3
Therese	5	2	5	2	1	1
Helle	3	5	3		1	1
Pietro	3	3	3	2	4	5
Ekaterina	2	3	2	3	5	5

---

[6] Linden et al., "Amazon.com Recommendations: Item-to-Item Collaborative Filtering." Available at www.cs.umd.edu/~samir/498/Amazon-Recommendations.pdf.

[7] B. M. Sarwar et al., "Item-Based Collaborative Filtering Recommendation Algorithms." 10th International World Wide Web Conference (ACM Press, 2001), pp. 285-295.

All customers have rated *Men in Black*, so you'll need to look at each user in turn. The first user is Sara, who also rated *Star Trek* (ST), *Braveheart* (B), *Sense and Sensibility* (SS), and *Les Misérables* (LM). You should add her ratings to the list of items rated together with *Men in Black*, so you have: MIB: [ST, B, SS, LM]. Next is Jesper, who rated movies already in the list plus *Ace Ventura* (AV). An item should only be added once, so you now have the following list: MIB: [ST, B, SS, LM, AV].

This is going to be a long story if I do this for all, so I'll skip ahead, but you as a dutiful reader should continue and do the model for all films. For the rest, this would be the result:

- MIB: [ST, B, SS, LM, AV]
- ST: [MIB, B, SS, LM, AV]
- B: [MIB, ST, SS, LM, AV]
- SS: [MIB, ST, B, LM, AV]
- LM: [MIB, ST, SS, B, AV]
- AV: [MIB, ST, B, SS, LM]

With these lists, you calculate similarities for each of the elements in the list for MIB. Again, I'll do it for the first one and then leave it as an exercise for you to calculate the rest. You'll use the adjusted cosine similarity function (the one that normalizes the item ratings based on the users average instead of the items) to calculate the similarity. To make the calculations fit, you again define $nr_{i,u} = r_{i,u} - \bar{r}_u$:

$$\text{Sim}(\text{"MIB"},\text{"ST"}) = \frac{\sum_u nr_{MIB,u} nr_{ST,u}}{\sqrt{\sum_u nr^2_{MIB,u}} \sqrt{\sum_u nr^2_{ST,u}}}$$

I have to admit that I'm in a bit of trouble here. I tried to write out the summations, but either the example got so small that it was too obvious, or I couldn't fit the calculations on the page. But let's do small steps and then it should work.

First, you want to normalize table 8.2 in table 8.3. Again, this is done by calculating the average rating for a user and subtracting the number of ratings. (This is only one way of doing it; in the code you'll use something a bit more complex.) With the normalized ratings, you can calculate the similarity between MIB and ST. To do that, look at each user in turn and sum it. You'll multiply each rating pair for each user and add them together (I've pointed out Jesper's contribution to the equation):

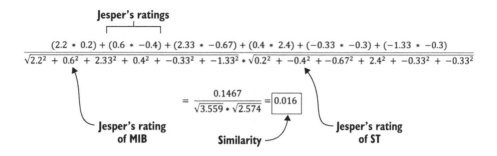

$$\frac{(2.2 * 0.2) + (0.6 * -0.4) + (2.33 * -0.67) + (0.4 * 2.4) + (-0.33 * -0.3) + (-1.33 * -0.3)}{\sqrt{2.2^2 + 0.6^2 + 2.33^2 + 0.4^2 + -0.33^2 + -1.33^2} * \sqrt{0.2^2 + -0.4^2 + -0.67^2 + 2.4^2 + -0.33^2 + -0.33^2}}$$

$$= \frac{0.1467}{\sqrt{3.559} * \sqrt{2.574}} = \boxed{0.016}$$

Jesper's ratings

Jesper's rating of MIB   Similarity   Jesper's rating of ST

Table 8.3   A repeat of table 8.2, but with normalized ratings according to the user's average

	MEN IN BLACK	STAR TREK		BRAVEHEART		
	Comedy	**Action**	**Comedy**	**Action**	**Drama**	**Drama**
Sara	2.20	0.20		-0.80	-0.80	-0.80
Jesper	0.60	-0.40	0.60		-0.40	-0.40
Therese	2.33	-0.67	2.33	-0.67	-1.67	-1.67
Helle	0.40	2.40	0.40		-1.60	-1.60
Pietro	-0.33	-0.33	-0.33	-1.33	0.67	1.67
Ekaterina	-1.33	-0.33	-1.33	-0.33	1.67	1.67

"Hmm," you might be thinking. "What does this tell me?" Well, you know that the adjusted cosine similarity function returns results between -1 and 1. And basically, you could interpret it as how many people who've rated both films gave both above average or under.

If you look at the ST and MIB numbers in table 8.3, you can see that Sara and Helle gave both films average ratings, while Pietro and Ekaterina gave below-average ratings. And Jesper and Therese like one movie more than the average but didn't like the other. It's Jesper and Therese who are the troublemakers here, but Sara and Helle gave different ratings, so none of the users agree on the two movies. This is visible in a similarity of 0.016.

If similarity is close to 1, then everybody agrees on the two films, so all users either put positive ratings on both films or negative ones. If all users are positive about one and not the other, the similarity is close to -1. If there's no correlation between users' ratings of the films, the similarity is close to 0. I calculated all the similarities in table 8.4.

Table 8.4 Similarity matrix between the six movies. The negative similarities are highlighted against a dark color, while the positive ones are written against a white background.

	MEN IN BLACK	STAR TREK	ACE VENTURA	BRAVEHEART	(Sense and Sensibility)	(Les Misérables)
MIB	1	0.63	1	-0.21	-0.88	-0.83
ST	0.63	1	0.35	-0.47	-0.64	-0.62
AV	1	0.35	1	0.01	-0.89	-0.83
B	-0.21	-0.47	0.01	1	-0.23	-0.32
SS	-0.88	-0.64	-0.89	-0.23	1	0.96
LM	-0.83	-0.62	-0.83	-0.32	0.96	1

To get a feel for how the similarity is distributed, it's a good idea to look at one on each end of the scale and one in the middle:

- *Close to 1*—LM and SS are interesting because you can see that they're dissimilar to all except themselves. They've a high similarity because all users agree on rating both either above or under. But then why is it not 1? Because the ratings aren't exactly the same. If they were the same, it would be 1, as is the case with AV and MIB.
- *Close to -1*—SS and AV are the most dissimilar, which also makes sense. I can imagine that most people who like *Ace Ventura* won't like *Sense and Sensibility*, and vice versa.
- *Close to 0*—The similarity between *Ace Ventura* and *Braveheart* is close to zero. This is an indication that some users like *Ace Ventura*, others don't, and vice versa. In this example, there are only three users who rated both, so it doesn't say much. Two users rate both films below average, while one is positive about *Ace Ventura* but negative about *Braveheart*.

When I calculated this in Python, I could have added an `if` statement that would only indicate similarity if the similarity function returned values above zero. That made the previous lists much shorter and easier to view. But in certain cases, it can also be worthwhile to use the negative similarities (or the dissimilarities). Would you consider recommending *Ace Ventura* to people who didn't like *Sense and Sensibility*?

BEWARE OF THE 1 OR 2 ITEMS IN COMMON PROBLEM

In the previous algorithm, if an item has only one rating, the average rating is equal to the that rating. This means it will be 0, which makes the similarity function undefined.

Next, if you've one user who's the only one who rated two items, then the similarity is 1, which is the highest similarity you can get.

Be careful about calculating similarity between users that have too few items in common. Imagine that it's only Helen who has watched both *Men in Black* and *Star Trek*, and she's rated them quite differently but the function says they're a top match:

$$\frac{2,17 \times 1.7}{\sqrt{2.17^2}\sqrt{1.7^2}} = 1$$

Always require a minimum of overlapping users—overlapping in the sense of the number of users who have rated both films. You shouldn't use collaborative filtering with users who have rated only one or two items. If there are too many overlapping users, it can also be difficult to find similarities because the recommendations produced will be too general. If everybody likes several items, it turns into a chart.

NOTE Remember, it's a tradeoff. Narrow the number of users and you risk not finding any content to recommend. Make it too wide and you risk that the recommendations contain content that's outside the user's taste.

Figure 8.6 shows how many users have only rated one item. Almost 20,000 out of the 45,000 users have only rated one movie in the MovieTweetings data set.

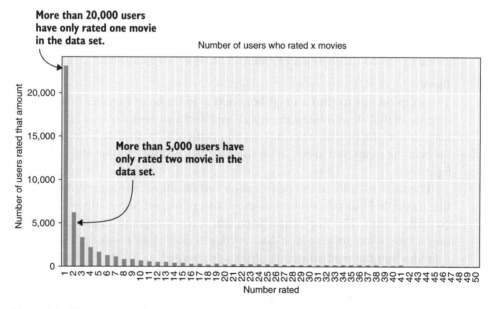

Figure 8.6 Histogram showing how many users have rated a certain number of movies. You can see that a bit more than 5,000 have rated two films (for x = 2).

8.5   *Ways to select the neighborhood*

A *neighborhood* is simply the set of items that are similar to the content you're currently looking at. We call it a neighborhood because we talk about items with a small distance between them. In this section, I'll cover three ways to define and calculate such a neighborhood: clustering, Top-*N*, and threshold.

CLUSTERING

In chapter 7, you learned how to implement clustering. If you performed user-based filtering, you could use these clusters as neighborhoods, or you could rig the clustering algorithm to cluster items instead and use that for the item-based approach. To do the clustering with this purpose, you'd probably want to add more clusters so your neighborhoods aren't too large, but it works the same way. The problem with this method is that you risk that the active user is on the border of a cluster or that the cluster has a strange shape and, therefore, you won't get the best neighborhood.

Instead of using the clusters directly as neighborhoods, the clusters can also be used to optimize the algorithm. That narrows the area where the system will look for neighbors. If you clustered your items into two clusters, the fact that you only have to look at one of them produces a large performance boost.

> NOTE   By narrowing the space where you search for neighbors, you also risk that they're suboptimal, so be careful.

I suggest doing test runs with and without clustering and compare whether there's a drop in quality (refer to chapter 9 on how to evaluate recommenders). If you use clustering to narrow the search area, you can use it in cooperation with Top-*N* or threshold.

TOP-N

The simplest way to find a neighborhood is to define a number *N* as the number of neighbors that should be in the neighborhood and then say that all items have *N* fellow items in the neighborhood. This allows the system to have items to work with, but they can be items that aren't at all similar. This is illustrated on the right-hand side of figure 8.7.

The two examples in the figures show the results of requiring three neighbors. The first example finds points close to the active point, while the other example needs to go further away. The Top-*N* approach can force the system to use points dissimilar to the active point, making it a bad recommender. For ensuring better quality, you should adopt the next approach, threshold, instead.

THRESHOLD

Another way to cut the cake is by saying that you only want items of a certain standard to be in the neighborhood by requiring that the similarity needs to be above a specific constant. This is shown on the left side of figure 8.7.

For the first point in the figure, this works great and gets similar items as the Top-*N* neighborhood. You can see problems with the second point because it doesn't have any nearby points. The neighborhood becomes small and lonely and potentially empty.

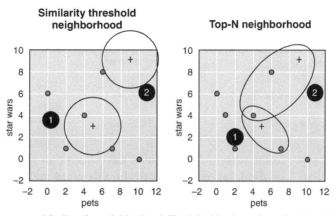

Figure 8.7 Two ways of finding the neighborhood. The left side shows how the threshold neighborhood works. Around the active point, you draw a circle (at least in 2D) and everything that's inside is a neighbor. On the right is the Top-*N* approach. It doesn't look at distance; it grows until it has *N* neighbors in the neighborhood.

TIP Choosing between Top-*N* and threshold is choosing between quantity and quality. Choose the threshold method for quality; Top-*N* for quantity.

No matter what you choose, you have a second question to answer: what should the threshold/*N* be? If you choose the Top-*N* approach to select the neighborhood, you need to find a constant *N*, indicating the number of points that should be in the neighborhood. The threshold method requires a threshold constant. The choice depends on both the data and how good you want your recommendations to be.

In a utopian data set, all items will be equally distributed throughout the area, and then *N* will be easy to select. But that doesn't happen often, and it's a matter of balancing between how good the recommendations should be for people liking popular things versus how good recommendations should be for people with peculiar tastes.

8.6 Finding the right neighborhood

Getting back to the example in section 8.4, now let's see what happens if you use either Top-*N* or threshold. Using the similarities calculated in section 8.4, the neighborhoods will look like those in table 8.5.

Table 8.5 Results of neighborhood calculations. Threshold returns elements that are similar, while the Top-2 mostly returns dissimilar objects.

Movies	Top-2	Threshold: 0.5
Men in Black (MIB)	ST: 0.63, AV: 1.00	ST: 0.63, AV: 1.00
Star Trek (ST)	MIB: 0.63, AV: 0.35	MIB: 0.63
Ace Ventura (AV)	MIB: 1.00, ST: 0.35	MIB: 1.00

Table 8.5 Results of neighborhood calculations. Threshold returns elements that are similar, while the Top-2 mostly returns dissimilar objects. *(continued)*

Movies	Top-2	Threshold: 0.5
Braveheart (B)	MIB: -0.21, AV: 0.01	
Sense and Sensibility (SS)	B: -0.23, LM: 0.96	LM: 0.96
Les Misérables (LM)	B: -0.32, SS: 0.96	SS: 0.96

As you can see in the table, *Braveheart* only has other items in the neighborhood if you use the Top-*N* method, but if you look at the threshold method instead, there are no similar items. If you're using the Top-*N* method, you could calculate recommendations based on the *N* similarities, even if they aren't similar at all. If you're using threshold, you can't recommend anything. Now that you've settled on the parameter for selecting a neighbor, you have the neighborhoods sorted and you can start calculating predictions.

8.7   *Ways to calculate predicted ratings*

The most common ways of calculating predicted ratings fall into two categories—regression and classification (for the machine language savvy!)—that I'll describe using two examples. Figure 8.8 gives an overview of the two methods. It glosses over the similarity values, which will have a place again when you calculate the rating predictions.

One method can be explained using an example of how to predict a sales price for a house using prices of similar homes. The second method is like counting votes at an election.

HOUSE PRICE (REGRESSION)

A way to understand how the regression method is implemented is by thinking about the example of pricing a house for sale. You want to put your home up for sale, but you don't know what you should ask for it. One way is to find similar houses sold in your area (comparables in real estate lingo) and take the average of the sell prices. This method is similar to regression.

Predicting ratings of items for specific users is done the same way. I'm not saying you're a house, but you can find similar users and average their ratings for an item.

FRIENDLY VOTERS (CLASSIFICATION)

Now consider that you have 10 people who are running for mayor in your town. You don't know which candidate to vote for, so you ask your neighbors who they're voting for. Then you count how many neighbors will vote for each candidate. When you're finished, you select the candidate with the highest score (count).

This method can easily be transferred to your domain. Instead of asking neighbors to rank a mayoral candidate, you're asking them to rate a movie. Hypothetically, if the active user has five users in their neighborhood, and they want to know what rating to

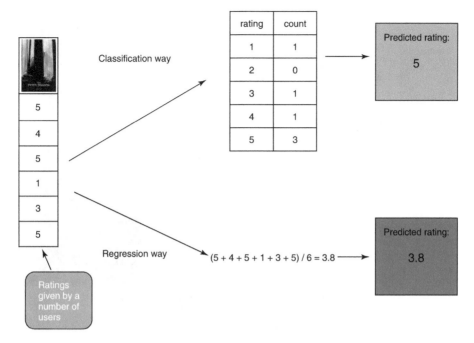

Figure 8.8 Two ways to calculate the predicted rating of *Pete's Dragon* for an active user whose neighborhood has given it the ratings listed on the right. Classification produces a rating of 5 by seeing which ratings are given more, whereas regression returns 3.8 by taking the average of the item-based ratings.

give a film, they first ask how many rated the movie one star, then asks about the number of two-star raters, and so on, until all rating values have been counted. The active user can now look at the rating count and choose the rating that most of the users in their neighborhood have. Instead of counting each neighbor as one vote, you can use the similarity score and make the votes count only as much as the similarity score.

These examples are simplified because they don't add any weighting to each of the ratings. In the next section, you'll look at predicting things in more detail using the regression technique. To recap, look at figure 8.9. You've an active user who has rated (interacted with) a list of items, and for each of these items you'll find similar items in the neighborhood. These similar items are the candidates for the recommendation.

8.8 Prediction with item-based filtering

Okay, so we're arriving at the core. You've created a list of similar items by looking in the neighborhoods around the user-rated items, and now you're ready to do predictions. How does that work exactly? Read on, and it shall all be clear.

In theory, you could take all the items in your catalog and calculate predictions, but because you're basing predictions on what the active user has already rated, you'll

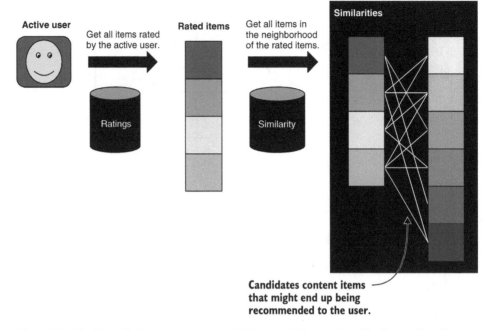

Figure 8.9 The items that become recommendation candidates are found by first getting the specific user's rated items and then locating the items in the user's neighborhood.

look only at items that are in the neighborhood. Expanding on the regression example from section 8.7, we'll look in more detail at how to predict the rating of an item.

8.8.1 Computing item predictions

When you find the neighborhood around an item, you can calculate the rating using a weighted average of ratings of the products that are similar to the item and that the active user rated. When you do it like this, you need to add the user's average rating to return the prediction to the same scale as the ratings the user put in. To put that into math, you'd write the following formula:

$$Pred(u,i) = \bar{r}_u + \frac{\sum_{j \in S_i} (sim(i,j) \times r_{u,j})}{\sum_{j \in S_i} sim(i,j)}$$

where

- $\bar{r}_u$ is the average rating of the user u.
- $r_{u,j}$ is the active user's u rating of item j.
- S_i is the set of items in the neighborhood that user u has rated.
- $Pred(u,i)$ is the predicted rating for user u of item i.
- $sim(i,j)$ is the similarity between item i and item j.

Let's say you want to predict Helle's rating for *Star Trek*.[8] You begin by looking at the similarity model calculated previously and, conveniently, use the movies where the neighborhood is the same no matter which method you used to find it. You'll have a list like this: ST: MIB: 0.63, AV: 0.35. Then it's a matter of filling in the numbers in the function:

$$Pred(Helle, Star\ Trek) \ = \ 2.6 + \frac{063 \times 0.4 + 0.35 \times 0.4}{0.63 + 035} = 3$$

If you've calculated the examples in this chapter, you should pat yourself on the back because you've calculated your first item-item prediction. But wait a minute! That was a prediction of a rating. How can that turn into a recommendation? That's easy. You do this for all items that are of interest, order them according to the predicted rating, and return the top 10. This is only if you can find 10 items to predict ratings for. If you implemented a threshold neighborhood, then it wouldn't be possible to predict a rating for *Braveheart*.

The next problem is that if your algorithm predicts ratings that are below average, do you then want to recommend them? Despair not. If you're still a bit confused, you'll soon look at a code example that even a machine can understand.

8.9 Cold-start problems

Collaborative filtering requires data, which is a problem when you receive new users as well as new items—you have no data for generating recommendations. Again, a way to get around this dilemma is to ask new users to rate a few items when they arrive. Alternatively, it's a good idea to create a new arrivals list to showcase new items because many users like to check out new products. We discussed this in detail in chapter 6. Another way could be to use exploit/explore methods, illustrated in figure 8.10.

In the figure, injecting new items occurs 1/6 of the time. Throwing a die (or using some random library), you get a number that either falls into the Exploit interval (1–5) or the Explore interval (6). *Exploit* means you exploit the knowledge you have and return recommendations. *Explore* means it shows a new item. This way the items gets exposed and users hopefully interact with them.

8.10 A few words on machine learning terms

Next, you're going to implement the item's collaborative filtering algorithm. First, let's put several terms in place.

One of the smart things about item-based filtering is that you can do much of the hard work before you have to serve recommendations to the active users. If you're new to the whole world of machine learning and data science, you might not know that doing work beforehand is called *offline model training*. Let's take a look at each of these words:

---

[8] Yes, it's already in the rating table, but let's go through the calculation anyway.

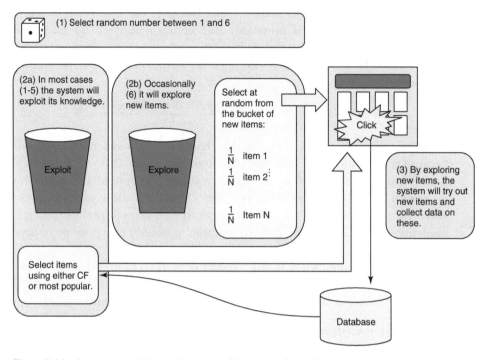

Figure 8.10   A way to sneak in new items is to inject those items into the mix a certain percentage of the time.

- *Offline*—Accomplishing something before using it live in production, not while the user is waiting. *(Online*—Doing tasks while the user is waiting.)
- *Model*—A process you can use to predict ratings (or other things depending on the machine-learning algorithm). A model can be created by taking the raw data, running it through a machine-learning algorithm that aggregates the data and produces a model. Creating a model is usually done offline.
- *Training*—A leftover term from the AI world where you consider machine learning as learning a new skill. In our case, the recommender is training (calculating the model) to find similar items.

Figure 8.11 shows what happens offline and online in item-item collaborative filtering.

To get everything into a real-life context, the next section looks at MovieGEEKs site. If you haven't already, download the site from GitHub and follow the instructions given in the README.md page at http://mng.bz/04k5. The README page also provides details on how to download and import the data.

8.11   *Collaborative filtering on the MovieGEEKs site*

You'll use the collaborative filtering recommendations in the second row of recommended items (figure 8.12), which, you might remember, lists products that are similar to items a user has already rated or bought. Let's get started building.

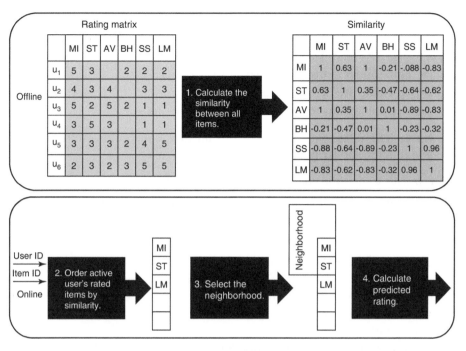

Figure 8.11 Collaborative filtering pipeline divided into offline and online calculations

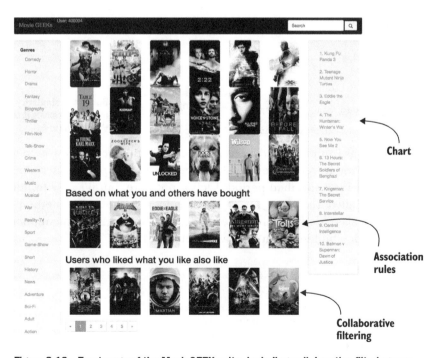

Figure 8.12 Front page of the MovieGEEKs site, including collaborative filtering recs

8.11.1 *Item-based filtering*

Hopefully after reading this far in this chapter it's crystal clear what you need to do now. If not, here's a little list of things you'll implement. They're also shown in figure 8.11.

- Find similar items to the ones the active user likes
- Calculate predicted ratings for these items
- Use predictions to calculate recommendations

> **NOTE** The difference between user and item collaborative filtering is how you find the similar items.

If you want to view the code, then you should look in two places:

- \builder\item_similarity_calculator.py, which is the offline training that shows the calculation of all the similarities
- \recs\neighborhood_based_recommender.py, which is the online part of it

CALCULATING ITEM SIMILARITY OFFLINE

To start with collaborative filtering, begin building the similarity matrix, which will be a database table with all the similarities calculated. It's better to create a Python script to run outside of the Django scope to do the model building. It might still take hours, but at least it's not days.

You need to create another builder as shown in listing 8.1. Overall, it gets data from the database, calculates the similarities, and saves them in the database.

Listing 8.1   Using a Python script to build and save a similarity model

```
import os
import pandas as pd

import database
import item_cf_builder

all_ratings = load_all_ratings()          ⟵   Gets the
                                                rating data

ItemSimilarityMatrixBuilder.build(all_ratings)   ⟵   Builds the similarity
                                                       model and saves it to
                                                       the database
```

Getting the ratings from the database is simple, but I still encourage you to glance at the code. If you use it, remember to add a time restriction to the query so that you only get the data for a specified period. I left it out here, but it's easy to find on Git (the method is called `load_all_ratings`). Let's look at the `build` method that will train/build/calculate/deduce/brew the model in listing 8.2. As mentioned, you'll find this in the file /builder/item_similarity_calculator.py.

Listing 8.2   Building the similarity matrix

```
def build(self, ratings, save=True):
    ratings['rating'] = ratings['rating'].astype(float)
    ratings['avg'] = ratings.groupby('user_id')['rating'] \
                     .transform(lambda x: normalize(x))   ⟵
```

Be sure the ratings are of type float, otherwise you might have problems later.

Normalizes the ratings based on the user's average and adds it to a column of data. You use the method normalize to do this.

Converts the user_ids as well as the movie_ids to categories. This needs to be done to use the sparse matrix.

Converts the ratings into a sparse matrix, called coo_matrix[9]

```
ratings['user_id'] = ratings['user_id'].astype('category')
ratings['movie_id'] = ratings['movie_id'].astype('category')

coo = coo_matrix((ratings['avg'].astype(float),
                 (ratings['movie_id'].cat.codes.copy(),
                  ratings['user_id'].cat.codes.copy())))
overlap_matrix = coo.astype(bool).astype(int) \
   .dot(coo.transpose().astype(bool).astype(int))

cor = cosine_similarity(coo, dense_output=False)
cor = cor.multiply(cor > self.min_sim)
cor = cor.multiply(overlap_matrix > self.min_overlap)

movies = dict(enumerate(ratings['movie_id'].cat.categories))
if save:
    self.save_similarities(cor, movies)

return cor, movies

def normalize(x):
    x = x.astype(float)
    x_sum = x.sum()
    x_num = x.astype(bool).sum()
    x_mean = x_sum / x_num

    if x.std() == 0:
        return 0.0
    return (x - x_mean) / (x.max() - x.min())
```

The overlap matrix

Calculates the cosine similarity between rows

Creates a dictionary of the movie_ids to find the items you're looking for

Saves to the database

Shows the normalize method used previously

Removes similarities not based on a big enough overlap

Removes similarities that are too small

A word or two of caution:[10] This code was changed and optimized from the original version so that it runs quite fast. You can run it while you watch it perform its magic; however, even if this is fast code, you should expect these things to take a while.

REMOVING SIMILARITIES THAT AREN'T BASED ON ENOUGH OVERLAPPING RATINGS

We've talked about how important it is to have enough overlapping ratings between two items. In many implementations of similarity methods, however, you don't have the option of defining a minimum number of overlapping elements.

Here's a way that works well in sparse matrices. You take your rating matrix, cast it first to Boolean (which makes everything more than zero `True` and the rest `False`), then you cast that to integers: 1 for `True` and 0 for `False`. You can now multiply the rating matrix with a transposed version of itself, and presto, you've a matrix where you

---

[9] For more information, see http://mng.bz/nLOL.

[10] You need time, patience, and lots of free RAM. When I first came up with a version of this code (being an optimist I thought I had the final version), two days passed before it finished. This version leaves me time to go for a run with my dog and eat dinner before it's finished.

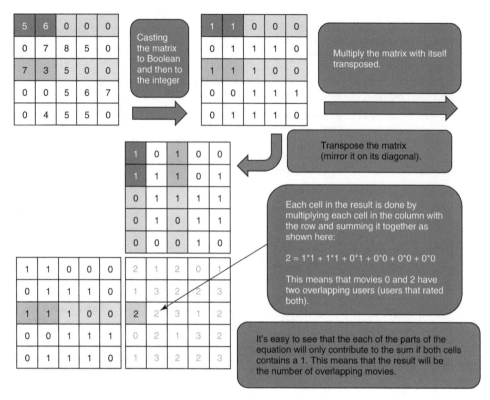

Figure 8.13   The fastest way to calculate overlap on your rating matrix

can look up overlapping elements. This is illustrated in figure 8.13 and done in the code in listing 8.3 (a snippet of the code from listing 8.2). You'll find this code in the file /builder/item_similarity_calculator.py.

Listing 8.3   Calculating an overlap matrix

```
overlap_matrix = coo.astype(bool).astype(int)
.dot(coo.transpose().astype(bool).astype(int))
```

With overlap matrices, you now have the option to say that you want all cells to be True if they're larger than a predefined minimum overlapping. If you only want to look at overlaps more than 2, for example, then all that are 2 or below are returned as False and the rest as True. If you cast that to integer again, then you've a matrix containing 1's where you're interested in saving the similarity. This can be done by writing this code as shown in /builder/item_similarity_calculator.py and listing 8.4.

Listing 8.4   Creating a threshold matrix

```
overlap_matrix > self.min_overlap
```

This expression returns a new Boolean matrix. When you've calculated the similarity, you do an element-wise multiplication, which means that you multiply each cell individually by the cell in the same position. Multiplying the similarity matrix with the Boolean overlap matrix will work such that all similarities that you aren't interested in will be multiplied by 0, meaning they'll return as 0, while the interesting ones will be multiplied by 1 and stay the same. In the following listing, the same trick is used to remove similarity values that are too small (or see /builder/item_similarity_calculator.py).

> **Listing 8.5 Removing similarity values**

```
cor = cor.multiply(cor > self.min_sim)
cor = cor.multiply(overlap_matrix > self.min_overlap)
```

Removes similarities that are too small

Removes similarities that aren't based on enough overlapping ratings

ONLINE PREDICTIONS

To use the model built with the methods shown previously, you need a prediction algorithm as illustrated in figure 8.14. Notice that you only go to the database twice—once to get the user's ratings and once to get the similarities of these. In fact, an easy way to optimize this is to join the data in the database before extractions, so that you've the similarities as well as the user's ratings.

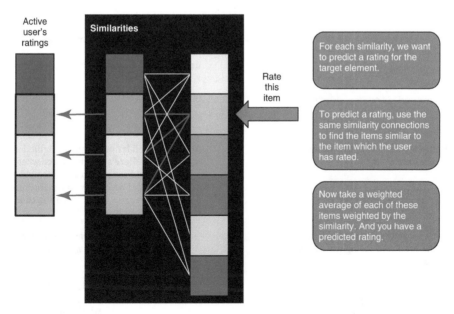

Figure 8.14 To predict a rating, use the similarity between the item in question and the items rated by the user. You multiply each similarity by the user's rating, sum that together, and divide it by the sum of the similarities. This creates a weighted average.

If the similarity script is finished running the offline calculations, it's time to look at the online part of the recommender.

Listing 8.6   The code when a user visits a page

**Creates a dictionary of
movie_ids and ratings**

**Finds all items similar to
active users' rated items**

```
def recommend_items_by_ratings(self, user_id, active_user_items, num=6):

    movie_ids = {movie['movie_id']: movie['rating']
                    for movie in active_user_items}
    user_mean = Decimal(sum(movie_ids.values())) / Decimal(len(movie_ids))

    candidate_items = Similarity.objects.filter(Q(source__in=movie_ids.keys())
                                    &~Q(target__in=movie_ids.keys()))
    candidate_items = candidate_items.order_by('-similarity')[:20])

    recs = dict()
    for candidate in candidate_items:
        target = candidate.target

        pre = 0
        sim_sum = 0

        rated_items = [i for i in candidate_items
                        if i.target == target][:self.neighborhood_size]

        if len(rated_items) > 1:
            for sim_item in rated_items:
                r = Decimal(movie_ids[sim_item.source]) - user_mean
                pre += sim_item.similarity * r
                sim_sum += sim_item.similarity
                if sim_sum > 0:
                    recs[target] = {'prediction': user_mean + pre / sim_sum,
                                'sim_items': [r.source for r in rated_items]}

        sorted_items = sorted(recs.items(), key=lambda
                            item: -float(item[1]['prediction']))[:num]
        return sorted_items
```

**Calculates
an average**

**Iterates
similar
items**

**Cuts the list to 20. This is
a choice you can play
around with to find a
good balance between
speed and quality.**

Adds the similarities

**Multiplies the normalized rating
by the item's similarity**

**Sorts all items based on prediction
value. Here's another place where
you could consider playing around a
bit and add other considerations
into the code.**

**Deducts the user mean
from the item rating**

**It's best if it's more than one rated item;
otherwise, the predicted rating will be the
same as the one item.**

**Appends the predicted rating to the
result, along with the rated items**

**From the target item, looks at all the
similarities present. That gives you a
list of the items the active user rated.**

**Ensures it doesn't add to zero (and
thereby cause a division with zero,
which throws an exception)**

You should now see another list of recommendations. What do you think? Do the recommendations look okay? Can you see them in figure 8.12? Open the site as your persona Helle and look at her analytics page (http://127.0.0.1:8000/analytics/user/400004/). You'll see that the recommendations are somewhat interesting (what's shown in figure 8.12).[11]

8.12 What's the difference between association rule recs and collaborative recs?

Let's take one last look at the recommendations, comparing the recommendations calculated with the association rules and the ones with collaborative filtering. The association rules look like they're closer to what Helle's taste is. But remember, you're looking at two different data sets: the association rules were based on the buys of your personas that are auto-generated by the script mentioned in chapter 3, while the collaborative filtering is based on the ratings in the downloaded data set. In a real system, those would be the same data set.

Associative rules aren't collaborative filtering because they're based on what's in a single shopping basket, not what a user buys over time. Collaborative filtering looks at what users buy or rate over time.

8.13 Levers to fiddle with for collaborative filtering

It isn't always enough to implement the algorithm to get good recommendations. Often there are things that need to be adjusted. For example, you previously adjusted the number of overlapping users needed before you could calculate a similarity. When considering what can be adjusted, refer to this list:

- Which ratings should be used for the active user?
  - Only the positive ones?
  - Only the most recent ones?
  - How should you normalize the ratings?
- When creating similarity
  - How many user's need to rate two movies for the similarity to be calculated?
  - Should you restrict similarities only to be added to the similarity list if they're positive?
- When creating the neighborhood
  - What method of selecting the neighborhood should you use?
  - How big should the neighborhood be (selecting threshold and/or *N* similarities)?
- When predicting the ratings
  - Should you use classification or regression?
  - Should you use a weighted average?

---

[11] To impersonate users, add a query string parameter called user_id. To see Helle's page (who has user_id 400004), you request the following URL: localhost:8000/?user_id=400004.

- When returning the recommendations, should you return all of them or only the ones with good predictions (that is, prediction above a threshold).

And the list goes on and on. … Each of these will narrow down a number of items going through the calculations. Take, for example, the overlap of users that you require. Figure 8.15 shows how the overlap affects the number of similarities you'll have in your model for the MovieGEEKs site. If you don't require a minimum overlap, you have around 40 million similarities. If you require two overlaps, you're already down to 5 million, and so on.

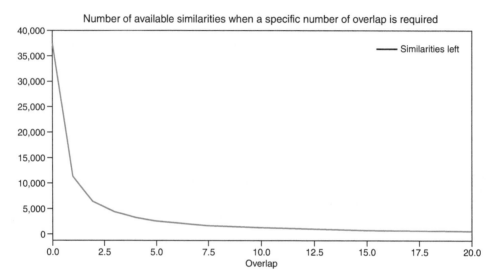

Figure 8.15   **Plot showing how many similarities you'll have when you add a higher required number of overlapping users. Note that the *y*-axis is in thousands.**

Figure 8.16 shows a plot dividing the movies into the number of ratings they've received. There are around 11,000 movies that have only been rated by one person. To calculate the similarity between movies, you need more than two users to have rated both movies, which means that you can't use these 11,000 items for anything.

Looking at the line above 2,000 in figure 8.16, you can see that there are around 4,000 movies that have been rated by two users. If you set a limit of a minimum of two overlapping ratings, then you can subtract everything to the left of it. Let's say you require at least two ratings, then you can see that you already cut away approximately 12,600 movies. That's a big number, considering you only have 25,000 movies to choose from.

TIP   The number of similarities saved in a database depends on many things, so it's hard to be specific about how restrictive you should be. My advice is to first try not being restrictive to see if that works, then try being more restrictive. You'll probably arrive at somewhere in the middle.

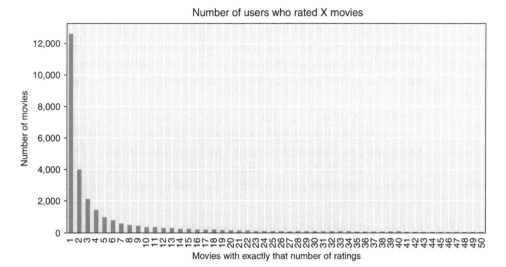

Figure 8.16 A chart that illustrates how many movies have received *X* ratings in MovieGEEKS site

Usually, the more users who've rated a film, the more popular, so as you require more overlapping users, you'll also look at more popular items and less personalized movies. The recommendations become better as fewer movies become candidates. Reading through the chapter, and indeed the book, should give you an idea of what to choose in each of the previous options.

In chapter 9, you'll look at how to evaluate a recommender. Before going crazy about how to select the correct values, read that and then return to this list, keeping in mind what you've read. A good reference for what values to start out with can be found in "Item-based Collaborative Filtering Recommendation Algorithms" by Badrul Sarwar et al.[12] But before moving on to chapter 9, look at figure 8.16, where several of the evaluation functions are plotted. And before summarizing the chapter, let's sum up the pros and cons of neighbor collaborative filtering algorithms.

8.14 *Pros and cons of collaborative filtering*

Even if it sounds fantastic, there are issues and drawbacks of collaborative filtering that you need to consider:

- *Sparsity*—This problem is one of the biggest. Most data sets aren't dense enough to recommend items other than the most popular ones. Because most users only have a few ratings and often an e-shop will have thousands of different items, it can be difficult to find neighbors.
- *Gray sheep*—As you recall from chapter 6, gray sheep are users who've such unusual tastes that it's impossible to find related users or items.

---

[12] For more information, see http://files.grouplens.org/papers/www10_sarwar.pdf.

- *Number of ratings*—As mentioned many times, to have good collaborative recommendations, you need many ratings from a user before you can trustworthily produce recommendations. This poses a problem because most systems don't like to sit around while collecting 20 or more ratings before starting to recommend things. It's known as the cold start problem that you read about in chapter 6.
- *Similiarity*—Collaborative filtering is content-agnostic and doesn't try to fit recommendations into specific subjects. It follows the users' behavioral trends, which tend to go toward the more popular content. Another way of saying this is that because it's based on similarity, the most popular items will have much in common with more content, which puts the popular items in the recommendations more often.

The fact that collaborative filtering is content-agnostic is also a great plus. You don't have to spend any energy adding metadata to your content or collect knowledge about your users. You only need the ratings and the interactions between items. In the next chapter, you'll look at how to evaluate recommender systems.

Summary

- The pipeline of neighborhood filtering can either use user-based filtering, looking at similar users, or item-based filtering, looking at similar items.
- Use user-based filtering if there are more items than users; otherwise, use item-based filtering.
- A similarity matrix makes it possible to quickly look up similar items.
- Using a similarity table enables the system to make neighborhoods using the clustering, Top-*N*, or threshold procedures.
- The neighborhoods you find let you calculate predictions when you've a small set of similar users.
- Amazon's first stab at a recommender system was item-based collaborative filtering.

Evaluating and testing your recommender

The Netflix Prize abstracted the recommendation problem to a simplified proxy of accurately predicting ratings. It is now clear that this is just one of many components in an effective industrial recommendation system. They also need to account for factors like diversity, context, evidence, freshness, and novelty.

—Xavier Amatriain et al.[1]

After studying this chapter, you'll gain experience in the following areas:

- Evaluating the effectiveness of a recommender algorithm
- Splitting data sets into training data and test data
- Building offline experiments to evaluate recommender systems
- A rough understanding of online testing

Why did you implement a recommender? What did you want to gain? Do you want to earn more? Have more visitors? Try out new technology? No matter what you answer, it might not directly translate into a way to calculate whether or not you're improving.[2] You often hear about algorithms that are better or slightly improved compared to the current cutting-edge algorithms, but improving what and how?

---

[1] Amatriain, Xavier et al., *Past, Present, and Future of Recommender Systems: An Industry Perspective* (Recsys, 2016).

[2] *Start with Why: How Great Leaders Inspire Everyone to Take Action* (Portfolio; Reprint edition, 2011) by Simon Sinek, is completely unrelated to recommender systems, but is an interesting book on how you need to understand why your business is there.

This chapter is about evaluating recommender systems, or rather, how to attempt to do so. General agreement among recommender system researchers is that it's close to impossible to evaluate a recommender system or algorithm without having a live system to test it out on. Still, it's important to know if your recommender system is going in the right direction.

9.1   Business wants lift, cross-sales, up-sales, and conversions

In this chapter, you'll work through how best to evaluate a system using the data you have. We'll also talk about how to test a live website. While you can simulate visitors and visits to give the data to run on, it doesn't make sense to simulate visits for evaluating recommenders.

Figure 9.1 illustrates the evaluation cycle of a recommender system; we'll look closer at each step as we progress through the chapter. Certain tasks aren't usually associated with the evaluation of recommender systems, but they're important if you want to develop and maintain one.

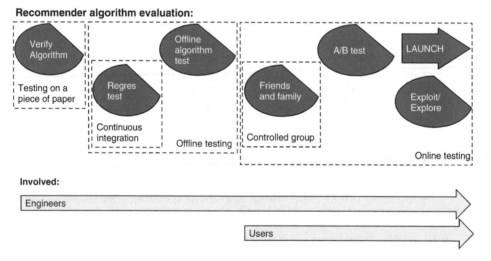

Figure 9.1   The evaluation cycle of recommender systems and who's involved in the process

One thing that's often forgotten is that all data applications are living things (not in the AI sense) and require maintenance and monitoring. Performance is a product of the data being used, which is updated constantly. The behavior of the system changes if the data changes, and the system's performance and predictive power might diverge or degrade.

Let's run through the tasks shown in figure 9.1 before going too deeply into the details. I recommend you start with the simplest algorithm first, then increase complexity if needed. When you've selected the algorithm, the first step is to verify it.

Take a small data set with something like 5 users and 10 items and see if the algorithm makes sense. Play around with it and if you're satisfied, then start implementing the algorithm. It's a good idea to have regression tests continuously running in such a way that if somebody makes an update to the data, it won't hurt the performance of the system. When the algorithm is coded and functionality is tested (continuously), it's time to do offline algorithm evaluation using a data set. If the offline evaluation is successful, you can introduce the output to humans.

Often, you'll start out with a control group, which many call *friends and family*. This is where you'll have to answer to your boss (who didn't read this book and doesn't know anything about recommender systems but is an expert and knows there's something wrong with his recommendations because they didn't look perfect to him). Friends and family will only get you so far, so to ensure everything is great with the recommender system, it can be unleashed upon the happy users—but only a small percentage to verify if it works and increases the Key Performance Indicators (KPI) that you're after. If that's successful, it's time to launch the algorithm for everybody.

Many people will probably stop there, but a trend that's gaining attention is exploit/explore, which means that you let the system decide which algorithm it should use based on how users respond to the output. We'll look at this briefly later in this chapter. Speaking of which, we've many things to talk about, so let's dig in. Before we start talking about how to evaluate your recommender, let's talk a little more about why you need to do this.

9.2 Why is it important to evaluate?

Is your recommender system running correctly? After having sworn, sweated, and bled to make a recommender system work, you don't want it to fail. Often, testing a recommender system is a quest for finding proof that it works. You also hope *not* to find signs that it might not work perfectly or that it returns unexpected results to more than half the users. It'd certainly be good to know this was going to happen before all your users did!

Often a system will be over-fitted to the taste of the stakeholders. The boss calls and says, "My daughter didn't like any of the recommendations your system produced. Fix it or you don't have to fix anything else." Of course, he says this late on a Friday afternoon and you've made plans for the weekend. Maybe I'm stretching it a bit, but you do need to understand who your customers are because different people want different recommendations.

With that in mind, it's important to have a clear idea of what question you're asking. Let's talk about Netflix again. One of its goals is retention of subscribers, but that's only measurable once a month. Netflix has deduced (probably by looking at the data) that user retention is correlated with the user watching more. But a user watching more content can also indicate other things, not necessarily that they'll be around a long time. Maybe the user's girlfriend left him and he has time on his hands; maybe it's something else entirely. More to the point, though, the goal might not be immediately measurable, and the things that are measurable might not uniquely indicate what you want to know.

Because we're only interested in the actual recommender system, we're interested in an evaluation that shows which recommender gives the best result based on the MovieTweetings[3] data that we're using in our example. To evaluate something that happens to many people (in MovieGEEKs' case, what happens is that a person receives a recommendation), we need to dive into statistics. I'm not going to teach statistics in this book, but I'll give you an overview of what you should consider when testing the recommenders you've implemented. First, we'll frame our question as a hypothesis.

HYPOTHESIS

A *hypothesis* describes the goal of the test. For us, that could be "Recommender *B* produces recommendations that are clicked more often than recommendations from Recommender *A*." The click event is also called the *click-through rate* (CTR).

Is the hypothesis clear enough to run a test? Will the mail carrier, to whom you've shown a copy of the hypothesis, understand it in exactly the same way as you do?

9.3 How to interpret user behavior

Figure 9.2 shows four scenarios for a visitor arriving on a website:

- *Visit 1 is simple.* Your system records that it showed the landing page and then nothing happened. Should you then assume—or not—that the visitor has seen the recommendations?
- *Visit 2 shows that several pages are viewed.* Here you must assume that the recommendations are presented but the visitor didn't show any interest because they clicked something different.
- *Visit 3 is ideal.* The visitor arrives and clicks a recommendation.
- *Visit 4 poses a question.* How should you value the visit? Does it count as one click or two? Possibly it could make more sense to say that a recommendation algorithm is successful if a user clicks one or more times on the recommendations. But again, that depends on the domain you're in.

9.4 What to measure

There appear to be two types of goals for recommender systems:

- To make your customers happy and hopefully earn money at the same time.
- To make as much money as possible and, if you must make your customers happy to do that, then you'll do it, but only enough to earn money.

You, the engineer, need to make your boss happy, which he will be if the customers are happy (and spending money). Customers' goals are nearly the same: they want to be

---

[3] For more information, see https://github.com/sidooms/MovieTweetings.

Unique visit

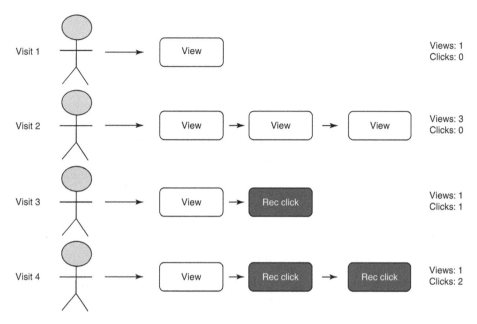

Figure 9.2 Different scenarios of user behavior. Visit 3 is ideal because the user viewed and clicked a recommendation.

happy and will spend money if they are, but they don't have your boss's goal of maximizing their spending!

Let's forget about the money for a moment and think about happy customers. How can you make the customers happy? The answer differs from individual to individual and from domain to domain, but here's what makes me happy when I shop online:

1   *The site understands my tastes.* I don't like to receive recommendations that are obviously wrong.
2   *The site gives me a nice variety of recommendations.* I want my recommendations like I want nature—full of diversity.
3   *The site surprises me.* I want to see things that I never knew I wanted, but now I want them.

As a site or content maintainer, you'd also want to add:

4   The site covers everything in the catalog.

We'll look more at the details for each of these.

9.4.1   *Understanding my taste: Minimizing prediction error*

One way of measuring how well a recommender understands my tastes is by saying that it must predict whether I like an item that I know and have already rated. This can be done by measuring how often the recommender gets close to predicting the correct rating.

Another way to look at it is as *decision-support metrics*, which divide the predictions into groups where the user will react in a similar way. If the system predicts a film above a 7 on a scale of 1–10, then I'd probably be interested in watching it. If it's below 7 but above 3, it's a film that I wouldn't refuse to watch if my wife wanted to watch it. Below that I'd put my foot down and say, "No way!" If the recommender predicts a rating that's somewhere inside the ranges that fit where I'd rate it, then it's probably okay. If it's in a different group, then it will make me lose time and/or lose good content. And, eventually, I'll lose confidence in the recommender if that happens too often.

9.4.2   *Diversity*

Let's take a quick detour into the Bible, where we find this in the book of Matthew:

> *For unto everyone that hath shall be given, and he shall have abundance: but from him that hath not shall be taken even that which he hath.*
>
> —Matthew 25:29, King James Version

You're probably asking how this relates to recommender systems. The Bible verse is the basis of what's called *the Matthew effect*. A more familiar interpretation is "the rich get richer and the poor get poorer." If you view a popular item as rich and unpopular item as poor, then the issue here is that you'll have items in your catalog that are recommended often because they're popular.

It's good that popular items are recommended often, but these items might show up in too many recommendations, thus becoming even more popular, while other potentially great items don't get shown because they aren't yet popular. With popular items always being favored, you're also creating what we call a *filter bubble*.[4] This can be a good thing, because you'll always get recommendations for what you like. But on the other hand, you'll never know if there's something slightly different that you might like even more than the popular item but haven't yet experienced.

In addition to the filter problem, there's also the fact that the original idea of a recommender system is to help users navigate a larger catalog than what is found on a single page of a shop. If the recommender only shows popular items, then that advantage is lost. (Okay, I know there are many other advantages as well, but this is an important one.)

It's hard, however, to measure whether your system is successfully diverse and also hard for your system to be diverse when it's personalized. Researchers have attempted

---

[4] For more information, see https://en.wikipedia.org/wiki/Filter_bubble.

to calculate a diversity measure by calculating the average dissimilarity between all pairs of the recommended items. Look at "Improving Recommendation Diversity" by Keith Bradley and Barry Smyth for more on the subject. You can find the article at www.academia.edu/2655896/Improving_recommendation_diversity.

9.4.3 Coverage

Diversity leads nicely into coverage because the better the diversity, the better the coverage. One of the main reasons for implementing a recommender system is to enable users to navigate the full catalog, which is known as *content coverage*. Coverage refers both to ensuring the algorithm will recommend everything in your catalog and whether it can recommend something to all registered users, which is called *user coverage*.

The brute-force way of calculating the user coverage is to iterate over all users, call the recommender algorithm, and then see if it returns anything. This can be done as shown in listing 9.1. You can view the script for this method in /evaluator/coverage.py.

Listing 9.1 Calculating coverage

```
def calculate_coverage(self):
    for user in self.all_users:           <——— Runs through all users
        user_id = str(user['user_id'])
        recset =                                       Gets recommendations
          self.recommender.recommend_items(user_id)    for the user
        if recset:                                     Checks if the
            self.users_with_recs.append(user)          recommender
            for rec in recset:                         returned a
                self.items_in_rec[rec[0]] += 1         recommendations
                                          Appends the user
                                          to the list of users
                                          that received recs
    no_movies = Movie.objects.all().count()
    no_movies_in_rec = len(self.items_in_rec.items())
    no_users = self.all_users.count()
    no_users_in_rec = len(self.users_with_recs)
    user_coverage = float(no_users_in_rec/ no_users)    <——— Calculates user coverage
    movie_coverage = float(no_movies_in_rec/ no_movies)     Calculates item
    return user_coverage, movie_coverage                    coverage
```

Shows each recommend item

Adds to the items in the rec

This method solves both coverage calculations—content and user. User coverage is defined as follows:

$$coverage_{user} = \frac{\sum_{u \in U} P_u}{|U|}$$

where

$$P_u = \begin{cases} 1 & : if\,|recset| > 0 \\ 0 & : else \end{cases}$$

$|U|$ = *number of all users*

$|recset|$ = *number of recommendationss the recommender returns for user u*

Using the result of the method execution, you can also calculate the catalog coverage, which is defined by:

$$coverage_{catalogue} = \frac{|all\ items\ in\ recs|}{|I|}$$

where $|I|$ = *number of items in the catalogue.*

For this coverage, you'll also need the total number of items in the catalog. Using the `calculate_coverage` method from listing 9.1, I found that the item-item collaborative filtering method implemented in chapter 8 has a coverage of 13%. Out of the 26,380 movie items in MovieGEEKs' data set, only 3,473 movies would make it into a recommendation.[5]

While running this code, I also collected which movies were recommended. This resulted in the histogram seen in figure 9.3, which shows how many movies were recommended only once between all the recommendations produced for all the users. The movies that are most popular are the ones that are in the long tail (which is a bit counterintuitive compared to the long-tail problem we talked about earlier). The figure was cut because there are movies that have appeared in more than 100 recommendation sets.

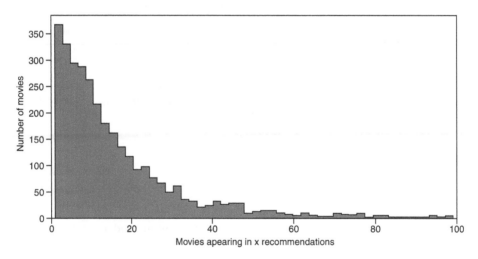

Figure 9.3   How many movies are shown *X* number of times. More than 350 movies are shown in only one recommendation. Counterintuitively, the movies that are most popular are the ones that are in the long tail.

Note that 3,473 movies out of 26,380 isn't many. Maybe it's a good idea to add a content-based recommender, which we'll talk about in the following chapter. The coverage code shown in listing 9.1 can be run by running this line in the following listing.

---

[5] This depends on which parameters you use to train it.

Listing 9.2   Running the coverage for the collaborative filtering algorithm

```
>python -m evaluator.coverage -cf
```

If you run `--help` instead (as shown in the following listing), you'll see that you've an option to run the coverage evaluation on each of the algorithms we'll look at in the rest of the book.

Listing 9.3   Running help for the collaborative filtering algorithm

```
Evaluate coverage of the recommender algorithms.

optional arguments:
  -h, --help  show this help message and exit
  -fwls       run evaluation on fwls rec
  -funk       run evaluation on funk rec
  -cf         run evaluation on cf rec
  -cb         run evaluation on cb rec
  -ltr        run evaluation on rank rec
```

But wait with running the others until you've trained models; otherwise, it'll take a long time to calculate the coverage.

9.4.4   *Serendipity*

You want to be surprised by finding things in your recommendations that you love but never knew you would. Serendipity is about giving the user that sensation, so that all their visits aren't more of the same. Serendipity is subjective and difficult to calculate, so I'll ask you to remember that it's important and to make sure that you don't constrain the recommender's returns too much. Constraining means less serendipity. You can read about attempts to apply metrics serendipity in the article *Beyond Accuracy: Evaluating Recommender Systems by Coverage and Serendipity.*[6]

You now have several different concepts of what you should measure and evaluate. You're one step closer to doing an evaluation or your recommender system, but first, as a former software developer, I've a few more things that I need to get off my chest.

9.5   *Before implementing the recommender...*

Another proverb: The lamp will only burn as well as the oil you pour in it, so here are a few steps to consider:

- Verify the algorithm
- Verify the data
- Do a regression test

Let's look at these in more detail.

---

[6] For more information, see http://mng.bz/nkGC.

9.5.1   *Verify the algorithm*

It's a silly thing to add, but you'd be surprised how often somebody reads a scientific article that sounds so cool, then spends months implementing it before somebody finally thinks to ask about the elephant in the living room. Too late they realize that this algorithm won't work with the data available or produce the output they need. Do yourself a favor and write down a simple scenario in which you can rigorously calculate your way through a small example where the algorithm is used. Consider carefully what data you can provide as input, and be sure to agree with stakeholders about what the output is going to be.

This simple scenario can also work as a way to verify that the system is running. For example, the algorithm you'll look at in this chapter takes a couple of hours to run on the full data set. If you're using that to debug the algorithm, you'll never finish. You'll do one correction and start the builder, then life happens, and when the algorithm finishes, you've forgotten everything. If you're unlucky, your next step is to do a new correction that basically undoes the correction you did first. Do yourself a favor and follow the steps in figure 9.4.

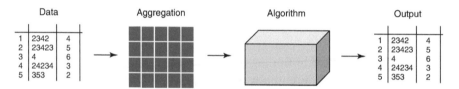

Figure 9.4   Execute the algorithm by hand to test if you've data and whether it produces the right output.

DATA

Test whether the data you need is either available or possible to produce. Is the data persisted far enough into the past to be usable? It's great if you save all users' ratings and behaviors, but if the system deletes everything that's a day old, you might have a problem.

You should also look at the diversity of the data. Do you have data of users who interact with all your catalog or only part of it? You need to do something special to get those untouched items into play.

ARCHITECTURE AND AGGREGATION

Having the data isn't enough. Can you retrieve it? If so, can you do the aggregation that you want? In SQL databases, it's easy to do joins between tables, but that might not be the case in a database such as MongoDB. It seems obvious, but consider this step before relying on the data.

ALGORITHM

How complicated is the algorithm? Is it easy to implement? Does it require mathematics that is difficult to implement or performance-wise too much to do on a computer? And if you create a small example using a small data set, is it possible to make a naive implementation in, for example, a Jupyter notebook to illustrate that it can be done? When these questions are satisfied, you can start implementing your algorithm.

9.5.2 *Regression testing*

As a software engineer, you should know about *regression testing*, which means that you should have a test set that can be run either nightly or at least every time somebody makes a change to the code base. Often people argue that these algorithms are way too complicated to run automatic tests on. If you run into one of those people, please rap them on their knuckles, especially if they claim that the business can't afford it.

Take, for example, the collaborative filtering algorithm. It's built as a pipeline with several steps. If you look at each, then you can test the pieces. For example, the similarity method can easily be tested if it responds correctly to simple vectors. If you call the similarity method with the same vector, the similarity should return one, while two vectors that are orthogonal to each other should be -1 or 0, depending on which similarity function you use.

Look at the tests I did in the test folder of the project.[7] One of the similarity function tests looks like that shown in the next listing. Again, you can view the code in the /item_similarity_calculator_test.py script.

Listing 9.4 Similarity function test

```
def test_simple_similarity(self):
    builder = ItemSimilarityMatrixBuilder(0)

    no_items = len(set(self.ratings['movie_id']))
    cor = builder.build(ratings=self.ratings, save=False)
    self.assertIsNotNone(cor)
    self.assertEqual(cor.shape[0], no_items,
      "Expected correlations matrix to have a row for each item")
    self.assertEqual(cor.shape[1], no_items,
      "Expected correlations matrix to have a column for each item")
    self.assertEqual(cor[WONDER_WOMAN][AVENGERS], - 1,
      "Expected Wolverine and Star Wars to have similarity 0.5")
    self.assertEqual(cor[AVENGERS][AVENGERS], 1,
      "Expected items to be similar to themselves similarity 1")
```

I created a small dataset to test, which lets me run small tests to verify that each step of the collaborative filtering pipeline is working. With this in place, it's time to look at the offline evaluation, which is typically where we start talking about the evaluation of machine-learning and recommender algorithms.

---

[7] For more information, see http://mng.bz/rS4s.

9.6   *Types of evaluation*

You have several ways to test a recommender algorithm. Not all of them are going to give you an accurate view of how the algorithm will perform if you add it to your website. The sad truth is that the only real way to know is to put one in action on your site. But before you do that, you can ease the transition by doing other evaluations.

We'll assume that you already have a data set containing ratings. To do a true evaluation, you need what's called a *complete ground truth set*, which is a data set containing information about all combinations of users and content. If you have that, however, you might not need a recommender system because the user already knows exactly how he feels about all items. If you don't have that set, you need to instead assume that the user-item combinations present in the data are the truth and representative of all users.

You can test in three types of scenarios: offline experiments, controlled user experiments, and online experiments. Recommender system researchers talk about offline experiments not working, and controlled and online experiments being too expensive, but sometimes it's hard to make everybody happy. Sean McNee and fellow researchers at GroupLens[8] point out that the focus on improving the accuracy of recommender systems has been misguided and even detrimental. Each experiment (offline, controlled user, and online) has a purpose. You only need to select the right one for the job.

9.7   *Offline evaluation*

The idea of offline evaluation is to use data that you regard as truthful. Then split the data into two parts and feed one part to the recommender. Use the other part to verify that the recommender predicts ratings on items in the set that were hidden to it; those that are close to the actual ratings or those that produce recommendations that contain items that were highly rated in hidden data as shown in figure 9.5. Or you can say that the users consumed items they rated even if they didn't like them, so the items still count for something.

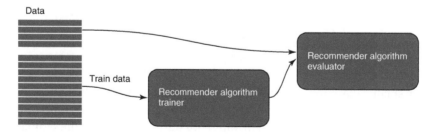

Figure 9.5   Offline evaluation splits data into training and test sets before testing the recommender algorithm.

---

8   Sean M. McNee et al., "Accurate Is Not Always Good: How Accuracy Metrics Have Hurt Recommender Systems," http://files.grouplens.org/papers/mcnee-chi06-acc.pdf.

This isn't regarded as a good way of evaluating recommenders, but so far it's been hard to come up with a better way—unless you're Netflix and you can do live A/B testing on all new features (which we'll talk about in a bit). Offline evaluation continues to be a way to measure the effectiveness of the recommender. To complicate matters further, a recommender can pass an offline evaluation with flying colors but still fail miserably in production.

There are many ifs and maybes, but you'll do this with the recommender you looked at in chapter 8. In the following chapters, we'll talk about how to evaluate the algorithms you look at. If you want to do research into recommender systems, it's best to have a good understanding of how to implement, test, and present new algorithms or dialects of existing ones. I recommend looking at Michael Ekstrand et al.'s article on the recommender research ecosystem.[9]

9.7.1 What to do when the algorithm doesn't produce any recommendations

Often you'll run into cases where the recommender doesn't produce any recommendations or maybe not a long enough list of them. This can be a problem when evaluating the system, so often you fill in the blanks with a simple algorithm, such as the most popular items, the average rating for the item, or an average of the user ratings. A slightly more complicated solution is something that's called baseline recommenders, which we'll look at in chapter 11. This is also briefly discussed in the article I recommended in the previous section.

9.8 Offline experiments

An *offline experiment* uses the data that you have and measures whether the algorithm is good. With offline experiments, you've limited options for finding out what you want to know. This is because the data you have will probably be based on the behavior of users where there was either no recommender system or there was one that you were hoping to demonstrate is inferior to the one you want to test. You can only test if it's as good (or as bad) as the one used to collect it.

We've agreed that a great benefit of a recommender system is providing users a selection of new items that they want to use. But if you only have data where the level of new (and surprising) items isn't high, then how can you test it? You'd need users to provide feedback on the complete catalog to know what a good recommendation is. For now, because you don't have any other way of testing your algorithms before exposing people to those, this will have to do.

One way you'll look at testing the algorithm is to see if you can make the recommender predict the user's rating. If you hide part of the high ratings as an alternative, you'll see how many of those hidden ratings are recommended by the recommender. So how will you measure what's good?

---

[9] Michael Ekstrand et al., "Rethinking the Recommender Research Ecosystem: Reproducibility, Openness, and LensKit," http://files.grouplens.org/papers/p133-ekstrand.pdf.

MEASURING ERROR METRICS

To determine what's good, you'll measure the difference between the ratings in your historical data set with what the recommender algorithm outputs. When we talk about *error*, it's exactly that—the difference between a user's rating and the recommender's prediction of that rating: $error = r - p$

In chapter 7, you looked at mean absolute error (MAE), mean squared error (MSE), and root mean squared error (RMSE). To quickly summarize the MAE takes the absolute value of each of the differences and finds the average of those. The reason for taking the absolute value is that if the recommender guesses low in one prediction and high in the next, those two would cancel out each other. But if you remove the sign, you'll see positive numbers, and this is what you want so that you can measure the distance between the two.

What these all have in common is that they sum up all errors (squared or not). If there are users who've many ratings, the recommender would have an easier time predicting the ratings, while users with only a few ratings would be difficult. The RMSE will put big penalties on big errors, such that one big error will count much more than several smaller ones. While if you use the MAE, big errors or outliers don't push the error much. If it's important that none of your users gets bad recommendations, then you should use RMSE. But if you realize that you can't make all users happy, then it's probably enough to use MAE.

Figure 9.6 illustrates two users. User 1 has added four ratings and let's say the system knows him well, so it's good at predicting ratings for him. User 2 has added only one rating, so the system doesn't know him as well. If you average all the prediction errors, you'll get $(1 + 1 + 1 + 1 + 3) / 5 = 1.4$, while if you average the users' errors first, then you get $((1 + 1 + 1 + 1) / 4 + 3 / 1)$. You have an average of 2 as the error, which better indicates the overall user experience.

If you look at each item instead, the popular items will be the ones easier to predict. If you've many items in the long tail, it might be worth thinking about what you're optimizing for. Maybe you can remove the popular items from the test set. Or you can divide the data (if you have enough) into a set with popular items and evaluate that, then separately evaluate the other data set with long-tail items.

If you take the average of all the rating errors, the bulk of your result will come from the user you know more about, while the one with the fewest ratings wouldn't contribute much. You get around that by measuring for each user and then taking their average. Then each user would contribute equally, and the evaluation won't favor users with more ratings. But if you're out to verify the predictive error on all the test data, then you should average over all of the users:

$$MAE = \frac{1}{|RECSET|} \sum_{r \in RECSET} |r - p|$$

where $RECSET$ = *the set of all recommended items for all users.*

Figure 9.6 Users should have equal weight in the evaluation. Here two users' ratings are shown. User 1 has added four ratings, while user 2 has only added one. If you average all ratings, then the bad experiences of user 2 will drown in the good ratings of user 1.

As mentioned, it might not be too important to the users if the recommender can predict their ratings down to a decimal (unless you're trying to win a competition). It's likely they'll want it the recommender to list only the things they like and leave out the things they don't like. Maybe you don't care if it's good at predicting things that the user has rated low.[10] (By the way, most people don't know how to describe what they do and don't like, so asking the recommender to do it is a bit of a complex requirement.)

Using the metrics we talked about here presents another issue (even if we only look at the good recommendations), which is that all ratings are considered equally important. If you look at the problem from a Top-*N* recommendation instead of a rating prediction, you'd be more interested in having good recommendations at the top but not care so much about what happens further down. Let's look at several rank-aware metrics.

MEASURING DECISION-SUPPORT METRICS

Decision support is about taking each element and asking if the system was right or wrong. If you consider a recommender system and look at each recommended item and compare it to a user's actual consumption, you can have four outcomes: for a given item, it can either be recommended or not, and the user can either have consumed it or not. If the recommender recommends the item, we say it's positive, and then if the user con-

---

[10] To account for this, you could say that the error of items rated below average by the user is something small, as long as the prediction is also below the user's average.

sumes the item, we say it was the right decision. We consider it positive if the item was rec-ommended and true if the recommender and the user agree, so you get these outcomes:

- *True positive (TP)*—Item recommended and consumed by the user.
- *False positive (FP)*—Item was recommended but the user didn't consume it.
- *False negative (FN)*—The recommender didn't include the item in a recommen-dation and the user consumed it.
- *True negative (TN)*—It wasn't recommended and the user didn't consume it.

This is often depicted as a table, which is shown in figure 9.7.

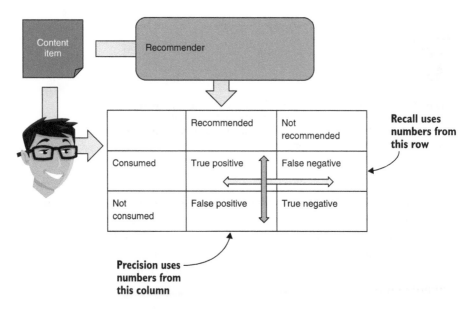

Figure 9.7   How precision and recall are calculated. comparing if users consumed the same things that were recommended by the recommender.

Having the outcome of your test in this format enables you to define two different metrics:

- *Precision*—What fraction of the recommended items the user consumed:

$$Precision = \frac{True\ Positive}{True\ Positive + False\ Positive}$$

- *Recall*—What, out of all the items that the user consumed, was recommended:

$$Recall = \frac{True\ Positive}{True\ Positive + False\ Negative}$$

Often a recommender system is implemented such that it should give the user at least one choice for what to buy or view next. It's important that there's always at least one relevant object in a Top-*N* recommendation. It's often considered more important to optimize precision, while not putting too much importance on whether the user gets all the possible relevant items (the recall).

How do you translate this into a metric that you can use for all your recommendations? Decision-support comes from information filtering, originally used for calculating the quality of search results. A search result can be long, so in the world of recommenders, they've restricted the measurement to look only at the *k* top elements.

PRECISION AT *K*

The *k* top elements are measured by taking the number of relevant items between the first *k* items. Relevance can be a hard boundary, considering that an item is relevant if the user has rated it more than four stars, or you could say it must be more than one star from the user's mean. If you're talking about implicit ratings, then it could also be items consumed or something altogether different. But relevance needs to be decided on.

If you're interested in the precision within the first *k* items, called *precision at k*, it's defined as follows:

$$P@k(u) = \frac{\#\{\ relevant\ content\ in\ the\ top\ k\ postitions\ \}}{k}$$

If you want to use precision, you can calculate the average over all users by summing up all precisions and then dividing by the number of users. But if you have a top 10, then you want to have relevant items all over the place, but most importantly at the top. For this reason, more and more companies are using ranking metrics to evaluate their recommenders. The first one we'll look at uses precision at k to calculate the mean average precision.

MEASURING RANKING METRICS

The first item recommended is always the most important one, then the second is second-most important, and so on. When evaluating, you should take that into account. In the following sections, we'll look at ranking metrics that do exactly that.

MEAN AVERAGE PRECISION (MAP)

The average precision (AP) can be used to measure how good the rank is by running the precision from 1 to *m*, where *m* is the number of items that are recommended (usually denoted as *k*). To take it a step further, take the average of the precisions over the first element, then the next two until you arrive at *m*. This is shown in figure 9.8 and in the following formula:

$$AP(u) = \frac{\sum_{k=1}^{m} P@k(u)}{m}$$

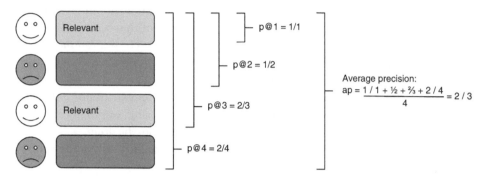

Figure 9.8 Calculating AP by taking the average of each precision at *k*, with *k* being from 1 to the number of items recommended.

This works per recommendation, so if you want to use it as a measure to evaluate a recommender, you can then take the mean of the average (or mean average precision—MAP) over all recommendations:

$$MAP = \frac{\sum_{u \in U} AP(u)}{|U|}$$

DISCOUNTED CUMULATIVE GAIN

The *discounted cumulative gain* (DCG) is hard to define but easy enough to understand. It's about finding each relevant item and then penalizing the items the farther down it is in the list. It's much like the MAP that you looked at earlier. But where the MAP only works with relevance, the DCG looks at levels of relevancy.

To determine DCG, you give each item a relevancy score. In the case of a recommender system, it can be the predicted rating or profit on the item. Here, relevance is also denoted as gain. You could have also called it the discounted cumulative relevance. The relevance is discounted by the position in the list: these relevance scores are added up to get the discounted cumulative gain.

$$DCG = \sum_{i=1}^{k} \frac{2^{rel[i]} - 1}{\log_2([i] + 2)}$$

DCG has an even stricter big brother called the normalized discounted cumulative gain (NDCG).

NORMALIZED DISCOUNTED CUMULATIVE GAIN

The thing about DCG is that it isn't easy to compare with DCG calculated in other evaluations. To get around that, one can use the big brother, NDCG, which when compared to the DCG, is written as a proportion of the optimal ranking. You'll have 1 if the ordering is optimal:

$$nDCG = \frac{DCG}{IDCG}$$

The NDCG is often used in competitions at Kaggle.com.[11] If you're interested in the implementations of these in Python or other languages, check out the GitHub repository at https://github.com/benhamner/Metrics.

9.8.1 Preparing the data for the experiment

With the different offline evaluation methods in place, you need to look at the data needed for the experiment. You'll need to go into tedious details about the data and how to divide it.

To start, figure out what data you have and whether it illustrates the reality you want to evaluate. You probably have too little data and too many users that you know too little about, or you have so much data that you're drowning. It's the usual problem: the grass is always greener on the other side. No matter what situation you're in, it'll seem like the opposite problem is the easier one.

HANDLING NEW USERS

An example of a challenge—one I've already talked plenty about in this book—is that you need data to personalize. If you've many users with only a few ratings, then it's a bit harsh to penalize the recommender if it can't recommend something sensible to a user that you basically don't know anything about. You'll usually filter users away with only a small number of interactions in your data. Another problem is what to do if you've too much data. In that case, you might need to try sampling.

SAMPLING

Sampling is about extracting a subset of the data that represents the same distribution across communities and oddities as the full data set. That can be difficult. At its simplest form, sampling is a matter of randomly picking items for your subset.

The more accepted way of sampling is something called *stratified sampling*. If you've a data set with 10% men and 90% women, then stratified sampling ensures that your sample will contain the same distribution of male and female users.

FINDING GOOD CANDIDATES FOR THE EVALUATION

For this experiment, you should remove all users with few ratings. In chapter 7, you learned that similarity only counts if there's an overlap of more than 20 items. To allow for that, you need to remove users with fewer than 20 items. In chapter 7, you also saw that 20 items was a large number. If you look at figure 9.9, you can see that a restriction of a minimum of 20 ratings will leave fewer than 10,000 users eligible for recommendations.

As with everything, it's up to you and the rules of the domain as to where to set the boundary. The algorithm won't work for users with only one rating. A user with only one registered rating also won't do anything for collaborative filtering algorithms, which work on binding items based on users having rated them. But removing all users who've rated fewer than 20 items also seems to paint a misguided picture of the

---

[11] For more information, see www.kaggle.com/wiki/NormalizedDiscountedCumulativeGain.

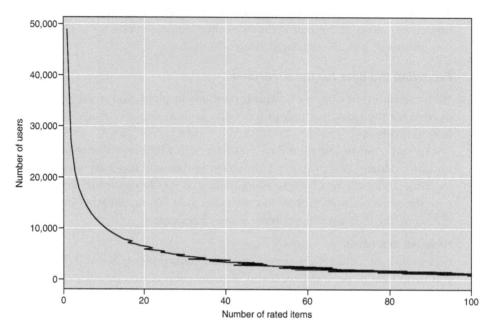

Figure 9.9 **The plot shows how many users remain in the data set if you specify a minimum number of ratings a user should have before they're included.**

e-commerce world, at least if you're making a recommender for something that has customers with similar buying habits, such as a bookstore.

In most e-shops, it takes time to arrive at 20 items. I'd test this a few times, putting the minimum as low as possible to determine the effect of the recommender on the result. No matter what you decide, you still need to split the data.

SPLITTING THE DATA INTO TEST, TRAINING, AND VALIDATION SETS

When performing the experiment, you need data for the recommender to train and calculate the predictions, but you also need data to test whether the predications work. To handle this, you'll split the data. You need three data sets: test, training, and validation.

The *test set* is where you calculate how good the algorithm is at predicting and producing ratings. But if you keep correcting the recommender system to run better on the test set, you'll end up with a recommender system that's good at predicting the things in the test set, but perhaps not so good at predicting untested material.

The test set should only be used once when you've finished optimizing the system. That leaves you with the training set. What you can do is to split the training set further, so that you've a training set (used to create the model) and a validation/dev set (used to optimize the variables of the recommender). In short, you'd split the data set into a test set and a training set. Then optimize the recommender (it could be the number of recommendations that should be returned, the minimum similarity that should be saved, and so on), then cut the training set into two sets for training and dev/validation.

You should optimize the recommender one parameter at a time. Or try your luck with grid search or even randomized search.[12] When you've an optimized model, use the test set to calculate the evaluation measure.

For the remainder of this section, we'll assume the test set is already separate. To use any of the metrics you spent so much time learning, you need two things—or more precisely—you need two data sets (well, 3, but we'e assuming that you took out the test set already). You'll get these by splitting your historical data set into two parts as shown in figure 9.10.

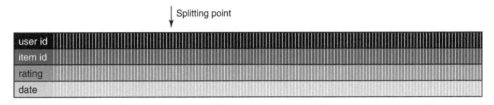

Figure 9.10 The historical data contains a long list of tuples, each describing a rating done by a user on an item. How the data is split greatly influences how the evaluation goes.

You'll use one part to teach the recommender algorithm and one part to evaluate what it has learned. Before you find a saw to cut the data set in two, let's consider what you're trying to do because that will affect how you should slice and dice the data.

Let's say you have a small data set. I cut table 9.1 out of the rating table in the MovieGEEKs site.

Table 9.1 A small sample of the MovieTweetings data set

user_id	movie_id	rating
1	0068646	10.00
1	0113277	10.00
2	0816711	8.00
2	0422720	8.00
2	0454876	8.00
2	0790636	7.00
3	1300854	7.00
3	2170439	7.00
3	2203939	6.00
4	1300854	7.00

---

[12] In theory, grid search and random search should return the same result. But a grid search is exhaustive while a random search isn't and is therefore faster.

We'll use this data to show how the different splitting techniques work.

RANDOM SPLITTING

Often when you deal with predictive machine-learning algorithms, it's normal to pick a percentage p of the data and use that for training, then use the rest for testing the trained algorithm. Many libraries will take care of this for you (Scikit-Learn to name one).[13] In a recommender system, you've the problem that splitting ratings randomly will make the recommender train with ratings that are added after the ones that it needs to predict.

> **NOTE** Recommenders often don't distinguish between ratings done now or a year ago, but a rating's age might have an effect on the recommender's ability to predict ratings.

It's a good idea to split the data around 80–20, but that isn't a rule. It's important to have as much data as possible to train the algorithm, but it won't matter if you don't have a nice selection of data to verify the result. Let's randomly select two rows and take them out using two examples where this wouldn't work well. Imagine the random selection was a bit lazy and took two from the top as shown in table 9.2.

Table 9.2 Unlucky random selection where only user 1's ratings are present in the validation data

user_id	movie_id	rating
1	0068646	10.00
1	0113277	10.00

The result is that the recommender doesn't know anything about user 1, therefore can't recommend anything. The same is the case if you pull out these two lines in table 9.3.

Table 9.3 Another unlucky random selection where item 1300856 is present in the validation set but not in the training set

user_id	movie_id	rating
3	1300854	7.00
4	1300854	7.00

Now the recommender can't find any similarity for movie 1300854 and it's lost. Taking out all the ratings of a certain value isn't a problem, however.

---

[13] For more information, see http://mng.bz/X5gZ.

SPLIT BY TIME

From a recommender system evaluation's point of view, it makes more sense to split the data based on time, saying that everything before a certain point is used for training the algorithm. Only you can't train with this data because you don't have a timestamp, so you'd have to skip this option (or update the data model because the MovieTweetings data set also contains timestamps).

If you've the ratings in figure 9.11 on a timeline instead as the brief example in table 9.1 shows, you've a snapshot of how the data looks at a certain point in time. You can even test the recommender with a sliding time scale and see how the recommender would work at any point.

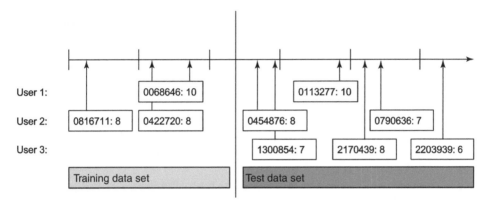

Figure 9.11   Splitting data by time creates timed snapshots of the data.

There's a cost of splitting data like that shown in figure 9.11; you'll have users who only appear in the test set, and the recommender has no idea what to do with that. Certain people would say that it's an excellent chance to see how it works with cold users, but for the evaluation of one algorithm, it doesn't seem like the right thing to do. If you're testing a hybrid that's implemented to handle cold-start users, this is perfect. Alternatively, you can clean the test data set for users who don't appear in the training set. One extreme case for this method is that you iterate through all ratings and attempt to predict it using only ratings with timestamps that are earlier than the current rating.

SPLIT BY USERS

The last option we'll look at doesn't divide the users between test and training sets. Instead, you'll divide each user's ratings between a training set and a test set. The ratings will be divided by taking the first *n* ratings in the training set and the rest in the testing set. This is illustrated in table 9.4.

Table 9.4 Data split by user

	user 1	user 2	user 3	user 4
1	0068646	0422720	1300854	1300854
2	0113277	0454876	2170439	
3		0790636	2203939	
4		0816711		

In table 9.4, the two first ratings of each user are put in the training set. Users 1 and 4 don't have any ratings in the test set, but this way all users will be in the training set, and you won't find any users in the test set that haven't been seen before.

It's a bit more demanding to split data this way because you need to order each user's rating. If you have timestamps, you can do something like this.

Listing 9.5 Getting the first two ratings of all users with SQL

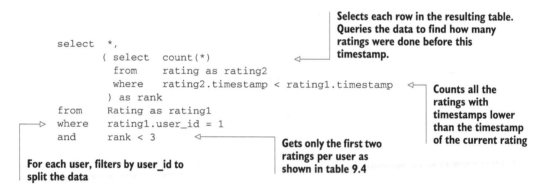

```
select   *,
         ( select   count(*)
           from     rating as rating2
           where    rating2.timestamp < rating1.timestamp
         ) as rank
from     Rating as rating1
where    rating1.user_id = 1
and      rank < 3
```

Selects each row in the resulting table. Queries the data to find how many ratings were done before this timestamp.

Counts all the ratings with timestamps lower than the timestamp of the current rating

Gets only the first two ratings per user as shown in table 9.4

For each user, filters by user_id to split the data

If you have many ratings, this takes more time, so you might be better off storing the number when you save the rating. Dividing the data like this is called the *given n* protocol; it's mentioned here because it's often used in research papers. Others would argue that this is the best way to collect one rating from all the users and will use that.

CROSS-VALIDATION

No matter how you split the data, there's a risk that you'll create a split that's favorable for one recommender. To mitigate this, try out different samples of the data for training and find the average and the variance of each of the algorithms to understand how one is better than the other. Figure 9.12 shows how the data can be divided.

k-fold cross-validations work by dividing the data into k folds then use *k*-1 folds to train the algorithm. The last fold is test data. You iterate through the full data set and allow each fold to be used as the test set. You run the evaluation *k* times and then calculate the average of them all.

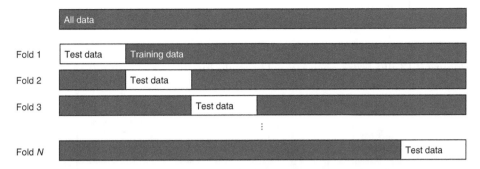

Figure 9.12 When you do k-fold cross-validation, you divide your data into chunks.

But the previous question still remains: how do you split the data? Do you divide the ratings into k different folds? But then you've the same problem: you might end up with users who are only present in one set.

Instead, you'll take all the user IDs and split those into *k* different piles. Then, you'll have the problem of users being in only one fold. To solve that, divide the ratings of the test users such that 10 ratings, for example, go into the training part and the rest are used for testing. Let's see if we can implement this.

9.9 *Implementing the experiment in MovieGEEKs*

As always, we'll look at an implementation in the MovieGEEKs website that can be found at http://mng.bz/04k5. (If you haven't done so, I recommend that you download it and run it on your machine.) The data set you'll use is called MovieTweetings, which can also be found on GitHub,[14] but if you're downloading the website, there's a script you can run to get all the data you need. For instructions on how to run the MovieGEEKs site, see the README file.

9.9.1 *The to-do list*

The implementation uses a k-fold cross-validation, where *k = 6.* The first 10 items of the test go to training the algorithm. This chapter describes an evaluation runner framework and shows how you can evaluate the algorithm from chapter 8. It uses the same evaluation framework throughout the rest of the book for each of the algorithms described. You'll evaluate it using the MAP. Figure 9.12 shows the pipeline we'll walk through. It goes through these steps:

- Cleans the data
- Splits the users into k-folds
- Repeats for each of the five folds
  - Splits data

---

[14] For more information, see https://github.com/sidooms/MovieTweetings.

  – Trains recommender
  – Evaluates recommender on the test set
  ▪ Aggregates result

Figure 9.13 illustrates each step. The code for this can be found on GitHub in the folder called\evaluator. The file is called evaluation_runner.py.[15]

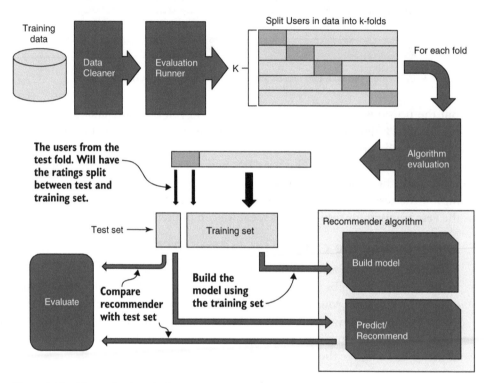

Figure 9.13   The evaluation pipeline

CLEANING DATA

Most data sets need a bit of housekeeping before you evaluate them. You can say that maybe it's cheating, but for your own sake, it's better to clean the data. Big data sets take forever to test, and in our case, all the users who rated only a few items don't help the recommender much, and the chance of recommending something sensible is small. In the code, I've chosen to do that as shown in listing 9.6. You can view this script in /evaluator/evaluator.py.

---

[15] For more information on the `split_users` method, see http://mng.bz/eL42.

Listing 9.6 Cleaning the data

Counts how many items to cut—the ones with fewer than the minimum number of ratings a user should have

With groupby, you need to reset the index to access the column by name.

```
def clean_data(self, ratings, min_ratings=5):

    user_count = ratings[['user_id', 'movie_id']]
    user_count = user_count.groupby('user_id').count()
    user_count = user_count.reset_index()
    user_ids = user_count[user_count['movie_id'] > min_ratings]['user_id']

    ratings = ratings[ratings['user_id'].isin(user_ids)]

    return ratings
```

Filters the ratings to only those from the users you filtered previously

Filters the list of user_ids to remove the users with fewer movie ratings than the min_ratings

Now that you have the data clean, spotless, and shiny, you're ready to proceed.

SPLITTING THE USERS

Splitting the users into k-folds isn't that hard, so we won't go into much detail about that here. This listing shows how you can use the Scikit-Learn tool. You'll find it in /evaluator/evalutation_runner.py

Listing 9.7 Splitting users into k-folds with the Scikit-Learn tool

```
def split_users(self, users, num_folds = 5):
    kf = KFold(n_split = num_folds)[16]
    return kf
```

Creates an instance of the k fold from sklearn[16] and initializes it to do num_folds folds

kf has a split method, which when called, returns a training set and a test set, corresponding to the next configuration of the k folds.

To get any benefit from the splitter, you can use it in a `for` loop (shown next) that runs the steps shown in figure 9.11 in the box called repeat *n* times. Again, you can see this in the /evaluator/evalutation_runner.py script.

Listing 9.8 Running the evaluation

```
def calculate_using_ratings(self, all_ratings,
                              min_number_of_ratings=5,
                              min_rank=5):

    ratings = self.clean_data(all_ratings, min_number_of_ratings)

    users = ratings.user_id.unique()
    kf = self.split_users()
```

---

[16] For more information about sklearn, see http://scikit-learn.org/stable/modules/cross_validation.html.

```
validation_no = 0
paks, raks, maes = Decimal(0.0), Decimal(0.0), Decimal(0.0)

for train, test in kf.split(users):
    validation_no += 1
    test_data, train_data = self.split_data(min_rank,
                                             ratings,
                                             users[test],
                                             users[train])

    if self.builder:
        self.builder.build(train_data)

    pak, rak = PrecisionAtK(self.K,
                            self.recommender).calculate(train_data,
                                                        test_data)

    paks += pak
    raks += rak
    maes += MeanAverageError(self.recommender).calculate(train_data,
                                                         test_data)

    results = {'pak': paks / self.folds,
               'rak': raks / self.folds,
               'mae': maes / self.folds}
return results
```

The kf.split provides the user_ids, but you still need to split the test users' data.

Calculates the mean average error

Returns the result, averaging over the number of folds

The builder is an instance of the recommender algorithm trainer class. Calling build means that it prepares the training data for recommendations. In the neighborhood algorithm, it builds the similarity matrix.

The precision at k evaluation that runs on the top five recommendations using the neighborhood recommender.

Before looking at the precision at k and the mean average error, let's look at a method for splitting the data.

SPLITTING THE DATA

As you learned in the previous section, you have k folds, where all ratings from the k-1 folds go directly to the training set, and the last fold is divided so that all items ranked lower than min_rank are in the test set and the rest are in the training set as shown in the next listing. The code can be viewed in the script evaluator/evaluation_runner.py.

> **Listing 9.9   Splitting the data into training and test data**

Creates a data frame with all the ratings of the train_users from the k-1 folds

Creates a data frame with all the ratings of the test_usersfrom the last fold

```
def split_data(self, min_rank, ratings, test_users, train_users):
    train = ratings[ratings['user_id'].isin(train_users)]
    test_temp = ratings[ratings['user_id'].isin(test_users)]
```

```
test_temp['rank'] = test_temp.groupby('user_id')['rating_timestamp'] \
                              .rank(ascending=False)
test = test_temp[test_temp['rank'] > min_rank]

additional_training_data = test_temp[test_temp['rank'] >= min_rank]
train = train.append(additional_training_data)

return test, train
```

Removes all items that rank higher than the min_rank

Ranks the content items ordered by timestamp for each user, so the item with rank 1 is the newest, and so on

Returns the two data frames

Takes all the items from the test users with ranks higher or equal to min rank . . .

. . . adds them to the training data

9.10 Evaluating the test set

Having done all these things, I'm afraid the sad truth is that you wouldn't have won the Netflix Prize with the algorithm implemented in chapter 8. That's also what they said at Netflix after they cashed out $1 million. They said that it wasn't a good way to evaluate whether a recommender is good.

The next brutal thing is that there are many parameters that you can adjust to make it look better (or worse). For example, you can restrict the users that are in the test. You can look at the precision at 10 or 100. But rest assured that everybody has received disturbingly low numbers the first time they ran an evaluation on their recommender. (I got a precision that was something like 0.063 the first time around.)

I guess I sound a bit like a sore loser, and yes, I was disappointed. But what you're looking for is a benchmark. If it's too close to zero, the recommender can't predict any of the films the users had in the test set. And that's bad. If you have something that's almost one, it means that all users in your test set receive recommendations that contain items the user has rated positively.

But before giving up, consider how often you click a recommendation and end up buying it. Let's say it's a movie site like MovieGEEKs, and you'll often arrive looking for something specific. How often do you think that you click something in the recommendations, buy it, and then rate it. That's what you're up against here. If you could create a recommender that would make a user click on a recommendation one out of 50 times, then that would be an okay start.

9.10.1 Starting out with the baseline predictor

Before you evaluate your new recommender, you should evaluate it on a simple recommender that, for example, always recommends the most popular items and see what numbers come out. Then you'll have something to compare. Listing 9.10 shows the code or you can view the script in /recs/popularity_recommender.

Listing 9.10   The most popular recommender method

```
class PopularityBasedRecs(base_recommender):

    def predict_score(self, user_id, item_id):
        avg_rating = Rating.objects.filter(~Q(user_id=user_id) &
        Q(movie_id=item_id)).values('movie_id').aggregate(Avg('rating'))
        return avg_rating['rating__avg']

    def recommend_items(self, user_id, num=6):
        pop_items = Rating.objects.filter(~Q(user_id=user_id))
                             .values('movie_id')
                             .annotate(Count('user_id'), Avg('rating'))
        sorted_items = sorted(pop_items, key=lambda item:
                             -float(item['user_id__count']))[:num]
        return sorted_items
```

The predict-score method finds all the ratings given to a particular item and averages that.

Returns a sorted list based on how many users rated it

The top-N recommender returns the items that have been rated the most.

Both methods in listing 9.10, `predict_score` and `recommend_items`, exclude all data for the current user, so the methods might give slightly different recommendations, depending on who's viewing. But for the rest, it's quite simple. The `predict_score` method calculates the item's average, and the `recommend_items` method takes the most rated items. You could also recommend items based on the highest average rating.

To evaluate this recommender algorithm run the script in listing 9.11. If you're measuring according to the MAP we talked about earlier, then test the most popular recommendation with $K = 2$ and then jump 2 until 20. The result is shown in figure 9.14. (Figure 9.15 is the same graph but for the neighborhood collaborative-filtering algorithm you saw in chapter 8.) The first evaluation (of the popularity recommender) was done by executing the script in the following listing.

Listing 9.11   Evaluating the popularity recommender in figure 9.14

```
>python -m evaluator.evaluation_runner -pop
```

The graph in figure 9.15 was done using the data created by running almost similar code as shown in this listing.

Listing 9.12   Evaluating the popularity recommender in figure 9.15

```
>python -m evaluator.evaluation_runner -cf
```

It's easy to see that you should choose this model over the popularity model because the MAP is much higher here. The problem is that to get this precision, you need to look at only the users who have rated 20 items.

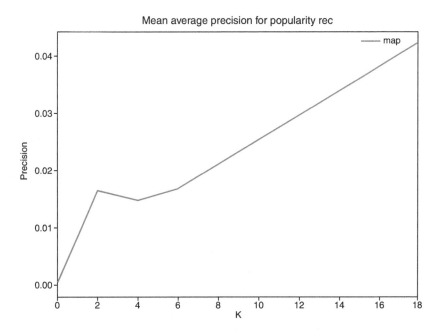

Figure 9.14   The MAP for the popularity recommender. An interesting hill appears at top-2 with a slight decrease for top-4 recs.

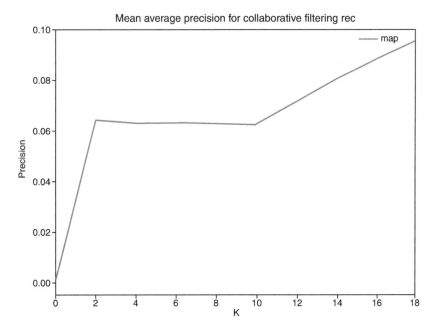

Figure 9.15   The MAP for the neighborhood model that you looked at in chapter 8

Even if the neighborhood model might not be good for recommending things to all users, it's still worth implementing and using over the popularity recommender because it has a higher precision. This is probably as easy a start as you could have to implement a hybrid recommender that will return results from the neighborhood model. When the user has too few ratings, it could spice things up a bit with results from the popularity recommender.

9.10.2 Finding the right parameters

You should begin taking away the test set. Then you should look at the training set, which is split further into smaller parts when you want to optimize the parameters of the model. The model implemented in chapter 8 has the parameters shown here and in /evaluator/evaluation_runner.py.

> **Listing 9.13 Splitting the training set**

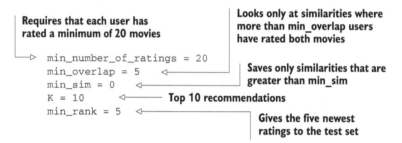

Requires that each user has rated a minimum of 20 movies

Looks only at similarities where more than min_overlap users have rated both movies

```
min_number_of_ratings = 20
min_overlap = 5
min_sim = 0
K = 10
min_rank = 5
```

Saves only similarities that are greater than min_sim

Top 10 recommendations

Gives the five newest ratings to the test set

You want these parameters to be set so they return the best evaluation. To do that, pick one and then run the evaluator for a range of values. For example, the parameter min_ number_of_ratings says something about the minimum number of ratings a user should have before being considered in the evaluation. Now do a simple for loop like that shown in the next listing. You can see this code segment in the file /evaluator/evaluation_runner.py.

> **Listing 9.14 Minimum number of ratings: evaluator/evaluation_runner.py**

Creates an instance of the model training class. In this case, it's the item similarity matrix. builder.

Runs through a range of values, where you're testing min_overlap

```
builder = ItemSimilarityMatrixBuilder(min_overlap, min_sim=min_sim)

for min_overlap in np.arange(0, 15, 1):
    recommender = NeighborhoodBasedRecs()
    er = EvaluationRunner(0,
                          builder,
                          recommender,
                          K)
    result = er.calculate(min_number_of_ratings,
                          min_rank,
                          number_test_users=-1)
```

Creates an instance of the recommender

Creates an instance of the evaluation runner

Runs the evaluation calculator

```
user_coverage, movie_coverage =
    RecommenderCoverage(recommender).calculate_coverage() ◁─── Calculates coverage
```

When that's finished, and you believe that you've an optimal number, you can move on to the next parameter. Go through all of the parameters, and if you want to do a thorough job, you can run through it all a couple of times in different orders. These are the manual steps in testing each parameter. Keep in mind that you'll have to fix the code, so it iterates over the parameter you're training.

This is it for offline experiments. I hope now you have an understanding about not only how you can use them, but also how many things can go wrong when you do. It's still a good idea to test so you can measure if you have improvements, just remember to evaluate the right things.

9.11 Online evaluation

Once you're satisfied that your recommender algorithm is spinning to the best of your knowledge, it's time to deploy the system and test it out on real humans. But you can do this in stages.

First, I'd recommend doing controlled experiments. Then when the feedback is good, move on to testing with random users in your system, doing what is called a *bucket test* or, more fashionably, A/B testing. But what is a controlled experiment?

9.11.1 Controlled experiments

You set up controlled experiments by inviting humans to perform a test in a controlled environment. You can invite people to follow a checklist; for example, in the case of MovieGEEKs, the goal is to have users insert their preferences (rate several movies), determine if the recommendations are good, show two different types of recommendations to the user, and see which seems to work better.

The good thing about controlled experiments is that you can monitor user behavior. You can ask users questions about what they thought. The downside is that users might behave differently in a controlled environment than they would if they were nonchalantly visiting your site. It might also be time-consuming and difficult to set up an experiment that you can learn from.

FAMILY AND FRIENDS

A way to do something similar is to provide access to a small group of people, which is normally termed *family and friends,* who you trust to try out the system and return honest feedback. This alternative will make everybody an expert in recommender systems, and they'll tell you how and why you need to update the recommender.... When that happens, remember to bow your head and listen to their feedback. Because even if they don't understand the new super-complicated algorithm you're testing, they're still representatives of the end-users.

9.11.2 A/B testing

Many things can influence how your application runs. You might have an increase in conversions because you added new content to your catalog, or Christmas is around the corner so people might go on a frenzied buying spree, or you might have a completely different reason. What I'm getting at is that there are many different factors that influence the state of e-commerce, including many that you can't control. This is important to consider because you might launch a new recommender system, or a change to an existing one, and when that something else happens, it might look like it's the recommender's fault. It's hard to test whether a recommender has a positive effect. To get around this, you can use A/B testing to see if your change has any effect.

With A/B testing, you can test a new recommender algorithm by redirecting a small part of the traffic to the new recommender and letting the customers (unknowingly) indicate which is better. In fact, usually it's business as usual for the customers. They won't know that they're part of an experiment. And that's the whole point.

How does A/B testing work? Let's say you finished a new algorithm implementation, the offline evaluation looked okay, and now it's time to step it up so you implement an A/B test. The test will show if there's a significant difference between the current recommender and the new one. In practice, it works by diverting a small percentage of traffic to the new feature as shown in figure 9.16.

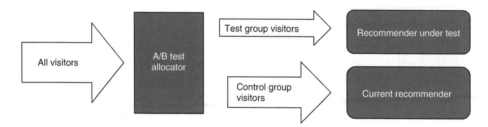

Figure 9.16 In an A/B test, visitors are split into two groups: the test group that sees the new feature and a control group that continues as usual.

A concrete example could be that you want to test two different settings of the neighborhood size, or you want to test if one recommender's performance is better than another. Registering all visitor behavior in the test group (as well as in the control group) lets you decide whether it's worth upgrading all traffic to the new algorithm.

One of the risks to consider with A/B testing is that if your new feature isn't good, then you might risk losing customers because they'd experience a drop in quality. But there's always a price to pay for a chance to do something better. Conversely, if you put new features in production without testing them, you might end up in much more trouble. At companies like Netflix with many millions of users, they A/B test everything before it goes into production.[17]

---

[17] Read more about Netflix's A/B test at http://mng.bz/FJUB.

A/B testing is something you'd want to look into more because it'll be the basis of feature development for data-driven applications in the future. A/B testing is one thing, and you need to do that, but another consideration is features that test well may not be good in the long run. It's a good idea to keep running tests, and one way of doing that is exploit/explore, which we'll summarize next.

9.12 *Continuous testing with exploit/explore*

A/B testing is about deciding whether to deploy a new feature. It's much easier instead to say, "I have these two algorithms running, and I believe that sometimes one is better, but other times, it's the other way around," and make the computer figure out which it should use. That's exactly what's behind the explore/exploit idea: you can either exploit the knowledge you've gained so far and use the one that you think is better, or you can explore another feature that the system doesn't know much about.

You can consider this as continuous A/B testing. Another way of thinking about it is this scenario: you've a long row of one-armed bandits (also known as slot machines) as shown in figure 9.17. As an experienced gambler, you know that machines 1 and 2 often give out something, but the payout may not be as much as the other machines you don't know much about. Should you then go for the safe bet and put your money in 1 or 2, or should you be daring and try something less known?

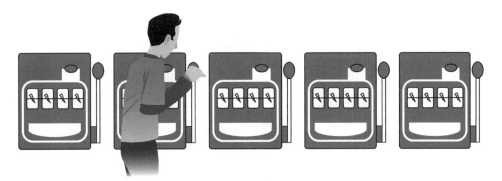

Figure 9.17 Exploit/explore is often explained as the problem of a gambler who needs to choose the next slot machine to play.

This problem is similar to the recommender system that knows that popular items are often good, but you might gain more by showing something new. This can be used not only when choosing between algorithms but also for items. For more on this subject, I recommend *Statistical Methods in Recommender Systems* by Deepak K. Agarwal et al., (Cambridge University Press, 2016).

Exploit/explore is also used at Yahoo! News to introduce new content so that it doesn't stay cold (remaining unseen). But it's tested among users first, allowing the system to understand what users' responses are to the new content.

9.12.1 *Feedback loops*

Collaborative filtering uses user behavior to create recommendations, but when you put your system in production, you should ask what the recommender does to the user's behavior. That's because if the recommender works, it might hinder diversity as discussed in section 9.4.2. NIPS (Conference on Neural Information Processing Systems) 2016 featured an interesting paper showing how to measure such diversity with feedback loops.[18]

It's a good idea to keep feedback loops in mind because it's about ensuring that users are given alternative ways to provide data for your tests. In figure 9.18, the loop represents what happens if users only consume things that are shown as in recommendations. This is something that Netflix has to consider because everything is a recommendation on its platform.[19] Somehow you need to introduce new items into this loop.

In figure 9.18, *X* could be a search, some manually added content, or even random items added to the feed as we talked about in the previous section. Remember, if you want diversity, you also need to enable the users to be diverse.

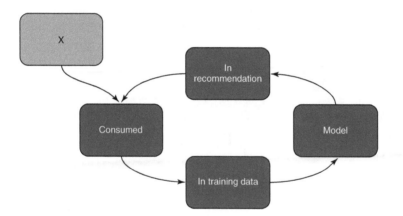

Figure 9.18   The feedback loop of recommenders

Recommender systems, although hard to evaluate, are about making many choices. You can either choose to measure prediction power or rank power as we talked about, or you can split your evaluation data into two sets in so many ways: random split, time split, or user splits. Is it a surprise that we've spent almost a whole book talking about how to implement recommender systems, and now it turns out that it's hard to evaluate whether they work or not? What you should remember from all this is that it's hard

[18] Sinha, Ayan et al., "Deconvolving Feedback Loops in Recommender Systems," https://papers.nips.cc/paper/6283-deconvolving-feedback-loops-in-recommender-systems.pdf.
[19] Look at the slides at http://mng.bz/0gw4.

to do one run and then understand if it's good. It's more important to do an evaluation and then use that as a basis for future evaluations.

Summary

- You should consider testing before implementing a recommender system.
- Regression tests guard your code against mistakes added unknowingly.
- Serendipity, the users finding things in your recommendations that they love but never knew they would, is hard to measure, but it's important.
- Different metrics are used to calculate whether the recommender is good or, at least, if it compares to a baseline.
- A/B testing (where visitors are split into two groups) is something you need to consider if you want to fine-tune your recommender system. An A/B test can also be done to test which parameters work better; for example, the size of the neighborhood in collaborative filtering or the number of latent factors in matrix factorization.
- The explore/exploit method is important if you want to keep optimizing your system when it's online.
- Watch out for feedback loops.

Content-based filtering

This chapter is all about content and users' tastes:

- You'll be introduced to content-based filtering.
- You'll learn how to construct user and content profiles.
- You'll learn to extract information from descriptions using term fequency-inverse document frequency (TF-IDF) and latent Dirichlet allocation (LDA) to create content profiles.
- You'll implement content-based filtering using descriptions of films in Movie-GEEKs site.

In previous chapters, you saw that it's possible to create recommendations by focusing only on the interactions between users and content (for example, shopping basket analysis or collaborative filtering). Although those work nicely, what about the things that you know about the content? For a movie that can include categories such as genres, actors, and directors. In other sites, it can be things such as clothing sizes and colors, or engine sizes for cars. Can you call a recommender system good if it doesn't take those things into account?

The answer is "YES!" as you've seen in the previous chapters, but it still seems as if you're missing something or losing out on certain information. I'll try to make up for that because this chapter covers what you know about content and users' tastes.

By the end of this chapter, you should have a clear idea of how to build a content-based recommender because you'll build one. We'll look at feature selection and how to process text to be used for content filtering. We'll also look at two different algorithms called term frequency–inverse document frequency (TF-IDF) and latent Dirichlet allocation (LDA). Sounds exciting, doesn't it? Let's start with an example to set the stage.

10.1 Descriptive example

On an average day, a conversation about movies could go something like the following:

> *Me:* I just saw *Ex Machina* (okay, still haven't watched it but I look forward to it).
> *Imaginary interested person:* Really, was it good?
> *Me:* Yeah, there were some very interesting subjects (imagining that I watched it).
> *Imaginary interested person:* All right, so you like robot people.
> *Me:* Well, yes (feeling like I shouldn't say yes).
> *Imaginary interested person:* Technology that goes bad. Then you must like *Terminator*.
> *Me:* Yes (relieved).

What transpired here? The *imaginary interested person* thought about categories containing *Ex Machina*, found the category "Robots that go insane," mentally looked up other movies in that genre (or maybe that isn't an accepted genre, so let's call it a category) and found *Terminator*. In this chapter, you want to implement a recommender that does the same.

You can use content-based filtering to create similar items recommendations, which are also sometimes called More Like This recommendations (see figure 10.1), or to provide personal recommendations based on taste.

Figure 10.1   More Like This recommendation from Netflix

The imaginary interested person never used any opinions about whether the movies were good or not, but only used the metadata of the content being discussed and recommended a movie based on that. To draw it, it might look similar to figure 10.2.

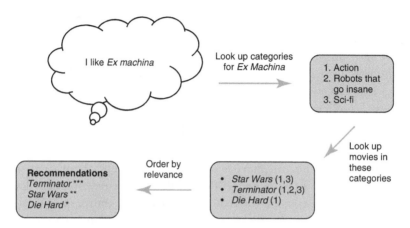

Figure 10.2   Example of content-based recommendation pipeline

That seems clear (at least to the imaginary interested person and me), but if you have to implement this into a recommender system, how would you get it to do the same? In figure 10.2, we took one film (*Ex Machina*) and found a recommendation based on that. To do that, we needed to look for a way to find content that visitors think is similar, That can be a bit hard because humans are strange machines. But let's make an attempt.

We'll start by talking more about what content filtering is when we look at a way to find important words using the TF-IDF algorithm. Using that and other tricks to extract features, we'll build a model where similar documents are close. In this chapter, you've a bit of road to follow, so let's see if I can provide directions to start with so you know where you're going. We'll start with an overview of what content-based filtering is. Then we'll look at several ways to describe content.

One element that's often used on the internet is *tags*. Tags are something that came out of the social internet or Web 2.0 (even if it had been there for a while). Tags let users of your website add keywords to your content. An example of this is seen on imdb.com as shown in figure 10.3. Another way to describe content is with textual descriptions, which is the next topic we'll address.

It's hard to make computers understand text-only content. Making computers read text is a complete research study in itself and, sadly, doesn't fit into this book. The field is called natural language processing (NLP) and it's a topic which is expanding

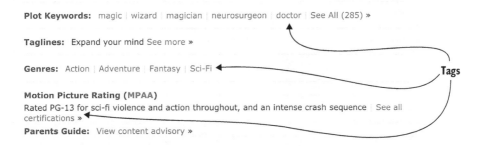

Figure 10.3 Screen from imdb.com showing tags

exponentially these days. If you're interested, a good place to start is *Natural Language Processing in Action.*[1] If you're going to recommend textual content, such as articles or books, then it's a good idea to look into NLP. If you're recommending content with only short descriptions, I don't know if it would be worth the effort. NLP can be many things and, indeed, most of what's in this chapter is also considered NLP.

Because we're trying to make the computer extract keywords, not read the text, we'll look at how to extract those words that are important while removing those that produces noise. You can remove noise in many ways, and we'll look at several. Then we'll calculate the most important words using the TF-IDF method.

You can use the important words you find to create a list of categories (also called *topics*) that capture similar trends in the descriptions by using the LDA algorithm.[2] *Latent* refers to the fact that the topics found don't compare to any category that you know, *Dirichlet* is the way the documents are described using these topics, and *allocation* means that words are allocated into topics. This isn't the complete truth, but without going too much into statistics, it's a good way to remember it. When you've a better understanding of these methods, we'll look at how they're implemented in the MovieGEEKs app. Now on to content-based filtering.

10.2 Content-based filtering

Content-based filtering seems a bit more complicated than collaborative filtering because it's about extracting knowledge from the content. You'll try to extract precise definitions of each content item and represent each item as a list of values. Described like this it sounds easy, but it does pose challenges. Figure 10.4 illustrates a simple version of how to train a content-based recommender (offline), while figure 10.5 shows how it's used when a user arrives at your site (online).

---

[1] Hobson Lane and Hannes Hapke, *Natural Language Processing in Action* (Manning, 2018).
[2] For more information on the LDA algorith, see http://jmlr.csail.mit.edu/papers/v3/blei03a.html.

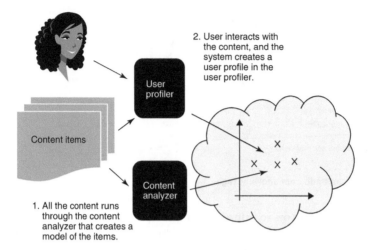

Figure 10.4   Training a content-based recommender offline

To sum up, you need the following to make things work:

1 *Content analyzer*—Creates a model based on the content. In a way, it creates a profile for each item. It's where the training of the model is done.
2 *User profiler*—Creates a user profile; sometimes the user profile is a simple list of items consumed by the user.
3 *Item retriever*—Retrieves relevant items found by comparing the user profiles to the item profiles as shown in figure 10.5. If the user profile is a list of items, this list is iterated, and similar items are found for each item in the user's list.

You have several ways to implement these steps, and this chapter is about how it works. Let's look at each of the three points in turn.

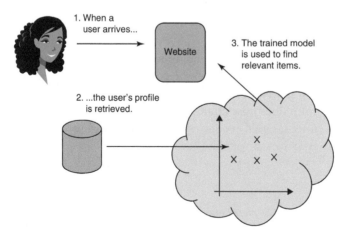

Figure 10.5   The item retriever returning recommendations with content-based filtering online.

10.3 Content analyzer

The content analyzer is the poor soul that's given descriptive data about your content and has the task of mapping that data into something, such as a vector, the machine can use. To implement a content analyzer, we need to chat a bit about content: what is it and how do you understand it? We also need to talk about feature extraction, which is extracting things that you think are important for your algorithm to work.

10.3.1 Feature extraction for the item profile

Data about data is called *metadata*. To avoid confusion, we call data about films metadata as well. Metadata about a film is everything that you can find on an IMDb page, such as genre, starring artists, and production year. It could also be something like the type of filming or the style of clothing worn by the actors in the film, or in other domains, the shade of paint on the car or the number of freckles on men on dating sites. I like to split the metadata loosely into two types:

- Facts
- Tags

This isn't a division normally used, but it's beneficial for you to think about. Because *facts* are the things such as production year or starring actors in a movie that can't be disputed, and you can also use them as input. Tags can mean different things to people and should be considered before adding them.

The social internet has made it popular for people to add descriptive tags to content. Tags can be something as simple as "uplifting" or more subjective like "breaking the fourth wall."[3] I've no idea what that means, but 10 people describing *Deadpool* said that it was relevant, and apparently it applies to a number of films across genres and decades.[4]

Another challenge with the tags that viewers put on films is that people have different ways of expressing themselves. A simple example is how people talk about a James Bond film. I'd probably say it's a "Bond film" and tag it as such. But looking at the data, you can see that there are several different ways to describe those files, predominantly using "007." To make your system understand that people are, in fact, talking about the same film, it's worth streamlining the tags to use the same word for the same thing as much as possible. Ideally, you also want to split tags that mean different things to people.

> **NOTE** Facts and tags have no clear divisions, so remember that facts are something that people often agree on, while tags can be a bit more subjective. In this light, you should probably put genres in the tag category, but that's a matter of debate also.

---

[3] Look for the most popular movies that have been tagged *breaking-the-fourth-wall* at http://mng.bz/uC72.
[4] For more information, see http://mng.bz/9971.

One of the biggest showstoppers for developers trying to use content-based recommenders is that they can't get the data about the items. What options do you have? You could try to build it yourself or you could hire people to go through the content and tag it. But beware, that can produce strange recommendations. Entire companies exist where people tag content for a living; can you guess where? Let's look at an example where you can get a feel for the differences between tags and facts.

TAGS VS. FACTS

Batman v Superman: Dawn of Justice (BvS) is an interesting film. The film from the IMDb site is shown in figure 10.6. Looking at the description of the film, you can see that the genres are action and adventure (and sci-fi, but I disagree with that) and that the film premiered in 2016. Much more can be said about the film; for example, it could say that Ben Affleck plays Batman. I'd also put that it's a long film.

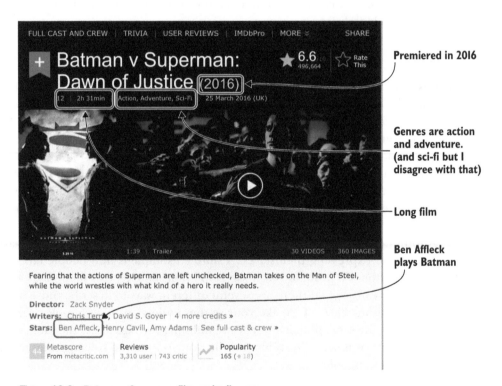

Figure 10.6 *Batman v Superman* film on imdb.com

To represent these film tags, you can make a simple vector such as the one shown in table 10.1. That isn't a vector but a table, but think of it as a list of key values. The table lists two types of values:

- *Binary values*—Like starring Ben Affleck and Action genre.

- *Quantitative values*—Such as explosions (if the number of explosions in the film could be considered as something worth having as a feature) and the production year.

Table 10.1 An item profile of *Batman v Superman*

	Year	Starring Ben Affleck	Action	Adventure	Comedy	Explosions	Long film	Dogs	Superheroes
BvS	2016	1	1	1	0	5	1	0	1

This table (vector) doesn't leave much space for features other than the ones for *Batman v Superman*, but you'll want to represent many different films using the same vector. Comedies should fit in there too. Films starring popular artists should also be there, and maybe a feature indicating how often they smoke, look at the rain, or whether any fish were hurt in the story. In the end, you'll have a long list of different features and movies. One of the funny parts about doing content-based recommenders is to figure out what's important and what isn't.

Now, if a user bought or liked BvS and other movies starring Ben Affleck, you could deduce that the user likes Ben Affleck. Then, with that knowledge, you can search the list of vectors for other films with a 1 in the *Starring Ben Affleck* feature and recommend those. It could also be for another reason that the user liked them; in which case, this wouldn't be a good direction to go. That other reason might be that the specific user likes a specific genre of films that's orthogonal to the usual genres and is therefore not normally used to classify movies. This type of hidden (or should we call it latent) genre is something that we'll look for when we introduce the LDA.

10.3.2 *Categorical data with small numbers*

Previously we talked about actors, but we could approach film features even more generally and say that everyone worth mentioning who's in the production of the content could be a feature. But while words that occur only once in a document are good to save if you're creating a search, you need to economize when you talk about recommendations.

For example, if there's an actor who appears in only one film, it's great if somebody likes the film, but it doesn't help find similar films because this actor isn't found anywhere else. You can't use an actor who's only mentioned once to find similar movies. In that case, you might as well leave the actor out.

10.3.3 *Converting the year to a comparable feature*

Most actors only appear in one role in a film, so the feature that indicates "starring X" is either 0 or 1. Except if we're talking about Eddie Murphy who typically plays everybody in his films. But would you make the category starring Eddie Murphy more if he plays five roles instead of one? If you like Eddie Murphy, then I guess you like Eddie Murphy.

Some features you'll want to keep as ordinal numbers (things that have an order—first, second, and so on), so it's clear one is positioned or ordered more or less than another and so on. Production year is a good example. If a user likes content from 1980, a film from 1981 is probably closer to his taste than one from 2000, so production year is something you want to keep ordinal.

When adding an ordinal feature, it's also worth considering how important this feature is. If you put an ordinal feature such as a production year into a system where everything is between zero and one, 2000 is a high number, even if it's supposed to represent a year. It's important that you normalize the data or scale it so that it's between zero and one, or close to it.

One way to compare films is by plotting them as shown in figure 10.7. It's easy to see that even if Harrison Ford doesn't star in *Harry Potter*, and *Star Wars* (1979) and *Harry Potter* (2001) were made 22 years apart, they still look similar in figure 10.7 (top), while in figure 10.7 (bottom) the production year has been normalized.[5] You could even subtract 1894 (the year of the oldest movie in the database) from all the production years or from the earliest production year to make the difference larger. With all the data having values between 0 and 1, it's easy to see that they're different.

Let's move on. Besides tags and facts, you can use descriptions as input for your algorithms.

10.4 *Extracting metadata from descriptions*

In the scope of content-based filtering, news articles are interesting because they're often only relevant for a short time, which means that they're hard to recommend using collaborative filtering (you know, that algorithm we talked about in chapter 8). But you might still want to recommend them.

Besides using popularity, you can analyze the content. One way of doing that is to look at what words are in the article, how many times each occurs, and how commonly they appear in all the news items in the database. This can be done using TF–IDF, which we'll look at soon. An article is text, so the content is in the description, while a movie has a description that's written by somebody.

10.4.1 *Preparing descriptions*

Getting good descriptions of content isn't easy because the quality of descriptions can vary. More work goes into tagging movies than books or TV shows, for example, but it's still a challenge to make computers read and understand text, at least for this purpose.

Before trying to extract information from the descriptions, you need to remove all the things that might confuse the machine. In the next sections, we'll look at exactly that. You start out pulling the text apart and putting it into a bag.

---

[5] By dividing each year with the highest year: 2001 => 1 and 1979 => 1979/2001 = 0.99.

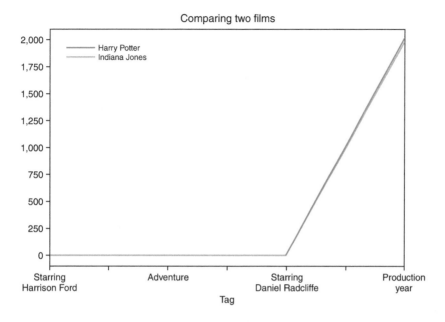

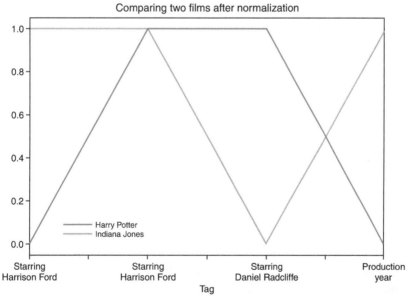

Figure 10.7 Illustrating why data needs to be normalized. At top, the production year isn't normalized, and the lines are more or less on top of each other. At bottom, the production year is divided by the max year and suddenly you can see that the two movies are different.

THE BAG-OF-WORDS (BoW) MODEL AND TOKENIZATION

To use the descriptions, you first need to make a bag-of-words (BoW) model, meaning that you split the description into an array of words:

"the man likes big ice creams" -> ["the", "man", "likes", "big", "ice", "creams"]

Notice that when using BoW, you're already losing a bit of information because "ice" and "cream" mean something when they're next to each other but different things when they're apart. This representation will also be the same for any permutation of the words used, such as "the big ice man likes creams" produces the same BoW, even if it's talking about something different.

Certain words won't add any knowledge to the BoW; these words are referred to as *stopwords*. You'll look at how to remove those next.

REMOVING STOP WORDS

Descriptions are full of filler words, in the sense that there are many words needed to make a human-readable description. But if you're deconstructing the documents into an array of words, you lose the value of words like *the* or *a*. Because the word *a* by itself doesn't give any descriptive information, it's best to remove that and similiar words of that type. The words you don't want in your model are the stop words.

The next step is to remove the stop words from the BoW. Stop words are, strangely enough, not synonyms of the word stop, but words that you're going skip in your analysis. A stop words list is dependent on both your language and your domain. The one you'll use here supports English but also many other languages (such as Danish). The package will be downloaded and installed executing the command line shown in listing 10.1 in the terminal window.

> **Listing 10.1   Installing the stop-words package**

```
>Pip3 install stop-words
```

After installing the package, you can get the stop words by importing `get_stop_words` as shown in the next listing.

> **Listing 10.2   Importing the stop-words package**

```
from stop_words import get_stop_words
```

This provides an array of words you probably won't be interested in including in your model. Calling `get_stop_words('en')` results in the list of words shown in the following listing.

> **Listing 10.3   English stop words**

```
['a', 'about', 'above', 'after', 'again', 'against', 'all', 'am', 'an',
    'and', 'any', 'are', "aren't", 'as', 'at', 'be', 'because', 'been',
    'before', 'being', 'below', 'between', 'both', 'but', 'by', "can't",
    'cannot', 'could', "couldn't", 'did', "didn't", 'do', 'does', "doesn't",
    'doing', "don't", 'down', 'during', 'each', 'few', 'for', 'from',
```

```
'further', 'had', "hadn't", 'has', "hasn't", 'have', "haven't",
'having', 'he', "he'd", "he'll", "he's", 'her', 'here', "here's",
'hers', 'herself', 'him', 'himself', 'his', 'how', "how's", 'i', "i'd",
"i'll", "i'm", "i've", 'if', 'in', 'into', 'is', "isn't", 'it', "it's",
'its', 'itself', "let's", 'me', 'more', 'most', "mustn't", 'my',
'myself', 'no', 'nor', 'not', 'of', 'off', 'on', 'once', 'only', 'or',
'other', 'ought', 'our', 'ours', 'ourselves', 'out', 'over', 'own',
'same', "shan't", 'she', "she'd", "she'll", "she's", 'should',
"shouldn't", 'so', 'some', 'such', 'than', 'that', "that's", 'the',
'their', 'theirs', 'them', 'themselves', 'then', 'there', "there's",
'these', 'they', "they'd", "they'll", "they're", "they've", 'this',
'those', 'through', 'to', 'too', 'under', 'until', 'up', 'very', 'was',
"wasn't", 'we', "we'd", "we'll", "we're", "we've", 'were', "weren't",
'what', "what's", 'when', "when's", 'where', "where's", 'which',
'while', 'who', "who's", 'whom', 'why', "why's", 'with', "won't",
'would', "wouldn't", 'you', "you'd", "you'll", "you're", "you've",
'your', 'yours', 'yourself', 'yourselves']
```

You probably want to add more words, but this list is a good start. Before using the BoW model, you want to go through each word of your description and check if it's a stop word if it's not, leave it; otherwise, remove it. You also want to keep derogative words (words that are sexual or hateful) out of your model.

REMOVING THE HIGH AND LOWS

It's also worth looking at words that appear in all documents and the ones that only appear a few times or only once in each document. The high-frequency words create background noise, while the low-frequency words add complexity to the model without adding content. The lowest frequency words can also be deleted, but if you remove too many, you run the risk that the model won't find nuances in the texts. The right amount is something to fine-tune in different data sets.

STEMMING AND LEMMATIZING

Words such as *run* and *running* are considered different words in the BoW model, and that might not be what you want. You have a number of ways to "normalize" that word. The best way is to use a lemmatizer, which will find the base of the word.

The base of both *run* and *running* is *run*. However, words such as *run, runner,* and *running* are easy words to handle because the base is the beginning of all the words. If this is all that's needed, then you can use a stemmer instead of a lemmatizer.

A *stemmer* usually refers to the heuristic process that chops off the ends of words in the hope of achieving this goal, correctly most of the time, while the *lemmatizer* is referred to doing things properly.[6] Their effectiveness depends on what type of text you're working with. Stemming is good in some cases, where there are words that when you strip them stay the same but weren't supposed to. It's generally considered that the good outweighs the bad. I discourage this on short documents because stemming does remove certain information. The best thing to do is to try this out and see if a stemmer or a lemmatizer improves things.

---

[6] In the words of Cristopher Manning et al. from "Introduction to Information Retrieval." Available online at http://mng.bz/OXR6.

Before moving on, let's be sure you know where you are and where you're heading. It should be clear by now what content filtering is and how to do feature extraction. We'll move on to the first of the two ways of extracting features from descriptions and create something that can be compared by a computer. First, we'll look at TF-IDF and then LDA. These are only two of many different types of feature extraction you can do in text.

10.5 *Finding important words with TF-IDF*

When you look at documents for information filtering or search, you often want to look at which words or phrases are in the documents. But, in addition to the stop words, documents are full of words that are so overused they don't add anything descriptive to the text.

Suppose you were to cut this book into small pieces. You'd probably have a zillion pieces containing the word *recommender*, so even if it's a mega-important word, it doesn't help to distinguish that word in the documents. If you have a collection of articles on the great things about computers, there might only be one article on recommenders and then the word *recommender* would be defining for the article, and probably even more if it's there many times. This is known as term frequency (*tf* in the equation) and a simple way to define it is as follows:

$$tf(word, document) \ = \ how\ many\ times\ does\ the\ word\ appear\ in\ document$$

But more often, this formula is used:

$$tf(word, document) \ = \ 1 + \log(word\ frequency)$$

The more times a word is present in one document, the higher the chance that it's important (assuming that you removed all the stop words). But, as mentioned previously, only if the word is only present in few documents. For this, you can use the inverse document frequency (*idf* in the equation), which is the number of all your documents divided by the number of documents that contain the word. Together, the product is `tf-idf`, which is defined like this:

$$tf-idf(word, document) \ = \ tf(word, document) * idf(word, document)$$

Look at the following words (let's pretend each line of text is a document):

- The superhero Deadpool has accelerated healing powers.
- The superhero Batman takes on the superhero Superman.
- The LEGO superhero Batman takes the stage.
- The LEGO superheroes adventures.
- The LEGO Hulk.

If you want to determine the importance of *superhero*, you can use the calculations in table 10.2.

Table 10.2 Showing TF-IDF of the word *superhero*. You aren't using stemming so *superhero* in document 4 doesn't work.

		TF *superhero*	IDF *superhero*	tf × idf
1	The superhero Deadpool has accelerated healing powers.	1	5 / 3	1.66
2	The superhero Batman takes on the superhero Superman.	2	5 /3	3.33
3	The LEGO superhero Batman takes the stage.	1	5 / 3	1.66
4	The LEGO superheroes adventures.	0	5 / 3	0
5	The LEGO Hulk.	0	5 / 3	0

If you've someone looking for a superhero movie, you can show document 2, which has the TF-IDF (*superhero*) equal to 3.33, followed by the two other documents with non-zero values. Try this on your own to calculate TF-IDF (*Hulk*).[7]

Why all this talk about words when you're looking at content features? Well, when you find words that provide large TF-IDF returns, you can add those to the list of features. If the previous sentences were actual descriptions of movies, you could add the word *superhero* to the list of features with the value of the TF-IDF.

Those formulas were simple. There's one correction, however. Usually you'd use the following IDF formula:

$$idf(term) = \log \frac{Total\ number\ of\ docs}{Number\ of\ docs\ containing\ term}$$

NOTE This equation keeps the final number more stable because the logs of numbers between 1-10 are close to each other.

TF-IDF was once king, but after the invention of LDA models, it's fallen out of grace. Everyone's first choice now is to use LDA models or similar topic models. However, before you believe I took up your time explaining something you might not use, it's worth mentioning that TF-IDF is something that you can use to clean the input of the LDA. TF-IDF is a classic method and has been widely used, but new algorithms are also gaining traction—one in particular called Okapi BM25.[8]

10.6 Topic modeling using the LDA

If you're a machine-learning professional, you've probably heard about the fantastic LDA models (figure 10.8) that can solve everything regarding text. Okay, word2vec is also quite popular, so let's say LDA is one of the popular ones.[9] The way that word2vec

---

[7] TF-IDF for the word *Hulk* is 0 for all except for string number 5 where it's 1(5 / 1) = 5.

[8] For more information, see https://en.wikipedia.org/wiki/Okapi_BM25.

[9] Mind, the LDA and word2vec models are usually used for different things.

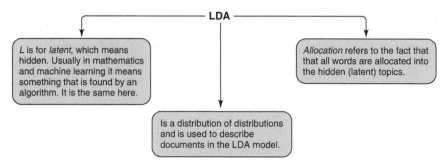

Figure 10.8   The LDA model (short for latent Dirichlet allocation)

and LDA are often described, it sounds like they'll give you a foot massage and wash your windows! Word2vec is the focus of chapter 6 in *Natural Language Processing in Action* (Manning, 2018) by Hobson Lane, et al.

If you aren't familiar with this, then sharpen your pencils and stay alert, because it's a bit complicated. Luckily LDAs are easy to use in the sense that there are many libraries out there that make it easy to have code up and running in no time. And in no time, you'll start having trouble because even if it did give you a foot massage, it doesn't respond in an easy-to-understand language.

Let's go through a bit of the theory of how LDA works and then return to what it produces. An LDA is what you call a *generative model*, so let's start with an example explaining what that is.

GENERATIVE MODEL EXAMPLE

This silly example will hopefully make a generative model clearer. You have three bags, each with shapes of one color: one bag with red shapes, one with blue shapes, and one with green shapes. If you form the row of shapes shown in figure 10.9, you'd need to draw three times from the red bag (triangles), two times from the blue one (squares), and finally five times from the green one (circles).

Figure 10.9   Row of shapes in a generative model example

Another way to indicate how to generate the row of shapes in figure 10.9 would be to say you'd have to draw a shape from the red bag 30% of the time, from the blue bag 20% of the time, and from the green bag 50% of the time. Or you could say that the row X in figure 10.9 is formed by the following equation:

$$x = 0.3 \times red + 0.2 \times blue + 0.5 \times green$$

If this were a recipe for generating documents, you could have also created the document shown in figure 10.10.

Figure 10.10   Another row, which could have been generated using this recipe: $x = 0.3 \times$ `red` + $0.2 \times$ `blue` + $0.5 \times$ `green`.

Now look at another row in figure 10.11.

Figure 10.11   And another row, which could have been generated using this recipe: $x = 0.2 \times$ `red` + $0.3 \times$ `blue` + $0.5 \times$ `green`.

The only difference between the first and the third rows is that a red triangle is replaced by a blue box. If you imagine each of these shapes is a piece of your description, then the idea is that you can write a formula to make documents easier to compare. Remember this mental image of the bags with shapes that can be used to generate rows of shapes.

What if, instead of bags, we call those items topics: the shapes are words, and the rows are descriptions. Then instead of colors, the topics could be something such as Superhero, computer science, and food, for example. Under the Superhero topic could be words such as *Spiderman, flying, strong, superhero,* and so on as shown in the following:

- *Superhero*—Spiderman, flying, strong, superhero
- *Computer science*—Computer, laptop, CPU
- *Food*—Eat, breakfast, fork

If you've a description like the following

`Z = Spiderman is home with his laptop to eat breakfast with a fork.`

and want to generate that from your three topics, you can draw *Spiderman* and *flying* from the Superhero topic, *laptop* from computer science topic, and *eat, breakfast,* and *fork* from the food topic. This can be summed up in the following generative formula:

$$z = 0.2 \times \text{Superhero} + 0.1 \times \text{ComputerScience} + 0.3 \times \text{Food}$$

That's simple, isn't it? It does get more complicated, however, because each word in a topic has a probability that says something about how important a word it is. But let's keep that in mind for now and skip on to how to create these topics.

An example closer to your MovieGEEKs site can be seen in figure 10.12. It shows how topics related to movie genres could be distributed.

I came up with the topics in figure 10.12, but normally the whole idea of topic models is that you want the computer to sort out topics from your database of descriptions.

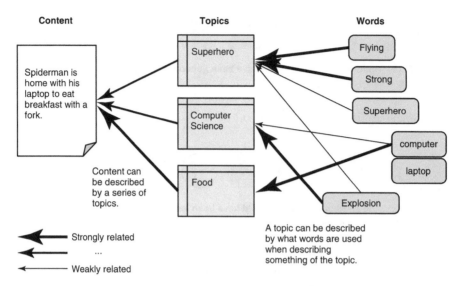

Figure 10.12 A topic model. Each topic is defined by a list of words and their respective probability of being drawn. A document can be described by selecting topics, using a formula of how large a percentage of the time you should draw from each topic.

GENERATING THE TOPICS

How do you generate topics? Figure 10.13 shows one way to do that. The idea, as shown in figure 10.13, is that input for the LDA algorithm contains several documents and a number K, where K is the number of topics the algorithm should create to produce a list of topics. The output of the algorithm is a list of K topics and a list of vectors, one

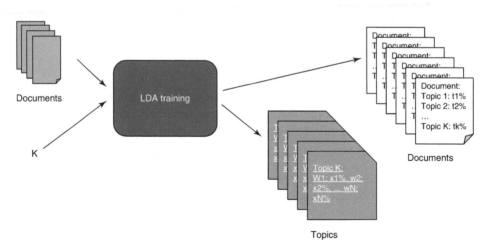

Figure 10.13 A model for generating topics when running an LDA algorithm with input from a list of documents and a variable K, representing the number of topics for the algorithm to create. The input documents can now be described using the generated list of topics.

for each document, that contains a probability of how often each topic appears in the document. Topics can be generated in several different ways; this is but one. In the next section, we'll look at how to connect the words, topics, and documents with Gibbs sampling.

GIBBS SAMPLING

Looking again at figure 10.13, let's elaborate on what data structures you have: you've K (which is the number of topics the LDA model should contain), and you've each document that's essentially considered a BoW (which means that you don't have any structure or idea which words are next to each other, only the words). The goal is now to connect words with topics and documents with topics. Let's start with the topics and words as shown in figure 10.14.

If you line up a list of K topics and all the words that are present in the documents, it's hard to imagine ever coming up with a solution. But because words related to the same topic are often found in the same document, then you already have information to start with. If you know one word is already in a topic, then you've information about whether another word should be there. This is what Gibbs sampling takes advantage of.[10]

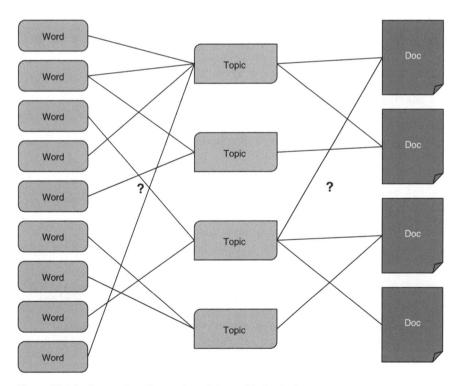

Figure 10.14 **Connecting the words and docs with the topics**

---

[10] Philip Resnik and Eric Hardisty, "Gibbs Sampling for the Uninitiated," https://www.umiacs.umd.edu/~resnik/pubs/LAMP-TR-153.pdf.

Gibbs sampling begins by randomly adding topics to documents and words to topics. Imagine the arrows set at random in figure 10.14. The Gibbs sampler goes through each document and each word, and, given the probabilities of all the remaining words in each document, it adjusts the probability of that word. This follows the premise that topics contain similar words. By fitting each word and distribution one step at a time, the Gibbs sampling algorithm slowly approaches a distribution of words and topics that seems magically to make sense.

I don't know if you need to know a lot of the information in the Resnik/Hardisty article mentioned in the footnote, but I do believe that you need to know how a model is trained and Gibbs sampling is used to train the LDA model. Guess what's next.

LDA MODEL

The Gibbs sampling produces K topics that look something like listing 10.4. Each topic is printed with the 10 (K) most probable words in each topic. If strange words appear with this sampling, such as *18genre*, it's my attempt to inject genres into the description. Instead of using names like *action* and *drama*, I added numbers to be sure they aren't confused with words in the description. This might change the importance of several of those words from the sampling In the listing, (0...) is the first topic, (1...) is the second topic, and so on.

Listing 10.4   Topic distribution created by Gibbs sampling

```
[(0,
  '0.037*18genre + 0.022*love + 0.021*s + 0.012*young +
  0.012*man + 0.011*story + 0.009*woman + 0.008*father +
  0.008*35genre + 0.007*10749genre'),
 (1,
  '0.010*vs + 0.010*even + 0.009*nothing + 0.008*based +
  0.007*boyfriend + 0.005*s + 0.005*music + 0.005*rise +
  0.004*writer + 0.004*hero'),
 (2,
  '0.012*one + 0.011*s + 0.011*gets + 0.011*three + 0.009*like +
  0.008*99genre + 0.008*years + 0.007*car + 0.006*different +
  0.006*marriage'),
 (3,
  '0.013*s + 0.010*28genre + 0.009*house + 0.009*two +
  0.009*878genre + 0.008*years + 0.008*daughter + 0.007*year +
  0.007*world + 0.007*old'),
 (4,
  '0.024*35genre + 0.015*girl + 0.011*10749genre + 0.010*year +
  0.009*old + 0.009*go + 0.009*falls + 0.008*s + 0.008*get + 0.008*four'),
 (5,
  '0.025*53genre + 0.016*80genre + 0.015*27genre + 0.013*28genre +
  0.011*18genre + 0.008*police + 0.008*s + 0.007*goes + 0.007*couple +
  0.007*discovers'),
 (6,
  '0.016*t + 0.016*s + 0.011*school + 0.010*friends + 0.010*new +
  0.009*boy + 0.008*first + 0.007*will + 0.007*35genre + 0.007*show'),
 (7,
  '0.013*99genre + 0.008*s + 0.008*fall + 0.007*movie + 0.007*documentary +
    0.007*power + 0.005*18genre + 0.005*wants + 0.005*will + 0.005*move'),
```

```
(8,
  '0.046*film + 0.011*friend + 0.010*past + 0.009*18genre + 0.009*directed +
     0.007*upcoming + 0.007*produced + 0.006*ways + 0.006*festival +
     0.006*turned'),
(9,
  '0.016*s + 0.014*will + 0.013*one + 0.010*10402genre + 0.009*life +
     0.009*journey + 0.008*game + 0.007*work + 0.007*time + 0.006*world')]
```

Each topic contains all words found in all the input documents, but many words have so little probability (close to zero) that they aren't interesting. The probabilities are the numbers in front of each word in the topic listing. If you try to generate a document from those topics, you'll draw that word with the lesser probability. If you have a document that was generated from topic 0 alone, then each occurrence of the word *love* has the probability of 2.2% as you can see in this listing.

Listing 10.5   Topic 0's probability for the word *love*

```
[(0,
  '0.037*18genre + 0.022*love + 0.021*s + 0.012*young + 0.012*man +
➥0.011*story + 0.009*woman + 0.008*father + 0.008*35genre +
➥0.007*10749genre'),
```

Another document could be generated by pulling words from the topics 2, 3, and 9, for example. The document could be represented in the LDA model as shown in the next listing.

Listing 10.6   A document's topic distribution

```
[(2, 0.02075648883076852),
 (3, 0.1812829334788339),
 (9, 0.78545976997831202)]
```

This listing shows that 2.1% of the time a word is generated from topic 2, while 18.1% of the time it's generated from topic 3, and 78.5% of the time it's generated from topic 9.

Now you know how it works, in theory at least. Much of the work in making an LDA function is how you process the text you're inputting. Understanding LDA models is difficult. You need to stare at the output for a while—well, maybe more like for a long time and then sleep on it before anything makes sense because the topics might represent something that's hard to understand from the input.

THE CORPUS WIKIPEDIA

We've only talked about adding descriptions and documents into the LDA, but what kinds of documents are they? The previous example and the implementation in MovieGEEKs that we'll soon talk about both use the same documents that you'll calculate similarity between. But it's a good idea to use a data set that describes (or at least provides) good examples of several of the topics you want to find.

The media company Issuu (https://issuu.com), for example, uses an LDA model to offer recommendations of what digital content to read. It uses the Wikipedia data set to create the models, which enables Issuu and other sites to create a model with easy-to-understand topics. Wikipedia also contains documents with classifications for everything, which ensures that the topic model is nicely distributed.

ADDING FEATURES AND TAGS TO DOCUMENTS

Pardon me for repeating myself: a document is presented as a BoW and not as connected words where the order is important. If you want to control the topics a document contains, you can also inject words into the descriptions. For example, if you want to include information such as actors or product year, you add them to the BoW. You saw an example of this in listing 10.4 where words such as *35genre* appeared. More details on that in a bit.

10.6.1 *What knobs can you turn to tweak the LDA?*

All this magic. Does it work? Looking at figure 10.15, it's easy to see that it leaves something to desire.

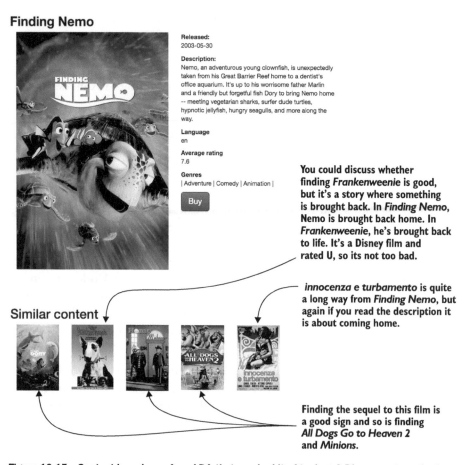

Finding Nemo

Released:
2003-05-30

Description:
Nemo, an adventurous young clownfish, is unexpectedly taken from his Great Barrier Reef home to a dentist's office aquarium. It's up to his worrisome father Marlin and a friendly but forgetful fish Dory to bring Nemo home -- meeting vegetarian sharks, surfer dude turtles, hypnotic jellyfish, hungry seagulls, and more along the way.

Language
en

Average rating
7.6

Genres
| Adventure | Comedy | Animation |

Buy

You could discuss whether finding *Frankenweenie* is good, but it's a story where something is brought back. In *Finding Nemo*, Nemo is brought back home. In *Frankenweenie*, he's brought back to life. It's a Disney film and rated U, so its not too bad.

innocenza e turbamento is quite a long way from *Finding Nemo*, but again if you read the description it is about coming home.

Similar content

Finding the sequel to this film is a good sign and so is finding *All Dogs Go to Heaven 2* and *Minions*.

Figure 10.15   Content-based recs from LDA that need a bit of tuning. A Disney cartoon that's similar to *Innonceza e turbamento* (Innocence and Desire) doesn't sound like the best of recommendations.

A model is only as good as the quality of the documents and good quality documents are examples of the types/genres/subjects that you want your model to represent. For example, the descriptions of the movies that you're using in this section aren't always good for this. Looking at the *Finding Nemo* description, it doesn't say that it's a cartoon or that it's about the sea. You can add the genres that will include that it's also animation, but unless you want to start handwriting better descriptions, it's hard to come up with ways to deal with a lack of information.

Something you can do is to see how the recommender responds to what you know has many similar items in the catalog, such as *Spider-Man* movies, as shown in figure 10.16. There's a lot of *Spider-Man* movies, so these recommendations would probably only appeal to the more hardcore *Spider-Man* fans. Besides the considerations around the input, you should also consider the number of topics you'd use.

Figure 10.16 The content-based recommender understands that all the different *Spider-Man* movies are similar.

WHAT'S A GOOD NUMBER OF TOPICS?

One thing that can make or break the LDA model is whether you've trained it with a good number of topics. And it's also one of the things that makes it into an art because there isn't any way to verify that you have the right number.

In the analytics part of the MovieGEEKs site (http://mng.bz/04k5), you've an interactive visualization of the model (http://127.0.0.1:8001/analytics/lda) as shown in figure 10.17, where it shows a circle for each topic. Hovering over a topic, you get a list of the most frequently used words in that topic.

It's important to find a number of topics that are distributed evenly. If you select a too low *K,* then many documents will look like each other as if you described all films using only the genres Action, Comedy, and Drama. But if you select too many topics, then you might end up with no similar documents because you have a million different dimensions (topics). Then you're back to the curse of dimensionality.

One way to visualize your model and better understand if your model distributes the topics nicely, is to use a tool called pyLDAvis (figure 10.17).

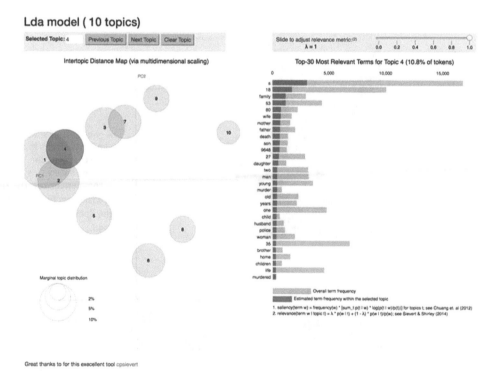

Figure 10.17   The pyLDAvis dashboard showing topic distribution

The pyLDAvis dashboard was created using a Python library called pyLDAvis[11] as described in a paper by Carson Sievert and Kenneth E. Shirley.[12]

It's a good idea to test the following when deciding on the right number of topics for training the LDA model:

- Check a view (such as the one in figure 10.17) to see if the topics are distributed and not on top of each other.
- Test if the LDA produces similar items.

Later in this chapter, you'll see how LDA is implemented in the MovieGEEKs site and where you can check to determine if it produces good recommendations. My first attempt produced the recommendations shown in figure 10.15.

The short answer to how the LDA model should look is that it should look right. Find several movies that you like and try to tweak them until the model makes sense. Then ask a friend to do the same and see if you can tweak it so you're both happy.

PLAYING WITH ALPHA AND BETA

You have two more parameters to play with when you're using LDA. You can change the parameters alpha and beta to adjust the distributions of both the documents and the words in the topics.

If you enter a high alpha, then you'll distribute each document over many topics; low alpha distributes only a few topics. The advantage with high alpha is that documents seem to be more similar, while if you have specialized documents, then a low alpha will keep them divided into few topics.

The same is true for beta: a high beta leads to topics being more similar because the probabilities will be distributed on more words that are used to describe each topic. For example, instead of having 10 words in a topic with a probability above 1%, you might have 40. This allows for bigger overlap. Most people I've talked with are careful to change the default values of alpha and beta because it can get a little rough, but if there's time to play, you should.

10.7 *Finding similar content*

Now that you've the LDA model, you've another way of finding similar items. By projecting two documents into the LDA model, you can calculate their similarity. Because the probability distribution can be seen as vectors, many use cosine similarity (one of the similarity functions that we talked about in chapter 7) for their calculations.

In principle, it's also possible to use the LDA model to compare documents that weren't used when creating the model. This is one of the more important features for content-based recommenders used for getting around the problem of cold products that we talked about in chapter 6. This can be used for the More Like This recommendation.

---

[11] You can view the documentation for pyLDAvis at https://pyldavis.readthedocs.io/en/latest/.

[12] Carson Sievert and Kenneth E. Shirley, "LDAvis: A method for visualizing and interpreting topics," http://mng.bz/qPf7.

Later in this chapter, we'll talk more about the implementation in MovieGEEKs and show a similarity calculation between two movies. For now, let's look at how to do personalized recommendations in a content-based recommender system.

10.8 Creating the user profile

If you like James Bond, then you might also like... This is a simple one that doesn't need any user profile. With the LDA model or simply the feature vectors we talked about earlier, you'll find the vector for a James Bond movie and then locate movies with similar vectors. But if you provide personalized recommendations, you'll need to create a user profile that encompasses all the movies the user likes. Let's look at how to do that with LDA, then with TF-IDF.

10.8.1 Creating the user profile with LDA

When creating a personalized recommendation function, you should look at the full list of items that the user likes and return other items that the user might also like. In real life, such a function isn't individual—the user might not be uniquely defined by the items consumed (even if most recommender systems probably will respond the same). But it's still much more personalized than a chart.

What you can do is to iterate through each of the items the user likes and for each, find similar products. When you get a list, order it according to the product of similarity and the users' ratings from the original list of consumed items. More formally, you could do the following for an active user:

- Get all consumed items (CI) by the active user.
- For each item I in CI:
    - Find similar objects using the LDA model.
    - Calculate a rating based on the similarity and the active users rating.
- Order items by rating.
- Order by relevancy (if you have any data about that).

An alternative way, described by Jobin Wilson et al., is that you can create an LDA vector of the user, and then find similar items.[13] It could also be interesting to see how that would work. The evaluation looks very good.

10.8.2 Creating the user profile with TF-IDF

With the vectors described previously regarding tags and facts, there's another way you could create a user profile. You can aggregate the vectors of the things the user likes and subtract the things the user doesn't like. Look at the insightful information in table 10.3.

---

[13] Jobin Wilson et al., *Improving Collaborative Filtering Based Recommenders Using Topic Modelling*, Feb 2014. Abstract at https://arxiv.org/abs/1402.6238.

Table 10.3   Vector representation of several movies

	Starring Ben Affleck	Action	Adventure	Comedy	Explosions[a]
BvS	1	1	1	0	5
Valentine's Day	1	0	0	1	0
Raiders of the Lost Ark	0	1	1	1	2
La La Land	0	0	0	1	0

a. These are made-up numbers.

If you have a user (you aren't doing collaborative filtering here, so it's enough to look at one) who rated 5 stars for *Raiders of the Lost Ark* (who doesn't love that movie?) and 3 stars for *La La Land*, you can now create a user profile multiplying the rating on the movie vector and adding it together as shown in table 10.4.

Table 10.4   Multiplying the users' ratings on the movie vectors and adding each element to create a user profile

	Starring Ben Affleck	Action	Adventure	Comedy	Explosions[a]
Raiders of the Lost Ark	0	5	5	5	10
La La Land	0	0	0	3	0
User's profile	0	5	5	8	10

a. These are made-up numbers.

You can now use that vector to find similar content for the user. You should probably normalize the values so that they're on the same scale as the movies, and the number of explosions should probably be downplayed into a film that does or doesn't contain explosions. In that case, the user profile looks like the one in table 10.5.

Table 10.5   Multiplying the user's ratings on the movie vectors and adding each element to create the user profile

	Starring Ben Affleck	Action	Adventure	Comedy	Explosions
User profile	0	5	5	8	5

I find this procedure to be truer to films. A good thing with this is that you can look for movies that have all the aspects of what a user likes (if you captured the right tags and facts, of course), but although I like chocolate and lasagna, that doesn't mean I like them together. The same can be said for many other attributes you could come up with for either food or movies. The takeaway is that you can use this to see that the user likes comedy more than action and adventure.

In the MovieGEEKs analytics part of the system, I've represented a user's taste by running through the user-rated movies and doing sums of the ratings for each genre as shown in the following listing. You can view the code in the /analytics/views.py file.

Listing 10.7 **Extracting tastes from ratings**

```
for movie in movies:          ◁─────┐  Calculated for each
    id = movie.movie_id             │  movie the user rated

    rating = ratings[id]      ◁──────┐
                                     │  Gets the rating
    r = rating.rating
    sum_rating += r
    movie_dtos.append(MovieDto(id, movie.title, r))
    for genre in movie.genres.all():          ◁─────

        if genre.name in genres_ratings.keys():
            genres_ratings[genre.name] += r - user_avg
            genres_count[genre.name] += 1

max_value = max(genres_ratings.values())
max_value = max(max_value, 1)        ◁──────── Makes sure it isn't below one
max_count = max(genres_count.values())  ◁───── Finds the max values
max_count = max(max_count, 1)        ◁──────── Makes sure it isn't below one

genres = []
for key, value in genres_ratings.items():     ◁──────
    genres.append((key, 'rating', value/max_value))
    genres.append((key, 'count', genres_count[key]/max_count))
```

Iterates over each movie genre and builds a dictionary with genre names as keys and sum of ratings as values

Finds the max values

Normalizes the values

This code is used to create charts like the one in figure 10.18 for user 100 (http://localhost:8001/analytics/user/100/).

10.9 *Content-based recommendations in MovieGEEKs*

As mentioned several times, we'll go through an implementation and use of a content-based LDA model building. First, we need to say a few words about getting the data.

10.9.1 *Loading data*

The data set you're using doesn't contain descriptions of movies, so again you're at the mercy of www.themoviedb.org to retrieve data. In the root of the code accompanying the book, there's a script called populate_sample_of_descriptions.py that retrieves the description of the most recent films. An example of what is downloaded can be seen in figure 10.19.[14]

---

[14] See http://mng.bz/1UXq.

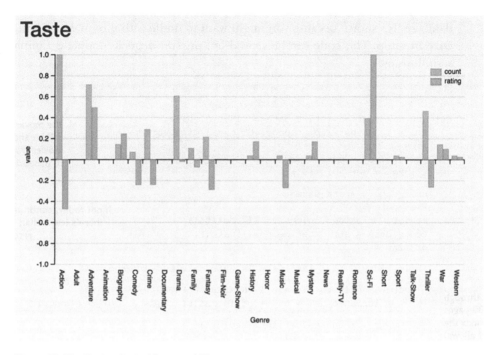

Figure 10.18 Taste charted for user 100

```
- {
    poster_path: "/z09QAf8WbZncbitewNk61KYMZsh.jpg",
    adult: false,
    overview: ""Finding Dory" reunites Dory with friends Nemo and Marlin on a search
    for answers about her past. What can she remember? Who are her parents? And where
    did she learn to speak Whale?",
    release_date: "20016-06-16",
  - genre_ids: [
        16,
        10751
    ],
    id: 127380,
    original_title: "Finding Dory",
    original_language: "en",
    title: "Finding Dory",
    backdrop_path: "/iWRKYHTFlsrxQtfQqFOQyceL83P.jpg",
    popularity: 27.117383,
    vote_count: 1234,
    video: false,
    vote_average: 6.69
},
```

Figure 10.19 The JSON object representing *Finding Dory*

The following listing's script shows how to retrieve and save the descriptions to the database. It's shown because you might want to fiddle with it to make it work for your current setup. This code can be viewed in /pre/moviegeek/populate_sample_of_descriptions.py.

Listing 10.8 Retrieving movie descriptions

```
def get_descriptions(start_date = "1990-01-01"):
    url = """https://api.themoviedb.org/3/discover/movie"""
    qs =
      """?primary_release_date.gte={}&api_key={}&page={}"""
    api_key = get_api_key()

    this_date = start_date
    last_date = ""
    MovieDescriptions.objects.all().delete()
    today_date = str(datetime.now().date())
    errorno = 0

    while today_date > last_date != this_date and errorno < 10:

        for page in tqdm(range(1, NUMBER_OF_PAGES)):
            formated_url = url + qs.format(start_date, api_key, page)

            r = requests.get(formated_url)
            r_json = r.json()
            if 'results' in r_json:
                for film in r_json['results']:
                    id = film['id']
                    md = MovieDescriptions.objects.get_or_create(movie_id=id)[0]

                    md.imdb_id = get_imdb_id(id)
                    if md.imdb_id is not None:
                        md.title = film['title']
                        md.description = film['overview']
                        md.genres = film['genre_ids']
                        last_date = film['release_date']

                        md.save()

            elif 'errors' in r_json:
                print(r_json['errors'])
                    errorno += 1
                break

        time.sleep(1)
```

The movie's API URL. It shows movies from 1990 to present.

If not today, continue if there's fewer than 10 errors

Runs through 1,000 pages (the max the API allows)

Runs through all films in the page

Saves it to the database

If an error occurs, increase the error counter and break out of the for loop.

The movie's API request contains the release data that has to be greater or equal (gte) than this. It is currently set to 1970. To retrieve these movie descriptions run this listing.

Listing 10.9 Downloading the movie descriptions

```
$ python populate_sample_of_descriptions.py.
```

This code downloads the descriptions you can use for the topic model. There might be issues running it because the descriptions are collected from www.themoviedb.org, and there might be a limit on how many requests you can make. I've added a `time.sleep(1)` in the code that requests it to sleep 1 sec between each request. It might not be enough, so if you keep getting angry messages from the server, go to the populate_sample_of_descriptions.py file and put in a higher number.

10.9.2 *Training the model*

You'll use a library called Gensim, which contains an implementation of LDA models. Other models exist, but this is one of the most popular, and my experience with it so far has been good.

You can install Gensim by running the command in listing 10.10. It's part of the general requirements for the MovieGEEKs site, so if you've installed that, then you should be good to go (besides running pip3 install –r requirements.txt).[15]

Listing 10.10   Downloading the Gensim package

```
$ pip3 install gensim.
```

Using the Gensim library, it isn't too hard to create the LDA model. You need the documents loaded and cleaned, as we've already talked about. That's done as shown in the next listing, whose code can be viewed in the /Builder/LdaBuilder.py file.

Listing 10.11   Building an LDA model

```
texts = []
tokenizer = RegexpTokenizer(r'\w+')          Goes through        Makes all the capital
for d in data:                               each document       letters in the text
    raw = d.lower()                                              small letters

    tokens = tokenizer.tokenize(raw)      Splits the text into an array

    stopped_tokens = self.remove_stopwords(tokens)   Removes the stop words

    stemmed_tokens = stopped_tokens   This line is where you stem the words.

    texts.append(stemmed_tokens)      Adds the concentrated document

dictionary = corpora.Dictionary(texts)      Creates a bag of words

corpus = [dictionary.doc2bow(text) for text in texts]

lda_model = models.ldamodel.LdaModel(corpus=corpus, id2word=dictionary,
                                     num_topics=n_topics)
                                                     Shows the LDA
index = similarities.MatrixSimilarity(corpus)        model being
                                                     built
self.save_lda_model(lda_model, corpus, dictionary)
self.save_similarities(index, docs)
```

Creates the corpus, which contains an array of all the documents represented as a bag of words

Saves the similarities in the database

Creates a similarity matrix

Saves the LDA model

---

[15] For more information on installing Gensim, see http://radimrehurek.com/gensim/install.html.

10.9.3   *Creating item profiles*

The item profiles are created with the model and are presented using the LDA vector, which we've talked about. In the builder you saw previously, I chose to go one step further and create the similarity matrix directly because doing the recommendations is a matter of looking up the item in question. This isn't always possible; you'll probably have many more items than we used here.

It's a good idea to look at how big the similarities are in the similarity matrix. If all are close to zero, then it might be worth coming up with more general data that will connect more items. To create the model and enable the MovieGEEKs site to produce content-based recommendations, run the LdaBuild.py file shown in the listing below.

> **Listing 10.12   Running the LDA model builder**

```
$ python -m builder.lda_model_calculator
```

10.9.4   *Creating user profiles*

I am definitely repeating myself: a user profile can be created in many ways. The simplest one, which you'll use in the next listing, is a list of the items that the user liked, and for each of them, you'll find similar items. You'll find this code snippet in the familiar script /recs/content_based_recommender.py.

> **Listing 10.13   Recommendation for a user at runtime**

You use all the ratings from the user, at least the 100 highest.

Using this method makes it easier to test because it receives a list of what ratings the user got.

```
def recommend_items(self,
                    user_id,
                    num=6):                         Calls the
                                            recommend_items_by_ratings

    movie_ids = Rating.objects.filter(user_id=user_id)
                        .order_by('-rating')
                        .values_list('movie_id', flat=True)[:100]

    return self.recommend_items_from_items(movie_ids, num)  ◄────

def recommend_items_by_ratings(self,
                               user_id,
                               active_user_items,   ◄────
                               num=6):
                                            Extracts all the IDs of
                                            the rated movies
    content_sims = dict()

    movie_ids = {movie['movie_id']: movie['rating'] \
            for movie in active_user_items}   ◄────      Calculates the
    user_mean = sum(movie_ids.values()) / len(movie_ids)  ◄── user mean

    sims = LdaSimilarity.objects.filter(Q(source__in=movie_ids.keys())
                        & ~Q(target__in=movie_ids.keys())
                        & Q(similarity__gt=self.min_sim))
```

You're only interested in iterating over the targets of the similarity, so get those.

Orders the similarities by similarity value and takes the top candidates. The number to take is something you should adjust, balancing performance and time.

Finds all the similarities that have that as a target

```
sims = sims.order_by('-similarity')[:self.max_candidates]
recs = dict()
targets = set(s.target for s in sims)
for target in targets:

    pre = 0
    sim_sum = 0

    rated_items = [i for i in sims if i.target == target]

    if len(rated_items) > 0:
        for sim_item in rated_items:
            r = Decimal(movie_ids[sim_item.source] - user_mean)
            pre += sim_item.similarity * r
            sim_sum += sim_item.similarity

        if sim_sum > 0:
            recs[target] = \
                { 'prediction': Decimal(user_mean) + pre/sim_sum,
                  'sim_items': [r.source for r in rated_items]}

return sorted(recs.items(),
        key=lambda item: -float(item[1]['prediction']))[:num]
```

Runs through those targets

Finds all the items that the user rated that are similar to the current target

Deducts the user mean from the rating

If it found rated items, it runs through them.

Adds the similarity to the sum

Multiplies similarity with rating

Sees whether there are any similarities . . .

Returns a sorted list of recs ordered by prediction

. . . if so, adds them as a recommendation

The `recommend_items` method can be called using the API, calling http://127.0.0.1:8000/rec/cb/ user/400003/ if you want to get the recommendations for user_id 400003. The result will look like that shown in the following listing.

Listing 10.14   Result of calling the cb user rec

```
{
user_id: "400003",
data:[
["1049413",{
  prediction: "10.0000",
  sim_items:[ "2709768"]}
],
["4160704",{
  prediction: "6.8300",
  sim_items: ["1878870" ]}
],
["1178665",{
prediction: "6.8300",
sim_items: ["1878870"]}
], …
```

The predictions are done based on the rating of only one film. You can decide whether it's beneficial to rate predictions this way, but it's at least an ordering that will provide a list where the items are more similar to the items that the user rated higher.

10.9.5   *Showing recommendations*

The content-based recommendations are shown on the Details page of a particular movie, so the current item is the featured film. You saw an example of this in figure 10.15.

For the personalized recommendations on the front page, iterate through all the user's items and calculate similarity based on their LDA vectors, and then order them before returning them to the user. An example that can be seen in figure 10.20.

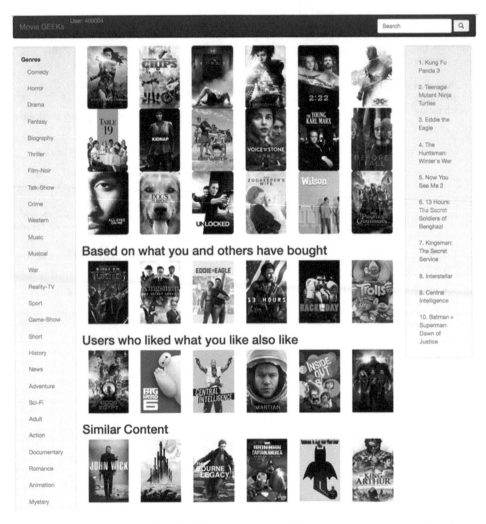

Figure 10.20   The personalized content-based recommendations can be seen on the front page of MovieGEEKs app in the row called Similar Content.

10.10 *Evaluation of the content-based recommender*

Before moving on, let's refer back to chapter 9 and think about how you could evaluate this recommender. In chapter 9, we talked about doing cross-validation of the data, but that doesn't work for content data. To evaluate this recommender, you can use the same code as used to evaluate the MAP. Well almost.

You need to make a recommender method that takes a list of ratings such that you can call it with the training part of the user's ratings. But you already had that as shown in listing 10.14. The next thing to consider is how you want to divide each user's data. Again, you can either do it so that you ensure that there's always a certain amount of training data or always a certain number of test ratings. Or it could be a specific point. You can run the evaluation by executing the code in the following listing.

> **Listing 10.15   Executing the evaluation**

```
> python -m evaluator.evaluation_runner -cb
```

This code creates a CSV file with the data used to show the evaluations. Figure 10.21 shows how the MAP looks.

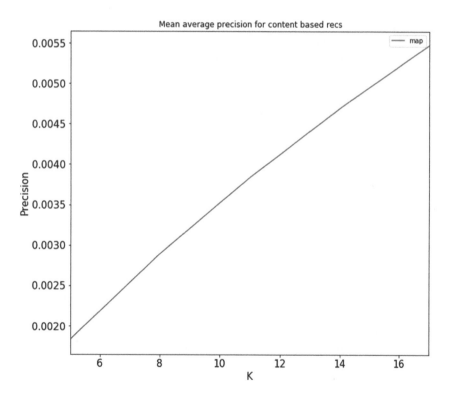

Figure 10.21   Evaluation on the content-based recommender. Using these measures won't put the content-based recommender in a favorable spotlight.

Content-based recommenders work by finding similar content. The result of the evaluation depends on whether your domain and users are one, where users stay within the same type of content, or on how adventurous the users are.

Another way to test this type of recommender could also be by looking at how different the recommended items are from the seeded (input) content. The good thing is that all users have rated one item, and there's a similar item that will receive a rating. The earlier test was done using similarities above 0.1 (at least), and that produced recommendations for 96% of the users. That's higher than a collaborative filtering algorithm.

10.11 *Pros and cons of content-based filtering*

Here are some things to consider when you build a content-based filtering algorithm:

- Pros:
  - New items are easy to add. Create the item feature vector, and you're set to go.
  - You don't require much traffic. Because you can find similarity based on content descriptions, you can start recommending things from the first visit or rating.
  - It recommends across popularity; content-based recommenders don't care which content is popular right now if it finds that a film nobody ever watched is as likely to be recommended as one that everybody watched.
- Cons:
  - Conflates liking with importance. If you like science fiction films with Harrison Ford, the system will also give you films with Harrison Ford that aren't science fiction.
  - No serendipity; it's specialized.
  - Limited understanding of content. It might be hard to include all features that mark the aspects that make content favorable to a user, which means that the system can easily *misunderstand* what the user likes.

An example of this is the first *Thor* movie. It could be that a user likes everything that comes out of the Shakespearian school, but normally dislikes action, but the system interprets a user liking *Thor* because it's an action film. Or as Joseph Konstan says in his "Introduction to Recommender Systems", if I like Sandra Bullock in action films and Meg Ryan in comedies, but if I hate Meg Ryan in action films and Sandra Bullock in comedies, there's no way for that to be captured in the feature vector.[16] That is, unless you start combining them to have a feature "Action film starring Sandra Bullock" and "Comedy starring Sandra Bullock," and so on.

You're doing great! Just the summary to go, and then you are finished with chapter 10.

---

[16] University of Minnesota courses, taught by Joseph Konstan, "Introduction to Recommender Systems: Non-Personalized and Content-Based," www.coursera.org/learn/recommender-systems-introduction.

Summary

- TF-IDF is easy, apart from remembering that its acronym means term frequency–inverse document frequency. You can use it to find important words in documents.

- Before feeding descriptions and texts to an algorithm, it's good to remove unwanted words and optimize for the algorithm. This can be done with removing stop words, popular words, stemming, and using TF-IDF to remove words that aren't important.

- Topic models create topics that can be used to describe documents.

- Latent Dirichlet allocation (LDA) creates a topic model.

- Evaluating content-based recommenders can be done by dividing each user's ratings into training and testing data (as you learned in chapter 9). Then run through each user and calculate the recommendations to see if it produced something that was in the test set.

- Content-based recommender systems are good because they don't need much information about the user.

- Content-based recommender systems will find similar items, which might not always be the most surprising and fun recommendations to get.

Finding hidden genres
with matrix factorization

11

The matrix is only numbers, and this chapter is about the matrix and how to create one:

- You'll learn about dimensionality reduction recommender algorithms.
- Reducing similarity will help you find latent (hidden) factors in the data.
- You'll train and use a singular value decomposition (SVD) to create recommendations.
- You'll learn how to fold in new users and items into an SVD.
- You'll look at another matrix factorization model called the Funk SVD, which is more flexible than the original SVD.

What have you learned so far? In chapter 8, we looked at collaborative filtering using neighbor-based filtering. In this chapter, we're going to return to collaborative filtering, but this time we're not talking about neighborhoods. Instead, we'll explore latent factors. In chapter 10, we talked about latent factors, but at that point, we talked about latent factors in the content data. Now we'll look at latent factors in relation to collaborative filtering, which means in behavioral data.

I'm throwing around many names. But let's get it settled: *hidden genres* are the same as *latent factors*. At least when talking about movies. The factors are said to be latent because they're defined by something that an algorithm calculates, not by humans. They're *trends* in the data that show or explain the user's taste. These trends or factors are also latent because even if they make sense data-wise, it might not be so easy to say what these factors mean. I'll explain this as we go.

Latent factor recommenders are a relatively new discovery, getting their real breakthrough when the Netflix Prize competition promised $1 million to anyone who could improve Netflix's recommendations by at least 10%. The winner was an *ensemble recommender algorithm*, which means mixing many different algorithms to produce the final result (and, incidentally, the topic of chapter 12). The winning ensemble was so complicated that it never went into production. Instead, another solution made by Simon Funk became famous for getting close to winning because he blogged about it. His finding has been the basis for many other solutions since.

In this chapter, you'll look at several solutions that were close to winning Netflix's prize. We'll also concentrate on something called the rating matrix. If you've only behavioral data or implicit ratings, you should first go through the steps of converting it into ratings as you did in chapter 4. The Funk SVD, which we talk about at the end of this chapter, can be modified to use behavioral data instead of ratings data.[1]

Before we move on, I want to set the stage. We'll start with much discussion about SVD. It's a well-known method from linear algebra, and there are many tools available to help you calculate matrix factorization. I'll show you one tool with scikit-learn, a machine-learning library for Python.

With a true SVD, you can add new users easily. However, it's terribly slow to calculate an SVD, and if you have a large dataset, then it will be time-consuming.[2] On top of that, there are strict requirements about what should be done about the empty cells in the rating matrix. To address this, we'll move on to the Funk SVD, which is becoming the one used most frequently. It's not as easy to add new users, but it can be done.

Finding latent factors is a task that can be done in many ways. In the scope of collaborative filtering, finding latent factors has been done primarily with matrix factorizations based on the rating matrix.

11.1 Sometimes it's good to reduce the amount of data

Everybody is always ranting about how it's good to have more data. What's up with that? Is this a covert attempt to go against the masses? Let me put you at ease and tell you up front that it isn't. But you need to look at how to get the most out of the data you do have.

A reason to reduce the dimensions could be to extract a signal from the data. For example, the top plot in figure 11.1 shows a scatter plot of noisy data, while the bottom one shows the actual signal—the information in the data. Simplifying the data can sometimes make it easier to understand the information hidden in it.

---

[1] It's a funky algorithm, but its name comes from the originator, Simon Funk, who popularized it.
[2] Michael Holmes et al., "Fast SVD for Large-Scale Matrices," http://sysrun.haifa.il.ibm.com/hrl/bigml/files/Holmes.pdf.

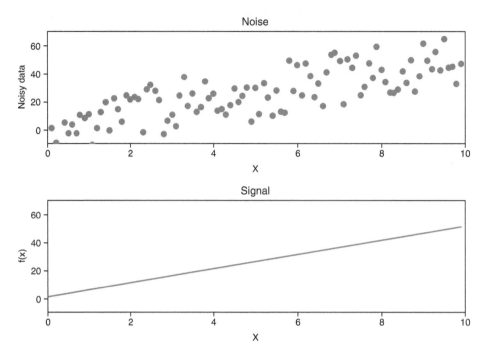

Figure 11.1   A scatter plot of noisy data (top) and the signals that uncover the information in the data (bottom)

In a sense, you could have the same information in the points as in the line as shown in the figure, only the points have noise too. The same principle applies when you do dimension reduction, where you have high-dimensional data.

Think about the data as a cloud of points, and you want to project the data into a lower-dimensional space where the distance between the objects is the same. Then the points that were further from each other before the reduction are also further away after the reduction, and nearby items are also closer after the reduction. You want to reduce the data so that only the directions that provide more information are retained. If the algorithm succeeds, then the vectors pointing in those directions are said to be *latent factors.*

To illustrate this in an example closer to home for us recommender people, let's look at a real-world story. Imagine that you are on a first date or stuck in an elevator with somebody (stress levels being equally high). To release part of the tension, you start talking about movies. It might start with something like "Did you see *X*?" Or it might be that you're in for a longer session and want to talk about movie tastes and say, "I like films with people dressed from a particular designer and with a slightly supernatural aspect, and preferably it makes me laugh and takes place in the seventies." The other person says, "Oh, so you like James Bond!" "Yes, but also *A Single Man* (a movie from 2009 directed by Tom Ford, who usually designs sunglasses and stuff) or *Clueless* (an even older comedy)." The other person says, "Cool," and goes off on ranting about *Dawson's Creek* (television series that ended in 1998) being such a cool series because they all wore clothing of a well-defined taste.

If you should do the same story with the usual set of genres, it would go something like this: "I like action movies, but also drama and comedy." And the other person would say, "Yes, I like TV series." This probably wouldn't turn out to be a fruitful conversation. The basic idea is that by looking at the behavioral data of users, you can find categories or topics that let you explain users' tastes with much less granularity than with each movie but more detail than genres. These factors will enable us to position the movies that users like closer to each other.

Talking about hidden things makes it sound as if there's always something there, so it's worthwhile to point out that if your data is random or it doesn't have any signal, the reduction won't provide any additional information. But by extracting factors from the data, you'll use more of the data collected for a user. The neighborhood algorithms discussed in chapter 8 uses only small sets of the data when calculating predictions; here you'll use more.

11.2 Example of what you want to solve

Let's get back to the rating matrix that I've been dragging around for the last several chapters (shown in table 11.1).

Table 11.1 Rating matrix

	Comedy	Action	Comedy	Action	Drama	Drama
Sara	5	3		2	2	2
Jesper	4	3	4		3	3
Therese	5	2	5	2	1	1
Helle	3	5	3		1	1
Pietro	3	3	3	2	4	5
Ekaterina	2	3	2	3	5	5

Again, you'll do a dimension reduction by factorizing the rating matrix (that's described in the following paragraphs). This will help you find important factors so that you've users and items in the same space, and you can recommend films that are interesting to the user by finding which are nearby. You can also find similar users.

Using the matrix factorization, I produced the plot shown in figure 11.2 using only two dimensions. First, you can say that the vertical axis indicates how serious, the films are: *Men in Black* (MiB) and *Ace Ventura* (AV) are not serious, while *Les Misérables* (LM) is serious.

It's important to note that this is my interpretation. I didn't try to fit the data to make it do a better factorization, so it's okay to be puzzled. I did try to come up with an interpretation of the horizontal axis but having *Ace Ventura* and *Sense and Sensibility* at the same point made it difficult.[3] It's also important to note that the system didn't choose the number of dimensions; I did that to make the result illustratable. More on that later.

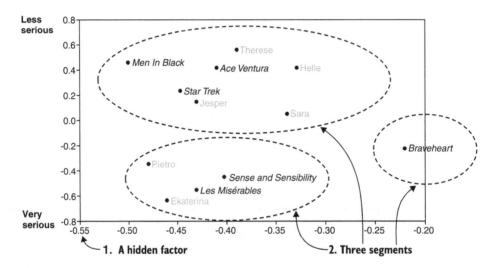

Figure 11.2   Plotting the movies and users in a reduced dimensional space. The reduced space has two dimensions: one is the seriousness of the movies (y-axis), while I can't see what interpretation to put on the x-axis.

The visualization in figure 11.2 shows three segments, which seems to correspond well with the rating matrix.

1   The top one contains Therese, Helle, and Jesper (he's hard to see because he's under *Star Trek*) and Sara who like all comedies and action movies.
2   Pietro and Ekaterina are down with the dramas.
3   The third segment contains only *Braveheart,* which is a bit outside of the other segments.

Looking at figure 11.3, where the segments are pointed out in the rating matrix, makes it easy to see why there would be these three segments in figure ll.2.

---

[3]   Please let me know on the book forum if you come up with something.

	Comedy	Action	Comedy	Action	Drama	Drama
Sara	5	3		2	2	2
Jesper	4	3	4		3	3
Therese	5	2	5	2	1	1
Helle	3	5	3		1	1
Pietro	3	3	3	2	4	5
Ekaterina	2	3	2	3	5	5

Segment 1 — Segment 3 — Segment 2 —

Figure 11.3 Showing the three segments in the rating matrix, which is shown in figure 11.2.

When I first saw the output from figure 11.2, it puzzled me that Jesper's position was near that of *Star Trek*. He didn't rate the movie that high, so why there? However, if you consider Jesper's ratings in figure 11.3, he gave four stars to *Men in Black* and *Ace Ventura* and three stars to *Star Trek* and the two dramas. Now, it seems sensible that Jesper's position is there because the matrix factorization attempts to push items and users that are more closely related. He's close to *Men in Black* and *Ace Ventura*, but still not too far from the two dramas.

Segment two also deserves another word. I think that *Braveheart* has won its own segment in the reduced space because it's the one film that all rated low. But again, that's my interpretation.

Calculating recommendations is done by looking into this factor space (the coordinate system shown in figure 11.2) and finding the ones that are closer to the user. Before you start plotting your factor space and looking for clusters, listen up: you'll find many tutorials and descriptions showing how you can interpret dimensions in a vector space into something understandable, but they rarely work. Use a vector space as a box that you ask about similarity among items and users. That's what it's good for.

Even if they're hard to interpret, I'm excited about this. It's so cool! I hope that this got you so interested that you're ready to learn a bit of math because you need to dip a bit into linear algebra.

11.3   A whiff of linear algebra

Linear algebra is a large field of mathematics. It covers the study of lines, planes, and subspaces, but it's also concerned with properties common to all vector spaces. Ideally the concept of matrix factorization is based more on linear algebra than what you're going to look at here.

11.3.1   Matrix

Matrix is Latin for *womb*.[4] You've looked at vectors, which represent user taste, but they can also mean so many other things. If you've two vectors like the following

$$v_1 = \begin{bmatrix} 1 \\ 1 \\ 1 \end{bmatrix} \quad \text{and} \quad v_2 = \begin{bmatrix} 0 \\ 2 \\ 1 \end{bmatrix}$$

then you could consider them as two arrows pointing in two directions. You could draw a plane that passes through them, and you can say that they span a plane, such as the plane shown in figure 11.4.

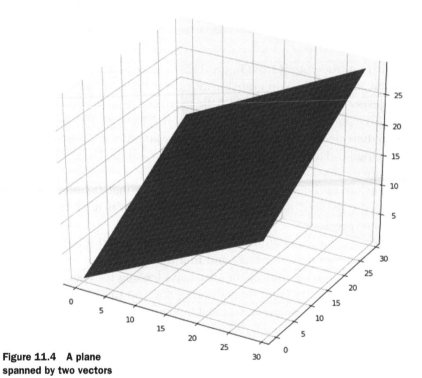

Figure 11.4   A plane spanned by two vectors

---

[4]   You can read more interesting facts about linear algebra at https://en.wikipedia.org/wiki/Linear_algebra.

One way to represent two or more vectors is as a matrix. The matrix M represents the vectors described previously:

$$M = \begin{bmatrix} 1 & 0 \\ 1 & 2 \\ 1 & 1 \end{bmatrix}$$

A *matrix* is a rectangular array of numbers and declared by a number of rows m and a number of columns *n*. A *vector* is a special case of a matrix that has only one column.

Now imagine you're rating vectors for your users. You have a dimension for each content item, which means that you're talking about a vector with thousands of dimensions. In a thousand-dimensioned space, you'll have something called a *hyperplane* that all the vectors lie in. A matrix is a way of describing one of those planes or hyperplanes.

The rating matrix shown earlier will span a kind of hyperplane in a six-dimensional space and will probably be difficult to imagine or draw, so I won't. Think of those as something in a space like this:

$$R = \begin{bmatrix} 5 & 3 & 0 & 2 & 2 & 2 \\ 4 & 3 & 4 & 0 & 3 & 3 \\ 5 & 2 & 5 & 2 & 1 & 1 \\ 3 & 5 & 3 & 0 & 1 & 1 \\ 3 & 3 & 3 & 2 & 4 & 5 \\ 2 & 3 & 2 & 3 & 5 & 5 \end{bmatrix}$$

But before you get too confident with this way of seeing the rating matrix as a matrix, you should remember that you don't have values to put in all the cells, and you can't have a matrix where only part of the cells have values. In the previous matrix, I filled in the empty spaces with zeros, but that isn't the best thing to do. You'll see later that much thought has to go into deciding what should be put in those empty cells.

In the following section, you'll multiply matrices. If you know how to do that, great; if you don't, that section provides a quick example.

MATRIX MULTIPLICATION

If you've two matrices *U* and *V*, they can be multiplied if *A* has the same number of columns as *B* has rows. Figure 11.5 shows an example of how to create a matrix by multiplying two of them.

The idea is that each cell in the new matrix is the dot product between the corresponding row (*U* in figure 11.5) in the first matrix and the corresponding column (*V*) in the second matrix. With this quick example done, let's move on to factorization.

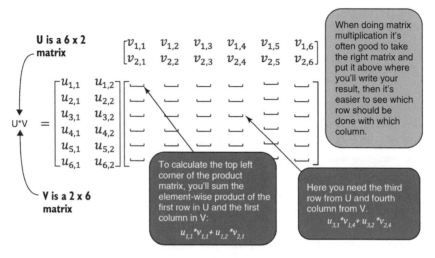

Figure 11.5   Crash course in matrix multiplication

11.3.2 What's factorization?

As discussed previously, you want to factorize the matrix. *Factorization* is about splitting things up. For example, you can split a number like 100 into the following prime factorization:[5]

$$100 = 2 \times 2 \times 5 \times 5$$

This means that you take a number and write it as a number of factors. In this case, you write it as a list of prime numbers.[6] Here, you don't have a number but a rating matrix. And what you can do in this case is to factor it into a product of matrices, so if you have a matrix R (R for rating matrix, blink blink) you can decompose it into the following form: $R = UV$.

If R has n rows and m columns (as in n users and m items), you call it an $n \times m$ matrix (read *n by m*); the size of U will be an $n \times d$ matrix and V is a $d \times m$ matrix. If you look at the matrix shown previously, you'll have a formula as follows:

$$
\begin{bmatrix}
5 & 3 & 0 & 2 & 2 & 2 \\
4 & 3 & 4 & 0 & 3 & 3 \\
5 & 2 & 5 & 2 & 1 & 1 \\
3 & 5 & 3 & 0 & 1 & 1 \\
3 & 3 & 3 & 2 & 4 & 5 \\
2 & 3 & 2 & 3 & 5 & 5
\end{bmatrix}
=
\begin{bmatrix}
u_{1,1} & u_{1,2} \\
u_{2,1} & u_{2,2} \\
u_{3,1} & u_{3,2} \\
u_{4,1} & u_{4,2} \\
u_{5,1} & u_{5,2} \\
u_{6,1} & u_{6,2}
\end{bmatrix}
\begin{bmatrix}
v_{1,1} & v_{1,2} & v_{1,3} & v_{1,4} & v_{1,5} & v_{1,6} \\
v_{2,1} & v_{2,2} & v_{2,3} & v_{2,4} & v_{2,5} & v_{2,6}
\end{bmatrix}
$$

---

[5] For more information, see http://mathworld.wolfram.com/PrimeFactorization.html.

[6] Interestingly, prime number factorization is unique due to the fundamental theorem of arithmetic.

This is called a *UV-decomposition*. Here you set the *d* to be 2, but it could also have been 3 or 4 or even 5 (since the original matrix is 6 × 6). The idea is that you want to decompose the matrix *R* into hidden features (read columns for users and rows for items) for items and for users. In the field of recommender systems, you'd call the *U* the user-feature matrix and the *V* the item-feature matrix.

MATRIX FACTORIZATION

To do the factorization, you need to somehow insert values in the *U* and *V* matrixes in such a way that *UV* is as close to *R* as possible. Let's start simple and say, for example, you want to fit the cells in the second row, second column from the upper left corner of *R* as shown in figure 11.6.

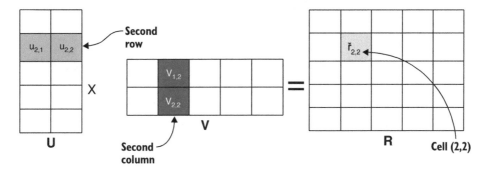

Figure 11.6   The fitted cells as the sum of the element-wise products of the second row in *U* and the second column in *V* by multiplying the first set (*U*) pair-wise with the corresponding column in the second set (*V*), then adding the product of the formula afterward.

As you saw in the figure, the cell is calculated using the dot product. The dot product isn't new to the careful reader; you looked at it before, so to refresh your understanding: if you've the row and the column from figure 11.6, then you've two vectors ($u_{2,1}$, $u_{2,2}$) and ($v_{1,2}$, $v_{2,2}$), and the dot product is:

$$\hat{r}_{2,2} = u_2 \times v_2 = u_{2,1}v_{1,2} + u_{2,2}v_{2,2}$$

Even if the vectors are longer, it works the same way. For each cell in the matrix, you've a similar expression, so that you've a long list of equations. To do factorization is to find the *v*'s and *u*'s that satisfy the equations. If you do that, you've successfully done a matrix factorization. In the next several sections, you'll look at two ways to do the factorization: with the SVD method, which is an old mathematical construct that's well-known and understood, and with the Funk SVD.

11.4   *Constructing the factorization using SVD*

One of the most commonly used methods for matrix factorization is an algorithm called SVD (singular value decomposition). You want to find items to recommend to users, and you want to do it using extracted factors from the rating matrix. The idea of factorization is even more complicated because you want to end up with a formula that enables you to add new users and items without too much fuss.

From the rating matrix M, you want to construct two matrices that you can use: one that represents the customer's taste and one that contains the item profiles. Using SVD, you construct three matrices: U, Σ, and V^T (also known as V^* depending on which book you look in). Because you want to end up with two matrices, you multiply the square root of Σ on one of the two others, and then you only have two left. But before doing that, you want to use the middle matrix that gives you information about how much you should reduce the dimensions. Figure 11.7 shows the SVD.

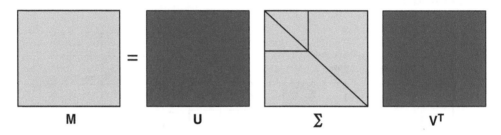

Figure 11.7   A matrix can be factorized into three matrices.

You call them:

- M—A matrix you want to decompose; in your case, it's the rating matrix.
- U—User feature matrix.
- Σ—Weights diagonal.
- VT—Item feature matrix.

When using the SVD algorithm the Σ will always be a diagonal matrix.

DIAGONAL MATRIX

A *diagonal matrix* means that it only has zeros except in the diagonal from the upper-left corner to the lower-right corner as shown here:

$$\begin{bmatrix} 9 & 0 & 0 \\ 0 & 5 & 0 \\ 0 & 0 & 1 \end{bmatrix}$$

REDUCING THE MATRIX

It might be hard to see how splitting a matrix into three matrices does any good, especially when I mentioned that it's time-consuming to create these. But the idea is that the central diagonal matrix Σ contains elements that are sorted from the largest to the smallest; the elements are called *singular values*, and the values indicate how much information this feature produces for the data set. A *feature* here means both a column in the user matrix U and a row in the content matrix VT. You can now select a number r of features and set the rest of the diagonal to zero. Look at figure 11.8, which illustrates what remains of the matrices when you set diagonal values to zero outside the middle box. This is the same as removing all right-most columns in the user matrix U and all the bottom rows from V*, keeping only the r top rows.

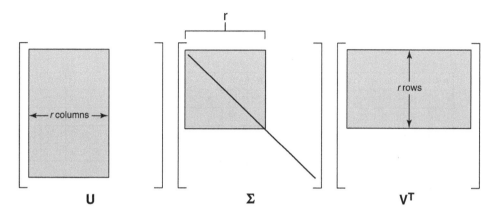

Figure 11.8   Reducing the SVD by setting small values in Σ to zero.

Let's look at an example using the rating matrix shown previously. You can make a Python Panda DataFrame[7] as shown in the next listing.

Listing 11.1   Creating a rating matrix

```
import pandas as pd
import numpy as np

movies = ['mib', 'st', 'av', 'b', 'ss', 'lm']
users = ['Sara', 'Jesper', 'Therese', 'Helle', 'Pietro', 'Ekaterina']

M = pd.DataFrame([
    [5.0, 3.0, 0.0, 2.0, 2.0, 2.0],
    [4.0, 3.0, 4.0, 0.0, 3.0, 3.0],
    [5.0, 2.0, 5.0, 2.0, 1.0, 1.0],
    [3.0, 5.0, 3.0, 0.0, 1.0, 1.0],
    [3.0, 3.0, 3.0, 2.0, 4.0, 5.0],
    [2.0, 3.0, 2.0, 3.0, 5.0, 5.0]],
    columns=movies,
    index=users)
```

For fun you can test whether it worked correctly and try out the following command:

```
M['mib'][ 'sara']
```

It prints 5.0, which is correct. To do the matrix factorization, you can use the NumPy implementation shown in listing 11.2.[8]

---

[7] If you're new to Panda, I recommend *Python for Data Analysis* by Wes McKinney (O'Reilly Media; 2nd ed., 2017).

[8] For more information on NumPy, see http://mng.bz/xYEl.

Listing 11.2   Doing an SVD on the matrix

```
from numpy import linalg      ◁————— Imports the linear algebra library of NumPy⁸
```

Imports the linear algebra library of NumPy[8]

```
U, Sigma, Vt = linalg.svd(M)      ◁————— Calculates the matrix factorization
```

This creates the three matrices shown in figure 11.9 (which looks like what you saw in figures 11.6 and 11.7).

-0.34	0.05	0.91	0.11	0.19	-0.00
-0.43	0.16	-0.31	-0.12	0.74	0.35
-0.39	0.56	-0.19	0.63	-0.32	0.02
-0.33	0.42	0.02	-0.76	-0.37	-0.05
-0.48	-0.34	-0.18	0.03	0.10	-0.78
-0.46	-0.61	-0.06	0.02	-0.40	0.51

17.27	0	0	0	0	0
0	5.84	0	0	0	0
0	0	3.56	0	0	0
0	0	0	3.13	0	0
0	0	0	0	1.67	0
0	0	0	0	0	0.56

-0.50	-0.44	-0.41	-0.22	-0.40	-0.43
0.46	0.17	0.42	-0.22	-0.49	-0.55
0.50	0.22	-0.78	0.26	-0.08	-0.13
0.34	-0.77	0.17	0.51	-0.02	-0.01
0.41	-0.36	-0.16	-0.76	0.19	0.25
-0.01	-0.03	0.01	-0.02	0.75	-0.66

U   Σ   Vᵗ

Figure 11.9   The matrices of the NumPy factorization

Does that make sense? Well, probably, not really. It's so much work to get three matrices exactly the same size as the original. But hold your horses a second. Look at the diagonal matrix in the middle (Σ), more significantly known as the *weights matrix*. Each of these weights can be an indication of how much information is present in each dimension. The first one provides much information (17.27), the next one, not so much (5.84), and so on, so you can reduce the size of the matrices. But by how much?

HOW MUCH SHOULD THE MATRIX BE REDUCED?

You could reduce the dimensions using only two, and still produce a chart like the one in figure 11.2. Another good reason for reducing the matrix to two dimensions is that by looking at the weights in the Sigma matrix (Σ), you'll get most of the information by using only two features.

With such a small example, reducing the matrix doesn't matter much. But a rule of thumb is that you should retain 90% of the information. If you add up all the weights, that's 100%, then you should continue counting weights until you have 90% of the information. Let's do the calculation for the matrix in figure 11.9.

The sum of all of them is 32.0, so 90% of that is 28.83. If you reduce it to 4 dimensions, then the weight is 29.80 so you should reduce it to 4 dimensions (factors). To reduce the matrices in code, you'd implement the commands in this listing.

Listing 11.3   Reducing the matrix

```
def rank_k(k):                 ◁
    U_reduced= np.mat(U[:,:k])          Returns the reduced
    Vt_reduced = np.mat(Vt[:k,:])       matrices
    Sigma_reduced = Sigma_reduced = np.eye(k)*Sigma[:k]
```

```
    return U_reduced, Sigma_reduced, Vt_reduced,
                                                        ┌─ Uses rank_k to
                                                        │  return the reduced
U_reduced, Sigma_reduced, Vt_reduced = rank_k(4)   ◁───┘  matrices

M_hat = U_reduced * Sigma_reduced * Vt_reduced     ◁──┐ Calculates the
                                                      │ deduced matrix M_hat
```

The M_hat matrix looks like the one shown in figure 11.10.

	mib	st	av	b	ss	lm
Sara	4.87	3.11	0.05	2.24	1.94	1.92
Jesper	3.49	3.46	4.19	0.95	2.62	2.82
Therese	5.22	1.80	4.92	1.59	1.10	1.14
Helle	3.25	4.77	2.90	-0.47	1.14	1.13
Pietro	2.93	3.05	3.03	2.11	4.30	4.67
Ekaterina	2.27	2.77	1.89	2.50	4.92	5.35

Figure 11.10   Showing the M_hat matrix

It's probably tempting to throw away the *U* and *V* matrices, but not if you want to add new users to the model. If you want to add them to the model, you must keep the factorized matrices. More on that in a bit. First let's see how to predict a rating.

PREDICT A RATING

With the factorization in place, it's now easy to predict ratings for users. Simply look it up in the new M_hat matrix, which contains all of the predicted ratings. To look up something in a matrix, you first denote the column (in the following listing, 'av') and then the index of the row (here 'sara'). The following listing shows a look-up (that's after it wraps M_hat in a data frame with nice column and index names).

Listing 11.4   Predicting a rating

```
M_hat_matrix = pd.DataFrame(M_hat, columns= movies,index= users ).round(2) ◁──┐

M_hat['av']['sara']  ◁──┐ Queries for Sara's predicted    Wraps the M_hat matrix in a data
                        │ rating for Ace Ventura           frame so you can query it as you
                                                           did with the rating matrix
```

Suppose you wanted to save the decomposed matrices only. To avoid doing three sets of multiplication, you'll take the Σ matrix and find the square root of it and then multiply that by each of the matrices. You can update the reduction matrix from the previous listing to that shown in the next listing.

Listing 11.5   Reducing the matrix

```
def rank_k2(k):                  ◁──────────┐ Reduces the size of the
    U_reduced= np.mat(U[:,:k])              │ decomposed matrices
    Vt_reduced = np.mat(Vt[:k,:])
    Sigma_reduced = Sigma_reduced = np.eye(k)*Sigma[:k]
    Sigma_sqrt = np.sqrt(Sigma_reduced)     ◁──┐ Takes the square
                                               │ root of all entries
```

```
    return U_reduced*Sigma_sqrt, Sigma_sqrt*Vt_reduced

U_reduced, Vt_reduced = rank_k2(4)        ◄─────┐  Calls the method to get
                                                │  the reduced matrices
M_hat = U_reduced * Vt_reduced            ◄─────┘

                                          To produce the M_hat
                                          matrix, multiply the two.
```

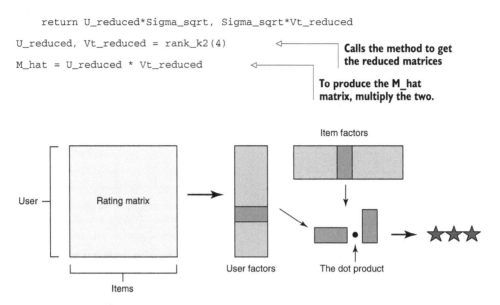

Figure 11.11 How to predict ratings using the factors

Now with these two matrices, you can predict a rating like the following listing (and illustrated in figure 11.11). Here you're indexing the matrix in the shape of NumPy arrays and not as data frames as you did before.

Listing 11.6 Calculating the ratings

```
Jesper = 1                                   Sets variables to make
AceVentura = 2                               it more readable
U_reduced[Jesper]*Vt_reduced[:,AceVentura]   ◄─── Calculates a predicted rating
```

Running the previous code shows that Jesper would rate *Ace Ventura* at 4.19, which is close to his actual rating. When you produce a rating on the same film for Sara, you get 0.048, which is also close to the zero you fed into the algorithm. Maybe filling all the empty spots with zeros wasn't such a good idea. To make the predictions better, you'll do something called imputation.

SOLVING THE PROBLEM OF THE ZEROS IN THE RATING MATRIX USING IMPUTATION
What do you do with all the data you don't know? The example you looked at previously had only a few unknowns, but often, you'll talk about situations where only 1% of the cells in the rating matrix have values. Something needs to be done. You have two common ways to approach this:

- You can calculate the mean of each item (or user) and fill in this mean where there are zeros in each row (or column) of the matrix.
- You can normalize each row, such that all elements are centered around zero, so the zeros will become the average.

Both methods are known as *imputation*. This solution takes you part of the way, but you can do better with something called baseline predictors, which I'll talk about soon. In the next listing, you'll fill in the cells with zeros with the averages of the product ratings.

Listing 11.7   Normalizing ratings

```
r_average = M[M > 0.0].mean()     ⊲── Calculates the mean of all movies
M[M == 0] = np.NaN                ⊲── Sets all entries equal to zero to NaN (not a number)
M.fillna(r_average, inplace=True) ⊲── Fills all NaNs with the averages
```

If you run it through the mill again, you get Sara's predicted rating for *Ace Ventura* as 3.47, which I think sounds closer to what it should be. It also sounds closer to the average rating for *Ace Ventura,* which is 3.4.

11.4.1 *Adding a new user by folding in*

One cool thing about the SVD method is that you can also add new users and items into the system (though not before there have been interactions). For example, you could add me to the factorization; my rating vector would look something like that shown in table 11.2.

Table 11.2   Ratings from Kim

	Comedy	Action	Comedy	Action	Drama	Drama
Kim	4	5		3	3	

Expressed as a vector, this would be:

$$r_{kim} = (4.0, 5.0, 0.0, 3.0, 3.0, 0.0)$$

What you want is to project this rating vector into your vector space. To do that, you can utilize the decomposition shown previously. To add a new user means to add another row to the rating matrix, which in turn means that the decomposed user matrix would also have another row, as illustrated in figure 11.12.

How do you do that? It's simple—you use the things you know already. You know the row of ratings, you know Σ and V^*. You have rules that come into play about how to work with matrices, but I'll leave that out here because it'll require lengthy discussion

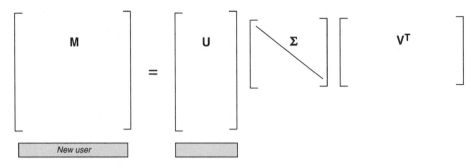

New user

Figure 11.12   The schematics of the SVD folding-in technique

about matrices.[9] I hope you'll trust me telling you that you can calculate the new row using the following formula:

$$u_{kim} = r_k V^t \Sigma^{-1}$$

where

- u_{kim} is the user vector in the reduced space to represent the new user.
- r_k is the new user's rating vector.
- Σ^{-1} is the inverse of the Sigma matrix.
- V^T is the item matrix.

To use this in Python, you implement the code in this listing.

```
from numpy.linalg import inv

r_kim = np.array([4.0, 5.0, 0.0, 3.0, 3.0, 0.0])
u_kim = r_kim *Vt_reduced.T* inv(Sigma_reduced)
```

Now you can predict ratings for user Kim as well. Similarly, you can fold in a new item using the following formula:

$$\hat{i}_{new} = r^T_{new\ item} U \Sigma^{-1}$$

where

- i_{new} is the vector in the reduced space to represent the new item.
- $r_{new\ item}$ is the new items user ratings vector.
- Σ^{-1} is the inverse of the sigma matrix.
- U—The user matrix.

As you can see, you need to have user ratings before you can add items. If you can add new users and items, then why ever recalculate everything, you might ask. Remember

---

[9] Look at "Using Linear Algebra for Intelligent Information Retrieval" for more details. See www2.denizyuret .com/ref/berry/berry95using.pdf.

that the reduction is done to extract topics from the data. These topics aren't updated when you fold in a new user or item; they're placed compared to the topics that are already there.

It's important to update the SVD as often as possible. Depending on how many new users and items you have, you should do it once a day or once a week. One curious thing about folding in a new user is that if the new user only has one rating, then it doesn't matter if it's high or low.[10] The list of recommendations will be exactly the same. Play around with the small matrix shown previously to understand why that's so.

11.4.2 *How to do recommendations with SVD*

Two ways you can make recommendations now are to calculate all predicted ratings and take the largest ones that the user hasn't seen before, or to iterate through each item and find similar products in the reduced space. A third way could be to use the new matrices you have to calculate neighborhood collaborative filtering as you did in chapter 8. The reason why that might be a good idea is that the matrices have all non-zero entries (at least if it's normalized). In this dense space, you've a much better chance of finding similar items or users.

PROBLEMS WITH SVD

I can keep on writing about SVD and its possibilities, but I want to move on to another type of reduction method, which is similar to SVD but much more efficient to calculate. The SVD you've seen so far has several problems: To begin with, it requires that something is done with the unfilled cells in the rating matrix. And it's slow to calculate large matrixes. On the positive side, there's the possibility to fold in new users as they arrive, but you need to keep in mind, the SVD model is static and should be updated as often as possible.

Further, SVD isn't at all explainable. People like to know why something is recommended but the SVD approach makes it difficult to understand why the machine is predicting high ratings for one item and not another. But before you move on, I recommend you read an article written by Badrul M. Sarwar et. al., from the GroupLens research group—people you should know if you're into recommender systems. The article is "Application of Dimensionality Reduction in Recommender System—A Case Study."[11]

The next matrix factorization algorithm is interesting, but as always, I'll sidestep a second and look at something called baseline predictors, which make it easier to add values to the empty slots of the matrix. Although these can be used as a recommender system, they're used here as a way to make the matrix factorization better.

---

[10] As pointed out in *"Fifty Shades of Ratings: How to Benefit from a Negative Feedback in Top-N Recommendations Tasks"* by E. Frolov et al. An abstract can be found at https://arxiv.org/abs/1607.04228.
[11] For more information, see http://files.grouplens.org/papers/webKDD00.pdf.

11.4.3 *Baseline predictors*

Besides item types and the users' tastes, there are other aspects of items and users to mention. If a movie is generally considered good, then the average rating of that film is probably slightly higher than the global average of all movies, and in turn, if a film was considered bad, its average rating is likely below the global average. If you had information like that, then you could add a slightly higher default rating on an item. At the same time, certain users are more critical than others (did I say grumpy old farts?) or, conversely, more positive. An item that's above or below the average you could say is *biased*. The same is true with users; you can say that users have a bias compared to the global average.

If you could extract the biases for the items and the users, then you'd be in a position to provide a *baseline* for your predictions, which is much better than using the average as you did before when filling out empty cells in the rating matrix. Using these biases, you can create baseline predictors. A *baseline predictor* is the sum of the global average plus the bias of the item plus the bias of the user. In math you'd use the following equation:

$$b_{ui} = m + b_u + b_i$$

where

- b_{ui} is the base prediction of item i for user u.
- b_u is the user bias.
- b_i is the item bias.
- μ is the average of all ratings .

All that sounds clever, but how do you calculate the user and item biases because they're both part of the ratings? Easy. You have an equation for each rating. If, for example, Sara rated the Avenger film *Civil War* only 3 out of 5 stars because she thought *Captain America* wasn't acting nice, you've the following equation:

$$b_{(sara, civil\ war)} = m + b_{sara} + b_{civil\ war} \implies 3 = 3.03 + b_{sara} + b_{civil\ war}$$

The global average of the example is 3.03 (sum all the cells divided by the number of nonzero cells). Can you answer what the values of the biases are? It's not possible to say which is what, but if you have many equations with the biases, you can get close by trying to solve it as a least-squares problem.

FINDING BIAS BY FINDING LEAST SQUARES

When discussing similarity in chapter 7, you learned about least squares. It's the same idea here; you want to find biases that make the baseline predictions as close to the known ratings. If you take the same rating as used previously, you'll ask what values you should set for the biases to make the following as small as possible:

$$\min(r_{(sara, civil\ war)} - b_{(sara, civil\ war)})^2 \implies$$
$$\min(r_{(sara, civil\ war)} - m - b_{sara} - b_{civil\ war})^2$$

To be sure I'm not losing anybody here, I'll go through this quickly. The equation means that you're trying to find the *b*s that makes the equation as small as possible or the minimum (min). When you have many ratings (or at least more than one), you can find the minimum of the sum of all of them. The reason for the equation to be squared is that it makes the values all positive as well as penalizes bit differences. When you have many ratings, you write it like the following:

$$\min_b \sum_{(u,i)\in K} (r_{(u,i)} - m - b_u - b_i)^2$$

where $(u,i) \in K$ is all the ratings you have so far.

A SIMPLER WAY TO CALCULATE BIASES

A simpler way to find these biases is to use the equations explained in this section. First, calculate the bias for each user (b_u), taking the sum of the difference between the users' ratings and the mean. Divide this by the number of ratings, which means the result is the average difference between the mean and the users' ratings:

$$b_u = \frac{1}{|I_u|} \sum_{i \in I_u} (r_{u,i} - m)$$

When all the users' biases have been calculated, calculate the item bias (b_i) the same way:

$$b_i = \frac{1}{|U_i|} \sum_{u \in U_i} (r_{u,i} - b_u - m)$$

These baseline predictors mentioned previously can be used to fill in the empty spaces of the rating matrix to make the SVD or, indeed most matrix factorization algorithms, work better. I've calculated the biases for the test data (using the Python code in listing 11.9) and they're shown in table 11.3.

> **Listing 11.9   Calculating biases**

Finds the global mean, which can be done by first finding the mean of each column and then finding the mean of that

Deducts the global mean from all the nonzero ratings

The mean of each row is the user bias.

```
global_mean = M[M>0].mean().mean()
M_minus_mean = M[M>0]-global_mean
user_bias = M_minus_mean.T.mean()
item_bias = M_minus_mean.apply(lambda r: r - user_bias).mean()
```

Deducts the user bias from each row, then takes the mean of each column giving you the item bias.

Table 11.3   User and item biases

User	User Bias	Item	Item Bias
Sara	-0.197222	*Men in Black*	0.644444
Jesper	0.402778	*Star Trek*	0.144444
Therese	-0.330556	*Ace Ventura*	0.333333
Helle	-0.397222	*Braveheart*	-0.783333
Pietro	0.336111	*Sense and Sensibility*	-0.355556
Ekaterina	0.336111	*Les Misérables*	-0.188889

Looking at the table, you'll see that certain users are more critical raters than others, and certain movies are generally considered better than others. I'm not sure this set of users is representative of the general public because I believe *Braveheart* to be a fantastic film. Besides the bias of users, there are other things that can be variable. Let's look at those next.

11.4.4 *Temporal dynamic*

We've talked about bias as something that's static, but a user could move from a happy rater to a grumpy old person, and biases should be adjusted to reflect that. The same is true for adjusting the item bias over time because items go in and out of fashion. Predictions of the ratings could also vary over time, so you could say your rating prediction function is also a function of time. In those instances, you should modify the previous equation to the following function of time:

$$b_{ui}(t) = m + b_u(t) + b_i(t)$$

where

- b_{ui} is the base prediction of item i for user u at time t.
- b_u is the user bias at time t.
- b_i is the item bias at time t.
- m is the average of all ratings.

It's something to consider if you implemented everything else and want to try to squeeze more precision out of the recommender. Whether this is something you want to do is also dependent on the size of your data.

If your data stretches over a long period of time and you have many ratings, then I'd say that you should look into the temporal aspect of things; otherwise, you might keep it simple to start with and then consider upgrading later. You can find much research out there describing how to approach this. A good place to start is *Collaborative Filtering with Temporal Dynamics* by Yehuda Koren.[12]

---

[12] The article can be found at http://mng.bz/52nP.

11.5   *Constructing the factorization using Funk SVD*

The SVD method puts much weight into the rating matrix, but that's a sparse matrix and shouldn't be relied on too heavily in the sense that finding a cell that's populated with a rating can be below 1%. Instead of using the whole matrix, Simon Funk came up with a method that only uses the things you need to know. You need to learn more math to appreciate it, but it's full of figures so that it will be over with in no time. The Funk SVD is also often referred to as *regularized SVD*.

You'll start by looking at the RMSE, which you first read about in chapter 7, to provide a measure of how close you are to the known ratings. With that in your toolbox, you'll look at something called *gradient descent,* which uses RMSE to walk (don't believe me? then you'd better read on) toward a better solution. When you have that, you'll look at how to use baseline predictors. I already mentioned them as a way to predict better than average rating information. Once you've learned all that, you'll look at the Funk SVD algorithm.

11.5.1   *Root Mean Squared Error*

When you're optimizing algorithms, your first approach should always be RMSE. Let's go through how that will make you happier. The problem you want to solve is to create two matrices U and V that when multiplied together will be as close to the original matrix as possible. Ideally you want to find u's and v's so the following is true:

$$\begin{bmatrix} 5 & 3 & 0 & 2 & 2 & 2 \\ 4 & 3 & 4 & 0 & 3 & 3 \\ 5 & 2 & 5 & 2 & 1 & 1 \\ 3 & 5 & 3 & 0 & 1 & 1 \\ 3 & 3 & 3 & 2 & 4 & 5 \\ 2 & 3 & 2 & 3 & 5 & 5 \end{bmatrix} = \begin{bmatrix} u_{1,1} & u_{1,2} \\ u_{2,1} & u_{2,2} \\ u_{3,1} & u_{3,2} \\ u_{4,1} & u_{4,2} \\ u_{5,1} & u_{5,2} \\ u_{6,1} & u_{6,2} \end{bmatrix} \begin{bmatrix} v_{1,1} & v_{1,2} & v_{1,3} & v_{1,4} & v_{1,5} & v_{1,6} \\ v_{2,1} & v_{2,2} & v_{2,3} & v_{2,4} & v_{2,5} & v_{2,6} \end{bmatrix}$$

You also saw earlier that this can be written as a long list of equations. And for each of them, you want the following to be as small as possible:

$$\min{}_{u,v}(r_{ui} - u_u v_i)$$

Because you want to do that for all cells, you can make a sum of these expressions and say that you want the minimum of all of them:

$$\min{}_{u,v} \sum_{(u,i) \in known} (r_{ui} - u_u v_i)$$

> **NOTE**   Remember that each row is a user (u), each column is an item (i), and each cell in the matrix is defined by (u,i).

The user-item notation makes it clear that all the ratings that the user u has given; is all the ratings you already know. The goal here is to find values for the two matrices that minimize the difference between the rating and the ones you calculate from U

and *V*. A way to minimize the difference is to use an algorithm called gradient descent, which you'll learn about in the next section.

You want the equation to penalize big errors, so you take the square of the difference. But you still want the error to come out to be on the same scale of the ratings so with that you end up with the RMSE:

$$RMSE = \sqrt{\frac{1}{|known|} \sum_{(u,i)\in known} (r_{ui} - u_u v_i)^2}$$

You square each element of the sum, and when everything is summed, you divide by the number of elements in the sum and then take the square root. You'll use this in a little bit. To make the explanation in the following more relevant, I'll point out that the previous RMSE can be seen as the following function *f*:

$$f(u_1, \dots, u_N, v_1, \dots, v_M) = \sqrt{\frac{1}{|known|} \sum_{(u,i)\in known} (r_{ui} - u_u v_i)^2}$$

And you want to find values $u_1, \dots, u_N, v_1, \dots, v_M$, which make the result of the function as small as possible. Because that's rather difficult to do by looking at it, as mentioned, you'll turn to something called gradient descent.

11.5.2 *Gradient descent*

To understand gradient descent, let's start with a general example and then go back to the problem at hand. *Gradient descent* is a way to find optimal points on a graph, where optimal means the lowest point (or the highest point). Consider that you've the following function *f* and you want to find x and y, which produce the smallest possible value:

$$f(x,y) = 12x^2 - 5x + 10y^2 + 10$$

If you plot, it looks like the one shown in figure 11.13.

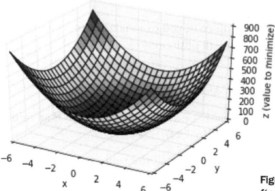

Figure 11.13   Plotting the function
$f(x,y) = 12x^2 - 5x + 10y^2 + 10$

The thinking behind gradient descent is to start somewhere (we'll get back to how to select that somewhere) and then look around to see if there's any direction that makes the function produce a smaller value. In math language, you want to find x' and y' such that:

$$f(x',y') < f(x,y)$$

In the example in figure 11.13, it boils down to understanding what side of the bowl you're standing on and then moving in the direction that points toward the bottom. Consider yourself standing on a mountain, it's foggy, and you can only see a meter in each direction. If you want to get to a point where you might find water, then the best choice is probably to go in the direction that leads downward. It's the same principle here. Figure 11.14 shows how to translate that.

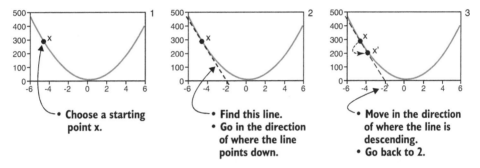

Figure 11.14 The gradient descent algorithm. Start out somewhere to find the direction that moves down, move a little bit in that direction, and repeat.

I'll divide the description of gradient descent into several steps in the next sections.

HOW TO START

How do you decide which point to start with? You can start anywhere because all functions aren't nicely bowl-shaped like the one in figure 11.14. Many times, you're looking at functions that have more than one local minimum like the one shown in figure 11.15.

Often the best suggestion is to try different starting points and see if they arrive at the same point. For example, if you continue with the previously described function and the steps in figure 11.14, you picked $x = -5$.

HOW TO FIND THE LINE THAT POINTS DOWN

To find the line pointing down, you find the derivative. If you don't know about derivation, then you'll have to take my word that the derivate of (this is the function after you set $y = 0$) is the following:

$$\frac{dy}{dx} = 24x - 5$$

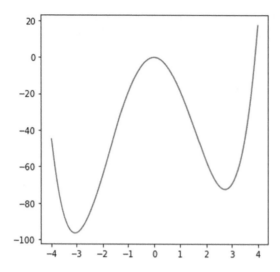

Figure 11.15   Function with more than one minimum ($1.2x^4 + 0.5x^3 - 20x^2$)

If you input your chosen starting point ($x = -5$), you get

$$\frac{dy}{dx} = 125$$

which means the original function at $x = -5$ slopes downward with a slope equal to a fall of 125 every time you move 1 to the right. If the derivate function produces something positive, you should move to the right to find the x that gives the minimum result.

To check that this is true, look at figure 11.14, where you can see that if you insert $x = 2$ into the derivate, you get $\frac{dy}{dx} = 43$, which means you should go left. If you're looking at a function with several variables like the one in figure 11.13, do this for each of the variables.

HOW TO FIND THE NEXT POINT

You know which way to go now, so how do you move on to the next point? How do you take that next step? Take this equation, for example:

$$x' = x - a * \frac{dy}{dx}$$

Don't stress because I added a Greek letter; it's an alpha (α). In the world of gradient descent, it's called the *learning rate*, which translates to how big a step you should take every time you want to move to the next point.

Again, there aren't any rules, other than if you take too large a step, you might miss the minimum altogether. Looking at step 3 in figure 11.14, if you take more than five steps, you'll miss the bottom and go back and forth between the sloping sides. And if you take steps that are too small, you'll never arrive. If you have more than one variable, you do the same for each variable.

WHEN IS IT FINISHED?

I can't tell you when you're finished (this is why it's called a *heuristic* and not a solution). But what you can look for is when your scoring function—the function you try to optimize—changes less and less. For example, if you take a step and the function only gets 0.0001 better, then it might be time to stop. Alternatively, you can say that you'll continue for 150 iterations (steps) and when you're done, you're done.

11.5.3 *Stochastic gradient descent*

The gradient descent algorithm described earlier is also known as the *batch gradient descent* because you calculate all the errors every time you move the value of the parameters—which can be a considerable amount of work. Consider that the data set you're using contains no less than 601,263 ratings. Every time the gradient descent algorithm does an iteration, you need to calculate all 601,263 subtractions as shown in this listing that uses the Django model interface.

Listing 11.10   Getting a count of all ratings

```
In[1]: Rating.objects.all().count()
Out[1]: 601263
```

Another way that's also proven both efficient and effective performance-wise, and also in the result, is what's called *stochastic gradient descent*, which looks at one rating at a time. The algorithm goes as follows. For each rating $r(u, i)$:

- Calculate $e = r_{ui} - q_i p_u$ where $q_i p_u$ is the predicted rating. You'll learn more about it soon.
- Update x so that $x \leftarrow x - a * e$ where α is the learning rate.

You'd be able to finish after one or more iterations over all the ratings! Sadly, this is it for the math lesson. I hope you learned something because it'll be useful in the next examples where stochastic gradient descent is used in the following sections.

If you're moving off into deep learning after reading my book,[13] then gradient descent is an important part of how you train deep learning networks.

11.5.4 *And finally, to the factorization*

What if you try to disregard all the cells with nothing in them and only calculate RMSE, looking only at the ratings you do know; thereby avoiding the problem of the sparse matrix and how to fill the empty cells? Don't get angry; you still need everything we talked about after the SVD. Trust me.

Our goal is to take all your ratings and create two matrices such that the ith row of the item factor matrix multiplied by the uth column of the user factor matrix provides something that's close to the actual known ratings. Putting that into a least squares problem,

---

[13] I'm reading *Machine Learning with TensorFlow* by Nishant Shukla (Manning, 2018) right now.

you can say that you want to find matrices Q and P, which will minimize the following for all known ratings. This can be done using the stochastic gradient descent algorithm.

$$\min_{p,q} \sum_{(u,i) \in K} (r_{u,i} - q_i p_u)^2$$

where

- q_i is the ith row in the item factor matrix Q.
- p_u is the uth column in the user factor matrix P.

For each rating, you'll update the two matrices Q and P, or rather a row and a column in the respective matrices. Before starting, you need to decide how many features you want to end up with.

In the Funk SVD, you don't have the Sigma matrix to calculate energy, so you'll have to run it for several different numbers of features and see which is best. You can use the following algorithm for each f in features and then continue until finished. (I'll explain what this algorithm does and then show you how to implement it in Python in a bit.)

For each rating r_{ui} in ratings, calculate

- $e_{ui} = r_{ui} - q_i p_u$
- $q_i \leftarrow q_i + \gamma * (e_{ui} * p_u - \lambda * q_i)$
- $p_u \leftarrow p_u + \gamma * (e_{ui} * q_i - \lambda * p_u)$

where

- γ is the learning rate.
- λ is called the regularization term.

First, this equation calculates how much the predicted rating is off, compared to the actual rating. You use this error to correct Q and P. You can now update the two vectors q_i and p_u using the error you calculated multiplied by the learning rate (γ), which is often similar to 0.001, and subtract its own vector times a regularization factor. (The last part is done to keep the length (values) of the vector small.)

Now when you run through all the known ratings once, you'll have two matrices that can be used to predict ratings. It's a good idea to shuffle the list of ratings before doing this algorithm because trends in the ratings might push the factorization in strange directions.[14]

11.5.5 Adding biases

We've talked about biases in a previous section. Even if the equation is already a bit complicated, it's worth adding them. But what does it mean to have both user factors (a row in P) and a bias?

---

[14] This means to randomize the ordering of the ratings.

The way I think of it is that the user likes a specific type of film, which is encoded in the user factors, while the negative (or positive) rater is encoded in the bias. A predicted rating is now the sum of four things as shown in figure 11.16.

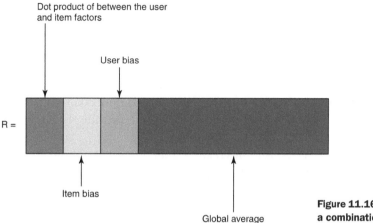

Figure 11.16   A predicted rating is a combination of these four things.

If you add those to the equation, the new function you want to minimize is the following:

$$\min_{b,p,q} \sum_{(u,i)\in K} (r_{iu} - m - b_u - b_i - q_i p_u)^2$$

And now your algorithm looks like the following (this is an extension of the previous one). For each feature f, continue until finished

- $e_{ui} = r_{ui} - q_i p_u$
- $b_u \leftarrow b_u + \gamma * (e_{ui} - \lambda * b_u)$
- $b_i \leftarrow b_i + \gamma * (e_{ui} - \lambda * b_i)$
- $q_i \leftarrow q_i + \gamma * (e_{ui} * p_u - \lambda * q_i)$
- $p_u \leftarrow p_u + \gamma * (e_{ui} * q_i - \lambda * p_u)$

where

- γ is the learning rate.
- λ is the regularization term.

Even if you aren't going to drag too much through these equations, it's worth knowing that you're doing it according to the stochastic gradient descent approach, and the equations are found by taking the derivate of the squared error.

11.5.6   *How to start and when to stop*

Now that you've all the math and structure in place, it's time to talk about the art of machine learning because good machine learning isn't only about knowing the math:

it's also about understanding how to initialize parameters and what the constants should be. The problem with any art is that it's hard to teach because there isn't a right or wrong. Although it's a bit of an art to arrive at good parameters, Simon Funk was nice enough to describe which values he used: learning rate $\gamma = 0.001$, regularization $\lambda = 0.02$ with 40 factors. This supposedly got him third place in the Netflix challenge mentioned in the beginning of this chapter.

But let's have a quick chat about how to figure good values for each of your parameters. The difference between what you're doing here and the evaluation you looked at in chapter 9 is that you're not only looking for more precision and recall (that's something you'll look at when you've finished fine-tuning the parameters), but you're also concentrating on training the algorithm to understand the domain. That sounds fancy, but let's remember your goal, which is to provide recommendations for users online.

How to emulate that best isn't by creating something that not only remembers the answers from the training data but also predicts ratings from the test data. It's about you wanting to have as little error as possible both on the data that you're training and on the data set that you test it on when you calculate or descend toward the two matrices for the user and item factors. As described in chapter 9, you split the data so that you can use the training data to *teach* the algorithm about the domain and to instruct the test data to know when it has extracted enough *knowledge.* If you teach the algorithm too little, you won't have a result that understands the domain, while too much and it'll be overfitted on the training data. Instead of understanding the domain, it'll have mastered only remembering the training data. The levers you'll use to manipulate the algorithm include the following:

- *Initialize the factors?*—Decides where the gradient descend should start walking.
- *Learning rate?*—How fast you should move at each step.
- *Regularization?*—How much should the algorithm regularize the errors? Should it be the same for all the expressions or should you split it into factors and bias?
- *How many iterations?*—How specialized should the algorithm become to the training data?

There are many ways you can interpret what effect you'll have on the result by setting these levers in different ways. I recommend that you strive to understand the effects of each of them. Also include a grid search, which means that you try many different values and see how each works. You'll be better equipped for your next recommender if you take time to understand what power the parameters have.

The last sentence should trouble you a bit, because the data you're using here most likely won't be the Netflix data set that was used in the Netflix Prize. You should try out different parameters to see if you can make your data set work better. This listing shows how you could test different parameters. If you like, you can view the code in /builder/matrix_factorization_calculator.py.

Listing 11.11 Testing how many factors to use

Trains one
factor at a time

Initializes all the
factors and constants

Splits the data
into training data
and test data

```
def meta_parameter_train(self, ratings_df):

    for k in [5, 10, 15, 20, 30, 40, 50, 75, 100]:
        self.initialize_factors(ratings_df, k)
        test_data, train_data = self.split_data(10, ratings_df)

        columns = ['user_id', 'movie_id', 'rating']
        ratings = train_data[columns].as_matrix()
        test = test_data[columns].as_matrix()

        self.MAX_ITERATIONS = 100
        iterations = 0
        index_randomized = random.sample(range(0, len(ratings)),
                                         (len(ratings) - 1))

        for factor in range(k):
            factor_iteration = 0
            last_err = 0
            iteration_err = sys.maxsize
            finished = False

            while not finished:
                train_mse = self.stocastic_gradient_descent(factor,
                                                            index_randomized,
                                                            ratings)

                iterations += 1

                finished = self.finished(factor_iteration,
                                         last_err,
                                         iteration_err)
                last_err = iteration_err
                factor_iteration += 1

                test_mse = self.calculate_mse(test, factor)
```

Continues until a
termination function is true

Each factor is trained
for 100 epochs that
runs through all the
training ratings 100
times.

With stochastic
gradient descent, it's
important that you
randomize the data.

Runs a stochastic
gradient on all the
training ratings (more
details later)

Calculates mean
square error on the
test data

Figure 11.17 shows the result of the testing in listing 11.11; each factor run has been plotted.

After running this test, which took approximately 12 hrs. on my MacBook with 2.7 GHz Core i7 from 2016, I came to the conclusion that 40 factors looked good. I also had to modify the number of iterations. Funk wrote that he trained each feature for 120 iterations each; with this data set, I stopped it at either 100 iterations or when the last error was smaller than the current one. I think maybe it was worth giving it some slack. For that reason, if the algorithm has started training a new factor, perhaps you should let it run for 10 iterations or so before stopping it. But I'll leave that as a test for you.

Funk also mentions that he had different ideas of how to calculate the prediction error. You have so many possible combinations of setting the levers, but the best way to go about it is to come up with a hypothesis and then do test runs as shown earlier.

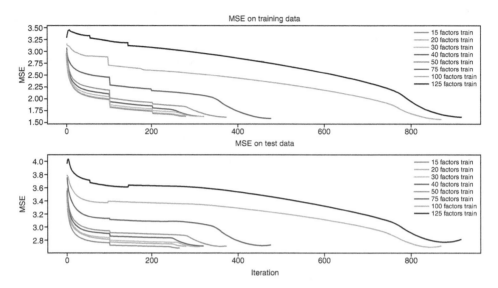

Figure 11.17   RMSE plotted for each iteration of the algorithm. The top is the MSE on the training data, while the bottom is the error on the test set.

Another way to look at the data is to compare the error of the training to the test error. This is shown in figure 11.18. It's important that the lines have a more or less 45-degree angle such that the test error is proportional to the training error.

Many advise you to run the test for a certain number of times, such as 50 or 100, while others recommend that you look at the RMSE for each iteration and when the change in RMSE is below a value, stop. If you do plot the MSE as in figure 11.18, it's a good idea to look for the elbows in the chart. The *elbow* is often where you stop fitting the algorithm to the known data and start overfitting the algorithm. A line in figure 11.18 shows the training of 75 factors. You can see the test MSE has a little elbow around 400 iterations. Here you should only use 20 factors because the 20 factor test line has a small elbow around 275 iterations, so that may be a good place to stop.

OVERFITTING

If your rating matrix is sparse, then you might run into *overfitting* problems, where the algorithm learns the training data too well and suddenly the MSE of the test data starts increasing. For example, overfitting happens when the matrices U and V can calculate precisely the right values for the existing ratings, but will be completely off when it comes to predicting new ones. A way to get around this is to introduce something call a *regularization factor*, so that what you're minimizing is the following:

$$\min{}_{uv} \sum_{(u,i)\in\ known} (r_{ui} - u_u v_i) + \lambda(\|u\|^2 + \|v\|^2)$$

The idea here is that you want the algorithm to find the best U's and V's, while not allowing any of them to become too large. The argument for doing this is not to let

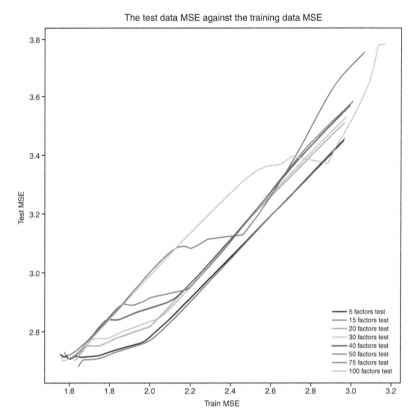

The test data MSE against the training data MSE

Figure 11.18 Comparing test MSE with training MSE shows if you're starting to overfit.

the factorization become too specialized toward the values that you're giving the training data because you want it to be good at predicting ratings on new data.

Overfitting is an interesting topic that requires more space than I have here.[15] In the Funk SVD, the fact that you can use the user factor to limit the item factor, and vice versa (and the same with the biases), should handle the overfitting problem.

11.6 Doing recommendations with Funk SVD

After all that work, you have four things:

1 *Item factor matrix*—Where each column represents a content item described by the latent factors that you calculated.

2 *User factor matrix*—Where each column represents a user described by the latent factors.

---

[15] Look at the Wikipedia page at https://en.wikipedia.org/wiki/Overfitting for more information.

3   *Item bias*—Where certain items are generally considered better—or worse—than others. The bias describes the difference between the global mean and the item's mean.

4   *User bias*—Encompasses different rating scales for different users.

With these four things, you can calculate a predicted rating for any item for any user using the formula we discussed earlier and shown here:

$$\widehat{r_{u,i}} = m + b_u + b_i + q_i p_u$$

And that's nice because compared to the methods you looked at before, you can now provide predicted ratings on *everything*! But recommendations are more than predicting ratings. You need to find a list of items that the user would rate high. The following describes two ways to do that—brute force and neighborhoods.

BRUTE FORCE RECOMMENDATION CALCULATION

Brute force is easy to describe: you calculate a predicted rating for each user for each item, then you sort all the predictions and return the top N items. While you're at it, you can also save all the predictions so that you have them ready when the user visits.

This is the no-nonsense way of doing stuff. The thing to remember is that it might take time to do and will require your system to do many calculations that might never be used for anything. You could optimize it a bit, but a better way would be to save the factors and the biases and use those to calculate the recommendations.

NEIGHBORHOODS RECOMMENDATION CALCULATION

I spent time describing neighborhoods in chapter 8, so I won't drag you through that again. The only thing that has changed in this chapter is that instead of using the original rating data, you can use the factors that you calculated. This means that you're calculating similarities where things are closer and in a smaller dimension, which makes it easier.

If you look at the factor space from earlier, again shown in figure 11.19, you can create user-based or item-based recommendations. Either way takes advantage of the created vectors representing users and items.

USER VECTOR

One way to create recommendations is to find the items with factor vectors that are close to the active user's vector. They're all in the same space, so why not. But if you do that, then you should consider that the user is placed in the middle between all the items the user likes. If the user likes only one type of movies, that's fine. If you're like me and like Italian dramas and superhero movies, then the neighborhood around you will be in between everything you like, and you might not like any of the things close to you.

THE ITEMS THE USER LIKES

We're back to figure 11.20 (the square from chapter 8 and repeated here) going through all the items that the user has rated positively and finding similar items, or finding similar users, and recommending items they liked.

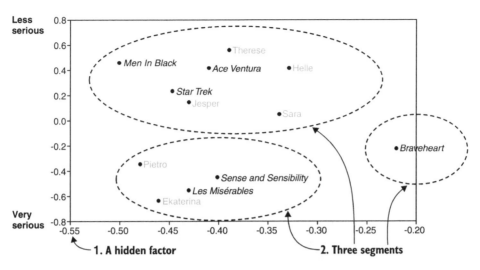

Figure 11.19 Coordinate system showing one interpretation of how the hidden space could be interpreted. Here you can see that Ekaterina and Pietro like *Sense and Sensibility* and *Les Misérables*. No one likes *Braveheart*.

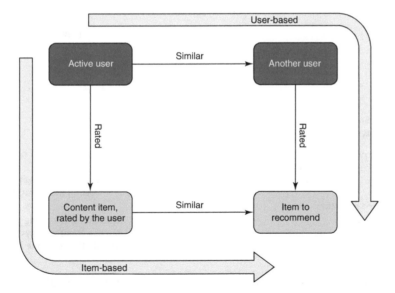

Figure 11.20 The different ways to go from active user to recommendations, either by finding similar users or looking at the active user's items and finding similar items

11.7   *Funk SVD implementation in MovieGEEKs*

Now let's return to the subject of implementing things in MovieGEEKs. You've already looked at a few implementations by now, so what you want to look at here are the recommendations and also how to verify if the model is working.

Listing 11.12   Building the matrix model

```
Python -m builder.MatrixFactorizationCalculator
```

You'll find the code to build the matrix model in /builder/MatrixFactorizationCalculator.py. In the following sections, you'll see what happens inside the the build.

TRAINING PHASE

The training phase initializes all the biases and factors and retrieves the ratings, as shown in the following listing. Because you'll run through the ratings a few times, it's better to load them up front and keep them in memory (if they fit), You'll find this listing's code in /builder/matrix_factorization_calculator.

Listing 11.13   Initializing biases and factors for MovieGEEKs

Creates a dictionary from user_ids to a number, so you can use NumPy arrays instead of pandas. You do that to make it faster.

Creates a set of all user IDs

Creates a set of all movie IDs

```
def initialize_factors(self, ratings, k=25):
    self.user_ids = set(ratings['user_id'].values)
    self.movie_ids = set(ratings['movie_id'].values)
    self.u_inx = {r: i for i, r in enumerate(self.user_ids)}
    self.i_inx = {r: i for i, r in enumerate(self.movie_ids)}

    self.item_factors = np.full((len(self.i_inx), k), 0.1)
    self.user_factors = np.full((len(self.u_inx), k), 0.1)

    self.all_movies_mean = self.calculate_all_movies_mean(ratings)
    self.user_bias = defaultdict(lambda: 0)
    self.item_bias = defaultdict(lambda: 0)
```

Creates two matrices of factors, all initialized with 0.1.

Calculates the average of all movie ratings

Creates a dictionary from movie_ids to a number, so you can use NumPy arrays instead of pandas. You do that to make it faster.

We need a way to test the error between the actual ratings and the calculated ones, so you need a predict rating method as shown in the following listing that you can view at /builder/matrix_factorization_calculator.py. The method is identical to the prediction method that will be used in the end.

Listing 11.14   Implementing a predict rating method

Calculates the dot product of
the current user's factors and
the current item

Sums the
biases

```
def predict(self, user, item):
    avg = self.all_movies_mean
    pq = np.dot(self.item_factors[item],self.user_factors[user].T)   ◁
    b_ui = avg + self.user_bias[user] + self.item_bias[item]
    prediction = b_ui + pq              ◁
                                            Sums things to create
    if prediction > 10:      ◁              the prediction
        prediction = 10
    elif prediction < 1:             Makes sure that the prediction
        prediction = 1              is between 1 and 10
    return prediction
```

With these, you're ready for the training algorithm. It's the same as described previously and is also found in /builder/matrix_factorization_calculator.py.

Listing 11.15   The training algorithm

Initializes all the factors and constal
shown in listing 11.13

Formats
the
rating
data

```
def train(self, ratings_df, k=20):

    self.initialize_factors(ratings_df, k)   ◁

    ratings = ratings_df[['user_id', 'movie_id', 'rating']].as_matrix()

    index_randomized = random.sample(range(0, len(ratings)),
                                     (len(ratings) - 1))   ◁

    for factor in range(k):     ◁                     Shuffles the data to
        iterations = 0                                ensure trends in the
        last_err = 0                                  ordering won't affect
        iteration_err = sys.maxsize        Iterates   the training
        finished = False                   through each of
                                           the k factors
        while not finished:
            start_time = datetime.now()
            iteration_err = self.stocastic_gradient_descent(factor,
                                                       index_randomized,
                                                       ratings)

            iterations += 1
            finished = self.finished(iterations,
                                     last_err,
                                     iteration_err)
        last_err = iteration_err
    self.save(factor, finished)
```

HOW MANY ITERATIONS ARE NEEDED TO RUN THE TRAINING?

As explained previously, there's no easy way to decide when to finish. The following listing shows the one I used while training, and you can view this snippet in the script /builder/matrix_factorization_calculator.py.

Listing 11.16   Are we there yet?

```
def finished(self, iterations, last_err, current_err):

    if iterations >= 100 or last_err < current_err:
        print('Finish w iterations: {}, last_err: {}, current_err {}'
            .format(iterations, last_err, current_err))
        return True
    else:
        self.iterations +=1
        return False
```

Moving on; incrementing the number of iterations

If more than 30 iterations have passed or the difference between the error has gone below 1, then it's time to stop and move on to the next factor.

SAVING THE MODEL

You wouldn't want all the work to be lost, so you should save the model to several files. Saving the model to JSON is one way of doing that, depending on how you want to use it. I've chosen to save each of the factor matrixes in a file as well as the biases as shown here. You can view these in /builder/matrix_factorization_calculator.py

Listing 11.17   Saving each factor matrix

```
def save(self):
    print("saving factors")
    with open('user_factors.json', 'w') as outfile:
        json.dump(self.user_factors, outfile)
    with open('item_factors.json', 'w') as outfile:
        json.dump(self.item_factors, outfile)
    with open('user_bias.json', 'w') as outfile:
        json.dump(self.user_bias, outfile)
    with open('item_bias.json', 'w') as outfile:
        json.dump(self.item_bias, outfile)
```

JSON in a file isn't that fast to retrieve, and you want to be fast, but that depends on what you want to do next. If you want to calculate the brute force recommendations and save all the predicted ratings in the database, then you need to take the dot product between all users and all items. Save the ones that are above a certain threshold in the database and do a simple look-up when needed.

Another way is to calculate similarities using cosine similarity as you did in chapter 8. Then calculate the ratings the same way you did in that chapter. In the next section, you'll do a slower version that loads the files every time it needs to return a recommendation.

ONLINE PHASE

Listing 11.18 shows how to do recommendations by calculating predictions and then ordering them according to the highest prediction. This snippet can be found in /recs/funksvd_recommender.py.

Listing 11.18   Ordering by highest prediction: recs/funksvd_recommender.py

Gets the IDs of all the movies the user has already rated. You don't want to show them again.

The user_factors are loaded from the files you saved during training.

```
def recommend_items_by_ratings(self, user_id, active_user_items, num=6):
    rated_movies = set(active_user_items.values('movie_id'))
    user = self.user_factors.loc[user_id]

    scores = self.item_factors.dot(user)
    scores.sort_values(inplace=True, ascending=False)
    result = scores[:num + len(rated_movies)]

    recs = {r[0]: r[1] + self.user_bias[user_id] + self.item_bias[r[0]]
            for r in zip(result.index, result) if r[0] not in rated_movies}

    sorted_items = sorted(recs.items(),
                          key=lambda item: -float(item[1]['prediction']))[:num]

    return sorted_items
```

Sorts the ratings in descending order

Creates the data format the frontend expects and cuts off the number that should be returned

Creates a dictionary, content id–predicted rating

Takes the head of the list containing only enough elements for the number of elements you want to return, leaving room for the case where all the user's rated items are found

Do a manual test and check a recommendation for somebody, then look at user 400005, whose taste profile is like that shown in figure 11.21.

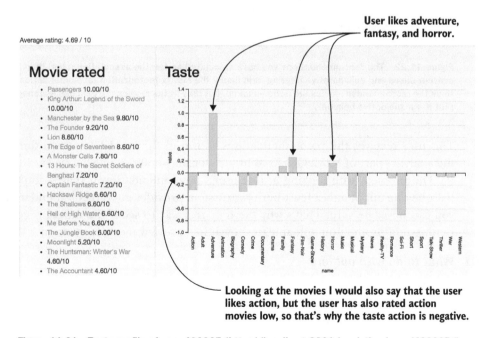

Figure 11.21   Taste profile of user 400005 (http://localhost:8001/analytics/user/400005/)

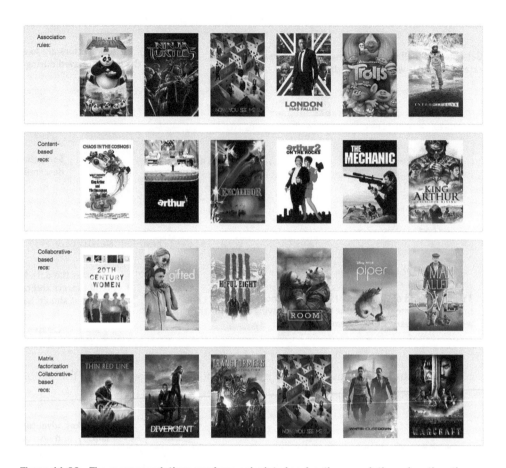

Figure 11.22   The recommendations you have calculated so far: the association rules, then the content-based and collaborative filtering, and finally the matrix factorization recommendations. I think the recommended movies are action-packed, but they fit the movies the user has watched well (but it's a subjective opinion).

This user receives the recommendations shown in figure 11.22 (screen dump from the analytics part of MovieGEEKs at http://localhost:8001/analytics/user/400005/).

The problem with looking at one user's recommendation is that it could potentially be one out of only a few where your system provides good recommendations, but you can never be sure. That's why the only real way to see if the model is good is by putting it in production and at least show it in a preview mode to someone.

11.7.1 *What to do with outliers*

In one of the earlier iterations of the recommender, I had gotten something that looked good when evaluating, and I thought everything was ready for sendoff. But then I came across a user who liked cartoons like *Kung Fu Panda* and *LEGO Batman*,

Figure 11.23   Several outliers have sneaked into the recommendations.

but the Funk SVD produced the recommendations shown in figure 11.23. Without having watched any of the recommendations, I thought it looked a bit odd.

It turns out that these aren't related to either *Kung Fu Panda* or *LEGO Batman*. The user's taste shows adventure, animation, crime, fantasy, and thrillers as a personal preference. A bit more poking around showed that those films were 5 out of the 5 items that had an item bias above 5. The algorithm does the dot product between the user and all the item factors, and then afterwards the item biases are added before you order them and take them from the top. Now I'm torn about whether you should order the items before adding the item biases or not.

If you change the algorithm to sort the items before adding the item bias, then they'll still boost the recommendations, but only within the list of items that are similar to the factors that the user likes. Doing this changed the recommendations into what's shown in figure 11.24.

Figure 11.24   Adding the bias after ordering the recommendations shows better recommendations.

Another thing I played around with was reducing the learning rate of the biases, which also helped with this problem because it made the biases smaller with more diversity in the user and item factors. It's a matter of taste about what's better, and it's something that can give you many sleepless nights, but also a sense of adventure. It's difficult to say what the best settings are, so you should continue to play around with them.

11.7.2 Keeping the model up to date

This model you created quickly goes out of date. Ideally, you should start a new run as soon as it's finished, but, depending on how much your data changes, you can do recalculate your model once each night or even once a week. But remember, every time a user interacts with a new item, it might be evidence that will show connections among the items and could give further inklings about the user's taste. And if you calculate weekly, also remember to remove items already consumed by the user from the recommendations. Finally, one last thing to keep in mind is that if you've used implicit data, then if there's a rating, it doesn't mean that the user has consumed the item.

11.7.3 Faster implementation

The previous matrix factorization is done using gradient descent, but if you have many millions of products and users, that might become a slow process. Another way is the alternating least squares (ALS) method, which isn't as precise as gradient descent, but should work fairly well anyway.

11.8 Explicit vs. implicit data

If you've a data set of implicit data, you could do as you did in chapter 4 and deduce ratings from it. Alternatively, you can use it directly by slightly changing the previous algorithm. For more information on how to do that, I recommend you read "Collaborative Filtering for Implicit Feedback Datasets" by Yifan Hu et al. (http://yifanhu.net/PUB/cf.pdf).

   If you want to skip directly to the implementation of it have a look at the Implicit framework, which is a fast implementation for implicit data and collaborative filtering.[16] I've heard that it's used in some production environments where there's a great deal of data. (I can tell you where, but then I'm afraid I'll have to kill you.)

   As mentioned, the implementation uses slightly different algorithms than described here. It can be a great exercise to look through the code to understand alternative ways to do it.

11.9 Evaluation

When you work with Funk SVD or other machine-learning algorithms, you often have many parameters to tune before starting the actual evaluation. Previously, we've talked about the error of the training data and compared it with the error on the test data. Then, when you're finished adjusting those variables, you can do the algorithm evaluation. Many would say that it's the same thing. But in the end you should test the algorithm on unseen data to see how it's working.

   You don't want to find hyper-parameters doing cross-validation because it takes too long. You almost always want to use cross-validation to evaluate the performance of the algorithm. The principle is exactly the same as the one described in chapter 9 and shown in figure 11.25.

---

[16] For more information, see https://github.com/benfred/implicit.

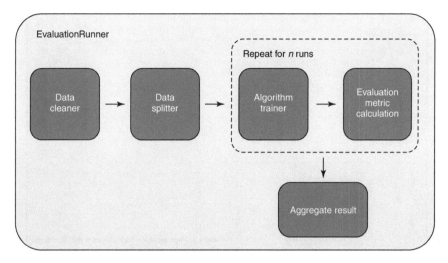

Figure 11.25 A diagram showing how the evaluation runner works

You clean the data, so you only have relevant information, then you split the users into k folds. Then for each of these folds, you hold one out and split it into train and test data for the users in that fold. The training data from the fold is merged and appended to the *k-1* other folds and used to train the algorithm. Then the algorithm is tested using one of the metrics described in chapter 9, and finally, you aggregate the result. You can run the evaluation by executing this listing.

Listing 11.19 Executing the evaluation

```
> python -m evaluator.evaluation_runner -funk
```

This command creates a CSV file with the data used to show the evaluations. I encourage you to check out the code and see how it's done.

The script doesn't run cross-validation out of the box; you need to tweak the code to run it. It's set to 0 folds, which means no cross-validation. I ran an evaluation on a model with 40 factors, calculating the precision and recall as you've done in the two previous chapters. The result is shown in figure 11.26.

Looking at the result of the matrix factorization, I think it's great to see that it can service 100% of the users, but I'm disappointed to see that it only recommends 0.11% of the items, which is a bit more than 3,200 items. (I tweaked the bias learning rate a bit to begin with: from 0.0005, which produced a model that only covered around 200 items, to 0.002, which yielded the final recommendation of more than 3,200 items. Much, however, is still missing to cover the full set of 28,700 items.) One reason for such a low percentage rate could be that more factors should be added to allow for more diverse taste profiles. But again, it's something to play with. And a great exercise for you to try out.

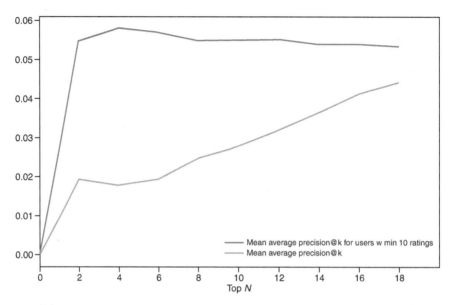

Figure 11.26 **Mean average precision of the Funk SVD. The bottom line tests all users, while the upper one restricts the test data to users who've at least 10 ratings.**

The precision in figure 11.26 is much better than the content-based algorithm, where both recall and precision were more than half this. The thing that you might make a fuss about is the fact that the neighborhood model gets a better recall than this one. But the difference here is that you have 100% user coverage, so users who only rated one item are also included; you took those away from the data before calculating the neighborhood model. If you remove all users with few ratings the way you did in chapter 9, then you'd probably have a superior precision and recall as shown in figure 11.27.

11.10 *Levers to fiddle with for Funk SVD*

You have so many levers and configurations that can be changed and tweaked when you use the Funk SVD algorithm. What makes it more complicated is that they're all *dependent*, meaning that you can't expect that optimizing one parameter will always be the best possible value if you then change another factor. You need to try all combinations to be completely sure which is best. That can be attempted with a grid search, or something similar.[17]

What ratings to add to the training for users who have only done one rating doesn't help your collaborative filtering algorithm much, so it might be good to take them out. The only thing they help is that they add to the average rating of the movies.

---

[17] For more information, see http://scikit-learn.org/stable/modules/grid_search.html.

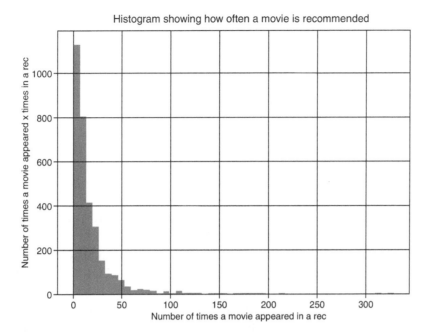

Figure 11.27 Plots how many movies are only shown a certain number of times. From this, you can see more than 1,000 movies are only recommended to one user.

Item and user factors are representations of users and items using the latent factors that you've been training. It's good to check that the factors aren't too large. I'd be worried if any vector had values that wasn't around 1. You can tune this by regularization; the larger the regularization the more the factors are kept close to 0.

Bias initialization matters too, because it determines how big the prediction error will be on the factors in the beginning. You don't want these to be too large. Consider that if you have an average rating of all the movies, then adding the user bias and item bias shouldn't take the average outside of the rating scale. The dataset you're using here uses a rating scale from 1–10. The average rating is around 7, so item bias and user bias shouldn't be too much above 1.5 each.

Determining the right number of iterations is also a matter of taste. If you run through too many iterations on the early factors, you risk the chance that all signals will be pushed into the first dimension, while the remaining factors will only have a small signal. Too few iterations and the vectors will never align correctly. Depending on how many iterations you decide on, you'll also have to settle on a learning rate for the factors as well as for the bias: too large and it might always overshoot the optimum; too small and it'll never move from its initial position.

This is a short list of things to play around with; there are many more. Remember to have a good measure of quality, then test it. Getting a low RMSE/MSE might not result in the best recommendations, but it shows how to do a function that captures that. Again, remember to make a hypothesis, be sure you know how to measure the result, and make the testing as easy as possible.

This has been a complex chapter, and you've learned a lot. Matrix factorization is a topic in itself and here we only scratched the surface. But if you understood this chapter, you can build on it and make much more complex things.

Summary

- SVD is a way of doing matrix factorization; it's well accepted in many libraries, which makes it a good method to use. The downside is that it won't work if your matrix isn't complete, meaning with no empty cells. You'll have to fill those cells in with something, and that something is hard to do because they're empty when you don't know what should be there.
- Baseline predictors are one way to fill in those empty cells. The same is true for items.
- Baseline predictors are used to understand user and item biases.
- A way that allows you to use a sparse matrix of ratings is with the method first tried by Simon Funk—the Funk SVD.
- Gradient descent and stochastic gradient descent are super tools for solving optimization problems like the one defined to train and optimize the Funk SVD.

Taking the best of all algorithms: Implementing hybrid recommenders

This chapter is a hybrid of many sections:

- You'll learn to combine recommenders to take advantage of the strengths and weaknesses of different types of recommender systems.
- You'll tour the overall classes of hybrid recommenders.
- You'll be introduced to ensemble recommenders.
- Having knowledge of ensemble recommenders, you'll look at how to implement a specific algorithm called feature-weighted linear stacking (FWLS).

Supposedly one of the most energy-efficient cars ever made is a hybrid: a Toyota Prius. At its core, Toyota combines two well-known technologies—the combustion engine and the electric engine.[1] Hybrid recommenders are basically the same idea—you combine recommender algorithms to get a more powerful tool. These not only improve the average result, but also attempt to mitigate the corner cases, where algorithms don't work well.

Figure 12.1 shows the four most acknowledged classes of recommender systems and their data sources. We've talked about each recommender system as something that runs alone and in a silo, but the world is far from being this ordered. To provide recommendations, you need to do a mix, or a hybrid, of more than one

---

[1] For more information, see https://en.wikipedia.org/wiki/Toyota_Prius.

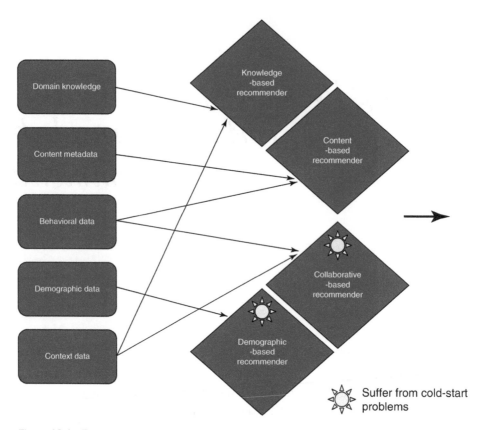

Figure 12.1   Four commonly recognized classes of recommenders and the type of data they consume

system. Also, if you've access to more than one of the data sources shown in the figure, it's a sin not to use all of them!

There are no limits to how you can combine algorithms, and if this chapter explained all of them, it would quickly become a book in itself. To avoid that, I'll start with a small survey of the different categories that are commonly considered. Then you'll look at the details for the FWLS algorithm. Finally, you'll see how to implement that algorithm in MovieGEEKs.

12.1   *The confused world of hybrids*

Hybrid recommenders are a common term for the different types of recommenders shown in figure 12.2. Here's how I like to look at hybrids.

The monolithic takes components of various recommenders and glues them together in new ways; the ensemble runs different recommenders and then combines the result into one recommendation, and a mixed recommender runs a number of recommenders, returning all of them. Each of these will be described in detail in the following sections.

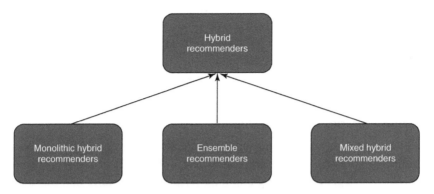

Figure 12.2 The three different types of overall hybrid recommenders

12.2 *The monolithic*

If you look up the word *monolithic*, you don't get a picture of something cutting edge. Instead, it means something that's made from one piece of stone, like the heads on Easter Island, or it refers to organizations that are powerful, rigid, and slow to change. While monolithic is probably not something you want to put in an ad for your company, nevertheless, it's what these recommenders are called.

In our case, a *monolithic hybrid recommender* is defined as the Frankenstein of recommenders. It contains parts from different types of recommender algorithms. Normally, a recommender contains many different components like item similarity or candidate selection, to name a few. A monolithic recommender mixes components from different recommenders or even adds new steps to improve overall performance. Figure 12.3 illustrates a monolithic recommender that uses the item similarity part of Recommender 1 and the candidate selection and prediction parts from Recommender 2.

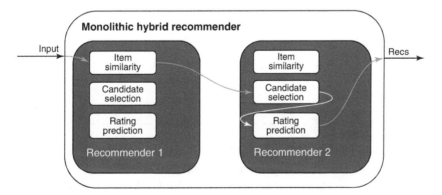

Figure 12.3 A monolithic hybrid recommender is composed of other recommender system parts.

As an example, you could use a content-based approach that finds all the items that are similar content-wise, mixing that with a collaborative filtering approach to calculate predicted ratings the same way you'd use simple collaborative filtering (which is how you did personalized content-based recommendations). The possibilities are endless. A monolithic recommender can also add another step as described in the following section.

12.2.1 Mixing content-based features with behavioral data to improve collaborative filtering recommenders

The whole point of hybrids is to take advantage of more types of data. An example of a monolithic hybrid recommender could be a collaborative filtering recommender with one extra pre-processing step that adds ratings to the rating-matrix, such that the collaborative filtering will connect things that are related content-wise. Say you have a list of films, as shown in table 12.1, all of them in the sci-fi genre.

Table 12.1   An example of a rating matrix

	Sci-fi 1	Sci-fi 2	Sci-fi 3	Sci-fi 4
User 1	4	4		
User 2	5	4		
User 3			2	4

Using neighborhood collaborative filtering on the rating matrix in table 12.1, you wouldn't get any similarity between the first two films and the last two, so you can't recommend anything to any of the users because there are no connections to unseen films. What you need is a user to bridge the content. Because you know you've all sci-fi films, it might be good to add another user who loves all films of that type into the matrix. You could then update the rating matrix as shown in table 12.2.

Table 12.2   An example of a rating matrix adding a sci-fi lover

	Sci-fi 1	Sci-fi 2	Sci-fi 3	Sci-fi 4
User 1	4	4		
User 2	5	4		
User 3			2	4
Sci-fi lover	5	5	5	5

This enables you to link sci-fi films and to also recommend films of the same genre. You could also take the next step and use the LDA model you implemented in chapter 10, where you create a pseudo-user for each of the hidden topics and then add those connections to the mix. There are more technical details to understand if this is a way you'd like to go. If so, I recommend that you read the article "Content-Boosted

Collaborative Filtering for Improved Recommendations" by Prem Melville et al., for more details.[2]

The previous example requires work, and monolithic recommenders, in general, probably require more effort to change current recommenders to operate within a hybrid recommender. If you already have recommenders in place, you might want to try mixed hybrids or ensembles.

12.3 *Mixed hybrid recommender*

A mixed hybrid doesn't do much mixing; a *mixed hybrid* returns the union of all the results. A way of using a mixed hybrid is one that I've used myself where you've a hierarchy of recommenders.

Consider the recommender as a scale of personalization. Make the first one as personalized as possible and then continue until you're using item popularity to give recommendations. Often the most personalized recommender only produces one or two recommendations, the next recommender produces several more and, in that way, you'll always have a good quantity of recommendations but with as much quality as possible. Figure 12.4 illustrates a mixed hybrid recommender.

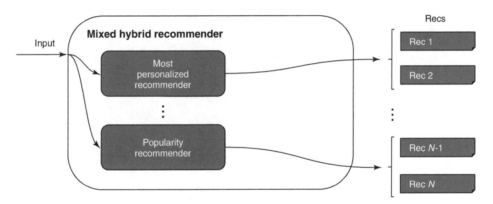

Figure 12.4 A mixed hybrid recommender, which simply stacks the output of several recommenders, starting with the most personalized recommender on the top, then the next most personalized, and so on.

If you've several good recommenders, each returning a score, then you can return a list ordered accordingly. Remember that the scores should be normalized so all the results are on the same scale. Keeping with the idea of having several recommenders running, let's now turn to ensembles.

---

[2] For more information, see www.cs.utexas.edu/~ai-lab/pubs/cbcf-aaai-02.pdf.

12.4   *The ensemble*

An *ensemble* is defined as a group of things viewed as a whole rather than individually. It's the same for ensemble recommenders: you combine predictions from different recommenders into one recommendation.

> **NOTE**   The difference between an ensemble and a mixed recommender is that the hybrid might not show anything of the result for one recommender, while the mixed hybrid always shows everything.

One of the takeaways from RecSys 2016—the annual recommender systems conference in 2016—was that if you're a start-up and want to get into recommender systems, you should start with matrix factorization (the topic of chapter 11) and add recommenders to create an ensemble recommender (see figure 12.5) as described by Xavier Amatriain in his presentation on "Lessons Learned from Building Real-Life Recommender Systems." Keep reading, and afterwards go and check out Xavier's slides because they contain more relevant advice.[3]

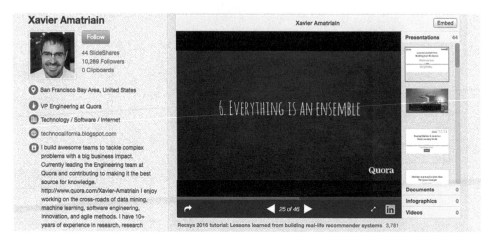

Figure 12.5   One of the takeaways from RecSys2016 was that everything is an ensemble.

If you've two recommenders running already, let's say content-based and collaborative filtering, then why not run them simultaneously as seen in figure 12.6 and then combine the result to get an even better outcome?

The idea with the ensemble is to calculate recommendations using several full recommenders and then somehow combine them. You can take the result of a number of recommenders and make them into one in many ways. For example, you can do a majority voting approach whereby the objects that occur most are the top ones, then the next ones, and so on.

---

[3]   For more information, see www.slideshare.net/xamat.

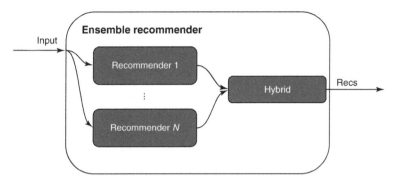

Figure 12.6 An ensemble hybrid runs a number of recommenders and combines the result before delivering it as one recommendation.

Figure 12.7 shows an example of how an ensemble recommender might work. Recommender 1 returns a recommendation for the top 3 movies 1, 5, and 6. Recommender 2 returns 5, 6, and 3. Then the hybrid returns 5, 6, and 1, depending on how you calculate ties. It recommends movie 5 because it occurs twice, once in each result, and it recommends movie 6 because it appears in both too, but below movie 5 because it was ranked lower. Then it recommends movie 1 because it appears as the first in Recommender 1, and movie 3 is dropped.

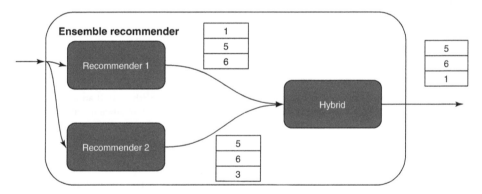

Figure 12.7 Example of how an ensemble recommender might work.

Often, you'll hear talk of switched or weighted ensembles. We look at those next.

12.4.1 Switched ensemble recommender

A switched ensemble recommender is about using the best tool for the job. If you have two or more recommenders, then a switched ensemble recommender will decide which of them to use given the context of the request.

For example, you might have two different recommenders for two different countries. When a user shows up from one country, the result of one recommender is shown, and if somebody from another country visits, then the second recommender produces the output. It can also be switched on time of day; maybe one works in the mornings, while another is just getting started in the evening. Or in a newspaper, the national news section should be filled with the latest news, while the cultural page might be more about content-based recommendations for specific books.

You can switch recommenders based on which section of the site a user is on. Or, in its simplest form, it could be one where the switch would be between users who rated fewer than 20 movies and the ones who rated at least 20 as shown in figure 12.8. Users with more than 20 ratings receive output from the collaborative filtering recommender, while users with fewer ratings receive it from the shopping basket recommender (see chapter 6).

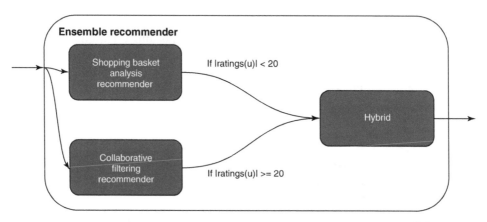

Figure 12.8   An example of a switching ensemble where users with more than 20 ratings receive output from one recommender, while users with fewer than 20 receive recommendations from another.

If a user is logged in, you know more details about the user. This might be a good reason to use a different recommender than you'd use if the user weren't logged in. But if you instead want to combine forces of the different recommenders, read on and learn about weighted feature ensembles.

12.4.2 *Weighted ensemble recommender*

Consider two algorithms you looked at earlier in this book: collaborative filtering (it doesn't matter if it's the neighborhood or SVD type now) and content-based filtering. Content-based filtering is good at finding similar content. If you know a user likes a topic, you can use content-based filtering to find similar things. The problem is that content-based filtering doesn't distinguish between good and bad quality; it's only concerned with topic or keyword overlap. Collaborative filtering, on the other hand, doesn't put any importance into items because it's about the same topic, only that certain people thought it was good quality and others didn't.

You can use them together to try to combine these strengths. You don't have to give them equal weight though, and this is where a *weighted hybrid recommender* comes into the picture. It's straightforward in the sense that you'll train two different recommenders and ask them both to produce candidates for recommendations. When two or more recommenders are combined like this, we call them *feature recommenders*.

You can feed all the candidates into both recommenders and then take the empirical mean of the two as illustrated in figure 12.9. To calculate an empirical mean, you select a weight, such as 60/40, which means that predictions from this hybrid would be calculated using the following formula:

$$\hat{r} = 0.6 \times \hat{r}_{collaborative} + 0.4 \times \hat{r}_{content}$$

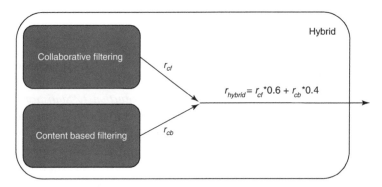

Figure 12.9 A feature-weighted hybrid. Here, the hybrid combines results from collaborative filtering and content-based filtering, using the weights 0.6 and 0.4, respectively.

The feature weights can be found in several ways. The simplest way is to guess, but that isn't too scientific and might result in strange recommendations. Another way is to do linear regression. Or you could do continuous adjustments to the weights using different values for different user groups and see who clicks more, using either A/B testing or multi-armed bandits (both mentioned in chapter 9). Let's have a quick look at linear regression.

12.4.3 *Linear regression*

Linear regression is about creating a function that minimizes the error between its output and the actual value. If you have the output of two recommenders, and you have the rating from a user (for example, data similar to table 12.3), then you can use linear regression to find how much the hybrid recommender should weight each output.

Table 12.3 An example of how predicted ratings from two recommenders could look compared to a user's ratings

Item	RecSys1	RecSys2	User rating
I1	4	6	5
I2	2	4	3
I3	5	5	5

Now create a function f that, given output of the two recommenders, predicts the user's ratings best. You want a function in which you can minimize the difference between its output and the user's rating r, for example:

$$RSS = \sum_{all\ ratings\ in\ training\ data} (f(u,i) - r)^2$$

The function could look more like the previous one:

$$f(u,i) = w_1 \times RecSys1(u,i) + w_2 \times RecSys2(u,i)$$

You want to find w_1 and w_2 such that the sum from the previous equation will be as small as possible. You have many ways to figure out what these values should be, some of them complex. I think we'll do as they do in *Introduction to Statistical Learning* (Springer, 2017) and move on after commenting that multiple regression coefficients estimates (which the previous equation is) have somewhat complicated forms.[4] And I should mention that there are many software packages out there that can easily solve it for you.[5]

It's good having weights for each recommender, but it's even better to have these weights change depending on the user or items. This is what you'll do in the following section.

12.5 *Feature-weighted linear stacking (FWLS)*

Previously you looked at feature-weighted hybrids, where you combined several recommenders using a fixed weight. This is similar to doing linear functions with the output of different recommenders, for example:

$$b(u,i) = w_1 \times r_{cf}(u,i) + w_2 \times r_{cb}(u,i)$$

Where

- $b(u,i)$ is the predicted rating for user u and item i
- w_1, w_2 are the feature weights.
- $r_{cf}(u,i)$ is the collaborative filtering predictor.
- $r_{cb}(u,i)$ is the content-based predictor.

---

[4] For more information, see http://www.bcf.usc.edu/~gareth/ISL/, a great book on machine learning.
[5] For example, Scikit-learn at http://mng.bz/P375.

You call the result here *for blend,* which is also a name for these feature-weighted hybrids.[6] In this example, you weighted the input of two recommenders (the weights are w_1 and w_2). You can use more than two; in fact, there's no limit to how many you use. In this section, you're going to look at how to make the weights into functions instead. It comes from an article by the same name by Joseph Sill et al.[7]

12.5.1 *Meta features: Weights as functions*

Let's say you want to make your recommender system even more flexible by saying that you want to use content-based recommendations if the user has only rated a few items, and collaborative filtering if the user has interacted with many items. To do that you can extend the previous example by replacing the weights with functions as shown in figure 12.10.

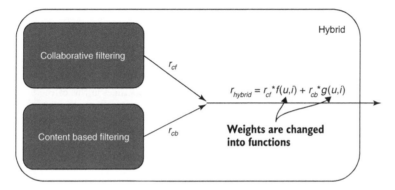

Figure 12.10 **Example of an FWLS recommender that replaces weights**

These functions are called *meta functions* or *feature-weights functions* and will make the prediction function look like the following:

$$b(u,i) = f(u,i) \times r_{cf}(u,i) + g(u,i) \times r_{cb}(u,i)$$

Figure 12.11 shows a selection of the meta functions used to win the Netflix Prize. They seem so simple that it's hard to believe there's enough power in these simple functions to almost win a million dollars. Those functions deserve respect!

---

[6]   The predicted rating is also often referred to as when looking at functions.
[7]   For more information, see https://arxiv.org/pdf/0911.0460.pdf.

Table 1: Meta-Features used for Netflix Prize model blending

1	A constant 1 voting feature (this allows the original predictors to be regressed against in addition to their interaction with the voting features)
2	A binary variable indicating whether the user rated more than 3 movies on this particular date
3	The log of the number of times the movie has been rated
4	The log of the number of distinct dates on which a user has rated movies
5	A bayesian estimate of the mean rating of the movie after having subtracted out the user's bayesian-estimated mean
6	The log of the number of user ratings
7	The mean rating of the user, shrunk in a standard bayesian way towards the mean over all users of the simple averages of the users
8	The norm of the SVD factor vector of the user from a 10-factor SVD trained on the residuals of global effects
9	The norm of the SVD factor vector of the movie from a 10-factor SVD trained on the residuals of global effects
10	The log of the sum of the positive correlations of movies the user has already rated with the movie to be predicted
11	The standard deviation of the prediction of a 60-factor ordinal SVD
12	Log of the average number of user ratings for those users who rated the movie
13	The log of the standard deviation of the dates on which the movie was rated. Multiple ratings on the same date are represented multiple times in this calculation
14	The percentage of the correlation sum in feature 10 accounted for by the top 20 percent of the most correlated movies the user has rated.
15	The standard deviation of the date-specific user means from a model which has separate user means (a.k.a biases) for each date
16	The standard deviation of the user ratings
17	The standard deviation of the movie ratings
18	The log of (rating date - first user rating date + 1)
19	The log of the number of user ratings on the date + 1
20	The maximum correlation of the movie with any other movie, regardless of whether the other movies have been rated by the user or not
21	Feature 3 times Feature 6, i.e., the log of the number of user ratings times the log of the number of movie ratings
22	Among pairs of users who rated the movie, the average overlap in the sets of movies the two users rated, where overlap is defined as the percentage of movies in the smaller of the two sets which are also in the larger of the two sets.
23	The percentage of ratings of the movie which were the only rating of the day for the user
24	The (regularized) average number of movie ratings for the movies rated by the user.
25	First, a movie-movie matrix was created with entries containing the probability that the pair of movies was rated on the same day conditional on a user having rated both movies. Then, for each movie, the correlation between this probability vector over all movies and the vector of ratings correlations with all movies was computed

Figure 12.11 Feature weights used for the Netflix Prize[8]

---

8   Found in the article "Feature-Weighted Linear Stacking" by J. Sill. Available online at https://arxiv.org/pdf/0911.0460.pdf.

12.5.2 *The algorithm*

Having a function like the one shown in the previous section is nice, but how do you figure out what the function should look like? The list of functions in figure 12.11 comes from a good knowledge of data, but probably also from an ample portion of wild guessing.

You can say that you've a series of recommenders, g_1, g_2, ..., g_L. Every g_i takes an input such as user and item and returns a predicted rating. With that you can write the simple linear function like this:

$$b_{FW}(u,i) = w_1 g_1(u,i) + w_2 g_2(u,i) + \ldots + w_L g_L(u,i)$$

It's called *FW* for feature weighting. As you saw in earlier chapters, there's an easier way to write this:

$$b_{FW}(u,i) = \sum_{j=1}^{L} w_j g_j(u,i)$$

That looks too simple, right? Make each of the w_j's into a function as you saw previously; these are called feature-weighting functions:

$$b_{FW}(u,i) = \sum_{j=1}^{L} w_j(u,i) g_j(u,i)$$

Now you have a short way to write linear functions so that you can add the really cool stuff. The feature-weighting functions can be defined as follows: Each weight w_j is defined as the sum of the functions with a weight v in front as shown in the following:

$$w_j(u,i) = \sum_{k=1}^{M} v_{kj} f_k(u,i)$$

But this is confusing, right? At least I thought so the first time I saw it. Each weighting function is the sum of all the meta features. The idea is that you want to let the machine decide what's better. You can say that you want the content-based recommender to provide 90% of the recommendation if the user has rated fewer than three items; otherwise, it should be 50/50. Let's look at an example. You could have two functions, such as function 1 and 2 in the following. The first function could be

$$f_1(u,i) = 1$$

and the second

$$f_2(u,i) = \begin{cases} 1 & \textit{if } u \textit{ has rated less than 3 items} \\ 0 & \textit{otherwise} \end{cases}$$

You had two predictors for collaborative filtering and for content-based filtering. You can make a blended recommender function b like the following:

$$b(u,i) = (v_{11} \times f_1(u,i) + v_{12} \times f_2(u,i)) r_{cf}(u,i) + (v_{21} \times f_1(u,i) + v_{22} \times f_2(u,i)) r_{cb}(u,i)$$

It's already a bit long. But can you guess what values you should give the v's? If you set the v's as highlighted in the following expression, you gain what you wanted:

$$b(u,i) = (\mathbf{0.5} \times f_1(u,i) + \mathbf{-0.4} \times f_2(u,i)) p_{cf}(u,i) + (\mathbf{0.5} \times f_1(u,i) + \mathbf{0.4} \times f_2(u,i)) p_{cb}(u,i)$$

If the user rated more than three items, then $f_2(u,i) = 0$ and $f_1(u,i) = 1$:

$$b(u,i) = (0.5 \times 1 + (-0.4) \times 0) p_{cf}(u,i) + (0.5 \times 1 + 0.4 \times 0) p_{cb}(u,i) = 0.5 \times p_{cf} + 0.5 * p_{cb}$$

If the user rated fewer than three items, then $f_2(u,i) = 1$ and $f_1(u,i) = 1$:

$$b(u,i) = (0.5 \times 1 + (-0.4) \times 1) p_{cf}(u,i) + (0.5 \times 1 + 0.4 \times 1) p_{cb}(u,i) = 0.1 \times p_{cf} + 0.9 * p_{cb}$$

This is what you wanted. To get back in theory mode, let's take the previous expressions and combine them so you get a more compact expression of r_{FWLS}:

$$r_{FW}(u,i) = \sum_{j=1}^{L} w_j g_j(u,i)$$

$$r_{FWLS}(u,i) = \sum_{j=1}^{L} \left[\sum_{k=1}^{M} v_{kj} f_k(u,i) \right] g_j(u,i)$$

$$w_j(u,i) = \sum_{k=1}^{M} v_{kj} f_k(u,i)$$

With this, you have FWLS, and figure 12.12 illustrates this. You can use this to blend the output of recommenders using weights that are functions that make those extremely flexible.

Manually setting the values is one thing, but you want the machine to look at the data and decide for itself which values are better. You want to train the algorithm. Let's call a shovel a shovel and admit that you're going to use machine learning.

Training the algorithm comes down to more or less the same problem as you saw in the previous chapter. You want to take the data you have in your database and use that to figure out what those weights should be. As an example, you could say that you have the usual user rating matrix shown in table 12.4.

Because you have six users and six items, you have $6 \times 6 - 3$ (the minus 3 is the empty cells in the table), meaning you have 33 data points, each containing a user ID, an item ID, and a rating; for example, (Sara, *Star Trek*, 3). You consider this to be true, and you can say that if you input (Sara, *Star Trek*) into the function, then you want it to return 3. The same is true for all the other 32 data points. You want the hybrid

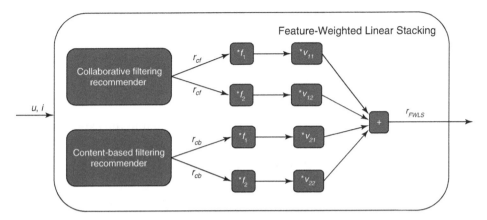

Figure 12.12 An example of an FWLS recommender, containing a collaborative filtering recommender and a content-based filtering recommender

Table 12.4 An example of a rating matrix

	Comedy	Action	Comedy	Action	Drama	Drama.
Sara	5	3		2	2	2
Jesper	4	3	4		3	3
Therese	5	2	5	2	1	1
Helle	3	5	3		1	1
Pietro	3	3	3	2	4	5
Ekaterina	2	3	2	3	5	5

recommender function to produce output that makes the difference between an expression and the actual ratings as small as possible. Looking only at the (Sara, *Star Trek*) example, you want to minimize the following:

$$r_{FSWL}(Sara, \ Star \ Trek) - 3$$

Well, you need to do something more, because if you set the rating to 0 in the previous expression, the result is -3, which is the smallest you can get. Let's aim for minimizing this instead

$$(r_{FSWL}(Sara, \ Star \ Trek) - 3)^2 \quad (1)$$

because then you can stick to the goal of getting it as close to zero as possible. The expression (1) is only for one of the 33 data points you have. And you need to be sure that the function works for all of them, so you'll want to do this for all users and all items. To do that, you get the following:

$$\sum_{u \in users} \sum_{i \in items} (r_{FSWL}(u,i) - r_{u,i})^2$$

What was the r_{FSWL}? In the following, r_{FSWL} is inserted into the expression:

$$\sum_{u \in users} \sum_{i \in items} \left(\sum_{j=1}^{L} \sum_{k=1}^{M} v_{jk} f_k(u,i) g_j(u,i) - r_{u,i} \right)^2$$

And this is what you want to make as small as possible. This is the algorithm.

You have many different ways to take it from here but keep it simple. To finish the example with the manually found weights, which gave us the following function:

$$b(u,i) = (0.5 \times f_1(u,i) + -0.4 \times f_2(u,i)) p_{cf}(u,i) + (0.5 \times f_1(u,i) + 0.4 \times f_2(u,i)) p_{cb}(u,i)$$

If you want to know how this recommender would predict what rating Sara would give the film *Avengers*, you'd call both feature recommenders (assume they predict 4 and 5, respectively), and run the two functions. Both return 1. That means the hybrid calculates the following:

$$b(u,i) = (0.5 \times 1 + (-0.4) \times 1) \times 4 + (0.5 \times 1 + 0.4 \times 1) \times 5 = 4.9$$

Now let's go back to the weights and see how you can machine learn yourself out of that problem.

WHEN THE FEATURE RECOMMENDER DOESN'T KNOW

One of the things you need to think about up front is what to do when one or more of the feature recommenders doesn't produce any recommendations. The easiest thing to do is take out the data where one of the recommenders doesn't respond. This reduces the training set, which might not be a viable solution. You can also try to guess by adding the average rating of the user, the item, the average of the two, or the baseline predictors described in chapter 11.

In the following implementation, you'll take the first solution and remove all the rows that don't contain predicted ratings from either of the feature recommenders. It could also be that a feature-weighting function isn't defined for all rows; in that case, you can also either remove the row or come up with a default value.

TRAINING THE BEAST

To prepare the hybrid recommender, you need to do a few things. It can be confusing and easy to make small mistakes that become big ones when you have a long pipeline such as the one shown in figure 12.13. You'll go through the following steps:

- Split the data into two sets for training and testing (not shown in figure 12.13).
- Train the featured recommenders.

- Generate predictions for each of the training data points.
- Execute each feature-weighted function on all training and data points.
- For each training data point, calculate the product between each predicted rating with each feature-weighted function result.
- Find the unknown values using linear regression.
- Test the hybrid on the test set.

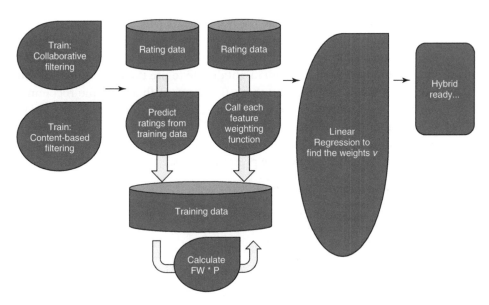

Figure 12.13 The FWLS hybrid recommender training pipeline

SPLITTING DATA

Before starting, it's a good idea to split the data and remove something like 20% of it to check how well the algorithm does. The problem is that if you use all the data to train the algorithm, then you'll measure its power on data that it's already seen. Instead, you need to cut part of the data so you can see how well it will do on not-seen data. And, as mentioned in an earlier chapter, splitting the data before training the feature recommenders means that the feature recommenders won't train on the test data.

To do this correctly, you should split your data into training, validation, and test sets. Use only the training data to train the feature recommenders and the hybrid. Then use the validation data to understand if the hybrid is a good model and to fine-tune the hyper parameters. The test set provides an unbiased validation of the model.

TRAINING THE FEATURED RECOMMENDERS

Here you're going to need many things that you learned in earlier chapters. Before beginning on the hybrid recommender, you need to prepare the recommenders that the hybrid will use. First, you'll prepare the item–item collaborative filtering recommender (which was described in chapter 8), and the content-based recommender (chapter 10). You could also have used something else, but those were the two I chose.

GENERATING PREDICTIONS FOR EACH OF THE TRAINING DATA POINTS

Here you could arrive at a strange problem: how will your recommender react when you try to predict ratings that already exist? Depending on how you implemented it, your collaborative filtering system might decide to use the most similar product to the current item that it can find and that's the same. In that case, the recommender will return the actual rating instead of a prediction. That isn't a good idea because it will skew the training of the hybrid.

Here you solve this by pretending that the current item hasn't been rated by the current user. Table 12.5 shows the present ratings.

Table 12.5   Training data for *Men in Black*

user	item	Actual rating
Sara	MIB	5
Jesper	MIB	4
Therese	MIB	5
Helle	MIB	4

When the recommenders are trained and they're ready to shine, you'll take the training data, which is the data you'll use to teach the hybrid algorithm to recommend, and run it by each of the recommenders to see what they'd predict for each user-item pairs. This gives you the data shown in table 12.6.

Table 12.6   Training data with the predictions added

user	item	Prediction collaborative filtering	Prediction content-based	Actual rating
Sara	MIB	4.5	3.5	5
Jesper	MIB	4	5	4
Therese	MIB	4	4	5
Helle	MIB	3	5	4

EXECUTE EACH FEATURE-WEIGHTED FUNCTION ON ALL TRAINING DATA POINTS

Now you want to run it past the two functions to get their results. This is shown in table 12.7.

Table 12.7 Training data with the predictions and function results added

user	item	Prediction collaborative filtering	Prediction cb	F1	F2	Actual rating
Sara	MIB	4.5	3.5	1	0	5
Jesper	MIB	4	5	1	1	4
Therese	MIB	4	4	1	1	5
Helle	MIB	3	5	1	1	4

For each training data point, calculate the product between each predicted rating with each feature-weighted function result, then multiply the predictions with the meta feature functions. You'll get the results shown in table 12.8.

Table 12.8 Training data with the calculated predictions and function results

user	item	Pcf * F1	Pcf * F2	Pcb*F1	Pcb*F2	Actual rating
Sara	MIB	4.5	0	3.5	0	5
Jesper	MIB	4	4	5	5	4
Therese	MIB	4	4	4	4	5
Helle	MIB	3	5	3	5	4

Now the training data is ready.

FINDING THE UNKNOWN VALUES VS. USING LINEAR REGRESSION

To find the v's (unknown values), you'll use linear regression. This means that you'll try to find a function that creates output as close to the actual data as possible. Such a function might not be possible to find, but we'll get back to that in a bit.

Linear regression is one of the first things that you'll learn in any machine-learning course. Whole books have been written about the subject, so I won't try to teach it here.[9] But I will tell you that the concept is basically the same as what you learned in the previous chapter, when you tried to find the unknowns in the Funk SVD, in the sense that linear regression will try to minimize the squared error over all data points.

TESTING THE HYBRID ON THE TEST SET

With the linear regression finished, you can now check the quality of the hybrid's results (compared to the ratings of the test set—the data you left out) and decide

---

[9] G. James et al., *Introduction to Statistical Learning* (Springer, 2017). This book is not totally about linear regression but it includes a good chapter about it.

whether it works. To do that, you'll examine how close the predictions of the hybrid fit the actual ratings. Now that you know it all, it's time to look at the code that can implement your hybrid.

12.6   *Implementation*

Let's see how an FWLS hybrid runs in MovieGEEKs. You'll follow the same steps as before but use code instead. If you haven't downloaded the MovieGEEKs code yet, I suggest doing it now, so you can follow along with what happens. MovieGEEKs is implemented to be ready and running in a few steps. You can find it at http://mng.bz/ 04k5. When you've downloaded the code, follow the installation instructions in the readme file.

During the installation you'll download the MovieTweetings dataset. When you have followed the instructions and populated all the data, you can train the FWLS hybrid algorithm by running this script.

Listing 12.1   Training the FWLS recommender

```
> python -m builder.fwls_calculator
```

While the script runs, you can see how it works. It starts out loading and splitting the data, of course.

LOADING THE DATA

You'll now load rating data. (I want to make sure you understand that it's made of the ratings collected from the users, either explicit or implicit.) The data is used to fine-tune the hybrid by providing both input and (expected) output. You'll find the following scripts in /builder/fwls_calculator.py.

Listing 12.2   Loading the rating data

```
def get_real_training_data(self):                                  Creates a Panda
    columns = ['user_id', 'movie_id', 'rating', 'type']            data frame of
    ratings_data = Rating.objects.all().values(*columns)               the data
    df = pd.DataFrame.from_records(ratings_data, columns=columns)  ◁──────
```

To get the data, you loaded all the ratings into memory. If there are red flags waving here, there should be.

It isn't a good idea to load the whole rating table into memory unless you're looking for trouble. But the size here is okay; if not, then you have to either stream the data chunk-by-chunk or take a data sample. The simplest thing might be to cut away old data until it all fits in memory. Moving on.

SPLITTING THE DATA

Here you split the data into the two sets: train and test data. This is done so you can see how good the result of our work is. You'll use the data to train the feature recommender and the hybrid recommender. For the hybrid, you'll use the training data to select good values for the weights and the test set to see how well you did.

Listing 12.3 Splitting the data for training and testing

```
self.train, self.test = train_test_split(self.train, test_size = 0.2)
```

TRAINING THE FEATURED RECOMMENDERS

The feature recommenders need to be trained, but you needn't do that here because you trained them in earlier chapters. But if you want to evaluate the algorithms, you should train those on the training data only; this is true for the collaborative filtering recommender at least. The content-based recommender uses content data, so hiding users from that won't change much. To train the feature recommenders, update the line in the following listing.

Listing 12.4 Calling the training method

```
fwls.train() # run fwls.train(train_feature_recs=True)
➥to train feature recs
```

GENERATING PREDICTIONS FOR EACH OF THE TRAINING DATA POINTS

With the ratings loaded, you can take each of the data points in the training data and see what each of the feature recommenders predicts. These will be added to the data frame.

Here are the methods that you'll call to do the predictions. The first one is collaborative filtering, which was described in detail in chapter 8 (see that chapter for more information). The code is shown in listing 12.5. Notice that the method takes a list of `movie_ids`. This is done to ensure that it doesn't mistakenly use the knowledge with which the user has already rated this item. The method is called with a list of all items rated by the user, except for the item you want to predict. You'll find the following scripts in /recs/neighbourhood_based_recommender.py.

Listing 12.5 Collaborative filtering

```
def predict_score_by_ratings(self, item_id, movie_ids):
    top = 0
    bottom = 0
    mc = self.max_candidates
    ids= movie_ids.keys()
    candidate_items = (Similarity.objects.filter(source__in=ids)
                                  .filter(target=item_id)
                                  .exclude(source=item_id)      ⟵──────┐
    candidate_items = candidate_items.distinct()                       │
                                  .order_by('-similarity')[:mc]        │
                                                                       │
    if len(candidate_items) == 0:                                      │
        return 0                             **Ensures that you**      │
                                             **don't use the**         │
    for sim_item in candidate_items:         **user's rating**  ───────┘
        r = movie_ids[sim_item.source]
        top += sim_item.similarity * r
        bottom += sim_item.similarity

    return top/bottom
```

The second recommender (listing 12.6) is the content-based recommender that uses the LDA. LDA was described in detail in chapter 10, but not this method. What happens is that you use the similarities and the user's ratings to predict a rating. Here you use the similarity from the LDA instead of the similarity based on user behavior as in collaborative filtering.

Listing 12.6   Content-based recommender

```
def predict_score(self, user_id, item_id):

    active_user_items = (Rating.objects.filter(user_id=user_id)
                            .exclude(movie_id=item_id)
                                .order_by('-rating')[:100])

    movie_ids = {movie['movie_id']: movie['rating'] for movie in
      active_user_items}
    user_mean = sum(movie_ids.values()) / len(movie_ids)

    sims = LdaSimilarity.objects.filter(Q(source__in=movie_ids.keys())
                                & Q(target=item_id)
                                & Q(similarity__gt=self.min_sim)
                                ).order_by('-similarity')
    pre = 0
    sim_sum = 0

    if len(sims) > 0:
        for sim_item in sims:
            r = Decimal(movie_ids[sim_item.source] - user_mean)
            pre += sim_item.similarity * r
            sim_sum += sim_item.similarity

    return Decimal(user_mean) + pre / sim_sum
```

You'll use these two methods on each of the ratings in the training data by applying them to each row and inserting the results into new columns as shown in the following listing. The script is found in /builder/fwls_calculator.py/.

Listing 12.7   Calculating predictions for training data

```
def calculate_predictions_for_training_data(self):

    self.training_data['cb'] = self.training_data.apply(lambda data:
self.cb.predict_score(data['user_id'], data['movie_id']))
    self.training_data['cf'] = self.training_data.apply(lambda data:
self.cf.predict_score(data['user_id'], data['movie_id']))
```

You now have a structure like the one you saw in table 12.2.

EXECUTING EACH FEATURE-WEIGHTED FUNCTION ON ALL TRAINING DATA POINTS

The functions you'll use in this step are simple and not much to talk about, but I deem that they're enough to show how FWLS works as shown in this listing. You'll find this script in /builder/fwls_calculator.py/.

Listing 12.8 Showing how FWLS works

```
def fun1(self):        <—— Always returns 1
    return 1.0
                            | Returns 1 if user has rated fewer
def fun2(self, user_id):  <—| then 3 movies; otherwise, 0
    user_ratings = self.rating_count['user_id']==user_id
    rating_count = self.rating_count[user_ratings]['movie_id'].values[0]
    if rating_count < 3.0:
        return 1.0
    return 0.0
```

Instead of calculating the function first and saving that data, you'll use the functions and compute the product of their result in one step.

FOR EACH TRAINING DATA POINT, CALCULATE THE PRODUCT BETWEEN EACH PREDICTED RATING WITH EACH FUNCTION

For each prediction, you want to return a column with the product of the prediction and each of the functions. You have two predictors and two functions, so you need to get four new columns as shown in the following listing. Once again, you'll find the script in /builder/fwls_calculator.py/.

Listing 12.9 Calculating feature functions for training data

Calculates the product of the content-based prediction and function 1

Calculates the product of the content-based prediction and function 2

```
def calculate_feature_functions_for_training_data(self):
    self.training_data['cb1'] = self.training_data.apply(lambda data:
                                        data.cb*self.func1())
    self.training_data['cb2'] = self.training_data.apply(lambda data:
                                    data.cb*self.func2(data['user_id']))  <—
    self.training_data['cf1'] = self.training_data.apply(lambda data:
                                        data.cf*self.func1())
    self.training_data['cf2'] = self.training_data.apply(lambda data:
                                    data.cf*self.func2(data['user_id']))  <—
```

Calculates the product of the neighborhood-based prediction and function 1

Calculates the product of the neighborhood-based prediction and function 2

You're finished the preparation for the linear regression to find the v's. This is also called *feature generation*. Often, when doing machine-learning applications, this is where you'll spend the most time.

FEATURE-WEIGHTED FUNCTION RESULT

You calculated the feature-weighted functions in the previous step, but it might not always be a good idea to do this in real life. Sometimes it's better to do only small steps, depending on your specific scenario.

Now for linear regression. You'll find these scripts in the train method in /builder/fwls_calculator.py.

Listing 12.10   Linear regression

```
regr = linear_model.LinearRegression(fit_intercept=True,
                                     n_jobs=-1,
                                     nomarlize=True)
regr.fit(self.train_data[['cb1', 'cb2', 'cf1', 'cf2']],
         self.train_data['rating'])
```

**Instantiates the
LinearRegression model
class of scikit-learn[10]**

**Fits the weights to build
the linear function**

To use these weights, you need to save them. You can put them in the database so that you can use them again later, or you can save them to a file as shown in the following listing.

Listing 12.11   Saving weights

```
with open(self.save_path + 'fwls_parameters.data', 'wb') as ub_file:
    pickle.dump(result, ub_file)
```

THE ONLINE RECOMMENDATION PREDICTION

You can implement the hybrid recommender by pre-calculating recommendations and saving them in the database. The lazier approach is to call all the feature recommenders and then mix the results.

To ensure a good ordering, both recommenders are requested to provide a Top-N five times larger than what the user is requesting. This is to allow for the linear functions to have enough elements to order them correctly as shown in the next listing. You'll find these scripts in the train method in /builder/fwls_calculator.py.

Listing 12.12   Ordering elements

```
def recommend_items(self, user_id, num=6):
    cb_recs = self.cb.recommend_items(user_id, num * 5)
    cf_recs = self.cf.recommend_items(user_id, num * 5)

    combined_recs = dict()
    for rec in cb_recs:
        movie_id = rec[0]
        pred = rec[1]['prediction']
        combined_recs[movie_id] = {'cb': pred}
    for rec in cf_recs:
        movie_id = rec[0]
        pred = rec[1]['prediction']
```

**Calls the content-based
recommender requesting
five times more elements
than needed**

**Calls the neighborhood-
based recommender
requesting five times more
elements than needed**

**Runs through all the
recommendations and
creates a dictionary of
dictionaries. Adds all items
from the content-based
recommendation.**

**Adds all the
items from the
neighborhood
model**

---

[10] For more information, see http://mng.bz/P375.

```
        if movie_id in combined_recs.keys():
            combined_recs[movie_id]['cf'] = pred
        else:
            combined_recs[movie_id] = {'cf': pred}
    fwls_preds = dict()
    for key, recs in combined_recs.items():          ◄────
        if 'cb' not in recs.keys():
            recs['cb'] = self.cb.predict_score(user_id, key)
        if 'cf' not in recs.keys():
            recs['cf'] = self.cf.predict_score(user_id, key)
        pred = self.prediction(recs['cb'], recs['cf'], user_id)  ◄─┐
        fwls_preds[key] = {'prediction': pred}
    sorted_items = sorted(fwls_preds.items(),
    key=lambda item: -float(item[1]['prediction']))[:num]  ◄─┐

    return sorted_items
```

Runs through the model and gets rating predictions from the recommenders that are missing

Calculates the predicted rating for all elements in the dictionary, using the predict method shown in listing 12.13

Orders result by prediction

The prediction method looks like the one shown in the next listing.

Listing 12.13 The prediction method

```
def prediction(self, p_cb, p_cf, user_id):        ◄──┐  Calculates the
    p = (self.wcb1 * self.fun1() * p_cb +                 predicted rating for
        self.wcb2 * self.fun2(user_id) * p_cb +          the item
        self.wcf1 * self.fun1() * p_cf +
        self.wcf2 * self.fun2(user_id) * p_cf)
    return p + self.intercept

def fun1(self):                    ◄─── Function 1
    return Decimal(1.0)

def fun2(self, user_id):           ◄─── Function 2
    count = Rating.objects.filter(user_id=user_id).count()
    if count > 3.0:
        return Decimal(1.0)
    return Decimal(0.0)
```

In the following section, you'll see a few recommendations produced with the hybrid.

HOW DOES THE HYBRID COMPARE?

The feature recommenders are correlated with the hybrid recommender, but how does the hybrid compare with the individual recommenders? To understand that, you can again see which of the three recommenders (collaborative, content-based, and hybrid) comes closest to the actual ratings.

In the first example where the user has only one rating, the neighborhood model doesn't return anything (figure 12.14). Then, if you look at a user who has several ratings registered, the combination of the two recommenders shows items that wouldn't enter into the top 6 of the content-based or the neighborhood-based recommenders (figure 12.15).

Content-based recommender will return something no matter how few ratings the user has.

User (user_id 386) has only one rating in the database, so the collaborative filtering doesn't return anything.

The hybrid only gets predictions from the content-based recommender. But it reorders it.

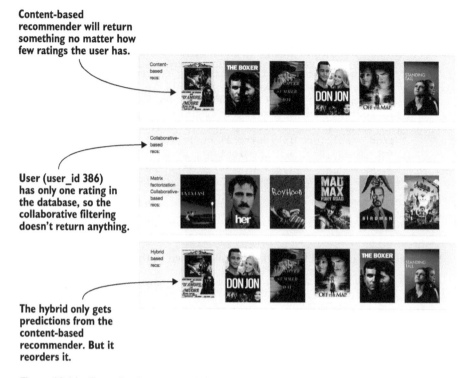

Figure 12.14   Example of recommendations returned by the hybrid recommender.

User has several ratings, so both neighborhood-based and content-based recommenders return a top 6.

The linear function rearranges the items returned from the two feature recommenders (content-based and collaborative-based).

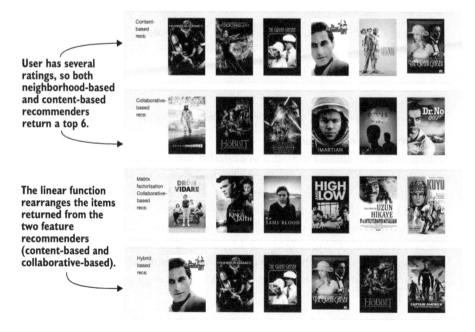

Figure 12.15   The recommendations from the hybrid recommender, where both feature recommenders predicted recommendations

TESTING THE HYBRID ON THE TEST SET

Did it work? How do you test that? Well, there's the offline evaluation that you learned about in chapter 9. That's where you did cross-validation as shown in figure 12.16.

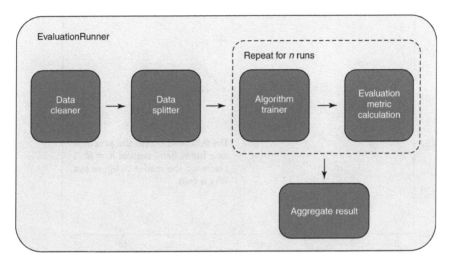

Figure 12.16 The evaluation runner is used to evaluate an algorithm. It's a pipeline where the data is first cleaned, then split into the k folds for cross-validation. Then for each fold it repeats training of the algorithm to evaluate it. When it's all finished, you aggregate the result.

Running this evaluation runner is similar to what's described in chapter 9, only here you need to train all of the included recommenders. You can run the evaluation by executing the code shown in the following listing.

Listing 12.14 Executing the evaluation

```
> python -m evaluator.evaluation_runner -fwls
```

The evaluator produces the data shown in figure 12.17. That evaluation (shown in figure 12.17) is special compared to the others you've seen because it's built on three machine-learning algorithms. But it's not the case that the final product is better when the two feature recommenders are optimal.

If I wanted to put this system into production, then I'd probably precalculate much of the algorithms to speed things up. A way to make the training faster is to sample the ratings used to do the linear regression, the way I did in this listing.

Listing 12.15 Executing the evaluation

```
self.train_data = self.train_data.sample(self.data_size)
```

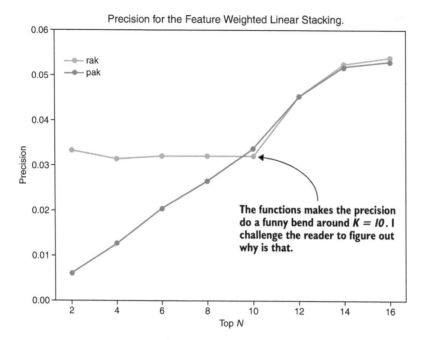

Figure 12.17 The evaluation of the FWLS algorithm.

The question is how big should the sample size be, so that it's representative of the whole data set, considering that you're training the four weights. It's a typical dilemma with machine learning. And I can say that I've had good experiences with a few hundred data points, but that's not many! But if you look at the precision in the chart in figure 12.17, then the algorithm looks good.

Many terms and combinations were thrown around in this chapter. If you're new to linear regression, then I highly recommend looking deeper into it. It's simple when you get to know it, and it can be used for so many things that it's silly not to have it in your tool box.

Summary

- A recommender system can be greatly optimized by adding the output of several algorithms.
- Hybrid recommenders enable you to combine the forces of different recommenders to get better results.
- Not all things that are complex are functional in the real world, although the algorithm that won the Netflix Prize also failed because it was too complicated to put into production.
- The feature-weighted linear stacking (FWLS) algorithm enables the system to use feature recommenders in a function-weighted way, which makes it strong.

13
Ranking and learning to rank

This book is all about learning, and in this chapter, you'll learn how to rank.

- You'll reformulate the recommender problem to a ranking problem.
- You'll look at Foursquare's ranking method and how it uses multiple sources.
- You'll go through the different types of Learning to Rank (LTR) algorithms and learn how to distinguish pointwise, pairwise, and listwise comparisons of ranks.
- You'll learn about the Bayesian Personalized Ranking (BPR) algorithm, which is a promising algorithm to implement.

Are all these chapters on recommender algorithms starting to look the same? If so, you're in luck, because now you're going to start something completely different. Instead of focusing on recommendations as a rating prediction problem, it sometimes makes more sense to look at how the items should be stacked. The catalog item that the user would find most relevant is on top, the second one next, and so on. To define relevancy like this takes away the need to predict ratings. You don't need to know how favorably users would rate something, only that they'd love it, or at least like it more than everything else that's available.

> **NOTE** Keep in mind that the catalog of content might not contain anything the user would love, but even when that's the case, you still want to provide a list of the best you can do with what you have.

I think this is going to be an exciting chapter. You're going to learn about a type of algorithm first introduced in the area of information retrieval (IR) systems—a posh word for search engines these days. Ranking powers the Microsoft search engine Bing, as well as most other search engines, and Facebook and Foursquare use it too. You'll see a difference between what they want to find and what a recommender wants, but in the end, most of the research done in the IR world has also been usable for recommenders.

You'll start this journey with an example of Learning to Rank from Foursquare to give you a sense of ranking. You'll then step back and look at LTR algorithms in general, which are divided into three subgroups. To have a concrete example of a LTR algorithms, you'll examine the BPR algorithm. It has a bit of complicated math, but you'll revisit it by coding the algorithm in MovieGEEKs so you can see it in action.

13.1   *Learning to rank an example at Foursquare*

Foursquare is a guide to cities. I use it to find places where I can maintain my coffee addiction (which I promise myself to stop when I finish writing this book). Imagine I'm standing in front of the beautiful St. Peter's Basilica in Rome. After an exhaustingly long wait in a queue to see the inside of the church, I decide I need coffee, so I flip out my phone and open the Foursquare app and click coffee near me. The result is shown in figure 13.1 (not completely, but it's the browser version of Foursquare's search for the same thing).

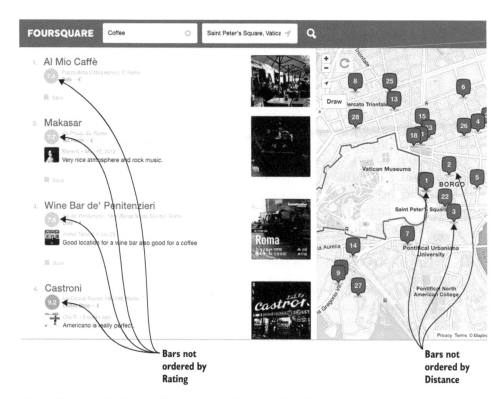

Figure 13.1   Looking for a coffee place near St. Peter's Basilica in Rome using Foursquare

As you can see, the recommendations aren't ordered by rating or by distance, so how are they ordered? How did Foursquare come up with this list?

Foursquare published an excellent article on how its recommender system works, describing their implementation of learning to rank.[1] I recommend that you read it because it's a fascinating insight into the challenges of finding points of interest near users. We'll look at a slightly simpler version than what they use to give you as a basic introductory example of learning to rank.

Like the hybrid recommenders from chapter 12, learning to rank is a way to combine different kinds of data sources, such as popularity, distance, or recommender system outputs. The difference here is that rank doesn't necessarily have to be from (or parts of) a recommender system. When ranking, you're looking for input sources that will give you an ordering of the objects. Figure 13.2 shows an overview of the list of features (called *features* in machine-learning lingo), which according to the article are utilized at Foursquare.

Feature	Description
Spatial score	$P(l \mid v)$
Timeliness	$P(t \mid v)$
Popularity	Smoothed estimate of expected check-ins/day at the venue
Here now	# of users currently checked in to the venue at query time
Personal History	# of previous visits from the user at the venue
Creator	1 if the user created the venue, 0 otherwise
Mayor	1 is the user is the mayor of the venue, 0 otherwise[5]
Friends Here Now	# of the user's friends currently checked in at query time
Personal History w/ Time of Day	# of previous visits from the user at the venue at the same time of the day

Figure 13.2   List of features used in Foursquare's algorithm to rank venues near you

Because you don't have access to the features listed in figure 13.2, let's stick to two features and see if you can make sense of the coffee rankings I got on the page shown in figure 13.1. The page shows the average rating of each venue; I found the walking distance using Google Maps. If you put this data into a table, it looks like table 13.1.

Table 13.1   The cafes recommendations from Foursquare

Ranking on Foursquare	Name	Walking time (distance)	Average ratings
1	Al Mio Caffé	2 min	7.4
2	Makasar	4 min	7.7
3	Wine Bar de' Penitenzieri	4 min	7.5
4	Castroni	10 min	9.2

---

[1]   Blake Shaw et al., "Learning to Rank for Spatiotemporal Search," http://mng.bz/vP25.

If you look at the table, it's easy to see that the rankings aren't based on ratings. If they were, Castroni would be at the top. It's also not ranked by distance, or Makasar would have to share its second place with the wine bar. Let's try feature engineering here and see if you can get closer to predicting the ranking for the four elements using only these two features—distance and average ratings.

First, you need to massage the data so that a higher value denotes a shorter distance and a higher average rating. Being far away isn't a good thing for a cafe, so you need to invert the distances. Inverting the distance will make places within a short walking distance (time) have a higher value. To do this, find the maximum, which is a 10-minute walk, and subtract each walking time from maximum. This makes the distance value of Al Mio Caffé be *10 – 2 = 8* and Castroni *10 – 10 = 0*. You rescale all the data so that everything is between 1 and 0 because if you don't, certain algorithms might not work well.[2] Rescaling can be done using the following formula:

$$x' = \frac{x - \min(x)}{\max(x) - \min(x)}$$

Normalizing the data will give you the data in table 13.2.

Table 13.2   Same as table 12.1, except with normalized data

Ranking on Foursquare	Name	Walking time (distance)	Average ratings
1	Al Mio Caffé	1.00	0.00
2	Makasar	0.75	0.17
3	Wine Bar de' Penitenzieri	0.75	0.06
4	Castroni	0.00	1.00

With this change, you've a distance ordering close to the ranking on Foursquare. Because Items 2 and 3 are tied for walking time, you need to get ranking from the ratings.

You're now at the core of the problem; you want to teach the machine to rank these items based on the input of ratings and distance. You can formalize this a bit more by saying you want the system to learn weights (w_0 and w_1), which when inserted into the following expression produce a value such that the four items get ordered as on the Foursquare page:

$$f(distance, rating) = w_0 \times distance + w_1 \times rating$$

Because you want to make the function produce an ordering like Foursquare's, you're trying to make an algorithm that's optimized to rank based on the output. In this

---

[2] For more information on rescaling, see https://en.wikipedia.org/wiki/Feature_scaling.

example, it's not too hard to guess the value for w_0 and w_1 if you set them equal to $w_0=20$ and $w_1=10$, you'll get the score values shown in table 13.3.

Table 13.3 Cafe data with a column showing the score calculated with the previous function *f*

Ranking on Foursquare	Name	Walking time (distance)	Average ratings	Score
1	Al Mio Caffé	1	0	20
2	Makasar	0.75	0.17	16.7
3	Wine Bar de' Penitenzieri	0.75	0.06	15.6
4	Castroni	0	1	10

Another way to approach the problem is to use linear regression to find the line that best represents the data set. Use the line to find the rank of each item by starting at the point furthest away from (0,0) and work inward. This is shown in figure 13.3. The angle of the line determines which of the two features (ratings or distance) will be given the most importance.

Figure 13.3 also provides a view of what you're trying to solve here. You have two different dimensions: the distance and the average ratings. By drawing the line as I did, I got the ordering as shown in the figure. If you change the angle of the line, the cafes might come out in a different order. I hope that helped.

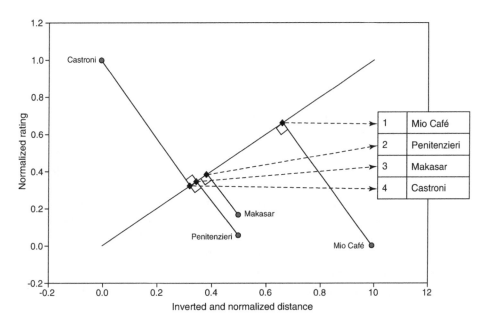

Figure 13.3 Projecting the points to a line shows an ordering of the items

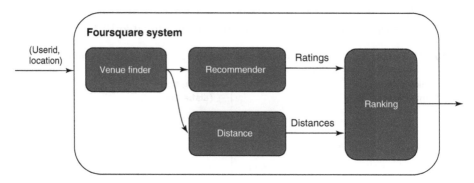

Figure 13.4   A simplified view of the Foursquare ranking system

Back to the Foursquare example: if you were Foursquare, you'd probably have a pipeline like the one shown in figure 13.4. Now the problem becomes slightly different because how do you (pretending you're Foursquare) optimize the function if you don't know what it's supposed to return? You use the check-in feature (read the articles for more details). Here I want you to note that finding data that describes how it should look isn't always straightforward.

13.2   *Re-ranking*

If you read about hybrids in the previous chapter, you might ask what's the difference between this and the feature-weighted hybrid. Remember that you're optimizing for two different things. A hybrid recommender always predicts ratings, while a LTR algorithm produces orderings. You'll look at how to define ordering in the next section.

Certain users would call the Foursquare ranking a re-ranking because it takes a list of venues that's found using a spatial index, meaning that it finds the items closest to you, and then reorders the list to also match the rating criteria.

A simple example of re-ranking in the recommender system is to use a popularity ordering as the base and then re-rank the items using the recommender. Popularity narrows the list to the most popular items and reduces the risk for showing items that are for particular (and maybe unpopular) tastes. This might remind you of a filter bubble, but remember that if a user likes unusual items more than popular items, the unusual ones would still bubble up in the list.

As an example, look at figure 13.3 again and find Castroni. It's far away but because its average rating is so high, it manages to get on the Top 4 list. The Mio Caffé doesn't have good ratings, but you were basically standing next to the cafe, so even if it's unpopular, it came first because it was the closest option.

Collaborative filtering algorithms are prone to recommend items liked by few people, but by people who really like the content. The algorithm has no concept of popularity and could be used for re-ranking instead of as the sole source for the ordering. This example is also described on the Netflix TechBlog.[3]

Instead of re-ranking items and rating predictions, why not start with the aim of ranking and then construct algorithms that optimize for that? This is the goal of LTR algorithms.

13.3 What's learning to rank again?

A recommender or another type of data-driven application that produces ranked lists is trained using a family of algorithms called *Learning to Rank* (LTR). A ranking recommender system has a catalog of items. Given a user, the system retrieves items that are relevant to the user and then ranks them so the items at the top of the list are the most applicable.

The ranking is done using a ranking model.[4] A ranking model is trained using an LTR algorithm, which is a supervised learning algorithm, meaning that you provide it with data containing input and output. In your case, that's a user_id as input and a ranked list of items as output. This family of algorithms has three subgroups—pointwise, pairwise, and listwise—which we'll quickly review.

13.3.1 The three types of LTR algorithms

LTR algorithms are distinguished by the way they evaluate the ranked list during training. Figure 13.5 illustrates the three different flavors.

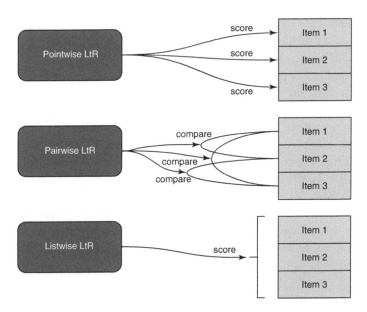

Figure 13.5 The three different subgroups of LTR algorithms: pointwise, pairwise, and listwise

---

[4] This definition is loosely taken from the article "A Short Introduction to Learning to Rank" by Hang LI. Available online at http://times.cs.uiuc.edu/course/598f16/l2r.pdf.

POINTWISE

The pointwise approach is the same as the recommenders you looked at in earlier chapters. It produces a score for each item and then ranks them accordingly. The difference between rating prediction and ranking is that with ranking, you don't care if an item has a utility score of a million or within a rating scale, as long as the score symbolizes a position in the rank.

PAIRWISE

Pairwise is a type of binary classifier. It's a function that takes two items and returns an ordering of the two. When you talk about pairwise ranking, you usually optimize the output so you've the minimal number of inversions of items compared to the optimal rank of the items. An *inversion* means that two items change places.

To do pairwise ordering, you need what's called an *absolute ordering*. An absolute ordering means that for any two content items in the catalog, you can say one is more relevant than the other or is tied.

> **NOTE** If you made a pairwise ranking by predicting ratings using the neighborhood model from chapter 8, you wouldn't have an absolute ordering because the algorithm can't predict ratings for all items.

LISTWISE

Listwise is the king of all LTR subgroups because it looks at the whole ranked list and optimizes that. The advantage of listwise ranking is that it intuits that ordering is more important at the top of a ranked list than at the bottom. Pointwise and pairwise algorithms don't distinguish where on the ranked list you are.

Consider, for example, a Top 10 recommendation; the pairwise recommendation will penalize you for getting the order of the last two items wrong as much as for getting the first two wrong. You know by now that that isn't good because users pay much more attention to the top of the list. To inject this into the algorithm also means that you need to look at the complete list and not each pair of items.

It sounds simple when explained like this: you have to create a ranking such that all items are always ranked correctly. But it turns out that it's hard to programmatically calculate whether one list is better than another one.

To have a look at a listwise ranking algorithm, I suggest CoFiRank (collaborative filtering for ranking), which was presented at NIPS (Neural Information Processing Systems) in 2007.[5] In the following section, you'll look at an algorithm that uses pairwise ranking.

---

[5] Weimer et al. Maximum. *CoFiRank Margin Matrix Factorization for Collaborative Ranking*. Available online at http://mng.bz/m0t1.

13.4 *Bayesian Personalized Ranking*

Once again, it's always a good idea to be sure you and your coworkers agree on the problem. That's true for this and so many other things in life. Let's start with a definition of the problem or task you want to solve. To solve it you'll use an algorithm called Bayesian Personalized Ranking (BPR), which was presented in a paper by Steffen Rendle et al.[6]

TASK TO SOLVE

The overall idea is that you want to provide customers with a list of items where the top one is the most relevant one, then the next best one, then the next, and so on. Up to now, I'm pretty sure that we understood each other: for each user you want to order the content items in such a way that the most relevant is on top. This is what you need to describe in a way that both you and the machine understand.

You need to define an ordering that says no matter which two items you hold up, the ordering will rank one better than the other. To make that work, you need three rules: totality, anti-symmetry, and transitivity. For example, for a given user, you want an ordering written such as $>_u$ and defined as the following:

- *Totality*—For all i, j in I (all items), if $i \neq j$, then you have either $i >_u j$ or $j >_u i$.
- *Anti-symmetry*—For all i, j in I, if $i >_u j$ and $j >_u i$ then $i = j$.
- *Transitivity*—For all i, j, k in I, if $i >_u j$ and $j >_u k$ then $i >_u k$.

It might not seem like it's important to spend so much time on this ordering, but it's needed to make the BPR work.

IF YOU HAVE IMPLICIT DATA

The algorithm we're talking about is often only used on implicit feedback. But here the problem is that you never have any negative feedback because you only have events that say "bought." Not having negative data is something that makes it hard for a machine-learning algorithm to understand when it's doing something wrong, so it also doesn't know when it's doing something right.

The absence of a bought event could indicate that the user doesn't know the item exists (they haven't seen it); they saw it, but didn't like it; or they saw it, liked it, but haven't bought it yet. In either case, you can assume that the *not* is something worse than the *bought* as illustrated in figure 13.6. Either a user has bought an item or not (the squared boxes). You then have different conditions for the user-item relationship.

If you've two items, one that's bought and one that's not, then when talking about ranking, you can define that a bought item is always more attractive than one that wasn't bought. With that clear, you can now turn to item pairs, which have two items

---

[6] Steffen Rendle et al., "BPR: Bayesian Personalized Ranking from Implicit Feedback," https://arxiv.org/pdf/1205.2618.pdf.

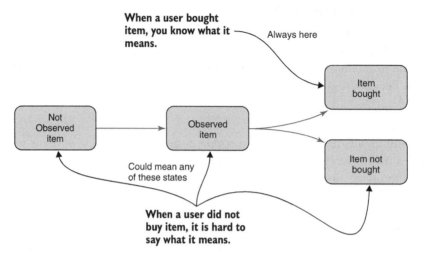

Figure 13.6   Different states of a user-item relationship. You know that when a user buys an item it's bought, but if a user doesn't buy an item, what does that mean?

that should be either bought or not bought, but you don't have anything to say about them just yet.

In figure 13.7, you can see the transformation of a user's buy log into an order matrix. Figure 13.8 shows how this expands your data because each user will have their own matrix.

That's all well and good, but you do have rating data, so how can you use that here? If you want more fine-grained sampling, you should look at MF-BPR (Multi-feedback Bayesian Personalized Ranking). Listen to this talk from RecSys 2016 on YouTube: "Bayesian Personalized Ranking with Multi-Channel User Feedback."[7]

WITH EXPLICIT DATA SETS

If you have explicit data—ratings—then you could make a similar order by saying non-rated items are below rated items (item rated = bought). You could ask if the not-rated item should be valued as an average rated item or as an item that's rated below all rated items. In figure 13.8, we'll assume rated means bought.

THE TRAINING DATA SET

With the approach described in the previous section, you can now collect a data set to be used to train a ranking recommender. This data set will contain all tuples *(u, i, j)*, where *i* has been bought and rated by the user, and *j* has not.

---

[7] To listen, go to www.youtube.com/watch?v=aKHLf4P3N08.

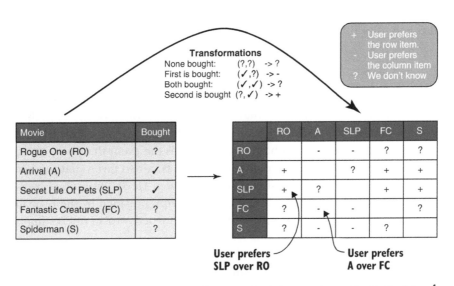

Transformations

None bought:	(?,?) -> ?
First is bought:	(✓,?) -> -
Both bought:	(✓,✓) -> ?
Second is bought	(?,✓) -> +

+	User prefers the row item.
-	User prefers the column item
?	We don't know

Movie	Bought
Rogue One (RO)	?
Arrival (A)	✓
Secret Life Of Pets (SLP)	✓
Fantastic Creatures (FC)	?
Spiderman (S)	?

	RO	A	SLP	FC	S
RO		-	-	?	?
A	+		?	+	+
SLP	+	?		+	+
FC	?	-	-		?
S	?	-	-	?	

User prefers SLP over RO

User prefers A over FC

Figure 13.7 How to transform one user's transaction into an order matrix. On the left, ✓ means that the user bought the item. In the matrix on the right, + means the user prefers a row element, and - means the user prefers the column element; for example, A is preferred over RO.

	RO	A	SLP	FC	S
Sara		x	x		
Jesper	x	x	x		
Helle	x		x		x
Pietro				x	x
Therese		x	x	x	

Create a new matrix for each user

Theresse	RO	A	SLP	FC	S
RO		-	-	?	?
A	+		?	+	+
SLP	+	?		+	+
FC	?	-	-		?
S	?	-	-	?	

Figure 13.8 The algorithm creates an order matrix for each user. Five users are in the rating matrix and will generate five matrices.

13.4.1 Ranking with BPR

Let's begin with the beast. You want to find a personalized ranking for all items and all users in your database. For personalized ranking, you'll use something called Bayesian statistics to solve this problem. Bayesian statistics are based on this simple equation:

$$p(A|B) = \frac{p(B|A)p(A)}{p(B)}$$

This equation states that the probability (p) of event A happening given that B happened is equal to the probability that A happens multiplied by the probability that B happens when A occurs, divided by the probability that B happened. To explain, you could say A is the event that it has rained, and B is the event that the street outside is wet. Then Bayes says that the probability that it has rained given that the street is wet ($p(A|B)$) is equal to the probability that it has rained ($p(A)$) multiplied by the probability that the street is wet given it has rained ($p(B|A)$) divided by the probability that the street is wet ($p(B)$). This simple equation has turned into an interesting branch of statistics, so I encourage you to look it up.

In the context of the ranking problem, you can formulate it by having an unknown ordering preference for each user, which you denote by $>_u$ for user u. $>_u$ is a total ordering, which given any two content items i and j from your catalog, the user will prefer one or the other. You'll also say that θ is the list of parameters you need to find for the recommender system (or, in fact, any machine-learning prediction model). If you're talking about the Funk SVD, remember that the problem boils down to making two matrices that you can use to calculate the predictions as shown in the following:

$$\begin{bmatrix} 5 & 3 & 0 & 2 & 2 & 2 \\ 4 & 3 & 4 & 0 & 3 & 3 \\ 5 & 2 & 5 & 2 & 1 & 1 \\ 3 & 5 & 3 & 0 & 1 & 1 \\ 3 & 3 & 3 & 2 & 4 & 5 \\ 2 & 3 & 2 & 3 & 5 & 5 \end{bmatrix} = \begin{bmatrix} u_{1,1} & u_{1,2} \\ u_{2,1} & u_{2,2} \\ u_{3,1} & u_{3,2} \\ u_{4,1} & u_{4,2} \\ u_{5,1} & u_{5,2} \\ u_{6,1} & u_{6,2} \end{bmatrix} \begin{bmatrix} v_{1,1} & v_{1,2} & v_{1,3} & v_{1,4} & v_{1,5} & v_{1,6} \\ v_{2,1} & v_{2,2} & v_{2,3} & v_{2,4} & v_{2,5} & v_{2,6} \end{bmatrix}$$

When you talk about θ in relationship to this, then θ is the set of all the $u_{i,j}$'s and $v_{i,j}$'s.

In a BPR, you want to find the model, θ, as defined, such that there's the highest probability that the model will produce a perfect ordering for all users. The probability can be written like this:

$$p(\theta | >_u)$$

(You read it by saying: the probability of seeing θ (theta) given the ordering $>_u$.) Due to Bayes' theorem, you know that if you want to maximize this, then it's the same as maximizing the following because they're proportional:[8]

$$p(>_u | \theta) p(\theta)$$

---

[8] For more information, see https://en.wikipedia.org/wiki/Bayes'_theorem.

Notice that the ordering $>_u$ and the model θ have changed places. Now you'll work on the probability of seeing the ordering $>_u$ given a specific model θ and multiply that with the probability of seeing that model.

> **NOTE** You'll need to do some math magic in the following section. Feel free to skip it if you're not interested in the nitty-gritty details.

Before going into the magic, however, let's stay afloat for a little bit longer and spell out exactly what's happening. You assume that in a perfect world there's a way to order all your content items flawlessly for each of your users, which is the total ordering $>_u$ that I keep mentioning. If there's such an ordering, there's also a probability that there's a recommender algorithm that can produce it.

$p(\theta| > u)$ is a question that you're asking. Assuming this ordering exists, what's the probability that you can find a model that will produce it? Then you mix Bayes into it, and you rephrase the question. Saying that $p(\theta| > u)$ is the same as asking what is the probability that there's θ times the probability that if you have θ, you then have the ordering. Is that clearer now?

13.4.2 *Math magic (advanced wizardry)*

Let's look at the two parts of the expression from the previous section. To refresh your memory:

$$p(>_u|\theta)\,p(\theta)$$

ASSUME THE PRIOR IS A NORMAL DISTRIBUTION

Let's start with the last part of the equation: $(p(\theta))$. Assume that the parameters of the model are independent and that each is normally distributed $(p(\theta) \sim N(0,\Sigma_\theta))$ with zero mean and a variance-covariance matrix Σ_θ.[9] Assuming that, you can write the last part as:

$$p(\theta) \,=\, \sqrt{\frac{1}{2\pi}}e^{-\frac{1}{2}\lambda\|\theta\|^2}$$

This infers you say that $\Sigma_\theta = \lambda_\theta I$.

Likelihood function

Moving on to $p(>_u|\theta)$, you can do some rewriting. When you say $>_w$ its only one user, but you want to maximize it for all users, so it means that you want to maximize

$$p(>_{u_1}|\theta) * p(>_{u_2}|\theta) * \dots * p(>_{u_n}|\theta)$$

This equation can be written more compactly as $\prod_{u\in U} p(>_u|\theta)$. You have a product of the probability where there's an ordering for each user, given such a model. The probability of an ordering for one user must be the same probability for all pairs of items where one has been bought and the other one not bought—there's an ordering.

---

[9] For more information, see https://en.wikipedia.org/wiki/Normal_distribution.

We said previously you're only looking at these cases. With some common sense and several clever tricks, you can reduce the previous product to a product containing probability of an ordering for each data point (u, i, j), meaning all your data D_s's become

$$\prod_{u \in U} p(>_u | \theta) = \prod_{(u,i,j) \in D_s} p(i >_u j | \theta)$$

You can take this one step further. Because θ is a recommender system model, you know that $(i >_u j | \theta)$ means that you're asking for the probability that a recommender exists that will predict ratings such that $(r_{ui} - r_{uj} > 0)$. You can rewrite the product again:

$$\prod_{(u,i,j) \in D_s} p(i >_u j | \theta) = \prod_{(u,i,j) \in D_s} p(r_{ui} - r_{uj} > 0)$$

RELAXING THE ORDERING

Earlier I said that the problem with ranking was binary, in the sense either it was (or wasn't) item i that was preferred. And because you've the total ordering, this describes a function that's called the *Heaviside function* (figure 13.9). The outcome of asking is $i >_u j$? can only ever be {yes, no} (yes or no), given a certain model. That means $p(i >_u j | \theta)$ is either 0 or 1.

You're only looking at the data where one item was bought by the user and the other one wasn't. That means there's no sliding on the function. It's 0 until there's a straight vertical line to 1:

$$p(i >_u j | \theta) = \begin{cases} 1 & \textit{if } i >_u j \\ 0 & \textit{otherwise} \end{cases}$$

Remember that in chapter 11 we talked about optimizing an analog, comparing it to standing on a foggy hilltop and looking for water and that it doesn't work if the function one minute is 1 and the next 0. With a Heaviside function, you can't see which way to go down safely. To solve this, you can use another function that's almost the same, one called the *sigmoid function*. The sigmoid function also runs in the interval from 0 to 1 and moves almost as the Heaviside function. The sigmoid is defined as:

$$\delta(x) = \frac{1}{1 + e^{-(x)}}$$

Figure 13.9 shows the sigmoid function in action. As you can see from the figure, you can insert the sigmoid without losing too much integrity. You get that

$$p(i >_u j | \theta) = p(r_{ui} - r_{uj} > 0) = \delta(r_{ui} - r_{uj}) = \frac{1}{1 + e^{-(r_{ui} - r_{uj})}}$$

where $r_{ui} - r_{uj}$ is the predicted ratings from a recommender system. You now have the building blocks to put everything together and come up with something you can stuff into some Python code and do ranking.

Once again, you want to find a set of parameters θ for a model such that you have the highest probability to produce a ranking for all users that's perfect. You can say

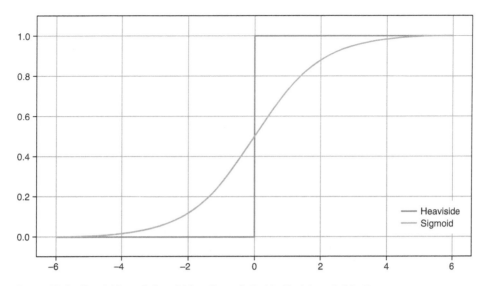

Figure 13.9   Heaviside and sigmoid functions plotted in the interval -6 to 6

you want to maximize the following (you use argmax when you want to say that you want to find the parameters that maximize an expression):

$$\operatorname*{argmax}_{\theta} p(\theta \mid >_u) p\theta$$

You'll use a trick that says that if you want to do that, then it's the same as maximizing the following because the function ln is continuous and always increasing:

$$\operatorname*{argmax}_{\theta} \ln(p(\theta \mid >_u) p\theta)$$

Inserting what you deduced, you get

$$\operatorname*{argmax}_{\theta} \ln \left(\prod_{(u,i,j) \in D_s} \delta(r_{ui} - r_{uj}) * \sqrt{\frac{1}{2\pi}} \, e^{-\frac{1}{2}\lambda\|\theta\|^2} \right)$$

where D_s is all the combinations you have in your data (user u bought/rated an item i but not the item j).

The function you added (ln) is short for the natural logarithm, and it has some nice properties shown here:[10]

$$(\ln(a * b) = \ln(a) + \ln(b) \text{ and } \left(e^{-\frac{1}{2}\lambda\|\theta\|^2} \right) = -\frac{1}{2}\lambda\|\theta\|^2)$$

---

[10] For more information, see https://en.wikipedia.org/wiki/Natural_logarithm#Properties.

You'll also set $\lambda: = \frac{1}{2}\lambda$, which you'll use to simplify the expression, at least a little bit. You'll call the part inside of the argmax for BPR optimization criteria (BPR-OPT).

$$\underset{\theta}{\mathrm{argmax}} \sum_{(u,i,j)\in D_s} \ln(\delta(r_{ui} - r_{uj})) - \lambda\|\theta\|^2$$

This is the task. Did everyone arrive here safe and sound? Let's recap.

The expression you arrived at is what the problem boils down to: you want to find the recommender system. Running with the set of parameters θ will make the whole expression as large as possible, meaning that it's the θ with the highest probability so that the system produces an ordering $>_u$ that matches all users' preferences. It's a noble goal, don't you think?

I'm afraid to say that this was only the problem; now you also need more work before you get at the algorithm that solves it. Remember, stochastic gradient descent from chapter 11? You'll use something similar here.

You want to find the gradient of the previous expression to understand which way you should move to get closer to the optimal ranking. I claim (without proof) that the gradient of the BPR-OPT is proportional to the following (∝ means proportional to):

$$\frac{\delta BPR - OPT}{\delta\theta} \propto \sum_{(u,i,j)\in D_s} \frac{e^{-(r_{ui} - r_{uj})}}{1 + e^{-(r_{ui} - r_{uj})}} * \frac{\delta}{\delta\theta}(r_{ui} - r_{uj}) - \lambda\theta$$

And this is the function you'll want to use to figure out which direction you should go to optimize the ranking method. With that you leave magic math mode and continue as though nothing strange has happened to optimize the expression found here.

13.4.3 *The BPR algorithm*

In the article where BPR is described, the author also suggests an algorithm called LearnBPR, which goes as follows:

```
1: procedure LEARNBPR(D_S,Θ)
2:     initialize Θ
3:     repeat
4:         draw (u, i, j) from D_S
5:         Θ ← Θ + α ( (e^{-x̂_{uij}})/(1+e^{-x̂_{uij}}) · (∂/∂Θ) x̂_{uij} + λ_Θ · Θ )
6:     until convergence
7:     return Θ̂
8: end procedure
```

This is it. I bet it's a bit like watching a complex whodunit movie and then sleeping through the last 10 minutes (where it was explained why the butler did it). But you've arrived at an algorithm that will produce a ranking. Up to now we haven't said much about the recommender algorithm, and, in fact, the step

$$\theta \leftarrow \theta - \alpha\frac{\delta BPR - OPT}{\delta\theta}$$

in the procedure depends on which recommender you plug into it. Most scientific articles use a matrix factorization algorithm, so you'll do the same. The thing to ponder is if you use the same algorithm and the same heuristic to solve it as you did in chapter 11, would it then produce the same results?

Perplexing I know, but now you have a new goal. Remember that in chapter 11 the goal was to reduce the difference between the ratings you have in your database and what the recommender predicts? Here you don't care what type of ratings are predicted, only the order of predictions—the ranking—which allows the learning to be more "free" (for lack of a better word). At this point, it's also worth mentioning the draw function, which can be implemented in several different ways and with different strategies. In the implementation, I used the simplest one, but there are other ways.

13.4.4 *BPR with matrix factorization*

If you don't remember what matrix factorization is, you can refresh your memory in chapter 11. You'll do many of the same things here. Predicting a rating in matrix factorization comes down to multiplying a row in the user matrix W with a column in the item matrix **H**, which is done by using the following summation

$$r_{u,j} = \sum_{f=1}^{K} w_{u,f} * h_{j,f}$$

where K is the number of hidden factors.

To fit it into the example expression, you need to consider how the gradient will look. You're taking the gradient in regards to θ, which is the union of all the parameters you're trying to find, meaning all the w's and the h's. With some careful thinking, you'll see that there are only three cases that are interesting (as in non-zero):

$$\frac{\delta}{\delta\theta}(r_{u,i} - r_{u,j}) \begin{cases} (h_{u,i} - h_{u,j}) & if\ \theta = w_u \\ w_u & if\ \theta = h_i \\ -w_u & if\ \theta = h_j \\ 0 & else \end{cases}$$

You may need to stare at the gradient expression before realizing this. But I'm afraid that I have to leave it as an exercise for you to do.

13.5 *Implementation of BPR*

The BPR was first described in section 13.4. The authors, along with several other people, implemented a recommender system algorithm library called MyMediaLite in C#; the code you'll see in the following is inspired by that.[11] Figure 13.10 shows an overview of what you're implementing in this section:

---

[11] For more information, see https://github.com/zenogantner/MyMediaLite.

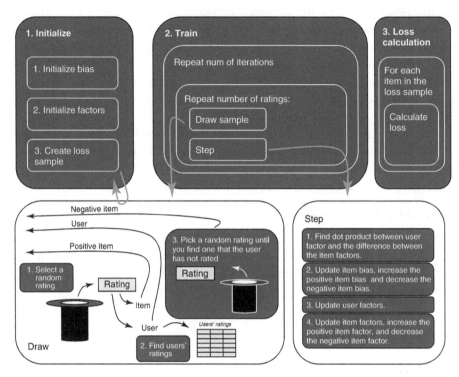

Figure 13.10   An illustration of what you implement in this section. You start by initializing everything, then you train. For each iteration, you run through the same number of ratings, and for each step, you draw a sample of a user and a positive and a negative item. Then you step, meaning that you move all the factors and biases in the right direction.

To run the training set, download the code from GitHub (http://mng .bz/04k5) and follow the install instructions in the readme file. Then go to the MovieGEEKs folder and execute the following listing.

Listing 13.1   Running the BPR training algorithm

```
> python -m builder.bpr_calculator
```

It outputs something close to this:

```
2017-11-19 16:23:59,147 : DEBUG : iteration 6 loss 2327.0428779398057
2017-11-19 16:24:01,776 : INFO : saving factors in ./models/bpr/2017-11-19
    16:22:04.441618//model/19/
```

To use this model, you need to take the folder name where the model (factors) has been saved and insert it into the recommender class. This could be done automatically in a real system. But it's good to have a manual step so you're sure you don't have faulty models suddenly running in production. Insert the path in recs/bpr_recommender.py in line 17 or as the default parameter to the init method, as shown in the following listing.The annotation mentions a relative path in the log. Is that what's output from listing 13.1? If so, mention full path.

Listing 13.2 `Init method of BRP recs`

```
def __init__(self, save_path='<insert path there>'):        Inserts path. The log only
    self.save_path = save_path                              prints out the relative path,
    self.load_model(save_path)                              but here you need the full one.
    self.avg =
      list(Rating.objects.all().aggregate(Avg('rating')).values())[0]
```

TRANSFORMING YOUR RATINGS TO DATA USABLE TO BPR

Before starting on the actual algorithm, you need to transform your rating data into something you can use. The BPR uses implicit feedback, which can either be clicks or purchases. If you consider the user-content lifetime that was described in chapter 4, then you could say that anything the user rated is something that they purchased. You could also say that all ratings are indications that the user bought something. The question then is whether you want to lose the information about whether a user has rated something high.

If you want to take advantage of the user's explicit feedback, you transform all ratings above a certain threshold that indicate a buy and the rest you delete. It's a matter of gut feeling. Here the first solution is taken, so you'll have more data to use.

LEARNBPR METHOD

First, you have the overall build method, which is where you control all of the build. The build method looks like that shown in this listing. You can view the code for the following listings in /build/bpr_calculator.py.

Listing 13.3 The overall build method

```
def train(self, train_data, k=25, num_iterations=4):
                                                                      Loops the num_iterations
Initializes  ┌─▷  self.initialize_factors(train_data, k)              4 times
the factors  │    for iteration in range(num_iterations):      ◁─┘

             ┌─▷      for usr, pos, neg in self.draw(self.ratings.shape[0]):
             │            self.step(usr, pos, neg)      ◁────────
             │                                              Calls the step
             Loops through all the samples created in the    method
             generate_samples method
```

If you were expecting a big light, then I guess this is a bit disappointing, so let's move on quickly. The `initialize_factors` method initializes everything. It doesn't do anything surprising, so I'll leave it to you to look it up if you're interested.[12]

After the initialization method loops the number of times indicated in the `num_iterations` parameter, in each iteration it loops through all the samples of u, i, j,

---

[12] For more information, see http://mng.bz/tjAO.

which are the users where item *i* was bought and item *j* not. In your case, it means randomly selected. For each of those, you call a step method (next listing).

Listing 13.4   Calling the `step` method

```
def step(self, u, i, j):

    lr = self.LearnRate
    ur = self.user_regularization
    br = self.bias_regularization

    pir = self.positive_item_regularization
    nir = self.negative_item_regularization

    ib = self.item_bias[i]
    jb = self.item_bias[j]

    u_dot_i = np.dot(self.user_factors[u, :],
                self.item_factors[i, :] - self.item_factors[j, :])
    x = ib - jb + u_dot_i

    z = 1.0/(1.0 + exp(x))

    ib_update = z - br * ib
    self.item_bias[i] += lr * ib_update

    jb_update = - z - br * jb
    self.item_bias[j] += lr * jb_update

    update_u = ((self.item_factors[i,:] - self.item_factors[j,:]) * z
                - ur * self.user_factors[u,:])
    self.user_factors[u,:] += lr * update_u

    update_i = (self.user_factors[u,:] * z
                - pir * self.item_factors[i,:])
    self.item_factors[i,:] += lr * update_i

    update_j = (-self.user_factors[u,:] * z
                - nir * self.item_factors[j,:])
    self.item_factors[j,:] += lr * update_j
```

- **Creates short nicknames for the learning rate and regularization constants**
- **Shows the same with the item bias**
- **Takes the dot product between user factor and the difference between the two item vectors**
- **Updates the item biases**
- **Updates the user's factor vector**
- **Updates the item factors**

The step method does exactly the same as the one you implemented for the matrix factorization in chapter 11. I encourage you to read through it again for any details (see the code in bpr_calculator.py and chapter 11). What's more interesting in this chapter is how the sample is done and how the prediction and loss functions look.

DRAW METHOD

A draw or a sample consists of a user ID and two item IDs, where one item is preferred by the user over the other. This can be implemented by saying that the preferred item is the one that the user purchased, and the other, the one that the user hasn't bought (or in our case, one is rated and one is not). To draw a sample like that with your rating data, you can do the following:

- Draw a random user rating to get the user ID and the positive item.
- Keep drawing random ratings until you have a item that isn't rated by the user.

This leaves assumptions about your ratings that you should remember. This data set, MovieTweetings only contains content if somebody has rated it, so all the content returns in the ratings data. Also, popular items appear more frequently than others because they're rated more.

The `draw` method in listing 13.5 uses `yield` instead of `return`, so when it arrives at `yield` it delivers the result. But that stays in the `for` loop so that `draw` will iterate through the entire index. You could do this by pushing all the samples to a list and then returning the list. But `yield` seems a nicer way of doing it. Note that the scripts for the following listings can be found in /build/bpr_calculator.py.

Listing 13.5 The `draw` method

```
def draw(self, no=-1):
    if no == -1:
        no = self.ratings.nnz
    r_size = self.ratings.shape[0] - 1
    size = min(no, r_size)
    index_randomized = random.sample(range(0, r_size), size)
    for i in index_randomized:
        r = self.ratings[i]
        u = r[0]
        pos = r[1]

        user_items = self.ratings[self.ratings[:, 0] == u]
        neg = pos
        while neg in user_items:
            i2 = random.randint(0, r_size)
            r2 = self.ratings[i2]
            neg = r2[1]

        yield self.u_inx[u], self.i_inx[pos], self.i_inx[neg]
```

Because you want to shuffle your data, creates an array of all the numbers in the index (0 until the end) and then shuffles.

Runs through the shuffled index

A rating is selected, now find all the users ratings. (Here's a place where you could probably optimize the code so you don't have to filter all the ratings every time.)

See the silly trick to get through the loop constraint the first time.

Loops until negative is an item that the user hasn't rated.

The loss function (`create_loss_samples` in listing 13.6) indicates if you're going in the right direction. It runs through the loss sample that was created in the initialization.

Listing 13.6 The loss function

```
Build\bpr_calculator.py
def create_loss_samples(self):
    num_loss_samples = int(100 * len(self.user_ids) ** 0.5)
    self.loss_samples = [t for t in self.draw(num_loss_samples)]
```

Draws the number of samples

Number of samples that should be taken.

The `loss` function shown in listing 13.7 runs through this loss sample and calculates

$$\sum_{(u,i,j)\varepsilon D_s} \ln(\delta(r_{ui} - r_{uj})) - \lambda\|\theta\|$$

Listing 13.7   Calculating the error on loss sample data

```
def loss(self):
    br = self.bias_regularization
    ur = self.user_regularization              Creates short
    pir = self.positive_item_regularization    nicknames for
    nir = self.negative_item_regularization    the constants

    ranking_loss = 0
    for u, i, j in self.loss_samples:
        x = self.predict(u, i) - self.predict(u, j)    Calculates the
        ranking_loss += 1.0 / (1.0 + exp(x))           ranking loss

    c = 0
    for u, i, j in self.loss_samples:
        c += ur * np.dot(self.user_factors[u], self.user_factors[u])
        c += pir * np.dot(self.item_factors[i], self.item_factors[i])
        c += nir * np.dot(self.item_factors[j], self.item_factors[j])
        c += br * self.item_bias[i] ** 2
        c += br * self.item_bias[j] ** 2             Ranking loss plus half
                                                     the regularization
    return ranking_loss + 0.5 * c
```

Regularization expressions

The `loss` function uses a prediction method, but the difference is that values, not ratings, are predicted. Listing 13.8 illustrates how the values are compared to the prediction of another item, which shows how those two should be ranked against each other.

Listing 13.8   Ranking one item against another

```
def predict(self, user, item):
    i_fac = self.item_factors[item]     Does the dot product
    u_fac = self.user_factors[user]     between the item factors
                                        and the user factors
    pq = i_fac.dot(u_fac)

    return pq + self.item_bias[item]    Adds the item bias and returns
```

Running this algorithm takes a long time. But there are many places where you could be smarter and optimize it to run several hundred times faster with a few tricks. As it stands here, it takes my MacBook 2017 model around two hours per iteration. At that rate, 20 iterations will take 40 hours, so you can go for a run or something. When it's finished, however, you can use it to make recommendations. Let's look at how you do that next.

13.5.1 Doing the recommendations

To hand test the recommendations, you can start MovieGEEKs and, if you trained the model, it will produce recommendations from the BPR using the method shown in the next listing. You'll find the code for the listings in this section in /recs/bpr_recommender.py.

Listing 13.9 Top *N* recommendation method using the BPR model

Makes a dictionary of the active user's
movies, which comes in handy when
verifying that you're not recommending
anything the user has already seen.

Be sure the model has seen the
user; otherwise, you can't
return any recommendations.

```
def recommend_items_by_ratings(self, user_id, active_user_items, num=6):

    rated_movies = {movie['movie_id']: movie['rating']
                        for movie in active_user_items}
    recs = {}
    if str(user_id) in self.user_factors.columns:

        user = self.user_factors[str(user_id)]

        scores = self.item_factors.T.dot(user)
        sorted_scores = scores.sort_values(ascending=False)
        result = sorted_scores[:num + len(rated_movies)]

        recs = {r[0]: {'prediction': r[1] + self.item_bias[r[0]]}
                    for r in zip(result.index, result)
                        if r[0] not in rated_movies}
    s_i = sorted(recs.items(),
                    key=lambda item: -float(item[1]['prediction']))

    return s_i[:num]
```

Orders
values
descending

Calculates the dot
product between
the active user
factor and all the
item factor vectors
so that you can
calculate which
are
more alike

Runs through the resulting
items, adding the item bias

Orders again and returns
expected numbers

Cuts the list down to the number that should be
returned plus the number of ratings the user has

To do this, you first have to load the model using the code in listing 13.10. The model
is saved in the last step of the training.

Listing 13.10 Loading the model

```
def load_model(self, save_path):

    with open(save_path + 'item_bias.data', 'rb') as ub_file:
        self.item_bias = pickle.load(ub_file)
    with open(save_path + 'user_factors.json', 'r') as infile:
        self.user_factors = pd.DataFrame(json.load(infile)).T
    with open(save_path + 'item_factors.json', 'r') as infile:
        self.item_factors = pd.DataFrame(json.load(infile)).T
```

13.6 *Evaluation*

How do you test the algorithm? One way is with the offline evaluation that you learned about in chapter 9, where you used cross-validation. The evaluation is shown in figure 13.11.

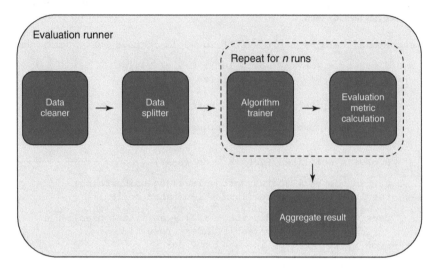

Figure 13.11   The evaluation runner for an algorithm. It's a pipeline where the data is first cleaned, then split into *k* folds for cross-validation. For each fold, it repeats the training of the algorithm, then evaluates it. When it's finished, you aggregate the result.

The following listing shows the evaluation method I added. This creates the data that's shown in the graph in figure 13.12. You can view the code for this listing in /evaluator/evaluation_runner.py.

Listing 13.11   The evaluation method

```
def evaluate_bpr_recommender():
    timestr = time.strftime("%Y%m%d-%H%M%S")
    file_name = '{}-bpr-k.csv'.format(timestr)

    with open(file_name, 'a', 1) as logfile:
        logfile.write("rak,pak,mae,k,user_coverage,movie_coverage\n")

        for k in np.arange(10, 100, 10):
            recommender = BPRRecs()
            er = EvaluationRunner(0,
                                  None,
                                  recommender,
                                  k,
                                  params={'k': 10,
                                          'num_iterations': 20})
            result = er.calculate(1, 5)

            user_coverage, movie_coverage =
    RecommenderCoverage(recommender).calculate_coverage()
```

```
pak = result['pak']
mae = result['mae']
rak = result['rak']
```

Measuring the precision gave the result shown in figure 13.12, which is nothing special. I've confidence that it can be better: it's good, but on small K it isn't great. I also calculated the coverage and it's also better. Item coverage is 6.4% and user coverage is 99.9%.

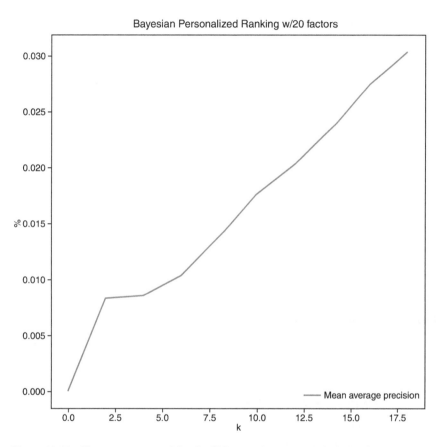

Figure 13.12 **Mean average precision for BPR on a short top *N*. It isn't that impressive, but I'm sure it can be tweaked to make it better.**

If you look at the larger numbers, then it suddenly looks much better as shown in figure 13.13. The thing about the graph in figure 13.13 and these numbers is that they're local to this data set, and you can't really use them for much other than as a benchmark that can be improved upon. This recommender only recommends 6% of the items, which isn't much. You should probably mix it with a content-based recom-

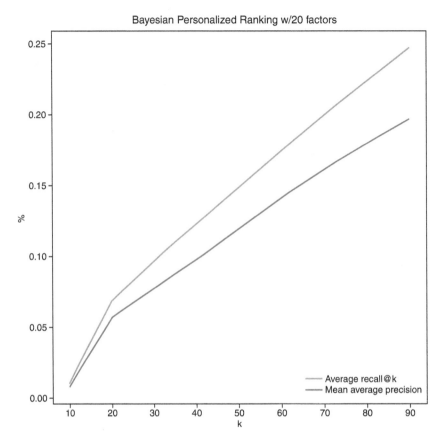

Figure 13.13   Precision and recall for the BPR algorithm

mender or use something else like the multi-armed bandit scheme to introduce more items into the system.

13.7 *Levers to fiddle with for BPR*

BPR is a complex algorithm and there are many decisions that were made before running it. Unfortunately, I glossed over many of them, such as how many factors should be included and what learning rate enables the system to optimize the learning problem best? That doesn't mean they aren't important here, but only that it's up to you to use what you learned in former chapters to evaluate the meta parameters. Let's take a quick walk through them.

You have the item bias and the user factors, so you need to decide how many factors you want to use. The number of factors should be determined by how complex your data domain is. For example, movies are divided into small sets of types (or genres), so it could be they don't need too many factors. But if you're making a wine recommender such as the Vivino.com example, then you probably need many more. This is something you should test based on your data set.

It's hard to give good advice about the learning rate. I found that a too high learning rate gave me large user factor values, meaning that the biases didn't have much to say, while a too low learning rate allowed the biases to take over the decisions. Regularizations try to keep things at bay, but if they need to be too large, then maybe it's a sign that the learning rate is too high.

I love the idea of comparing items and then pushing them in different directions (I'm talking about the item bias here). This can be adjusted with positive and negative item regularization. These will also affect how much a negative item is pushed away, and that might hurt new items if there aren't many users who have consumed those yet.

The data set that you used contained ratings, so you could have removed the low-rated items so they didn't figure as positive items in your training set. But even if a user didn't like a movie, and it was still something they'd consumed, it's good to use those also.

As we conclude this chapter, did you learn everything you needed? If not, then you can reread this chapter again. But it's hard, and unless you're going to implement the BPR, maybe you don't need to remember all the details. But if you're planning to implement a recommender using BPR, then it's a good idea to know how it works. Learning to rank is also something you'll have to consider when you work with search machines, so it's not a bad thing to know a little bit ranking.

This is it. One more chapter to go, then you can go to GoodReads.com and mark this book as read. Remember to review it where you bought it, good or bad. Recommender systems need feedback, so please support that.

Summary

- Learning to Rank (LTR) algorithms solve a different problem than that of the classic recommender problem of predicting ratings.
- Foursquare uses a ranking algorithm to combine the ratings and the locations of venues, which is a great example of how to combine relevant data into one recommendation.
- A challenge with the LTR algorithm is that it isn't easy to come up with a continuous function that can be optimized.
- This chapter touched upon the Bayes theorem, so even if it wasn't the subject of this book, you should look into it because it's used in many scenarios. I recommend *Practical Probablistic Programming* by Avi Pfeffer (Manning, 2016) for additional information.
- The Bayesian Personalized Ranking (BPR) can be used on top of the matrix factorization method you looked at in chapter 10, but also with other types of algorithms.

Future of
recommender systems

14

In this final chapter, you'll go back to the future:

- You'll look at a short summary of the book.
- I'll provide a list of topics to learn next if you want to continue your voyage into the exciting world of recommender systems.
- Although nobody knows what the future of recommender systems holds, I'll give you my best bet and then some final thoughts.

It has taken me three years to arrive at writing this sentence; I hope your travel time has been a bit faster. I wish I could say that now you know everything about recommender systems and that you can venture forth as an expert who understands all recommender algorithms. And, more importantly, that you'll never be surprised by anything on this topic again. You've come a long way, but from here to becoming an expert is still a long journey.

In this book, you learned the basics, enough to get you started and equip you for digging deeper into the subject. But don't only read. Play around with new algorithms or get more intimately familiar with the ones described in the book. You'll find many improvements and tricks to make each of them work better.

Hopefully, the MovieGEEKs site provided the basics for how to load different kinds of data and try out some of the things you learned from reading this book. Remember that MovieGEEKs was implemented to make recommender systems and algorithms easy to understand and has many places where it can be optimized.

But before you go out into the world of recommender systems alone, I want to talk about a few things that didn't fit into this book. My editor would probably call it the cliffhangers for the next book, but my wife says no way—so you'll probably be on your own from here. First, let's have a quick run through of what topics we looked at in the book.

14.1 *This book in a few sentences*

In this book, you learned about recommender systems, which can be described by the pipeline shown in figure 14.1.

You started out learning about collecting data or *data ingestion.* In Pedro Domingo's famous paper called "A Few Useful Things to Know about Machine Learning," he

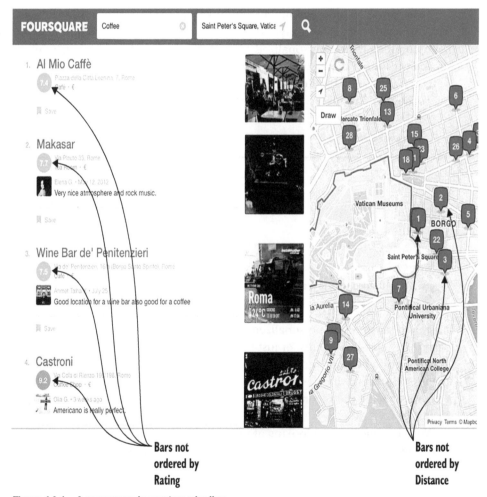

Figure 14.1 A recommender system pipeline

points out that more data beats a more complex algorithm.[1] That's also true for recommender systems, only data collected isn't always a source of truth.

Explicit ratings can be a reflection of mood or a result of social influences and can't always be trusted to indicate what the user wants. *Implicit ratings* are, as the name implies, implicit, and you or the machine have to deduce what the collection of events that have occurred between each user and item indicate. And, no surprise here, people's tastes change over time, so old data might be misleading. It isn't always straightforward to understand what the behavioral data means. Turning events into ratings and clustering users is part of preparing the data for creating a recommender model. It's often referred to as *data pre-processing.*

While data is important for understanding what the user wants, it's equally important to have a way to see how the system is performing, which is why you looked at analytics that will be useful for keeping an eye on how things are going.

Calculating recommendations often uses a model, so you looked at *model training.* You can divide the different types of recommendations into levels of personalization, from completely non-personalized to very personalized as shown in figure 14.2. We started with the non-personalized because those don't require that you know the user well or, frankly, much other data at all. This enables you to have a soft launch into adding recommendations to your site.

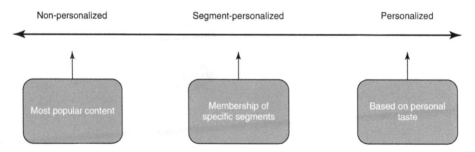

Figure 14.2   Grades of personalization

First, you saw the non-personalized recommendations that helped find the most-sold items, the most-liked items, or just the trending items. All users start out as cold users, so we spent a chapter (chapter 6) on one of the more difficult problems in recommender systems, which is to figure out what to do with new users and items. An attempt to solve the recommender problem for new users is to look at shopping basket analysis.

You then moved into looking at how you can segment things (chapter 7) to undertake semi-personalized or demographic recommendations. Before getting all per-

---

[1] For more information, see https://homes.cs.washington.edu/~pedrod/papers/cacm12.pdf.

sonal, you looked at distance and similarity measurements between items and between users, which is something that haunts nearly every recommender system algorithm.

The first personalized recommendation method was *collaborative filtering* (in chapter 8), which provides recommendations based on similar behavior, either between users or between items. This can be done using ratings explicitly inserted into the system by the user, or by implicitly deducing the results of data in your logs.

There are two types of collaborative filtering. You started with the one known as *neighborhood-based*, in which the algorithm uses similarity measures to find neighboring items or users to the current one. With one algorithm under your belt, you then looked at evaluating algorithms (in chapter 9). Looking at many different metrics for evaluating a recommender, you then implemented the Mean Average Precision (MAP) for the system.

If you don't have much user data (or you have well described content), then it's worth it to consider *content-based* recommenders. You have several ways to do that, but the core is that you look at the content and calculate similarities on that basis. You looked at creating vectors using first *term frequency–inverse document frequency* (TF-IDF) and then topic vectors using *latent Dirichlet allocation* (LDA) topic modeling (in chapter 10).

After the LDA, we returned to collaborative filtering, only now you looked at *model-based filtering*. You can do model-based filtering in many ways, but the main way is *matrix factorization* (chapter 11). This is also where you started to look seriously at training machine-learning algorithms. We talked about the traditional *singular value decomposition* (SVD) and then moved on to the Funk SVD, which got excellent results in the Netflix Prize competition.

With a good toolbox of different recommender algorithms, you started looking at how to combine them, which you can do in many ways. You explored several ways in the chapter on hybrids, where you implemented one called *feature-weighted linear stacking* (FWLS), which was the method that won the Netflix prize. Next, you looked at a new type of algorithm called *Learning to Rank* (LTR), which doesn't care much about correctly predicting ratings, but rather focuses on producing lists of items that are ranked appropriately. The algorithms can be divided into three different types as shown in figure 14.3.

Each ranking method has advantages and disadvantages. I picked one that's often referenced when talking about learning to rank, the *Bayesian Personalized Ranking* (BPR) algorithm.

At this point you might ask which algorithm should you implement? It depends on what kind of data you have. I suggest going with matrix factorization. When that's implemented, you can build the LTR model on top of it. Or you can add another implementation and make it into an ensemble.

And finally, we arrived at the future of your recommender journey and the future of recommenders in general. Let's start with the first one.

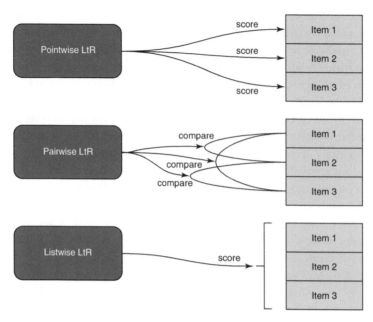

Figure 14.3   Different types of LTR algorithms

14.2   *Topics to study next*

Here's what I recommend as the next steps in your pursuit of mastering recommender systems.

14.2.1   *Further reading*

First, if you want more details and more ways to do recommendations, there's so much more research to dive into. I can heartily recommend *Recommender Systems Handbook* by Francesco Ricci and Lior Rokach. (Springer, 2015 ed.). It's a brick of a book, but it covers more than what I managed to fit into this book.

I'd hoped to cover more about online testing in this book. I did get to talk a bit about A/B testing in chapter 9, but for this, the next topics you need to learn about are exploit/explore methods and multi-armed bandits. For that purpose, I recommend *Statistical Methods for Recommender System* by Deepak Agarwal and Bee-Chung Chen from LinkedIn (Cambridge University Press, 2016).

Beyond books, keep an eye on GroupLens (https://grouplens.org/) and look for the ACM Recommender Systems (RecSys) conference. Many interesting papers come out of that conference, and YouTube videos also have their own channel for recommender systems (http://mng.bz/ta38).

Reading this book, you might get the impression that collaborative filtering as mentioned in chapter 8 is largely a historical approach, but it's still a method where much research is on-going, and it's the way that many companies produce their recommendations. For example, the paper of the year at RecSys2016 was "Local Item-Item Models for Top-N Recommendation."[2] You can catch Evangelia Christakopoulou, the author, on YouTube talking about it.

Recommender algorithms are a subfield of machine learning. Few people will get away working with only the algorithms deemed recommender algorithms. I suggest that to continue your journey into becoming an expert in delivering relevant recommendations, you study machine learning in general, beyond what you learned here. Two books worth looking at are *Real-World Machine Learning* by Henrik Brink et al. (Manning, 2016) and *Algorithms of the Intelligent Web*, 2nd ed., by Douglas G. McIlwraith et al. (Manning, 2016).

Search engines are a topic that is closely related to recommendations. My view of search engines is that they're seeded recommendations, so searches are a special case of recommender systems. But search engine people like Doug Turnbull would say that recommenders are search machines. This could quickly become a chicken-or-the-egg discussion. At most places where recommenders are implemented, there's also a search index to manage, so take a look at *Relevant Search* by Doug Turnbull et al. (Manning, 2016).

14.2.2 Algorithms

Turning now to algorithms, those called Learning to Rank (LTR) are popular. Also popular are the listwise ones, which are more complex than what you saw at in chapter 13.

Nowadays every serious machine learner will look to deep learning for improvements in all areas, and there's also intensive research going on in the subject of recommenders. Things are moving so quickly that it would be foolish to add any pointers here because I'm sure those will be terribly outdated before this book is even printed. Still, look at the Deep Learning Workshop at the 2016 RecSys conference (http://dlrs-workshop.org/dlrs-2016/program/).

One of the issues with the algorithms described in this book, and one of the largely unresolved problems of recommender systems, is that most recommenders are optimized to show items that are as similar as possible to content already seen by the user. But what you want a recommender to do is find items that are undiscovered, serendipitous, and novel. It depends on which domain you're using as to how much you need this, but it's worth thinking about; it'll also add a little bit of chaos into the recommendations. Another problem is also that people might not want to see the same Top-*N* list of recommendations over and over again.

14.2.3 Context

Recommender systems are moving from being stationary (something that you only see on your desktop monitor) to portable (with all sorts of mobile devices). Users

---

[2] For more information, see http://mng.bz/5c7E.

could have one session in Europe and the next one in the U.S. Because a device is mobile, it can also be influenced by weather and other conditions.

I've discussed this idea throughout the book, but without providing any concrete solutions. Depending on the domain you're in, it's worth also considering the context. For example, you learned about Funk SVD in chapter 11 that can be extended to also handle context, or you could use the re-ranking method described in chapter 13.

14.2.4 *Human-computer interactions*

As a data scientist or machine learning nerd (as in single-minded), you'd probably like to forget about anything regarding the frontend, but to create a good recommender, you also need to serve it in the best way. UI is important.[3]

14.2.5 *Choosing a good architecture*

Let's face it. The MovieGEEKs site doesn't perform well. With one concurrent user, it's okay, but I fear that it wouldn't handle many more! It's a good idea to look for a stronger platform to run a recommender and website on.

Django is performant, but it needs a real database. I've used SQLite because that's what requires the least setup, but I recommend upgrading to a PostgreSQL or similar database before letting your site go live. In saying this, however, I don't intend that you start moving everything to a new architecture and buy new hardware. First, figure out if a recommender will provide you with what you want. If you can't test it on all your traffic to begin with, it doesn't matter: create something smaller and show it to only 1% of your customers and see how they react. Only remember that the more data you give a recommender, the better it works (this is a general rule).

But let's imagine that you have this step sorted already and you want to roll out your recommender full-scale. In that case, the following sections cover things that I'd consider.

THE CLOUD DOESN'T SOLVE ALL YOUR PROBLEMS

We're all bombarded with ads about how one cloud service after another beats all the others in being the best, fastest, and cheapest. But before moving things to the cloud, consider the following:

- *Data needs to be in the cloud to be usable.* If you have an on-premise solution (meaning that you have your servers locally), then you'll have to somehow move all your data into the cloud for your system to do the calculations necessary to create the recommendations. Bandwidth, storage, and so on can quickly turn an economical solution into something far too costly.
- *The off-the-shelf recommenders such as the Microsoft Cognitive Services Recommendation API are probably an easy start.* But there might be restrictions on how many items

---

[3] For more information, see http://mng.bz/933q. Another question is does the way items are recommended need to be the same for all people? People have different temperaments and moods, so it could be your recommender needs to be more discrete with certain people and more in-your-face with others.

you can have in your catalog or how often it can be called. Carefully research the restrictions; do those make it feasible to have your application or site rely on such a third-party solution.

- *Privacy should be taken seriously.* If you have any sensitive data, remember that in the cloud means *somewhere in the world,* and it's the country where the server is placed that dictates the laws that are applied to the data stored on it.
- *Data is your most valuable asset.* Don't show it to others before considering what values you're providing to your competition.

On the plus side, a cloud service takes away much of the pressure of keeping a server running and scaled up in peak periods. I'm not saying you should disregard such a service, but do consider the circumstances around it.

WHAT PROCESSING PLATFORM TO CHOOSE

And finally, here it comes… ta da.… Spark has so much hype that this wouldn't be a good data book if I didn't mention it at least once.

Spark is a distributed computing platform that can handle machine learning in a distributed, performant way. If you're interested in doing the calculations across many computers, then Spark is an excellent choice. If you look at Spark.MLlib (https://spark.apache.org/mllib/), it's possible to create the matrix factorization we talked about in chapter 11. If you want to do a content-based recommender, such as the one from chapter 11, there's an implementation for doing an LDA model, but I haven't found a tutorial on it yet. But do keep your eyes on my blog (https://kim-falk.org); it might appear there soon.

14.3 *What's the future of recommender systems?*

Predicting the future proves to be difficult, and only the ones who predict it correctly will be remembered, so let's hope the entries in the following sections will be remembered. But know that chances are the future will be entirely different.

One thing I'm certain about is that recommenders will be something that will pop up everywhere. They'll be the new JavaScript for the web and applications. They'll run on everything and provide their humble services in virtually any decision-making process.

USER PROFILES

In Denmark, we've had many discussions about the fact that everything is becoming electronic and accessible only online. The Danish state has stopped sending out paper letters and will only communicate using an electronic mailbox. State policy and the speed-of-light innovations don't, however, make all people in Denmark inclined to jump on the bandwagon. This creates an increasing gap between the people who are on the bandwagon and people who aren't.

Why is this important in this context? People on the bandwagon are those we recommender system engineers like because they're the ones who give us more evidence to work with. Tracking and knowledge about people who use the internet are only going to increase, which means that we can get a good picture of what they like.

Facebook and LinkedIn are teaching people to have a public human-readable profile. I think in the not-too-distant future either Facebook or another company will provide a public machine-readable profile for machine-learning algorithms.

Having a public profile will enable your systems to access and use those profiles to understand who your customers are. Using lists of movies or books a person likes works well for the entertainment industry. But public profiles might also contain segment details, such as whether someone is a homeowner, a car owner, or a parent as shown in figure 14.4, which will help other types of recommenders.

A machine-readable profile like that will also enable people to be much more conscious about what information to share, or whether to share information at all. Currently, sites such as Facebook let people use their profile for logging in to different sites without much effort. In essence, you're allowing another company to access your profile.[4] In a certain sense, the profile is already there, which means readily available

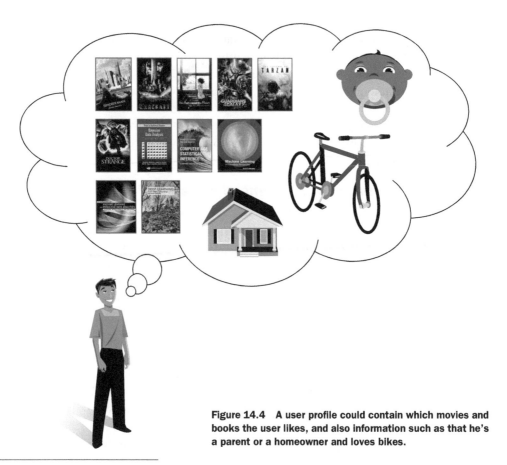

Figure 14.4   A user profile could contain which movies and books the user likes, and also information such as that he's a parent or a homeowner and loves bikes.

---

[4]   Many will point to the General Data Protection Regulation (GDPR) at this point, and for good reason. But I am afraid that the new laws will not stop the harvesting of users' data; it'll just make the user agreements longer, and that doesn't matter because nobody reads those anyway.

data. Having a format for a machine-readable profile may also enable better privacy because you can decide how much you want to reveal about yourself, such as letting a system know that you've recently read the latest Peter F. Hamilton novel and are crazy about new trends in organic raw food dishes.

For people who don't allow access to their details, there are companies in the business of generating profiles about users, and they're on the rise. This means that no matter what you do, an online business will probably know something about you from day one.

It probably will be even harder to serve recommendations to people who aren't on the web but who use non-internet mobile apps. As the new generations grow up, not knowing how it was before everybody had a smartphone, this segment will likely grow smaller by the year. And in the near future, you'll still have problems with cold customers.

CONTEXT

Devices and choice are also becoming more dynamic. I believe that recommenders will eventually be used in many different contexts. Not only because almost all devices are now portable, with GPS and other tools to understand the current context (figure 14.5), but also because soon all devices will contain so much content that people will need a recommender to figure out what to do. I'm not talking only about buying stuff. Recommenders will also be used to make decisions in many other scenarios.

For example, *Next Best Action recommenders* are becoming bigger and bigger in marketing and banking. This isn't necessarily for the end user but to help bankers suggest to customers what options are better or to help lawyers handle a case, or even to help you find the love of your life.

Current research and most publicly available knowledge about recommenders are about algorithms that do all the calculations offline. This lends itself to further research and allows you to validate the algorithm on a test set. You can even enlist the aid of others to come up with a better result. As mentioned several places in this book, this doesn't guarantee you'll produce a good recommender using this approach. I think that the future of recommenders lies in dynamic recommender algorithms, though, of course, with a core of offline calculations similar to the ones you've learned here. And the idea of reinforced learning will have a much more important role.

The context could also be that your phone is connected to your smart watch, which looks at your body functions and predicts that you need a drink because you're low on fluids, so it recommends a juice bar around the corner. Or it notices that your heart rate indicates you might be a little stressed because that algorithm is just not coming together, so it plays some calming music. Maybe a recommender will become a general recommender.

For more in-depth discussion about context-aware recommender systems, I again suggest the *Recommender Systems Handbook* by Francesco Ricci et al. (Springer, 2015 edition). Its chapter on context-aware recommenders is available online.[5]

---

[5] To access the PDF, go to https://www.researchgate.net/publication/220605653_Context-Aware_Recommender_Systems.

Figure 14.5   Context can be many things; the weather can have an impact, whether the user is happy or sad, alone or with friends, or even driving or just being at home lying on the sofa. Each would mean different things in different domains.

ALGORITHMS

When I first started working on recommender systems, I thought of them as the natural evolution of search engines. Everything was so data-overloaded that information needed to be filtered before recommending. With that perspective, recommenders become something similar to data retrieval, where your query is your taste profile combined with the context, your mood, and more.

Mohammed Hossein Taghavi, Netflix senior researcher engineer, stated in his presentation at RecSys2016 that the ideal state of their recommender system was if you'd "Turn on Netflix, and the absolute best contents for you would automatically start playing" (http://mng.bz/2152). But to do this, you'll need algorithms that can incorporate a larger model and that also include much more knowledge of the current users: is the user happy, with other people, tired, writing a book, and so on.

In chapter 12, we talked about everything being an ensemble, which is also something that could support more input and more different models. Again, deep learning is also seen as something that's expected to improve everything. What algorithms are around the corner are hard to say; maybe you'll be the one to come up with the next big thing.

PRIVACY

With the social internet, you'll have more and more data about people and their social connections. Even if collaborative filtering is good because it connects users' behaviors, in the future, you'll also see that people want to have recommendations based on close and trusted friends rather than a group of people that happen to have the same taste. Trust-based recommenders are already out there and this area will grow.

As I review this book, the Facebook data scandal is rolling. Coupled with new privacy laws like the European Union GDPR, that will probably make this an explosive field of discussion over the next couple of years. I fear that even with new legislation, people will soon forget all the fuss, going back to giving up their privacy to free services and then being surprised that their data is being sold. But I hope all this trouble will make people realize that they need to think about what they put on the internet, and that businesses will be a bit more careful about handling their users' data. As a data scientist, I urge you to use the data sensibly and respect other people's privacy.

ARCHITECTURE

A recommender system will naturally be requested where there's too many choices. In the future, I suppose there will be numerous choices everywhere, not only in an entertainment business such as Netflix. With huge amounts of data, the recommender algorithms will start having problems, and it will be too time-consuming to get recommendations based on terabytes of data. We'll have to look for new types of algorithms that can handle huge data loads or at least optimize the ones we have now.

Recommenders will become something that runs everywhere, and you'll need recommenders that run on smaller devices. But with the rate that phones and other devices are developing, it's likely that it won't be a problem because they'll have the same power as our servers have today. I could imagine, for example, that a topic model could be trained on a large amount of data and then the model could be used locally on your phone to do content-based recommendations on your local library.

SURPRISING RECOMMENDATIONS

One of the biggest problems of recommenders is that they aren't good at providing surprising recommendations. We need to figure out better ways to cut across categories and recommend things from the catalog on a wider scale. This will be one of the bigger problems to solve in the future.

You'll see many proposals out there about how it could be done. In *Novelty and Diversity Metrics for Recommender Systems: Choice, Discovery and Relevance*, Pablo Castells et al. list different methods to measure novelty and diversity of recommendations.[6] But doing so successfully is far from straightforward.

14.4 Final thoughts

I should admit that I never read the last section in a machine-learning nonfiction book because I spend my time researching what people tend to write. My conclusion is that most authors don't write any final thoughts, but I'll leave with a few of my own.

As a parting thought about writing this book, I've met many people who've hinted that they had a great idea for a similar book and that if they bothered to write it,

---

[6] P. Castells et al.: *Novelty and Diversity Metrics for Recommender Systems: Choice, Discovery and Relevance*. Available online at http://ir.ii.uam.es/rim3/publications/ddr11.pdf.

they'd have written a much better book than what you're reading now. Probably so. However, most of these people never started on the project. And for a good reason.

Writing a book is a humongous project, one that will teach you so much, both on the subject that you're writing about and on the art of writing. In addition, it'll test the strength of the bonds of those with whom you are the closet.

Regarding writing and recommender systems, I still have much to learn. Regarding those personal bonds, I'm happy to say that they are strong enough, even if I have at least a couple of years of making up for lost time with family and friends. If you do get the crazy idea of writing a technical book, then I can't recommend Manning Publications enough because they've made it a great experience.

Most would say that writing such a book was a full-time job that wouldn't support you in any other way than giving you the gratifying feeling of the weight of the printouts. That may be. Writing this book, I have nonetheless learned *a lot*. I've met many people and have gained numerous new contacts. I've had fun, and I hope you have too while reading; hopefully you learned what you wanted. I'll part with these wise words:

> *We are stuck with technology when what we really want is just stuff that works.*
>
> —Douglas Adams (2002)

index